Unruly Examples

On the Rhetoric of Exemplarity

CONTRIBUTORS   Daniel Boyarin

Cathy Caruth

Alexander Gelley

Irene E. Harvey

Thomas Keenan

David Lloyd

John D. Lyons

Louis Marin

J. Hillis Miller

Stephen G. Nichols

Herman Rapaport

Ewa Ziarek

Unruly Examples

ON THE RHETORIC
OF EXEMPLARITY

EDITED BY Alexander Gelley

Stanford University Press

Stanford, California   1995

Stanford University Press, Stanford, California
© 1995 by the Board of Trustees of the
Leland Stanford Junior University
Printed in the United States of America

CIP data appear at the end of the book

Stanford University Press publications are distributed
exclusively by Stanford University Press within
the United States, Canada, and Mexico;
they are distributed exclusively by
Cambridge University Press throughout
the rest of the world.

Contents

Contributors

DANIEL BOYARIN is Taubman Professor of Talmudic Culture at the University of California at Berkeley. His most recent books are *Carnal Israel: Reading Sex in Talmudic Culture* and *A Radical Jew: Paul and the Politics of Identity*. He is currently working on a project called "Jewishness as a Gender; or, The Invention of the Jewish Man."

CATHY CARUTH is Associate Professor of English at Emory University. She is the author of *Empirical Truths and Critical Fictions: Locke, Wordsworth, Kant, Freud* and *Unclaimed Experience: Trauma, Narrative, and History*, and has edited *Trauma: Explorations in Memory*.

ALEXANDER GELLEY is Professor in the Department of English and Comparative Literature at the University of California at Irvine. He is the author of *Narrative Crossings: Theory and Pragmatics of Prose Fiction*.

IRENE E. HARVEY is Associate Professor of Philosophy at Pennsylvania State University. She is the author of *Derrida and the Economy of Difference* and of numerous articles on deconstruction, postmodernism, and contemporary French thought. She has completed a study on the issue of exemplarity and is currently working on essays concerning feminism and spirituality.

THOMAS KEENAN teaches in the English Department at Princeton University. He is the author of *Fables of Responsibility* and coeditor, with Werner Hamacher and Neil Hertz, of Paul de Man's *Wartime Journalism, 1939–43* and of *Responses*.

He is at work on *Windows of Publicity*, a book on television and the public sphere.

DAVID LLOYD is Associate Professor of English at the University of California at Berkeley. He is the author of *Nationalism and Minor Literature* and *Anomalous States: Irish Writing and the Post-Colonial Movement*, and coeditor, with Abdul Ben Mohammed, of *The Nature and Content of Minority Discourse*.

JOHN D. LYONS is Commonwealth Professor of French at the University of Virginia. He is the author of *Exemplum. The Rhetoric of Example in Early Modern France and Italy* and coeditor, with Mary McKinley, of *Critical Tales. New Studies of the Heptameron and Early Modern Culture*.

LOUIS MARIN (1931–1992) was director of studies at L'École des Hautes Études en Sciences Sociales in Paris. He was the author of over 300 essays and of sixteen books, including *Utopics: The Semiological Play of Textual Spaces*, *Le Critique du discours: Études sur la "Logique de Port-Royal" et les "Pensées" de Pascal*, *Portrait of the King*, *Food for Thought*, and *Des pouvoirs de l'image*.

J. HILLIS MILLER is Distinguished Professor of English and Comparative Literature at the University of California at Irvine. His most recent books are *Versions of Pygmalion*, *Ariadne's Thread*, *Illustration*, and *Topographies*.

STEPHEN G. NICHOLS is James M. Beall Professor of French at the Johns Hopkins University. He is the author of *Romanesque Signs: Early Medieval Narrative and Iconography*, *The New Medievalism*, *The New Philology*, *Boundaries and Transgressions*, and *Commentary as Cultural Artifact*. He is currently working on a book entitled *Modernism and the Politics of Medieval Studies* and another called *Seeing Great Beauty: Myth, Image, and Culture in the Early Middle Ages*.

HERMAN RAPAPORT is Professor of English and Comparative Literature at the University of Iowa. He is the author of *Heidegger and Derrida: Reflections on Time and Language* and *Between the Sign and the Gaze*. His essay in this volume is part of a forthcoming book on the inhuman.

EWA ZIAREK is Assistant Professor of English at the University of Notre Dame. Her publications include articles on Melville, Kafka, Joyce, Levinas, Kristeva, and Marianne Hauser. She was a Lilly Fellow during the 1991–92 academic year and is currently completing a book entitled *Rhetoric of Failure: Skepticism, Modernism, Deconstruction.*

Unruly Examples

On the Rhetoric of Exemplarity

Introduction

$\mathbf{T}$he use of example in discourse is so pervasive, so routine, and at the same time so various that one might hesitate to dignify it with a theory. "No art examines the particular," Aristotle wrote.[1] The example is a particular. But it is a particular kind of particular. Examples do not fall into speech like leaves to the ground. Yet a "fall" of a kind—a link to circumstance, to a momentary revelation—plays a part in their effectiveness in rhetoric and argumentation.

Already in Greek thought we find the logic of exemplarity developed along two strands. In Plato the primary philosophical sense of *paradeigma* (Lat. *exemplar*) is that of a model, a standard. It is related to the theory of ideas, those primal and universal forms that are the generative source for the characteristics of objects. And this sense of the exemplar—as archetype deriving from a transcendent source—continues in later Platonism and medieval theology. But there is an alternative, rhetorically oriented conception of example that comes from Aristotle. Here *paradeigma* functions inductively: the instance serves as vector pointing to a principle or conclusion.[2] Whereas the Platonic model displays a vertical directionality, from a primary exemplar down to multiple instantiations, for Aristotle example involves something like a lateral movement: "neither from part to whole nor from whole to part but from part to part, like to like, when two things fall under the same genus but one is better known than the other."[3] What is at work here is a form of induction whereby particulars are linked and traced so as to produce, as George A. Kennedy glosses, "an 'unmediated inference,' or unspoken recognition of the universal proposition."[4]

Thus at the start of the Western philosophical tradition appear two kinds of exemplarity, one primarily oriented to a pragmatic function, to rhetoric, the other to a cognitive principle and to ontology. How are they related? If the example as model, as paradigm, derives from a thetic act—the elevation of a singular to exemplary status—then its meaning becomes dependent not on the instance itself but merely on its application. Is the example merely *one*—a singular, a fruit of circumstance—or *the One*—a paradigm, a paragon? The tactic of exemplarity would seem to be to mingle the singular with the normative, to mark an instance as fated.

Example, sample: the Latin etymology tells us that they denote a part taken out of some whole: *eximere* (cf. "exemption").[5] The cut or part stands for the whole. But *stands*, how? And what *whole*? These questions lead to the heart of the effectivity—and enigma—of example. In the fabric of discourse and debate, example, like citation, has no autonomous standing. Whatever is designated as example functions as a nexus of converging articulations. Where are these to be sought? Is it in a vector back to a source, a whole from which the example derives? Or is it in a vector forward—to an addressee, an agency for whom the example has been prepared? Finally, what of the status or standing of the example: what makes the example exemplify, gives it the capacity to *stand for*, to represent and exhibit, some other entity?

"Stands for": not as symbol, not as analogue, but rather—this we learn from the rhetorical tradition—as illustration, as an aid in understanding, in visualizing.[6] How does such an aid work? Does it draw its power, its effectivity from what it's a part of, or is there a power in the part itself, in the part as part?

As for the *whole*, the source, whatever the example is an example *of*: Where is it found? How is it constituted? Often this source is determinate and easily identified (e.g., the writings of an author, the Bible). But in other instances, especially when the context of discourse is persuasive or rhetorical, the source may be altogether hypothetical—the speaker's assumption of a body of evidence to support his position. Here example is derived proleptically—first of all in being oriented toward a conclusion, a truth or principle that the speaker may have in view but that has not yet been established, but also in being oriented to an interlocutor, an addressee, for whom the example has, to a certain extent, been selected and fashioned. As we will see, it is this outward reach to an agency of reception that constitutes the rhetorical—I would prefer to say pragmatic—dimension of example.

In this sense example cannot assume a whole on which it draws. Rather, it is oriented to the recovery of a lost whole or the discovery of a new one. But will we know it when we see it? Can we ever expect to see the whole since we have been shown only a part? Perhaps, though, the function of example is precisely to divert us from the two limiting terms—the whole *from which* and the whole *toward which*—and disclose an *in between*, an opening for picturing, for illustrative realization. We come here to another puzzle regarding example: is it, semiotically, sample or illustration? Does it work by way of synecdoche (part for whole) or analogy (similitude)? While one might wish to draw firm boundaries, in practice the difference is hard to pin down. Usually one would say that the analogical function is decisive. Thus anecdotes, fables, narratives of all kinds are offered as examples for general truths or principles, which in turn may be formulated as maxims or sayings. Here the narrative is not of the same form but only *like* the maxim. It illustrates by way of a different substance, an image or simulated enactment that is analogically related to a proposition or general truth. But it is very easy for this strategy to shift from an analogical to an iconic mode. As has already been indicated, the function of pictorial realization in ancient rhetoric, *eikon* and *imago*, was closely linked to the structure of example.[7] But in a rhetorical sense not only does the example picture, it may also induce an imitative reproduction on the part of the receptor or audience. The mimetic effect here is linked not, as is usual, to techniques of representation but to forms of behavior, to a goal of ethical transformation. The example turns into an exemplar and its function becomes that of propagating itself, creating multiples.

The kind of alternative that I have outlined in terms of ancient Greek thought—the Platonic cognitive sense of paradigm contrasted to the Aristotelian rhetorical focus—could be viewed diachronically, in terms of stages of a historical mutation of the dominant forms of example. (And it should be kept in mind that the alternative models are to be taken in no sense as mutually exclusive but as boundary features of a complex function.)

The medieval exemplum served as a staple of Christian didacticism. Collections of exempla were widely disseminated for use in sermons. Since the truth of the Christian teaching was not open to question, exempla served to educate and persuade, not to analyze or test doctrines. The sources of examples seem indiscriminately various. An example's authority was based on effectivity in promoting established dogma rather than on any criterion of factuality or even Christian origin. As Hugo Friedrich writes:

But the actual exemplum (and this is the case also in Dante) is always characterized in its content by the presentation of human action that is renowned, preserved in "memoria," and validated through transmission. Quite irrespective of whether it derives from mythology, from profane history, from sacred narratives or saints' lives, from legend or from incidents of recent date, it is seen as having actually occurred, and everything depends upon this conviction in those who propound it as well as those who receive it.[8]

The status of exemplum as an imitable model in medieval Christianity facilitated its projection into everyday reality as a means of validating the immediacy of experience through image and word. As Hans-Robert Jauss has pointed out, the Christian-typological sense of history could stress both the factuality and the pictorial immediacy of example by constant reference to the ultimate exemplar, the deeds and the life of Christ, and thus play off a "norm-creating function" of Christian exemplarity against what were characterized as the invented examples of pagan rhetoric.[9]

The Classical tradition provided a quite different basis for the authoritative status of historical examples. This basis can be traced back to Hellenistic rhetorical principles and its motto was Cicero's *historia magistra vitae*. History here does not yet have the modern sense of a sequential, unitary process but is rather taken as an aggregate of instances designed to serve as guides for behavior and action. The conceptual mutation that led to the modern idea of history may be illustrated, as Reinhart Koselleck has shown, through the semantic shift of the German word *Geschichte*. Up to the eighteenth century the term could be taken as a collective plural, as *Geschichten*, or "historical narratives," but its gradual shift into a collective singular— "history" in the modern sense—marks a definitive conceptual transformation. In this new sense, "the context of action was incorporated into the knowledge" of history, Koselleck writes, in line with "Droysen's formula that history is only knowledge of history. . . . History as unique event or as a universal relation of events was clearly not capable of instructing in the same manner as history in the form of exemplary account."[10] Koselleck's study shows that whereas the classical sense of *historia* envisioned a series of instances linked inductively to produce a conclusion, history in the modern (or at least Hegelian) sense situates particular events in a totalizing schema that assimilates the exemplary function.

In both the classical and the Christian traditions the authority of exempla was predicated on their truth, whether this was understood in a transcendent or a factual-historical sense (and, of course, the two were often interwoven).[11] With the waning of this sort of authoritative support in the modern era, the forms of discourse and textuality that had earlier realized the principal functions of exemplarity may well have ceased to be operative. But this should not lead us to conclude that the functions themselves disappeared, though their label, their place in the taxonomy of cultural practices, may have shifted. Hans Blumenberg has reminded us that the mutation of the "great questions" in a cultural canon must not blind us to the persistence of certain fundamental human concerns across epochal thresholds. A culture may harbor certain "answer positions" for which the questions have been forgotten or are not yet formulated.[12] If we follow Blumenberg's lead, the answers made available by exemplarity in its rhetorical and religious forms correspond to functions that have persisted in spite of the waning of those forms. Our task, then—and this is the motive that has guided the selection of the papers in this volume—is to identify and begin to chart this new space, a modern tropology of exemplarity.

When Walter Benjamin, in "The Storyteller," lamented the fact that narrative in the modern era, the era of information and of the novel, was no longer capable of providing counsel for living, he identified a deep-seated and persistent rationale for narrative itself. The didactic purpose that is typically associated with exemplary narrative represents, I would venture, a restricted application of Benjamin's wider insight. For it is not simply a single truth, a moral lesson, that the traditional storyteller conveys by means of a tale but a form of wisdom: "Counsel, woven into the fabric of living existence, is wisdom. The art of narration is approaching its end because the epic side of truth, wisdom, is dying out."[13] Benjamin's argument is that the exemplarity of storytelling derives from both an accumulated wisdom of experience and a regulated practice of transmission. Yet it should not be thought that with the notion of counsel for living Benjamin meant to signify an edifying core at the heart of a story since this would presume a kind of universal subject as the model receptor of the narrative act. In its core Benjamin's essay conveys not a technique of interpretation but rather a conception of narrative that is embedded in a life process: thus, a situated praxis encompassing the telling, the listening, the absorbing, the preserving, the passing on.

In other texts, notably the writings on Kafka, Benjamin is especially attuned to the parabolic side of narrative, to its capacity to render a paradox—whether theoretical, practical, or spiritual—in empirical embodiment. What Benjamin saw in Kafka's writing was a modern version of a form found in virtually all cultures: narratives as vessels of hidden truths, of mysteries. Benjamin's remark that Kafka had "failed in his grandiose undertaking of transposing fiction into doctrine [die Dichtung in die Lehre zu überführen]"[14] may be understood in the context of his reflections in "The Storyteller" on the historical mutation of narrative practices. By way of the paradoxical characterization of Kafka's "failure," Benjamin indicates a specific historical manifestation of a perennial goal of parabolic narrative, the (unattainable) transposition of fiction, of poetic creation into universal meaning, into truth.

These considerations lead us back to the issue of just what form exemplarity takes in modernity, in a context where the kind of veridical criteria that we found in the classical and Christian uses of example are no longer operative. The proximity of example to fable was already noted by Aristotle.[15] What links them is, as we have seen, an underlying narrative basis, and then a distinct metatextual orientation, a pointing beyond to another text, a *con*text that enlarges and assimilates the instance. What differentiates them may be clarified by focusing on the relation of the particular to the whole or the universal. As Karlheinz Stierle writes: "In the fable, the general appears *as* the particular; in the exemplum, it appears *in* the particular. In the first case, the general is represented, in the second it is implied."[16] Fable, in this model, functions analogically, in the manner of allegory. But what Stierle designates as a relation of implication (of embedding, I would add, "*in* the particular") points to another kind of linkage between particular and universal: the need to *think* a universal that we can never *know* in order to be capable of speaking of the particular at all.

It is in terms of Kant, and especially of the "aesthetic" project of the third *Critique*, the *Critique of Judgment*, that I want to develop this problematic, however schematically. Such an approach will also allow us to see in certain tendencies of deconstruction a marked reaction to what I would term a meliorist strain in Kant's approach to example, a willingness to work with an accessory function in full awareness of its logical fallibility.

The issue of example surfaces at various levels in Kant's work,[17] understandably so since his thought repeatedly confronts an incommensurability between an absolute and an empirical dimension, between the noumenal and the phenomenal. And far from dissimulating or evading this discrepancy, Kant regularly thematizes it. In the *Critique of Pure Reason*[18] he distinguishes between the understanding, as the faculty concerned with formulating and grasping rules or principles, and judgment (*Urteilskraft*), whose special function consists in the application of rules, or more precisely, of *subsuming* or incorporating instances and examples under the appropriate rules; it is "a particular talent that cannot be studied but only practiced [or exercised: *geübt*]" (*CPR*, A 133). Kant likens judgment to a native, ingrained wit, *Mutterwitz*. This aptitude, then, involves the ability not only to discern general principles but also to select concrete cases in relation to a principle ("whether a case falls under it in concreto" *CPR* A 134). He goes on, "This is also the singular and great use of examples: that they sharpen the judgment" (ibid.). Thus judgment, exercised and "sharpened" by this exemplifying practice, takes charge of the understanding and puts it into practice.

A differentiation that Kant makes between *Exempel* and *Beispiel* is instructive in this connection:

> How to take an *Exempel* and how to cite a *Beispiel* for clarification of an expression involve quite separate concepts. The *Exempel* is a special case of a *practical* rule, insofar as it conceives the practicality or impracticality of an action [*sofern diese die Thunlichkeit oder Unthunlichkeit einer Handlung vorstellt*]. Whereas a *Beispiel* is only the notion of the particular (concretum) standing within the concept of the general (abstractum), and merely the theoretical presentation of a concept.[19]

While this terminological distinction is not operative in Kant's writings as a whole, the passage is relevant for its separation of a pragmatic from a logical function of example and, further, for its foregrounding of the former, the pragmatic. In a sense, of course, this might be taken merely to refer to the traditional didactic goal of exemplarity, the instance serving as a guide and stimulus to practice. But Kant goes in a new direction in emphasizing the methodological status of reasoning through examples, whereby reflection draws on particulars not merely as guides for behavior but as aids to reason and judgment. Thus in his ethical philosophy Kant offers those "casuistic" instances, borderline cases devised to illustrate what in itself cannot be empirically demonstrated, such as the concept of freedom.[20] The focus is less on the singularity of the instance than on the manner whereby the instance points the way for an activation of the moral judgment and the imagination. Analogously in the *Critique of Judgment*, the aesthetic theory, exemplarity is critical in defining such key concepts as genius and the aesthetic (reflective) judgment.[21] Thus the distinction drawn between *Nachfolge* (connoting discipleship, tradition) and *Nachahmung* (connoting mechanical imitation, copying) is intended to explicate the ability of aesthetic judgment to reach its conclusions not by means of fixed models or exemplars (*Mustern*) but in consequence of a reflexive turn that finds in its own workings the basis for an objectification of judgment. The example, Kant writes here, rather than functioning as model, serves to "trace out" ("auf die Spur zu bringen") how reason is led to "seek in itself the principles that govern its operations" (*CJ*, sec. 32).

The methodological status of exemplarity in Kant's philosophy is especially evident in his elucidation of the reflective (as distinct from the determinant) judgment—a central category of the aesthetic theory. Kant conceived the reflective judgment as a way of establishing a form of generality or finality that is neither apodictic (derived from a rule) nor empirical (based on experience) but "only *exemplary*," defining it as "the necessity of the agreement of *all* [men] in a judgment that can be considered as an example for a general rule that cannot be stated" (*CJ*, sec. 18). Exemplarity here involves a principle of communality (*Gemeinsinn*) that serves as a basis for the general communicability of cognitive data (*CJ*, sec. 21). The "general rule that cannot be stated" signifies not a hidden or inaccessible truth but the *positing* of such a generality as the condition for predication and communicability. While the standard invoked here may be "a merely ideal norm" (*CJ*, sec. 22), it serves as the necessary bridge between subjective judgments of taste and any general standard of aesthetic value. In summary, the plurality of functions that Kant denotes as example is designed to allow us to grasp what cannot be grasped otherwise, conceptually or iconically.

In section 14 of the *Critique of Judgment*, "Elucidation by Examples," Kant characterizes "pure aesthetic judgments" (as opposed to "empirical" ones) in a negative manner by citing features of aesthetic objects that might be assigned an "extrinsic," or supplementary, function but that are not "an intrinsic constituent" of an object's beauty. He terms these "ornaments (*parerga*)" and provides as illustration the frames of paintings, the drapery of statues, and the colonnades around monumental buildings (*CJ*, sec. 14). This effort to separate out ancillary or ornamental features (*par-ergon* = what is outside the work) from the work proper, the work in its essence, provides the basis for a far-ranging critique by Jacques Derrida of Kant's aesthetic project. Kant's attempt to draw a clear line of separation between a work of art and its frame or setting is symptomatic for Derrida of a fundamental split in the concept of aesthetic judgment: if the singular instance, the "case in concreto," is intended to exhibit the process of judgment, as Kant maintains elsewhere, the argument of this part of the *Critique of Judgment* significantly attenuates the criteria for any judgment of beauty and betrays what Derrida terms a combination of "inner infirmity" and "intrinsic ideality" in regard to the example.[22]

Repeatedly in his writings, Derrida challenges the grounds for stipulating a division, a potential barrier in any construct of ideas or concepts. Thus, in regard to the seriation and segmentation at work in the idea of genre, he writes:

What is at stake is exemplarity and its whole *enigma*—in other words, as the word enigma indicates, exemplarity and the *récit* which works through the logic of the example. . . . The trait that marks membership inevitably divides, the boundary of the set comes to form, by invagination, an internal pocket larger than the whole; and the outcome of this division and of this abounding remains as singular as it is limitless.[23]

For Derrida, virtually any form of articulation or segmentation will unravel the very unity that the instance, the example, was designed to underwrite.[24] Where Kant, in the *Critique of Pure Reason*, acknowledged the facilitating but auxiliary function of examples by characterizing them as wheelchairs or strollers for the judgment ("Gängelwagen der Urteilskraft," *CPR*, A 134), Derrida makes light of the image with a series of fanciful variants. "These exemplary wheels are finally prostheses which replace nothing."[25] However assiduously Kant might seek to rein in or restrict the example, what is operative, Derrida insists, is "a principle of contamination, a law of impurity, a parasitical economy."[26]

Another version of the deconstructive critique of example may be found in Jean-Luc Nancy's imputation of a constitutive fall, a lapsarian fallibility, at the heart of judgment. Nancy's argument inverts the Kantian presentation and asks what judgment would be if we were to begin with its product, the instance or case that is meant to signify the rule. His model is a juridical one: *case* stands for *example*. In the logic of law, of justice (*le droit*), Nancy argues, law should be a universal code: each case should be foreseen. In practice, each needs to be situated and legitimated, case by case. The "essence" of law is thus placed in a singular relation with the essence of accident. "What is at issue here is the necessity of the accident."[27] The judge establishes what is right or just (*le droit*) by determining the relation of law to the case *hic et nunc* in question. The case is thus raised—*relevé, aufgehoben*—to the level of law. But what is pronounced is always only "the law *of* this case and *in* this case." If the judgment is conceived as the agency responsible for selecting the case, isn't this very choice nothing more than a confirmation of the circumstantial nature of the case, the way the case in its irreducible singularity is made *to fall* into place as a prop for the law? For either the judgment, in choosing, fashions or constructs the case to fit the rule, or it is nothing but a formal sanction for a "fall" (*lapsus*) that takes place with or without it. "The logic of the case is to fall or slip on itself: logic of the relapse." Here judgment is reduced to staging a fall, the accident of a fit between case and law.

For both Derrida and Nancy example is only another of the ruses whereby metaphysics seeks to validate its proximity to meaning or truth, a ruse to guard against but at the same time to subject to constant testing. "On guard—example ahead," they seem to warn, but by this very move do they not set up another law, a law of the regulated and systematic disabling of example, which leaves in its wake the Other of example: *lapsus, différance*, trace?

It is in this sense that Irene E. Harvey argues that Derrida's persistent, ever renewed concern with example and exemplarity constitutes less the working-through of an enigma than a version of his own entanglement in the ontological system that he has so massively deconstructed.[28] Of course, the practice of deconstruction cannot rid itself of entanglement, nor does it claim to. But the kind of reservation that Harvey expresses still deserves attention. Thus, in discussing Derrida's treatment of Hegel in *Glas*, she writes:

[H]e reveals that non-exemplarity—the Jews, Antigone, the signature—*obeys another law*: the law of the Other, one might call it. In this way, as instance of the trace of differance, these non-examples are precisely what they are not: examples. Has metaphysics ever done anything else? Namely, is metaphysics itself not constituted by the very process of turning the non-example into an example (of something else ostensibly more general)? (196)

Harvey's critique of Derrida on this issue is less an attempt to challenge or refute than to foreground a pattern, to demonstrate that insofar as the logic of exemplarity is the regulated instantiation of a conceptual framework, it cannot be elided or bypassed but only, as it were, displaced and reiterated. Derrida's work has the great merit, as we have seen, of insisting that the rule, the conceptual principle underpinning the logic of exemplarity, is both internal and external, that it is typically played out at the level of the frame, the boundaries, the switch of inclusion-exclusion. Though Harvey maintains, "Derrida does *not question*, nor can he question the strategy of exemplarity itself" (207), she can conclude, "[h]e performs it instead" (215).[29]

In a traditional rhetorical context, as we have seen, the effectiveness of example is based on the availability of a repertory of instances accredited by memory and tradition. In addition to providing models, paradigms in an ethical and religious sense, traditional forms of exemplarity give scope to an illustrative and pictorial function in argumentation and narrative. Where the applicability of examples diverges significantly from an established normative basis, they come to serve not as confirmation of a rule but as an instrument of testing, of possible revision. My discussion of Kant was designed to underscore a shift in the status of exemplarity, a shift from a level of communal discourse where exemplarity is allied to practical wisdom to one where the very constitution of the subject becomes dependent on exemplarity. In place of the subject as an agent of experience (i.e., of examples) Kant puts forward the notion of a self-regulating subject that draws on examples at the point where the limits of conceptual exposition are reached. The deconstructionist critique—in one sense a reaction to this Kantian tactic—is to expose the risk of a "metaphysical" residue in exemplarity, of any tendency to arrest the slippage of signifiers in the name of a master signified.

In conclusion I want to focus on the performative and ethical aspect of a rhetoric of exemplarity. At the level of praxis there is a continual need to judge in the absence of definitive criteria, whether in aesthetic terms ("Is it beautiful?") or in moral terms ("Is it right?"). Far from being unconsidered or merely intuitive, this form of judgment operates in the manner of Kant's reflective judgment, that is, by invoking a "general rule that cannot be stated." Though the rule or law as such cannot be formulated, its point (or *pointing*) emerges from what Lyotard has termed a "symbolization . . . through permutations of instances."[30] The example does not stand alone but inaugurates a dynamic that displaces the instance. Each variant or alternative, whether introduced for clarification or for refinement, shifts the direction of the argument, the point of the example.

It is in the Wittgenstein of the *Philosophical Investigations* that we find a sustained reflection on the effect of a series, the tendency or "drift" that multiple instances set into motion. "You give him examples,—but he has to guess their drift."[31] The focus here on the level of practices rather than foundations reorients the issue of the singular and the universal. Rules are taken as "sign-posts" along a path (see *PI*, sec. 85). They may be limiting but are not mandatory or prohibitive in any absolute sense. You can always not follow a rule, though you may pay for it. At the same time any instance of a rule in practice can raise questions as to how it is to be taken, what application it has in a given case. Wittgenstein finds a radical paradox in the need to link a rule to an interpretation. For the true test of a rule is how it is acted upon, what practice or form of life it gives rise to, but our need to supply cognitive validation, to *know* what the rule means, draws us repeatedly into a mode of interpretation, into an attempt to formulate the fit between the rule and the case at hand. The paradox to which this gives rise—that we are supposedly guided by a rule, but can only know the rule by looking at the behavior that enacts it—is reflected in the convergence of existential urgency and logical blockage that may be found in the *Philosophical Investigations*. Wittgenstein's sense of the indetermination of the rule in relation to the act of judgment illuminates the pragmatic aspect of example, its way of bringing together a model and a directive.[32] For the example is never merely an instance; it is an instance plus its vector of reception. Nothing guarantees that a reception, an "uptake" in Austin's sense,[33] will come out right. Nor need the form of the uptake be precisely calibrated. But as example, the particular is projected beyond itself, not so much toward a formulable rule, a universal, as toward what Wittgenstein termed "a form of life." And in the process rules of a kind, arising from the seriation of instances, may be repeatedly invoked and displaced.

What is most at stake in the use of example is perhaps the stake itself, the imputation that a particular functions in such a way that a judgment is called for. The rhetorical force of example is to impose on the audience or interlocutor an obligation to judge. Whether it be in argument or narrative, the rhetoric of example stages an instance of judgment, and the reader, in order to grasp the point at issue, must be capable of occupying, however provisionally, the seat of judgment. The reader does not simply occupy a post of reception, as in a communicative transmission, but is drawn into the process of weighing alternative arguments or cases. Yet the scandal of example, its logical fallibility, lies in the fact that this ethical summons—the obligation to judge—is predicated not on a law or rule—thus at the level of the general or universal—but on the instance in its particularity, an instance that cannot in itself suffice to justify the principle in question. Yet this situation is in no sense exceptional. As readers, as interpreters, we are continually and inescapably called upon to make judgments on insufficient grounds. It is this condition that the studies in this volume seek to elucidate.[34]

*

The aim of this collection is to demonstrate that while example has a rich genealogy in the rhetorical tradition, it involves
as well questions of practice and structure that converge with
central preoccupations of present-day theory in literature and
philosophy. Most of these essays were written expressly for this
volume. Some grew out of papers delivered at sessions of the
1987 and 1988 annual meetings of the International Association for Philosophy and Literature; others were solicited; and
three were published previously. They are grouped here according to certain common orientations, as explained below, though
these groupings cannot do justice to the multiple and complex
linkages among them.

Daniel Boyarin's and Stephen G. Nichols's studies deal with
example within a larger historical context of rhetoric and figuration—Boyarin treating the ancient Jewish form of midrash,
and Nichols a central strand of medieval and Renaissance writing. Two other essays—by John D. Lyons and Louis Marin—offer detailed analyses of instances in the Renaissance (Montaigne's *Essays* and *The Logic of Port-Royal*, respectively).

Four of the essays focus on the status of example within literary structures. The illustrations extend from Aesopian fables
(the essays by Thomas Keenan and Alexander Gelley), to Kleist
(Gelley), Nietzsche (J. Hillis Miller), and Kafka (Ewa Ziarek).

The final four essays situate the issue of example more specifically in philosophical and political terms. Irene E. Harvey's
study of Rousseau deals with a use of example as applied, or political, rhetoric. David Lloyd's and Cathy Caruth's essays examine, in very different ways, the status of exemplarity in Kant.
And Herman Rapaport uses a photograph as an occasion for reflecting on image and responsibility in the context of Emmanuel Levinas's thought.

Historical Forms of Exemplarity

Daniel Boyarin's study deals with the ancient Jewish genre of
midrash—a tradition of biblical commentary that flourished in
the first four centuries A.D.—a genre predicated on a faith in the
referential validity, the absolute truth, of the biblical narrative

but nonetheless oriented to a highly self-conscious process of questioning and eludication. Drawing on elements of recent rhetorical and narrative theory, Boyarin shows that, within the form of commentary, the Rabbis developed a complex structure of fictive and, in a sense, performative discourse that runs tributary to the primary text.

It is hardly surprising that a highly developed culture of interpretation such as that of midrash should go far in thematizing its own procedures. Boyarin develops in detail one instance, a midrash on Exodus 14:19, where the interpenetration of two narrative strands—one a story from the Bible, the other a figurative narrative adapted to it—seems at first sight to be abbreviated since it does not make explicit any relation of simile or allegory between the narratives. Yet it is precisely the elliptical presentation, the way that the "parable proper" functions as a "shadow double" to the "real narrative" (the referential biblical account) that makes the structure as a whole figurative of its own practice, a parable of parable. For what is operative here is not a model of reflection where one strand mimes the other but a model of mutual implication where the meaning is sought by way of a third, implicit factor, the label or code marking the features that make the collocation of narratives possible at all.

In his analysis of Montaigne's art of quotation Stephen G. Nichols emphasizes a graphic and performative dimension of *exemplum* that derives from a systematic breaching of traditional rhetorical and narrative patterns. The initial point of reference of this essay is Homeric epic, taken as representative of a congruence between *nomos* and *ethos*, between a level of custom, sedimented in folkways and law, the *dire* of a culture, and one of practical ethics and behavior patterns, the *faire*. Whereas the representational style of Homeric epic aimed at a congruence between the two, Montaigne's use of exemplary instances tends in the opposite direction, bent on exposing the continual risk of disjunction between *faire* and *dire*.

What Nichols undertakes, then, is to sketch a context for Montaigne's innovation through a wide-ranging survey of medieval allegorical and rhetorical practices—from Saint Augustine in the fourth century to John the Scot (Eriugena) in the ninth, and finally to Dante in the thirteenth. Eriugena, in his *Commentary on the Gospel of Saint John*, represents a mediating stage between Dante's high medieval mode of *historia*, in which questions of meaning and action are projected onto a transcendent symbolic plane, and a more mixed allegorical mode—that of *allegoria facti et dicti*, allegory of word and deed—which gives greater scope to a level of behavior and action to intervene in the interpretation. Nichols lays out a complex historical fabric, showing that the achievement of the Montaigne essay, its "knowledge gleaned from insufficiency," represents a highly original and forceful application of principles that a long tradition had made available.

John D. Lyons's essay focuses on the interplay of similarity and difference as the basis for Montaigne's practice of example. What makes Montaigne's thought so instructive is its persistent testing of fundamental, elementary principles of discrimination. The practice of citation utilized by Montaigne derives from a long-standing tradition, but the determined application of a principle of selectivity capable of linking historical instances and personal experience represents a significant departure.

Lyons's study illuminates the patience and ingenuity of a mind turned on the proliferating multiplicity of nature and the endless diversification of experience. The disclosure of pattern arises from a kind of controlled intervention, the "uncoupling movement," in Lyons's analysis, that is able to sift through the accumulation of notations and observations. Montaigne's "internalization of the logic of example," is indicative of an ongoing reflection on the process of example formation in the *Essays*.

Louis Marin has, in numerous writings, evolved a powerful and supple semiological analysis of the relations of representation and power. In *Food for Thought* he argued that the use of the "example" of the consecratory utterance ("This is my body") "sheds light on how the sign functions as a representation during the act in which the speaking subject articulates a judgment."[35] By "representation" Marin suggests a quasi-performative model, thus a function that is not merely illustrative but foundational. In the present essay he develops this issue, showing that *The Logic of Port-Royal* allows an empirical enunciation—the discourse-of-the-example—to provide a rational prop for a "theological model," a model that had hitherto been guaranteed primarily by a " 'mysterious' theology of the sacramental sign."

When Marin states that maps and paintings as icons of signs show that "the example is the icon of discourse and it is inside discourse," we understand his "inside" as signifying both a structural feature and a disarticulating or "disappropriating" effect. The sign, he continues, works through an "excitation" or "transport" from the sign as operation to the sign as thing represented. The example, then, will function analogously: the example as icon of discourse will transpose its effectivity to the example as product of discourse: the map or painting will be endowed with a quotient of "reality" by virtue of this transfer. The argument thus leads back to the paradigmatic status of the eucharistic enunciation, "This is my body," and its consequences in the structure of representation and power (e.g., "The portrait of Caesar is Caesar," as developed by Marin in *Portrait of the King*).[36] Or, in the terms of the conclusion of the text discussed in the present essay, "when dealing with propositions . . . we are able, on some occasions, to affirm the things signified."

Exemplarity in Literature

"The fable is a dangerous snare." La Fontaine's saying is cited in both Thomas Keenan's essay and my own. What is at issue is the double track of all didactic narrative—part story, to be interpreted and enjoyed, part address, to be responded to. The reader or auditor is caught between two rhetorics (genres of discourse, Lyotard would say) that do not mesh.

In narrative theory the narratee signifies an agency of reception insofar as it is encoded in the narrator's discourse. Keenan's essay explores what may be termed a performative or appellative aspect of this function. "The fable at once thematizes and calls, is addressed to (about *and* for, subject matter *and* destination) the second-person singular—in general," he writes. While the formulation of a "general" addressee is reminiscent of the way that Kant's reflective judgment brings about a shift from the singular to the universal, Keenan's position is resolutely un-Kantian and even anti-Kantian in insisting on the fragility of the subject position and the impossibility of using it as a springboard for a generalized subject. (In the Kantian model, it should be added, the shift is from the first to the third, not the second, person.) Keenan's analysis brings out that the exemplarity of a narrative is always dependent on a prior positing of a subject position, whether at the level of address, of reception, or of nomination, yet this positing is just what the fable is designed to secure. Thus the element of risk—La Fontaine's snare—contaminates both the discourse and the message. "Responsibility begins in the bad example," is Keenan's provocative entry into this problematic.

My own essay takes its point of departure from a tripartite model of parabolic narrative that distinguishes a factor of principle or truth (the moral or rule), one of illustration (the narrative "proper"), and one of effectivity or performative potential (the moral or injunction). While these three elements constitute the implicit structure of exemplary narrative (as Susan Suleiman has shown), they are by no means isomorphic, nor can it be assumed that they will function coordinately. "[C]an any example ever truly fit a general proposition?" Paul de Man asked: "[I]s not its particularity, to which it owes the illusion of its intelligibility, necessarily a betrayal of the general truth it is supposed to support and convey?"

Thus we begin with something like a functional rhetorical structure—a machinery of pedagogy and persuasion—and introduce a fundamental challenge to its integrity, its operativity. But the structure has its uses. When we single out the constituent elements and test their workings in specific instances, we find that the two ends of the parabolic structure—the principle or rule and the moral or injunction—can give rise to a dynamic not accounted for by the model. Heinrich von Kleist's "Über das Marionettentheater" (On the marionette theater) is one of the counterexemplary narratives discussed in this light.

Both Ewa Ziarek and J. Hillis Miller deal with parable as a species of exemplification—"parable" here understood as a narrative form that both thematizes and occludes a performative or ethical dimension. The "darkness" of parable demands an interpretive investment that is motivated by more than curiosity—a form of risk or moral testing. Parable's resistance to interpretation reflects an implicit tension. On the one hand it operates by shifting or transposing meaning, as indicated in the Greek derivation of metaphor—*meta-pherein*, movement across, transport. On the other hand, it involves a form of resemblance or mimesis, as indicated in the German word for parable, *Gleichnis*. What this suggests is not a mere alternative derivation or multiplicity of functions but rather a constitutive overdetermination: parable is both mobile and specular, an agency of displacement and a form of similitude. The essays by Ziarek and Miller explore certain implications of this paradox.

In *Zarathustra* Nietzsche sought to present a number of his central philosophical concepts in narrative form. What interests Miller is that the very form of such "presentation" involves a narrative apparatus that is itself suspended or displaced by Nietzsche's conception of language. Miller argues that the radically indeterminate figurality of *Zarathustra* represents an elaboration of a theory of tropes, and of a concurrent epistemology, already evident in Nietzsche's early lectures on rhetoric and the essay fragment "On Truth and Lying." The rueful self-characterization that Nietzsche puts in Zarathustra's mouth— "I speak in parables and limp and stammer like poets"—may be taken, then, as a fundamental reflection on the status of language.

Ewa Ziarek draws on Walter Benjamin's striking insight into Kafka's project: "he sacrificed truth for the sake of clinging to its transmissibility." Interpreting Benjamin's reading of Kafka in the larger context of his theory of translation, Ziarek argues that this "sacrifice of truth" questions the exemplary meaning of the parable not only in epistemological terms—that is, with reference to the foundation of truth—but also in communal terms—with reference to the ideal unity of the community sustained by ways of talking. The material constructs that Kafka evokes as frame or setting for communal life—tower, burrow, wall, bridge—generate those enigmatic narratives of an ordained yet repeatedly aborted transmission, a pattern that Ziarek identifies as "the double bind of the exemplary narrative itself, in which the moral relies on the mediation of both the redundant narrative and incomplete figural language." Despite this critique of the traditional tasks of the parable, Benjamin's interpretation of Kafka nonetheless preserves a paradoxical sense of obligation, which he stakes against both the oblivion of the past and the "negative theology" of aestheticism.

Exemplarity in Philosophy

Irene E. Harvey deals with one of the fundamental concepts of Rousseau's *Social Contract*, the status of the legislator. If, in constituting a state, the legislator establishes the laws as its foundation, where is a foundation for the legislator to be sought? To say that it is in some fiat or revelation from a divine source is to displace but not resolve the issue, for the form of any such revelation needs to be mediated by the legislator. At a rhetorical level Rousseau repeatedly invokes the pattern of example, which draws on a principle of similarity or analogy, in order to constitute the Exemplar, which draws on the principle of singularity or uniqueness.

In analyzing the examples of legislators from ancient history that Rousseau recurrently cites—notably, Moses, Lycurgus, and Numa—Harvey discloses a consistent tactic (what she terms a "ploy") designed to validate the founding principle of a legislative polity. It is a tactic that involves the coordinate and imbricated operation of a rhetorical and a religious-mythic model. At the level of religion and myth Rousseau consistently exposes the pretensions of miracles and other signs of divine sanction insofar as they are taken as violations of the natural order, while he acknowledges their effectiveness, indeed their necessity, as a manifestation of the legislator's singularity. The operant procedure necessitates the subordination of *some* instances in favor of *one*, which becomes the goal, the telos, the Exemplar.

David Lloyd turns to an issue that has come increasingly into prominence in recent years: the paradox of Kant's turn to aesthetics in the third *Critique* as a way of providing a new foundation for the moral philosophy developed in the second *Critique*, a foundation based primarily not on the categorical imperative but on the idea of a communal consensus that would not be subject to an ethics of obligation. In examining the *sensus communis*, the basis of the category of taste in the third *Critique*, Lloyd underscores the extent to which this concept is founded on an appeal to example—both specifically, insofar as empirical examples are repeatedly invoked, and generically, in that "the exemplarity of the example . . . is not a characteristic of the object itself . . . but must be referred . . . to the judging subject." What results is a thoroughgoing formalization of the judgment, whereby the example that should mark its link to experience undergoes a transformation into the exemplar as product of an idealizing aesthetic-pedagogic projection.

Lloyd finds evidence in Kant for a fundamental shift in the ideology of pedagogy in the period in question. But the special interest of his argument for our topic lies in its focus on the paradox implicit in the third *Critique*, whereby the status of example as singular instance (*Beispiel*) is displaced by its regulative function in the system of pedagogy as exemplar or paradigm (*Muster*). The aesthetic sphere becomes, in consequence, prey to a contradictory necessity: the subject, in the formation of its critical autonomy, requires the positing of an *idea*, a "concept of reason" in Kant's sense, but any instantiation that it elicits as example must fall short of the model that is sought.

Cathy Caruth's essay addresses a fundamental assumption in Kant's thought. "It was the innovation of critical philosophy," she writes, "to question the attempt to model philosophical understanding on mathematics or scientific law, by rigorously examining the principle of their difference." It should be noted that the *modeling*, in her argument, involves "the principle of their difference." The difference remains, but the foregrounding of the *principle* of the difference points to the "transcendental" turn of the Kantian criticism.

Caruth shows that transcendental thought operates by way of a kind of "negative self-reflection," an exercise of self-limitation with reference to an "externality" that is "no longer precisely mathematical (or empirical) but conceptual." It is at this juncture in the argument that the function of example as a narrative articulation of a conceptual relation emerges.

In Caruth's demonstration a narrative example intervenes at "points of articulation within the system," and testifies to a structure that has been overburdened, that betrays an imbalance (or "asymmetry") needing to be righted. To put it another way, the "righting" of the imbalance, the effort to stabilize an asymmetry, is just what provides the occasion for a leap from concept to narrative, from symbol to illustrative example. A distinction that Caruth draws between the symbol—that is, "the thinking of the relation of the sensible to the supersensible" and its *concept*—"the definition of the symbol in critical discourse"—allows her to specify this latter stage as "a kind of positing that cannot be recuperated symbolically. This nonrecuperation would be marked by the proliferation of examples, not 'empirical' examples, but examples in the argument, linguistic examples, which would always eventually take the form of a narrative." What is termed "linguistic" here, it should be noted, designates not merely language or fictionality but the possibility of realizing the self-reflexivity of the symbol by way of an exemplary structure.

Herman Rapaport takes a certain photograph, a "snapshot," and thus in a sense the most circumstantial trace of a historical moment in its mimetic immediacy, and reflects on its possible impact in various contexts: as image, as historical document, as an instantiation of ethical law. The most striking feature of the photograph is the face of a child, a victim of a Nazi roundup of Jews in Warsaw, his face expressing the most poignant sense of dread and abandonment. Rapaport raises such questions as, How may this photograph be read? More specifically, What allows us to draw a lesson from the image of this face? And further, Who is addressed by this image?

Rapaport draws on the work of Emmanuel Levinas, a thinker representative of both Jewish theology and phenomenology (Husserl, Merleau-Ponty, Heidegger). It would appear that in regard to the image as a representational and ethical medium, these orientations would be radically incompatible. In Husserl and Merleau-Ponty the image is a fundamental constituent of an epistemology that has marked ontological tendencies. By contrast, in the Judaic tradition the significance of the pictorial image is altogether eclipsed in favor of the word and the text. For Levinas, as Rapaport reminds us, "the Judaic notion of the law is an anti-mimetic or iconoclastic imperative."

At the same time, Levinas has insisted on the paradigmatic status of the face as a phenomenal irruption that is foundational for ethics though it is anterior to any social polity. As Rapaport makes clear, Levinas's position would not endorse anything like an "epiphantic disclosure" of the divine by means of the face as image or icon. Yet, in spite of the iconoclastic disposition of the Judaic tradition that Levinas draws on, Rapaport proposes an exemplifying function for the image, not as icon but as singular, nongeneralizable instance of an ethical summons. In suggesting the possibility of assimilating a radical singularity to a form of ethical obligation, Rapaport's essay develops something like a limiting condition for exemplarity.

PART I

Historical Forms of Exemplarity

Take the Bible for Example

Midrash as Literary Theory

> All fiction is exemplary.
> —Michael Riffaterre

The nature of biblical narrative is hotly contested territory in recent critical writing. Robert Alter threw down a certain gauntlet when he wrote, "prose fiction is the best general rubric for describing biblical narrative,"[1] and the challenge was taken up by Meir Sternberg, who argued that the "narrative . . . illegitimates all thought of fictionality on pain of excommunication."[2] In a recent paper I have addressed the controversy between these two critics and argued that the very terms of their disagreement are based on an incomplete conception of literary history, for the organization of narratives into fictions and histories in the way that we know it is a production of a particular sociocultural moment—not the one in which the Bible was produced.[3] The notion I developed there was that the distinction we make between fiction and historiography is essentially one of reading practice; accepting the reliability of the "omniscient implied author" (not necessarily narrator, of course) and "suspension of disbelief" being two of the most reliable markers of a practice of reading a text as fiction. From this point of view, it is clear why Alter and Sternberg must disagree; on the one hand, ancient receivers of the Bible almost surely accepted the reliability of the omniscient implied author (God!), but on the other hand they did not suspend disbelief. They believed, on pain of excommunication indeed. From the perspective of our reading practice, then, biblical narrative is suspended in an ambiguous position somewhere between fiction and historiography.

In this paper, I wish to approach the problem from another angle entirely, the angle of semiotic structures in narrative itself. When we consider other characteristics traditionally utilized to distinguish forms of narrative, we see that narrative, even in our cultural system, does not divide itself up so neatly into historiography and fiction. Historiography, as shown so elegantly by Hayden White in his several works, is as "artificial" in its narrative structures, its plotting, as fiction, and indeed very close to fiction in its semiotics. Therefore we are no longer prohibited from regarding a narrative text as historiography by the discovery of structured plotting, rhetorical artifice, linguistic play, and the like in that text, nor *a fortiori* are we compelled, as Alter argues we are, to regard a narrative as fiction by the fact that "virtually every utterance of biblical narrative reveals the presence of writers who relished the words and the materials of storytelling with which they worked, who delighted, because after all they were writers, in pleasing cadences and surprising deflections of syntax, in complex echoing effects among words, in the kind of speech they could fashion for the characters and how the self-same words could be ingeniously transformed as they were passed from narrator to character or from one character to another."[4] On the other hand, fiction is clearly a carrier of vital truths for us, truths that we may not be excommunicated for disregarding but that often have other effects just as dire (or even more so). If anyone needs convincing of that, the wave of suicides among European youths after the publication of *The Sorrows of Young Werther* ought to do the job. Michael Riffaterre is the theoretician who has most sharply inquired into the seeming oxymoron of "fictional truth." Riffaterre argues: "All literary genres are artifacts, but none more blatantly so than fiction. Its very name declares its artificiality, and yet it must somehow be true to hold the interest of its readers, to tell them about experiences at once imaginary and relevant to their own lives. The paradox of truth in fiction is the problem for which I propose to seek a solution."[5] So, in a sense, both Alter and Sternberg are right; the Bible is a kind of fiction that banishes all thought of fictionality on pain of excommunication. We have the paradox of "truth in fiction" with a vengeance here. I wish in this paper to explore a solution to this problem offered by some of the most ancient readers of the Hebrew Bible, the Rabbis[6] of the midrash and Talmud. These assiduous readers of the Bible made extensive use of the notion of exemplarity in their reading; indeed, the exemplum or parable was the privileged hermeneutic device. Although their discursive practices were, of course, entirely different from our Platonic-Aristotelian ones and many of their cultural assumptions were different, I think we can learn something about how exemplarity is related to historiography, truth, and fiction by studying their use and discussion of the parable as a hermeneutic form.[7]

In the Hebrew of the midrash and of the Talmud, the same words mean "example" and "parable." The Rabbis actually use the word "dugma," a normal word for "sample" or "example," as another name for the mashal, or midrashic parable, that special kind of exemplary narrative that they deployed as a hermeneutic key for the understanding of the Torah. It is not insignificant that these two words derive from different lexical sources in Hebrew, "dugma" being of course a Greek-derived word while "mashal" is of Semitic origin. "Dugma," from Greek deîgma carries with it from its *etymon* more abstract senses of "pattern," "model" as well as "sample" or "example," while "mashal" has an original and basic sense of "likeness."[8] We learn the partial equivalence of these two vocables from the following text:

And not only that Kohellet was wise, he moreover taught knowledge to the people, and proved and researched, and formulated many meshalim [= parables] [Ecclesiastes 12:9]—"and proved" words of Torah, "and researched" words of Torah; he made handles[9] for the Torah. You will find that until Solomon existed, there was no *dugma*.[10]

The last sentence in the midrash, "until Solomon existed there was no *dugma*" is a paraphrase of the last phrase in the verse, "formulated many meshalim." It follows that the midrash has translated "meshalim" (the plural of "mashal") by "dugma." "Dugma," it is clear, is a synonym for "mashal." "Example" means "parable."

Moreover, the categories of parable and of fiction are perfectly coterminous in the literary theory of the Rabbis. The consequence of all this is that fiction is inextricably bound up with exemplarity in rabbinic textual theory. The next citation makes this dramatically clear:

R. Eliezer says: the dead whom Ezekiel raised stood on their feet, uttered a song, and died. What song did they utter? God kills justly and resurrects mercifully. R. Yehoshua says: they uttered this song: God kills and resurrects, takes down to Sheol, and will raise up [I Samuel 2:6]. R. Yehuda says: in reality it was a mashal [= parable and example]. R. Nehemiah said to him: If a mashal then why "in reality," and if, "in reality," then why a mashal?! But, indeed, he meant that it was really a mashal. R. El'azar the son of R. Yosi Hagelili says: the dead whom Ezekiel raised went up to the Land of Israel, took wives and begat sons and daughters. R. Yehuda ben Beteira stood on his feet and said: I am one of their grandchildren, and these are the phylacteries which my grandfather left to me from them.[11]

This text draws a very strong contrast between parables and referential claims of truth. They are considered to be mutually exclusive opposites. This is indicated in the text in two ways: first of all by the self-contradiction that R. Nehemiah claims to find in R. Yehuda's statement that in reality the story of the Dry Bones is a parable and secondly by the attempt to contradict the parabolic status of the text by asserting its actual concrete referentiality—to the extent that there are "real" objects in the world that certify this. Something cannot be a parable and be real. If something is real then it cannot be a parable. The parable is thus coextensive with fiction. Indeed, it may be the only name that the Rabbis have for fiction, as opposed to lying, a category into which they obviously do not place parables. This same view of things is presupposed by other rabbinic statements as well, such as "Job never was created and never was, but it (the Book)/he (the man) is a parable."

The claim of the Rabbis that all the exemplary is fiction provides an elegant counterpart to Riffaterre's apothegm that all fiction is exemplary. In any case, having established that the mashal is synonymous in rabbinic literary theory with fiction, we can see that at least for this culture, the problem of the referentiality of the fiction is crucially bound up with the notion of the example and its semantic-semiotic problematic. A good starting place for our analysis would seem to be then a study of the notion of the example itself. In my analysis, I shall make use of a paper of Nelson Goodman's published several years ago that draws important distinctions in the semantics of exemplification and in particular analyzes the way that exemplarity intersects with the problem of referentiality.[12] I shall claim an essential isomorphism between the conceptualization of this issue in the Rabbis and in Goodman.

Exemplification was one of the most significant modes of expression in rabbinic thought. They spent great efforts at determining for themselves what an example is and how it works or teaches, particularly in the privileged type of rabbinic discourse, interpretation. To be sure, they never use the abstract and systematic discursive modes favored in our philosophy, but rather speak (consistently with their whole stance) about examples in examples. As we shall see by closely analyzing several texts, they arrived at quite a complex understanding of exemplification in general and of its relation to the conundrums of fictional/parabolic reference:

And command you the Israelites that they will bring olive oil [Exodus 27:20]. *Your eyes are doves* [Song of Songs 1:15]. Rabbi Yitzhaq said, God said to them, Your dugma is like that of a dove. One who wishes to buy wheat says to his associate, show me their dugma, you also your dugma is *like that* of a dove. How so? When Noah was in the ark what is written? *And he sent the dove* [Genesis 8:10], *and the dove came to him in the evening [and behold, it was grasping an olive leaf in its mouth]* [Genesis 8:11]. Said the Holy One to Israel, Just as the dove brought light into the world, also you who have been compared [*nimšalt*] to a dove, bring olive oil and light before me, for it says, *And command you the Israelites that they will bring olive oil.*[13]

This is a complex and interesting text that justifies a somewhat lengthy analysis. In typical midrashic fashion, it uses a passage from the later Holy Writings to interpret a passage from the Five Books of Moses. This is a midrashic text of the type called "petihta," the motive of which is to show how all of the Prophets and Holy Writings can be shown to be commentary on the Torah. Accordingly, R. Yitzhaq demonstrates here that the verse of Song of Songs is a commentary on a passage in Exodus.[14] As

we shall see presently, the way that the Song of Songs is understood to interpret is by its being a mashal. This hermeneutic
connection is adumbrated in the cited text by the focus upon
one highly privileged instance of interpretive use of the Song,
namely the metaphorical depiction of Israel as a dove. The key
to the midrash is its opening move, which I cite here from its
original source in the midrash on Song of Songs: "*Your eyes are
doves* [Song of Songs 1:15]. Your dugma is like that of a dove."[15]
This hermeneutic assertion is based on an elaborate pun. The
Hebrew word "'ayin" ("eye") also has the meaning "color."
From this sense derives a series of prepositions, such as
"me'ein" and "k'ein," which mean "according to the likeness
of," or "following the example of."[16] From this there develops a
midrashic topos by which verses that include the word "eye"
can be glossed as having the sense of "dugma" as form or likeness, "figure" in both the sense of plastic form and the spiritual
or moral significance.[17]

Thematizing the notion of example directly, the text of R.
Yitzhaq constitutes a meta-midrash, a rare and precious explicit rabbinic comment on hermeneutics. The text depends for
its effect on the fact that "dugma" is polysemous. In fact, I
would suggest that the text plays with this polysemy deliberately, creating examples within examples, each of a slightly different type. This polysemy exploited by our midrash is a powerful key to the complexity of the notion of exemplarity and
thus of the exemplarity of fiction as well.

In his initial move after "translating" *Your eyes are like
doves* by "Your dugma is like that of a dove," Rabbi Yitzhaq explains the meaning of "dugma" by exemplifying it with the little narrative of one who goes to the market to buy wheat and
brings home a sample first.[18] The primary usage of "dugma" is
thus that of "sample" in the sense of a small portion of a substance that serves as a way of communicating to others the
properties of the substance, as, for instance, a small amount of
colored wool that a dyer would carry about as an indication of
the quality of his wares and work:

The tailor should not go out at the advent of the Sabbath with the needle in his garment, nor the carpenter with the splinter on his collar, nor

the dyer with the dugma on his ear, nor the money changer with the dinar in his ear. (*Tosefta Shabbat*, 1:8)

This text describes craftsmen whose custom is to advertise by carrying a small sign of their trade. The dyer would attach to his ear (or put in his ear) a small sample of dyed cloth, so that people would know what his work was, just as the money changer would advertise himself with a coin and the carpenter with a splinter. The dugma, here then, has two signifying functions. It serves as a conventional sign of the trade of its bearer but also as a sign of his ability and standards. If we compare it to the other two signs mentioned in the text, which are not called "dugma," this point will become clearer. On the one hand, the dugma of the dyer functions like the needle of the tailor or the splinter of the carpenter. It tells people that the trade of this person is such and such. On the other hand, the dugma stands in a part-whole relationship to the dyer's product and as such signifies directly the quality of his work. The word "dugma" here signifies a concrete portion of a mass (a "fusion" of all such similar objects) which through its characteristics manifests the characteristics of the entire mass. The mass which it signifies is just as concrete as the portion of the mass, as the dugma. In English we would use the word "sample" or "specimen" to convey this meaning. Dugma, then, clearly has the sense of "sample" or "example" as a portion or member of a class chosen and pointed out to show the characteristics of the entire class.

When God addressed Israel with the metaphor *Your eyes are doves*, what He really meant, according to R. Yitzhaq, was the dugma of Israel is like that of a dove. In order to illustrate this point, the rabbi gives an example of the literary form "dugma," that is to say, a dugma about dugma. The first dugma is very concrete indeed. It refers to the simplest usage of the word that I considered above, that of a sample of merchandise. This dugma of dugma (the dugma of the comparison of dugma to the sample of wheat) has its own parabolic application, namely, it *exemplifies* the type: parabolic signification. It is a dugma of the class "dugma" in *exactly* the same way that the dugma of the sample of wheat is a dugma of all of the wheat. Everything is equally concrete. The sample of wheat is as concrete as the silo full of wheat from which it was taken. Similarly, the example of the "wheat" is as concrete as the group (fusion—not class) of other instances of parabolic discourse to which it is being compared. Goodman too has discussed exactly this type of exemplification as its very prototypical form:

> Exemplification is reference by a sample to a feature of it. A tailor's swatch, in normal use, exemplifies its color, weave, and thickness, but not its size or shape; the note a concertmaster sounds before the performance exemplifies pitch but not timbre, duration, or loudness.
>
> Exemplification, then, far from being a variety of denotation, runs in the opposite direction, not from label to what the label applies to but from something a label applies to back to the label (or the feature associated with that label). . . . Exemplification is not mere possession of a feature but requires also reference to that feature; such reference is what distinguishes the exemplified from the merely possessed features.[19]

Goodman thus gives as his most basic type of example precisely the type that R. Yitzhaq adduced as his, the sample used by the merchant or tradesman to show off his wares.

Following the self-reflexive exemplification of dugma, the relation of the dove to Israel is discussed as similar to the relation of a sample of wheat to all of the wheat, or of this particular dugma (= example) to the whole category of dugma (= exemplification). Israel's dugma is a dove, just as the dugma of the wheat is the sample. This comparison is, however, considerably more complex. It is not nearly so straightforward as the one that compares the ratio of an example to the class "exemplification" with the ratio of a sample of wheat to the fusion "wheat," for, after all, a dove is not a member of the fusion "Israel." What we have here is what Goodman calls "complex reference." The way that "Israel's dugma is like a dove" works is most similar to the following case cited by Goodman:

> I may answer your question about the color of my house by showing a sample rather than by uttering a predicate; or I may merely describe the location of the appropriate sample on a color card you have. In the latter case, the chain of reference runs down from a verbal label to an instance denoted and then up to another label (or feature) exemplified. And a picture of a bald eagle denotes a bird that may exemplify a label

such as "bold and free" that in turn denotes and is exemplified by a given country.[20]

Note that this is almost precisely the way that "Israel's dugma is like a dove" functions. The word-picture "dove" denotes a bird that exemplifies a label that in turn denotes and is exemplified by a given people, Israel. However, we must also recognize (as certainly Goodman does) that the exemplification of the label "bold and free" by a bald eagle—actual, depicted, or denoted—is a culturally determined or intertextual function. The process of interpretation by exemplification is thus a picking out of the feature to which the exemplification will refer. The phrase "your dugma is like a dove" means a feature that you possess is like a feature of a dove, and by pointing out that feature in the denotation, "dove," that feature is referred to— exemplified. And what is that? Both the dove and Israel are light-bringers. The dove brought light to the world by bringing an olive branch, the concrete symbol of light, and Israel brings light to the world by bringing oil to the Temple.[21] It is important, however, to make clear that the Rabbis are not thereby exhausting the description of a dove or *a fortiori* of Israel. There is no abstraction here (in either a nominalistic or a realistic sense) but a placing of a concrete entity beside another concrete entity in such a way that characteristics that are obscure in the one are revealed by association with those same characteristics in the other, where they are obvious or explicit. This possibility of exemplifying Israel by a dove, once established on conventional, cultural, intertextual grounds, can be (as we shall see) very productive of other exemplifications. In other words, the very process of reading by example produces knowledge. It is certainly illuminating to note once more how close this brings us to Goodman's descriptions:

Such correlative chains must be understood as schematic constructions, and *not by any means as providing literal translations for metaphors.* The transfer of "mouse" from mice to a man may not be via the label "timid" or any other specific predicate. Moreover, metaphorical transfer need not follow antecedently established coexemplifications of a feature or label, verbal or nonverbal; the metaphorical application itself may participate in effecting coexemplification by the mice and the man of some one or more of their common features; and just what is exemplified may be sought rather than found.[22]

In the hermeneutics by example which rabbinic midrash practices, this becomes a doubly productive process, for once a certain mashal is established on the grounds of a given verse, that very metaphorical coexemplification is used precisely to seek that which is exemplified. The common midrashic questions "Why is the Torah compared to water?" and "Why is Israel compared to a dove?" are exact references to this process of search.

"Dugma" also conveys the meaning of the whole correlative chain or schematic construction that effects a coexemplification and points to common features between the denoted object and the example. We find this usage with reference to the unknowable essence of God Himself:

Tsofer Hana'mati said to Job: *Will you discover the extent of God's nature [ḥêqer]? . . . His measure is longer than the Universe* [Job 11:7 and 9]. Who can research [yaḥqor] His dugma, but indeed, *will you grasp the height of the heavens?* [verse 8]. What is the meaning of *will you grasp the height of the heavens?* Are you able to describe the One who made the heavens and the earth? Even Moses, who arose to the firmament and received the Torah from hand to hand did not understand His form.[23]

"Dugma" here obviously does not mean "example" or "sample" but something like "God's essential form." This emerges from the context, where it is clear that what is being talked about is the inability of humans to perceive or understand the essence of God. Even Moses, who was closer to God than any other human being, to whom God showed Himself, could not understand God's dugma or describe Him.[24] The biblical Hebrew word חקר (ḥêqer), which I have translated "extent of God's nature," is glossed here by "dugma";[25] so understanding "ḥêqer" may give us some insight into "dugma."

The verb from which the biblical noun is derived means to delve, to search out, to explore. The noun, as the object of the activity of the verb, often connotes that which is deep, hidden, essential, and unsearchable. Thus the sea is described in Job 38:16 as having no ḥêqer. The most significant text for our exploration here is, however, the following passage from Isaiah:

Unto whom will you compare Me, and to whom am I similar, says the
Holiness. Raise up your eyes to the heavens and see Who created these.
. . . Do you not know, have you not heard? The Eternal God, . . . His
wisdom is unfathomable [has no *hêqer*]. (Isaiah 40:25–28)

The second quoted verse follows logically from the first. God's
wisdom is unfathomable *because* there is no one to whom He
can be compared, that is to say in rabbinic parlance, He has no
dugma, that is, there is no other member of His class. It seems
quite likely that this text of Isaiah is what lies behind the gloss-
ing of "hêqer" by "dugma" in the midrash. We thus disclose
something of the significance of dugma itself. It is by placing an
individual into a class that we can understand its nature. Or
better, because this formulation almost inevitably leads us into
Greek-style abstraction: by placing an individual beside others
and denoting those others, we see what the features are that
characterize that individual and understand them. God, in
being sui generis, is thus beyond our understanding. "Dugma"
is thus a denoted object that refers to a label or feature coexem-
plified between the object we wish to understand and the
dugma. At the same time, however, it is also the exemplified label or feature itself. This explains, by the way, the vacillation
between "your dugma is a dove," "your dugma is like a dove,"
and "your dugma is like that of a dove."

As in Rabbi Yitzhaq's discourse, moving from example as a
denoted object to example as a denoted narrative raises the
complexity of analysis geometrically. However, when we study
the mashal, we will see a correspondence between the semantic
complexity of the notion of example and the semiotic complexity of the functioning of the example narrative. A mashal is an
explicitly fictional narrative that is placed beside a biblical narrative as a means of filling in its gaps. There is here, accordingly,
both a fictional text and a textual representation of the "actual"
events, standing in the relation of example and exemplified, as
the dove stands to Israel. The figure of Israel as a dove became,
in fact, one of the most productive sources of the mashal. One
such text is found in *Song of Songs Rabba*, on the verse "My
dove in the clefts of the rock, let me hear thy voice" (Song of
Songs 2:14):

The one of the house of R. Ishmael teaches: In the hour in which Israel went out from Egypt, to what were they similar? To a dove that ran away from a hawk, and entered the cleft of a rock and found there a nesting snake. She entered within, but could not go in, because of the snake; she could not go back, because of the hawk that was waiting outside. What did the dove do? She began to cry out and beat her wings, in order that the owner of the dovecote would hear and come to save her. That is how Israel appeared at the Sea. They could not go down into the Sea, for the Sea had not yet been split for them. They could not go back, for Pharaoh was coming near. What did they do? "They were mightily afraid, and the Children of Israel cried out unto the Lord" [Exodus 14:10] and immediately, "The Lord saved them on that day" [Exodus 14:30].[26]

With this text, we can begin to see the systemic ambiguity of the operation of the mashal within the hermeneutic practice of midrash. The text here rests on two common rabbinic assumptions—the identification of Israel with a dove, one of the sources of which we have seen above, and the identification of the entire Song of Songs as a dialogue between God and Israel at the time of the Crossing of the Red Sea.[27] What is going on in this text? First of all, the figurative utterance, "My dove in the clefts of the rock, let me hear thy voice," is being expanded into a full narrative, or rather it is being provided with a narrative context in which it can be read. What is the dove doing in the clefts of the rock? Who is addressing her? Why does he want to hear her voice, or why is it necessary that she make a sound? All of these questions are being answered by filling in the gaps of the narrative.[28] The dove is in the rock because she is afraid. But the rock is not a sufficient protection for her. The speaker is her master, and she must cry out so that he will save her. However, the claim is being made that this figure refers to a concrete situation in Israel's history, the crisis situation at the shore of the Red Sea. In order that we experience that situation fully, that we understand the predicament of the People, why they cried out unto the Lord and why He answered them, the verse of Song of Songs is associated with it by means of the mashal or narrative figure. The way that this parable is linked to the biblical story is identical to the way that the dove is linked to Israel in the meta-midrash above.

This is an interpretation, then, not so much of a verse of Song of Songs as of a verse of Exodus. The Rabbis explicitly refer to the Holy Song as a mashal, which, as we have seen, is for them synonymous with fiction; and, moreover, they clearly refer to the hermeneutic function of the fictional text:

The rabbis say: Do not let this mashal be light in your eyes, for by means of this mashal one comes to comprehend the words of Torah. A "mashal" to a king who has lost a golden coin from his house or a precious pearl[29]—does he not find it by means of a wick worth a penny? Similarly, let not this "mashal" be light in your eyes, for by means of this "mashal" one comes to comprehend the words of Torah. Know that this is so, for Solomon, by means of this "mashal" [i.e., the *Song of Songs*], understood the exact meaning of the Torah. Rabbi Judah says: it is to teach you that everyone who teaches words of Torah to the many is privileged to have the Holy Spirit descend upon him.[30] From whom do we learn this? From Solomon, who because he taught words of Torah to the many was privileged to have the Holy Spirit descend upon him and utter three books, Proverbs, Ecclesiastes, and Song of Songs.[31]

It follows that for the Rabbis, the Song of Songs is the parable that Solomon formulated in order that the people will understand the Torah. The fictional text interprets the "real" one by being put beside (para-bole) it and thus exemplifying some feature that is discovered as common to it and the "real" story (and thus present in the real story). Since in the mashal what is being referred to is a story, it is the meaning of the story that is the exemplified label or feature. The meaning of the events in Exodus is revealed by associating this text with another narrative. This placing of a fictional narrative beside a real one is the association of the concrete with the concrete—the fictional particular with the actual particular. The figures of the Song of Songs are made concrete by being identified with particular situations and characters from the Torah history. However, those situations and characters are also made more intelligible and concrete by being associated with the very homely figure of the dove, the dovecote, and the dove's master. This double concretization is achieved, however, by an exemplified label, the dugma, with respect to which the characteristics of the two concrete examples can be said to be alike. The text always explicitly or implicitly cites a specific feature or label under which the comparison of the two particulars is applicable, to which the exemplification refers.

However, as we have seen, the word "dugma" has a double meaning. In the case of a sample of wheat, "dugma" means the sample, but in the case of the dove and Israel, it means rather the exemplified feature or label (or even the potential set of such exemplified features or labels). Once more, that is why the text says there "Your dugma is like a dove," and not "Your dugma is a dove." Goodman remarks, "Exemplification is never fictive—the features or labels exemplified cannot be null or vacuous—for an exemplified feature is present in, and an exemplified label denotes, at least the sample itself."[32] The example, however, can be fictive. A picture of a unicorn will function in precisely the same way as a picture of a bald eagle. So, as exemplified feature, the mashal is not (cannot) be fictional, but as sample it certainly can be and indeed *must* be fictional, because what it exemplifies is meaning, which is a construction. In the mashal structure, the fact that both the example and the exemplified are stories makes for some very intriguing ambiguity. When "dugma" is taken to mean "sample," then the concrete story in the Torah, the "true" story, is a dugma of the category to which it belongs. However, when "dugma" is understood as a name for the category itself, then the metaphorical application, the fictional tale that effects the exemplification, is the dugma.[33] In the next text that we will read, we will see this doubleness or ambiguity explicitly thematized by the text itself:

And the angel of God, going before the Camp of Israel, moved and went behind them. And the Pillar of Cloud moved from before them and went behind them [Exodus 14:19]. R. Yehuda said: This is a Scripture enriched from many places. He made of it a mashal; to what is the matter similar? To a king who was going on the way, and whose son had gone before him. Brigands came to kidnap him from in front. He took him from in front and placed him behind him. A wolf came behind him. He took him from behind and placed him in front. Brigands in front and the wolf in back, he (He)[34] took him and placed him in his (His) arms, for it says, "I taught Ephraim to walk, taking them on My arms" [Hosea 11:3].

The son began to suffer; he (He) took him on his shoulders, for it is said, "in the desert which you saw, where the Lord Your God carried you" [Deuteronomy 1:31]. The son began to suffer from the sun; he

(He) spread on him His cloak, for it is said, "He has spread a cloud as a curtain" [Psalms 105:39]. He became hungry; he (He) fed him, for it is said, "Behold I send bread, like rain, from the sky" [Exodus 16:4]. He became thirsty, he (He) gave him drink, for it is said, "He brought streams out of the rock" (Psalms 78:16].[35]

A semiotic analysis of this text will reveal how complex the re-lations of exemplification are within it. Let us begin by looking more closely again at "mashal" itself. The term translates as "likeness" in English, a translation expanded as well by the phrase "to what is the matter similar?" in the introductory for-mula to the midrashic mashal. That which the mashal (fiction) is like is itself a narrative, namely, in this case, the story of God's tender treatment of the Israelites in the Wilderness. Now the biblical narrative certainly makes referential claims. It claims not only that these events could possibly have happened out there in the world, but that they certainly did happen.[36] The mashal, explicitly a fiction, makes no such claim in its dis-course that the events did happen.

Let us see then what this text does. The narrative in the verse upon which R. Yehuda is commenting contains gaps. The mo-tivation for the movement of the Angel of God, who was accus-tomed to go before the people, is not made clear. Moreover, there is a doubling in the verse. "And the Angel of God, going before the Camp of Israel, moved and went behind them. And the Pillar of Cloud moved from before them and went to a place behind them." The higher critics theorize a join between two sources, J and E, in the middle of this verse;[37] R. Yehuda, in con-trast, puts in his story. The story, like much of midrash, is an explicit representation of the kind of activity of concretization of a text that readers must perform when encountering a gapped narrative. This paradoxical moving around first of angel then of pillar is explained as an instance of a paradigm of God's protec-tive behavior toward the Israelites in the Wilderness, which is like the behavior of a father protecting his infant son. The story that R. Yehuda adds, which answers to the gapping in the verse, is built entirely out of concrete materials drawn from other parts of the biblical canon itself, as he himself avers by his state-ment "This is a Scripture enriched from many places." What then is the function of the mashal? It is a story and yet not a story; it is a kind of shadow or double of the "real" story, one that no one claims actually happened. As a literary structure it is a genre code, which enables and at the same time constrains the possibility of new narrative to fill in the gaps. As a hermeneutic structure, it is the uncovering of that code as the key to the significance of the narrative; that is, the mashal says in effect, This is not just something that happened, but something that happened and that means something specific. Our mashal text assigns the particular example, the concrete event, of the movement of the Pillar of Cloud and the Angel from before to behind the People to a class of such events, a paradigm. The mashal is both the description of that paradigm and the other examples that enable us to abduce this description.

Now, as I have suggested above, our midrashic text explicitly thematizes the ambiguity that I have been approaching asymptotically throughout this essay. Let us go back to the text and read it once more. R. Yehuda is interpreting the verse of Exodus 14:19. Doing so, he makes two moves that seem at first glance to be unrelated. He claims that the verse is only intelligible in the context of several other verses, and he claims that a mashal will interpret the verse. These two moves are, in fact, rigorously connected. However, this connection will only fully appear through a consideration of the ambiguity that I am talking about. The other verses that will enrich or make intelligible our verse are other members of a paradigm, of the paradigm set: God's behavior toward the Israelites during the Desert Wanderings. The mashal is the paradigm set itself, the rubric under which all of the verses can be gathered together and which reveals them to be a paradigm of the behavior of a father toward his infant child. The instances of God's behavior toward the Israelites in the Wilderness are shown to be intelligible and coherent, because they are like the behavior of a father toward his infant. But notice: the Rabbis never attempt to state their categories as abstractions; their drive is always toward concretization and more concretization. Even the pattern or category to which all of the instances of God's behavior are assimilated and which explains them is a concrete story. The double meaning of "dugma" as "sample" and "paradigm" makes this operation

possible. We could capture this double meaning by translating
"He made of it a mashal" as "He made of it an example," which
would mean both: R. Yehuda took this text and assigned it to a
class as a sample-member of that class *and* R. Yehuda produced
an exemplum that assigns the text significance as a model of
the class.[38]

Strikingly enough, our mashal explicitly marks this signifying ambiguity. It begins as if to tell us a parabolic tale, which
will then be decoded by an application. We expect to be told the
entire story of the father and his son, and then to find something
like: "Similarly, God led us through the wilderness. When we
were threatened from behind, He moved behind us to protect
us, as it says. . . . When we were threatened from in front, He
moved in front of us. When we were troubled by the sun, He
spread His cloud above us, as it says. . . . When we were hungry,
He fed us, as it says, . . . and when we were thirsty, He gave us
drink, as it says." But this is exactly what we do not have here.
The parable begins telling us a story about a father and a son,
but in each case, by citing the relevant verse having to do with
God and Israel, it immediately signifies that there really is no
such story at all. There are not two narratives here but only one,
the story of God's treatment of infant Israel in the Wilderness;
the other story exists only as a shadow double, as an abstract
structural pattern behind this one, as it were. The parable no
more signifies its application than a paradigm in grammar signifies the members of the paradigm; it does explain what they
are doing together and how they are related to each other. I have
tried to capture this ambiguity by my translation "he (He)."
What creates this story, however, and assigns significance to
our verse by making it a member of this paradigm (= dugma) is
the other examples (= each a dugma) that R. Yehuda cites. One
signifier is folded into the other here, thematizing the Möbius-
strip-like interpenetration of parable and example, concrete and
abstract in the parabolic system. As Louis Marin has argued,
"The function of the parabolic narrative therefore appears
through an ambiguity which gives it great practical efficacy: the
parable designates in its fiction a real narrative (situation, position) that it assimilates to itself in the process of showing that

this narrative is the revealing figure of one term of the code by which the parable was encoded into a fictive narrative."[39] The explanation of this ambiguity is that as code (dugma) the parable is more abstract than the "real narrative," but as "revealing figure" the "real narrative" is an example (dugma) of the code (or member of the paradigm) that the parable represents. R. Yehuda's mashal fits this description precisely. The verses R. Yehuda quotes in order to interpret the verse he addresses are the revealing figures of the code by which the parable was encoded into a fictive narrative. The double meaning of "figure" here, like the double meaning of "dugma," which it parallels, captures exactly the ambiguity encoded in our text by the slippage between the parable and its application. The "real" story is an example of the code by which the mashal was encoded into a fictive narrative, and by being so encoded, the mashal assimilates the "real" story to a cultural code and assigns it significance. The example may be fictive; the exemplification is not.

The mashal that I have just been discussing is actually quite atypical in form. In general, the mashal has precisely the unambiguous structure of parable followed by explicit application—that is, precisely the structure that I claim our text rejects. Accordingly, the question could be raised, and indeed has been raised: in what sense is it legitimate to use the atypical case as an illustrative dugma for a paradigm most of the members of which it does not exactly resemble? David Stern has raised this question with regard to my analysis. He prefers to see this text as an early mashal in which the form has simply not yet been regularized.[40] I agree with him; the difference between us is that on my understanding this "unregularized" form reveals the underlying semiotic undecidability that the later regularized form, with its strict textual and terminological distinction between "mashal" and "nimshal," plasters over.

Apparently other readers have found the undecidability of this midrashic text disturbing as well. The printed texts of the midrash have smoothed out the form and regularized it so as to pin down the undecidability. Thus we find in the critical edition and translation of J. Z. Lauterbach:

And the Angel of God . . . removed, etc. R. Judah says: This is a verse rich in content, being echoed in many places. To give a parable, to what is this comparable? To a man who is walking on the road with his son walking in front of him. If robbers who might seek to capture the son come from in front, he takes him from before himself and puts him behind himself. If a wolf comes from behind, he takes his son from behind and puts him in front. If robbers come from in front and wolves from behind he takes the son up in his arms. When the son begins to suffer from the sun, his father spreads his cloak over him. When he is hungry he feeds him, when he is thirsty he gives him drink. *So did the Holy One, blessed be He, do, as it is said:* "And I taught Ephraim to walk, taking them upon My arms." . . . When the son began to suffer from the sun, He spread His cloak over him, as it is said: "He spread a cloud for a screen." (Italics added. The italicized passage was inserted by a later medieval editor of the text adopted by Lauterbach.)

This version of the text (which contradicts the evidence of all of the manuscripts) partially occults the very ambiguity that gives signifying power to the text. However, even in this version an ambiguity remains, as pointed out by Robert Johnston: "Another notable aspect of this item is the blurred distinction between *Bild* and *Sache* as worked out in the application. Sun, hunger and thirst are repeated as sun, hunger and thirst. More strikingly, the son is still 'the son,' and not Israel, as one might expect."[41] On my reading this blurring is an uneradicated relic of the original ambiguity of reference at the very heart of the "mashal."

This conception is, I would like to claim, a more than adequate understanding of the actual functioning of the midrashic parable. In all of the cases we have considered, the parable is a fiction that concretizes in its fiction a story with real referential claims. This is certainly true of the rabbinic examples we have read, where the biblical text is being designated and interpreted via the mashal, and the biblical narrative (except in the instances, like the "Dry Bones," Job, or the Song of Songs, when it itself is read *as* a mashal) certainly makes strong referential claims, not only that the events could have happened but that they certainly did happen.[42] Why, then, must a mashal be a fiction? According to the rabbinic insight only a fiction can be an exemplary text, a text that carries significance. One understanding of this claim would be that only fiction can be exemplary because only it is the product of a signifying practice, while a "true" story would be meaningless in itself. The way to assign meaning to a "true" story is to assimilate it to a mashal, a code, of which it is then shown to be the revealing figure." An alternative understanding would be that the "true" story *does* have meaning but the meaning is not transparent by itself.[43] The function of the mashal in this formulation is heuristic in that the mashal picks out from the welter of facts that constitute the historiographical record those that are significant for perceiving the meaning of the narrative. (I rather suspect that the Rabbis themselves would prefer this latter formulation.) The movement of the Angel of God and the Pillar are by themselves facts without meaning or the meaning of which is opaque, as R. Yehuda explicitly remarks. They only become meaningful (or their meaning is only understood) when they are shown to be part of a pattern, examples of a class. "R. Yehuda said: This is a Scripture enriched from many places. He made of it a mashal" by associating it with the other (concrete) instances under the rubric of the mashal. Once more, the mashal works in two ways at the same time: by simplifying the structure of the biblical narrative it picks out the structurally significant elements, and by doing so it enables us to generalize from those elements. No wonder, then, that the Rabbis considered the mashal the royal road to the significance of Scripture, or in their own words: "Until Solomon invented the mashal, no one could understand Torah at all"; that is, until Solomon invented the form of the mashal as a means of understanding and formulating the underlying codes by which the biblical narrative was encoded as meaningful, the meaning was ungraspable. This interpretation of history through fiction is very similar to the interpretative truth that fiction-writing makes in our culture, not necessarily (but often enough) with regard to historiographical materials, but even more commonly with regard to quotidian reality. This is, after all, what Riffaterre meant when he said that all fiction is exemplary, and what the Rabbis meant when they said that all the exemplary is fiction.[44]

The rabbinic interpretation of biblical narrative suggests,

then, a way out of the dilemma posed by Alter and Sternberg. Historiography and fiction for the Rabbis are not alternative genres to one or the other of which biblical narrative must be assigned, but different semiotic functions within the text. That is why it is possible for them to speak of the clearly historiographical narratives of the Torah as having a "mashal," a term which always signifies fiction for them. Both the historiographical and the fictional functions of the biblical text make truth claims—one referring to external reality and one to the significance of the events. Interpretation of the historiography of the Bible is, for the Rabbis, precisely the discovery of those "fictions," the meshalim that structure its discourse. Notice how close this brings us to Hayden White's unsettling of the dichotomy between historiography and fiction, and in almost the same terms. Historical narratives are for White "metaphorical statements which suggest a relation of similitude between such events and processes and the story types that we conventionally use to endow the events of our lives with culturally sanctioned meanings." Writing history is the articulation "of a complex of symbols which gives us directions for finding an icon of the structure of those events in our literary tradition."[45] Those icons are the meshalim. White has explicitly remarked on the function of the fictive in historiography:

A historical interpretation, like a poetic fiction, can be said to appeal to its readers as a plausible representation of the world by virtue of its implicit appeal to those "pre-generic plot-structures" or archetypal story forms that define the modalities of a given culture's literary endowment. Historians, no less than poets, can be said to gain an "explanatory effect"—over and above whatever formal explanations they may offer of specific historical events—by building into their narratives patterns of meaning similar to those more explicitly provided by the literary art of the cultures to which they belong.[46]

In this way the insights of both Sternberg and Alter can be preserved. History is "what happened"; fiction is the stories we denote (by telling them) in order to exemplify the labels that constitute the culturally constructed meaning of what happened. All fiction is, then, by definition, exemplary, as the Rabbis (and Riffaterre) have claimed.

Example Versus *Historia*

Montaigne, Eriugena, and Dante

> Je veux qu'on commence par le dernier point.
> (I want to begin with the last item.)
> —Montaigne, "Des livres"

Le *Dire est autre chose que le faire* ("saying is quite another thing from doing"). Montaigne inserts this epigram early in "De la colère" (Of anger) chapter 31 of Book II of his *Essais*. Subtly, he shades this saying toward the subgenre of moral example (exemplum) by adding a second apothegm, *il faut considerer le presche à part et le prescheur à part* ("you have to separate the sermon from the preacher").[1] Saying and doing are now contrasted in a manner that suggests skepticism as to the value of the word when measured by the actions of the speaker.

This might appear to be simply a consequence of the context, an essay on anger—a mood in which, as Montaigne points out, actions frequently belie precepts: "Il n'est passion qui esbranle tant la sincerité des jugemens que la colere" ("No passion upsets the sincerity of judgment so much as anger," 692a). Although, like many of Montaigne's *Essais*, "De la colère" takes a classical model for its pretext—Seneca's *De ira*—neither the classical subtext nor the subject matter can account in themselves for the opposition between word and act that we find so starkly contrasted here. Montaigne quite deliberately poses the question of the gap between sign and referent in discourse; he raises the question of the adequacy of written language to represent *le fait*, acts in the world, in a sufficient manner.

There is good reason to explore Montaigne's preoccupation with saying and doing, but first we should recognize the historical dimensions of the issue he confronts with apparent nonchalance. In his pithy way, Montaigne brings his skeptical gaze to bear on this keystone of the mimetic mode in classical and medieval narrative, particularly epic and historiography. For two millennia prior to Montaigne's time, saying and doing defined the literary representation of history for exemplary purposes. Speaking, particularly eloquence, and its gestural equivalent, heroic action, linked narrative and event in a tight web of referentiality thought to be essential for guaranteeing the truth of the story, and consequently the utility of its moral and historical lesson.

Eric Havelock, in his *Preface to Plato*, asserts that from Hesiod's *Theogony*, the power of poetry in the Greek epic derived from the poet's ability to match the custom-laws and folkways—*nomoi* and *ethea*—of society with the content of his song.[2] *Nomos* meant, in archaic Greece, "force of usage and custom before it was written down, and also the statutory law of advanced Greek societies when it was written down."[3] *Ethos* meant "personal behavior-patterns or even personal character and so in Aristotle supplied the basis for the term 'ethics'."[4] The epic poet, Havelock recalls from Hesiod, is to celebrate the conjunction of doing and saying as paradigmatic of the community: "As servant of the Muses, [the bard] chants the mighty deeds of former men, And the blessed gods."[5]

The beginning of Homer's *Iliad* is a principal locus for the *faire/dire* paradigm in early classical poetry, and here, as we know, anger is both theme and (negative) example:

> Anger be now your song, immortal one,
> Akhilleus' anger, doomed and ruinous,
> That caused the Akhaians loss on bitter loss.[6]

The seer, Calchas, in a speech illustrating both *nomos* and *ethos*, uses anger to provide a lesson on the realities of political power.[7]

> A great man (king) in his rage is formidable
> For underlings: though he may keep it down
> He cherishes it burning in his belly
> Until a reckoning day
>
> (*Iliad*, ll. 80–83)

It is the focus of all this wrath, Achilles, who is also the example of the epic hero trained to be "a sayer of words and a doer of deeds" (*Iliad*, 1. 443). Saying and doing are seen as requisites for the epic hero because, as Odysseus and Aeneas illustrate, the epic hero is both doer and teller of the tale, both its focus and its motivating force. As benchmarks for historical and ethical behavior in the society at large, the hero's actions take on special meaning. The interpreter of these actions, the bard or epic poet, is thus avatar or surrogate for the epic hero. Not only is the truth of the epic tale assured by the link between principal actor and principal teller, but the historic and exemplary truth of epic was attested by the referential web spun between event, hero, poet, and poem.

Mimesis, as Erich Auerbach showed, is symbolized by Odysseus's scar.[8] But that scar by which Odysseus's old nurse recognizes him when he returns, disguised, to Ithaca symbolizes not simply the recognition of a culture hero by the social ecology, "the people," but also the way in which the laws and customs that made up the culture could be embodied in the hero, through his own words and deeds. This is why, for example, the Greeks and Hebrews linked mastery of the epic form and mastery of the epic action in heroes like Achilles and David, as Havelock has observed:

While in modern conception the prince's honeyed powers would be merely an extra talent . . . for Hesiod this talent was an inherent part of his job. He had to be able to frame executive orders and judgments in verse; at least his effectiveness increased as he was able to do this, for in this way his authority and his word carried further and was remembered better. Through this power, exercised in a society which relied on the oral preservation of communication, a man might find a ladder to political leadership. The career achieved by the minstrel David in Hebrew society may provide an analogy.[9]

Saying and doing, as Montaigne knew, represented more than a simple narrative concept or mode. They were held to address directly the social function of poetic representation. This tradition had been as true for the Middle Ages as for the classical period, as we shall see in due course. Montaigne advances the essay form as a means of speculating on human behavior, of examining the claims that *nomos* and *ethos* do in fact coincide. The essay studies *nomoi* and *ethea* in concrete instances of observed human behavior, often chosen, like anger, for their universality. The transhistorical nature of a given behavioral manifestation or human condition—anger, sadness, idleness, fear, old age, friendship, sexuality, and so on—allows Montaigne to juxtapose his own experience with discrete cultural examples of the phenomenon as part of what Antoine Compagnon has called the "work of quotation" in the essays.[10] The task of quotation for Montaigne—*Je ne compte pas mes emprunts, je les poise* ("I do not count my borrowings, I weigh them," 387c)—is to infuse the essays with an active system of allusion to the cultural heritage that linked saying and doing, *nomos* and *ethos*, by way of illustrating the assumptions Montaigne examines so skeptically through the eyes of the essays.

This dynamic scrutiny of the relationship of words and action implicates one of his principal expressive modes, the example (exemplum), a compressed form of spoken and written discourse in which image, the graphic representation of the experiential world of the author, takes precedence over rhetoric, seen as an abuse of language to rewrite reality. What is said must be measured against actions: language against image, where image appears as gesture (act). Montaigne identifies rhetoric and narrative as the agents that attempt to abolish or obfuscate the gap between *faire* and *dire*. "Le vray miroir de nos discours est le cours de nos vies" ("The true mirror of our discourse is the conduct of our lives," 168c), he says in "De l'institution des enfans," a concept spelled out even more explicitly later on in the same essay:

Je veux que les choses surmontent, et qu'elles remplissent de façon l'imagination de celuy qui escoute, qu'il n'aye aucune souvenance des mots. Le parler que j'ayme, c'est un parler simple et naif, tel sur le papier qu'à la bouche; un parler succulent et nerveux, court et serré, (c) non tant delicat et peigné comme vehement et brusque.

I want the substance to stand out, and so to fill the imagination of the listener that he will have no memory of the words. The speech I love is a simple, natural speech, the same on paper as in the mouth; a speech succulent and sinewy, brief and compressed, c not so much dainty and well-combed as vehement and brusque. (171a, c; *127*).

The *choses* here are the human actions that form the object and excuse for the example Montaigne builds his essays upon. He places the *Essais* under the sign of the example, the moral lesson not dissimilar to the parable of the New Testament or the moral sentence developed in the Middle Ages for the purposes of preaching. The force of the example lay in its ability to transpose complex philosophical ideas into precepts applicable to human behavior. As he remarks in "De l'institution des enfans," *Aux exemples se pourront proprement assortir tous les plus profitables discours de la philosophie, à laquelle se doivent toucher les actions humaines comme à leur reigle* ("To the examples may properly be fitted all the most profitable lessons of philosophy, by which human actions must be measured as their rule," 158a; *117*).

As Montaigne uses it, the example continually mediates between doing and saying. As he recognizes himself, it has a double status of written and spoken language. Its very compression authorizes the startling quality of "succulence" he ascribes to the apothegm in the passage from "De l'institution des enfans" just quoted. The orality is crucial here because it suggests why Montaigne could exempt the example from the opposition between *faire* and *dire* so frequently repeated in his *Essais*. Like Plato in *Phaedrus*, 275d–276b, Montaigne consistently manifests suspicion regarding the written word, although in his case, it is the overwritten, narrative word that is primarily in question. Montaigne's preference for oralizing expression reiterates the skepticism Socrates voices to Phaedrus:

You know, Phaedrus, that's the strange thing about writing.... Written words seem to talk to you as though they were intelligent, but if you ask them anything about what they say, from a desire to go on being instructed, they go on telling you the same thing forever. And once a thing is put in writing, the composition, whatever it may be, drifts all over the place, getting into the hands not only of those who understand it, but equally of those who have no business with it; it doesn't know how to address the right people, and not address the wrong.[11]

Plato's critique is that writing is insufficiently action, or more specifically, insufficiently interactive; detached from its context, it remains simply rhetorical, raising questions that must be answered for it without regard for the accuracy of the intelligence supplied. Speech, a close relative of written expression, retains its quality of gesture, of action:

Socrates: But now tell me, is there another sort of discourse that is brother to the written speech, but of unquestioned legitimacy? Can we see how it originates, and how much better and more effective it is than the other?
Phaedrus: What sort of discourse have you in mind and what is its origin?
Socrates: The sort that goes together with knowledge, and is written in the soul of the learner, that can defend itself, and knows to whom it should speak and to whom it should say nothing.
Phaedrus: You mean no dead discourse, but the living speech, the original of which the written discourse may fairly be called a kind of image. (276a–b)

Parenthetically, we might note that the conditions under which Plato does authorize writing sound very similar to Montaigne's project and situation: "he who has knowledge of what is just, honorable, and good [will] write when he does write by way of a pastime, collecting a store of refreshment both for his own memory, against the day 'when age oblivion comes,' and for all such as tread in his footsteps" (276c–d).

The compression of the example, which Montaigne identifies as its oral profile, offers minimal scope for narrative elaboration. At the same time, its gnomic force renders it difficult of access, thus helping to assure one of Plato's criteria: that it address the right people. Misinterpretation and misdirection, the cardinal sins of writing for Plato, seem circumscribed by the example as Montaigne formulates it. Montaigne rarely misses an opportunity, it seems, to denounce poetic narratives in one form or another. As we know from *Essais*, Book III, chapter 5, "Sur des vers de Virgile," doing and saying are never so far apart for him as in poetic narratives, and, by implication, the lives of the authors may serve as one index of the sincerity of their writing: "Je ne voy jamais autheur, mesmement de ceux qui traictent de la vertu et des offices, que je ne recherche curieusement quel il a esté" ("I never see an author, including those who write of virtue and duty, without avidly seeking to learn what kind of a man he was," 694a). But in poetic narratives, the doing represented has already taken place; it is an action purported to have occurred, and thus a fact of history reported and interpreted by the poet.

Mais de ce que je m'y entends, les forces et valeur de ce Dieu se trouvent plus vives et plus animées en la peinture de la poësie qu'en leur propore essence. . . . Elle represente je ne sçay quel air plus amoureux que l'amour mesme. Venus n'est pas si belle toute nue, et vive, et haletante, comme elle est icy chez Virgile . . . Ce que j'y trouve à considerer, c'est qu'il la peinct un peu bien esmeue pour une Venus maritale.

But from what I understand of it, the powers and worth of this god are more alive and animated in the painting of poetry than in their own reality. . . . Poetry reproduces an indefinable mood that is more amorous than love itself. Venus is not so beautiful all naked, alive, and panting as she is here in Virgil. . . . What I find worth considering here is that he portrays her as a little too passionate for a conjugal Venus. (826–27b; 645)

Montaigne's skepticism comes from his perception of the gap between what the poet says and what he could have known. He is less skeptical about the role of history per se than about the rewriting of history for rhetorical purposes. The exemplary can be heuristic only to the extent that it is also pragmatic, that is, grounded in practical, evaluative observation. Historical examples abound in Montaigne's work, but generally are associated with corroborating contemporary observations from his own experience (as in the final sentence of the above quotation). Example is a critical methodology that must carry conviction by self-verifiability. What is said cannot simply be confirmed by reference to history; it must also conform to experience, to critical observation.

Unlike the poetic narratives Montaigne decries, the example has a different status vis-à-vis time and thus a different status as representation. Reducing narrative mode almost to a zero state, or attempting to do so, the example offers itself as a temporally neutral or else proleptic descriptor of human behavior: "Celuy qui a faim, use de viande; mais celuy qui veut user de chastiement, n'en doibt avoir faim ny soif" ("He who is hungry eats meat, but he who wishes to punish should have neither hunger nor thirst," 693b). As a moral precept it is hortatory, offering a model on which action may subsequently be based. It does not pretend to narrate past action, but suggests a possible future narrative. Like Augustine's famous "Tolle, lege" from *Confessions*, a text Montaigne indirectly refers to more than once, Montaigne's examples tend to be imperatives or optatives, but unlike Augustine's example, they tend not to motivate a narrative sequence, even when biographical: "Quand je me courrouce, c'est le plus vifvement, mais aussi le plus briefvement et secretement que je puis" ("When I get angry, it's as keenly, but also as briefly and privately as I can," 697b; *544*).

Montaigne's examples are not mimetic. They do not attempt to reproduce an ideal or true form of behavior and so may not be said to be specular—reflections of an ideal as defined by social and cultural tradition. Nor are they representations of actions purported to have occurred. They are images, vignettes, but images as signs that stress differences between *ethos* and *nomos*, that emphasize, in short, the disjunction between how people are said to behave and how they may be observed to behave.

Montaigne's examples are thus much more on the order of philosophical fragments, propositions or models for human conduct where the emphasis falls not on the relation between the real and the ideal so much as on the *écart*, or disjunction between the model and recognized norms of human behavior. The example, then, posits a failed representation; it shows the distance between paradigms of ideal behavior and actual norms of conduct. From this standpoint, one may say that Montaigne's examples fit the distinction drawn by Claude-Gilbert Dubois between mimetic and semiotic forms of representation. In his terms, they are semiotic, that is, "a 'mise en sens' of an enigma to be deciphered, a symbolic construct belonging to the world of signs."[12] The examples do not simply propose paradigms but stress the interferences between philosophical model and human conduct.

That is the meaning of Montaigne's rather abrupt opening sentence to "De la colère": "Plutarque est admirable par tout, mais principalement où il juge des actions humaines" ("Plutarch is admirable throughout, but especially where he judges human actions," 691a; *539*). Montaigne says nothing about Plutarch's qualities as a historian but rather praises his ability to critique human behavior. In other words, he applauds Plutarch's vision in construing human conduct as a text whose meaning is secondary to the questions it poses.

The gap between word and deed that Montaigne underscores—"Le dire est autre chose que le faire"—turns out to be the literary space in which the example inserts itself. Far from attempting to close that gap, Montaigne exploits it. For literature to be a socially engaged activity, for it to have the weight of the Latin authors he most admires, Seneca and Plutarch,[13] it must mediate rather than reinforce the distance between saying and doing. The mediation comes from his use of the example as gesture, a form of verbal act that minimizes the word as writing in favor of what we might call "graphic speech," a sort of "fairedire," from its effort to use language as a speech act that critiques human conduct. It is a form of expression that is neither fully a "dire," owing to its ostensible rejection of narrative and rhetoric, nor yet completely a "faire." At once self-assured as regards the rigor of its precepts, it takes a skeptical view of traditional representative modes.

Central to this conceit is the dual status of the apothegm marked by orality and thus perceived as an immediate verbal gesture, vaunted for its sinewy spoken language—un parler succulent et nerveux, court et serré—and for its visual dimension. Montaigne himself sums up this dual status in a memorable chiasmus: "Si voux le voyez, vous l'oyez; si vous l'oyez, vous le voyez." In the editions prior to 1595, the quotation was introduced by a revealing claim about the ability of the example to mediate between doing and saying: "Voicy mes leçons [où le faire va avec le dire . . .]. Celuy-là a mieux prouffité, qui les fait, que qui les sçait. Si vous le voyez, vous l'oyez; si vous l'oyez, vous le voyez"; "Here are my teachings (where saying and doing coincide). Whoever practices them will benefit more than he who simply learns them. If you see him you hear him; if you hear him you see him" (167c; 124). Hearing and seeing suggest the immediacy of participation in an event, rather than the distance of narration. It is the absence of narrative mode that Montaigne sees as setting example apart from poetic discourse.

By substituting hearing and seeing for saying and doing as key elements in the exemplary mode, Montaigne avoids the distortions narrative inevitably introduced. *Ethos* was his primary concern, not *nomos*; or rather, folkways interested him only insofar as they provided data that his own observations or those of his favorite authorities might contradict. In effect, Montaigne sets *ethos* against *nomos*, suggesting that the main problem with historical narrative lay in perpetuating the mimetic myth of the consonance of saying and doing.

In casting his project in these terms, Montaigne was breaking not simply with the classical tradition that linked word, deed, and history but also with its Christianized medieval variation, the compound allegorical mode of historiography called *historia*.[14] Since Augustine, this compound mode was known technically as *allegoria facti et dicti* and it purported to link word and deed in an allegorical narrative of vernacular history seen as the exemplary handmaiden of Salvation History. In this context, it is important to remember that in the Middle Ages allegory was a form of "exemplum," since as Jean Pépin reminds us, its primary meaning was "teaching," a connotation differing somewhat from the current one.[15]

In addition to the compound mode of *allegoria facti et dicti*, there was a second kind of allegorical discourse, also exemplary, based on word alone with no reference to historical event and thus a simple rather than a compound discourse mode, known as "allegory of word but not event," *allegoria dicti sed non facti*. Since the compound mode of *allegoria facti et dicti* posed the world as event in discourse, it was called "mystery"; the second avoided confrontation with real events in the world and thus was perceived as symbolic. Both were narrative discourse modes, but the first incorporated "real" historical events while the second expressly exchewed them.

Although Augustine was the first to see the importance of linking *factum* and *dictum* for the exemplary purposes of Christian exegesis, it was John the Scot (Eriugena) in the late ninth century who first made the distinction between the two allegorical models, and who made of them a full-blown theory of historical and symbolic exemplarity in which the symbolic is considered the higher—in the sense of more theologically privileged—of the two modes. Thus we must look briefly at John the Scot to understand fully the system of hierarchical exemplarity that Montaigne is challenging in his *Essais*.

Historical Versus Symbolic Exemplarity in John the Scot

In his late-ninth-century *Commentary on the Gospel of Saint John*, Eriugena interprets the account of the miracle of the five barley loaves and two fish in a radical departure from previous commentators, particularly Augustine.[16] In a movement whose importance for medieval theories of representation has yet to be fully appreciated, he proposed that historical event *in its discursive form*, rather than truth per se, be taken as the criterion for distinguishing history from other forms of symbolic expression. In other words, history should be viewed as text. By thematizing history as a narrative component, he creates an allegorical architecture susceptible of infinite mutations. "Mystery" was the term used to suggest the labyrinth of potential variations.

Commenting on John 6:14—"Homines ergo uidentes quod fecit signum iesus, dicebant: Quia ipse est uere propheta qui uenit in mundum" ("The people, seeing this sign that Jesus had given, said 'This truly is the prophet who is to come into the world'")—John the Scot observes that the account shows the people's imperfect understanding of signs by emphasizing their insistence on interpreting simply the visible sign (operation) rather than its potential for meaning (*PL*, 344b; 348–49). Even Augustine, he says, did not fully appreciate the richness of the passage, because, like the people, he commented on what was said—the intelligible sign—rather than what was not said, the mystery.

The "profound mystery of which Augustine does not mention so much as a word in his commentary" (*PL*, 344c; 350–51) is not the miracle of the loaves and fishes itself, as the people thought, but the whole story of the feast and the "cleaning up." Why, he asks, does the account mention the twelve hampers that the disciples filled with the remains of the barley loaves, but not the fish? What happened to the remains of the fish?

Rather than concluding that the story simply does not tell us what became of the fishbones, Eriugena believes the omission to have been intentional. He argues that we are meant to note the asymmetry between the bread and the fish and to work out the significance. In modern terms, the silence regarding the fish would be an example of what Gerald Prince calls disnarration: "an event that does not happen but that is nevertheless referred to, in a negative or hypothetical mode."[17] More specifically, the disnarrated

calls for alethiological expressions of virtuality (unrealized) or of impossibility ("Joan thinks that *x* is possible but *x* turns out to be impossible"), deontological expressions of prohibition (respected), epistemic expressions of ignorance, ontological expressions of nonbeing, purely imagined, desired, or intended worlds, unfulfilled wishes, unjustified beliefs, dashed hopes, failed initiatives, mistaken calculations, errors, and so forth.[18]

The disnarrated covers many instances when the writer wishes to make the reader aware of significant information that has been suppressed in the narrative. It may function in a variety of ways, not the least of these being to heighten the symbolic dimension of the narrative by skirting the boundaries of the ineffable. That is how Scotus Eriugena intends it, and Montaigne will also use it to suggest psychic depths beneath the conversational style of the essay at certain moments. Through the disnarrated, historical narratives reveal mysteries, and that is what sets history apart from parable, the other common biblical mode. Although Scripture often gets the two terms confused (*PL*, 345c), mystery and symbol, he argues, are two distinct allegorical modes. Mystery, the first allegorical mode, is the more complex. It is an allegory of events and words ("Mysteria itaque proprie sunt, quae iuxta allegoriam et facti et dicti traduntur, hoc est, et secundum res gestas facta sunt, et dicta quia narruntur"—"mysteries are thus properly conveyed by an allegory of word and deed, that is, according to events that have happened and the words that are narrated [about them]," *PL*, 344d).

"Mystery" is thus both historical event and the narrative of that event. Moses' tabernacle (Numbers 7:1) was constructed according to history; in Scripture, according to Eriugena, it appears both as historical fact and as narrative (*PL*, 344d; 352–53). Similarly, the circumcision was performed in the flesh and narrated in word (*PL*, 345a; 352–53). In the New Testament, the same may be said of the mystery of baptism and that of the body and blood of Christ (*PL*, 345a). Signs of this sort, which on the one hand "have actually happened and on the other have been transmitted by letters, are visible signs, properly called by the Holy Fathers 'allegories of event and of discourse'" (*PL*, 345a; 352–53).

The allegory of *facti et dicti* emphasizes the visibility or presentation of the event for contemplation. It is less the factuality of the happening that seems to matter here than its ability—as a compound artifact—to stimulate reflection not just on the factual event but on the represented event, the event as text. Eriugena does not downplay the importance of historicity so much as take it as a given not requiring proof. The historical dimension of the allegory of event and discourse *must* matter for John the Scot because it is the connection to the physical world—revealed in its opaqueness, like the language that conveys the event—that makes the mystery.

"Symbol" is what Eriugena calls the second kind of allegory characterized by him as simple rather than compound: "allegory of words but not of events" (*allegoria dicti non autem facti*), so called because it consists solely of narrative and moral teachings. Unlike mysteries, symbols are not historical events but discourses recounting for didactic purposes things that did not actually happen *as though they had happened* (*PL*, 345a–b; 352–55). With the *allegoria dicti sed non facti*, Eriugena, like Montaigne after him, goes beyond the simple mode of saying and doing that connects *nomos* and *ethos* in a referential discourse. The purely symbolic mode of *allegoria dicti* addresses the ethical dimension of human behavior against a backdrop of virtual acts. Folkways are not omitted so much as suspended; they are disnarrated, intended to be filled in by the reader. The didactic dimension of the *allegoria dicti* derives precisely from the reader's ability to perceive the disjunction between the ethical behavior proposed by the symbolic narrative mode and the customary behavior observed in everyday life. The allegory of word offers an implicit judgment on the conjunction of saying and doing in the world. *Nomos* represents an erosion or naturalization of *ethos*.

Examples of the narrative symbolic mode (*allegoria dicti*) are found in both testaments. The New Testament, according to John the Scot, contains many discursive symbols; the parables of Christ, like the story of Lazarus and Dives, for example, are rich in allegory of the word (*PL*, 345b–c; 355–57). The New Testament parables rely on figural language, and the exact name for the figural language of the parables is "symbol" (*proprieque simbolica nominatur*), but, he adds in a wonderful aside, "Scripture has a habit of calling 'symbol' what is properly 'mystery' and 'mystery' what is 'symbol' " (*PL*, 345c; 355–57).

We cannot pursue the intricacies of Eriugena's distinction between mystery and symbol for biblical exegesis. Suffice it to say that the five loaves represent the five bodily senses while the two fishes represent the two testaments. Together, the loaves and the fishes are the sacraments. The multitude—whom he calls the fleshly faithful—take the sacraments, that is, the historical sense alone. The spiritual adepts gather the crumbs, the remains signifying the spiritual meaning (*PL*, 346b; 358–61), so they wind up with both history and the deeper meaning in the form of its hermeneutic accretions.

In John the Scot's view, all mystery contains the double address to the bodily senses and to the mind, each corresponding to the literal and the spiritual meaning. History cannot signify, at least in any profoundly meaningful way, unless it contains the element of mystery, of otherness, which makes it allegory. Mystery, his name for the hidden sense, may also be identified as a sign of the mental activity triggered by the discourse in a search for deeper meanings. Mystery thus corresponds to the term and process of invention that played so important a role in vernacular lyric and narrative in the Middle Ages under such terms as the Provençal "trobar" and the Old French "trover," which both mean "to discover," "invent," "compose" and which gave us the terms for poets, "troubadour" and "trouvère." Discovery or invention by the intellect working on the enigmas posed by the world: that is Eriugena's driving principle.

With symbol, the unitary rather than the combinatory principle obtains. In the everyday world, Eriugena would argue, symbol is less complex than mystery, but that is precisely what gives it a higher value from a transcendent viewpoint. Symbol, free from ties to the physical world of history, represents, allegorically, the undivided language of pure spirituality. As he explains in chapter 6 of his *Commentary on the Gospel of Saint John* (*PL,* 346d–347a; 364–65), the two fish represent the allegory of spiritual teaching that is an "allegory of words and not of (historical) events." This allegory is allied with the number two because its perception involves two senses only, sight and sound: we read it with the eyes and hear it with the ears. Or, as Montaigne would say six hundred years later: "Si vous le voyez, vous l'oyez; si vous l'oyez, vous le voyez."

With the allegory of word we enter the realm of the example, ethical language tightly constructed for eye and ear: the sinewy spoken language of the apothegm we found in Montaigne. The pithy orality of the *allegoria dicti* is not just an effect of language but seeks also to be an image of the indivisibility of the symbol. The allegory of word alone is the indivisible symbol: one can't "break it" like the bread because it's already single, an allegorical discourse without historical content. In effect, Eriugena interprets the "disnarrated" here by explaining why we find no mention of the disciples gathering up the remains of the fish after the miracle of the loaves and the fishes. The fishes are symbol because they cannot be divided, like the bread, into the historical (literal) sense (the part consumed) and the spiritual meaning (the crumbs gathered by the disciples). Whereas the bread may be twice used—first whole, then as crumbs—the fish may be consumed only once: like Christ, for whom the fish was a symbol, the body disappears leaving only the symbolic (Logos) behind.

In principio erat uerbum, et uerbum erat apud deum, et deus erat eurbum ("In the beginning was the Word, and the Word was with God, and the Word was God," John 1:1) is Eriugena's arche-

typal example of the allegory of word alone. The statement conveys no historical event or fact (*PL*, 848a; 366–67). It must be
taken whole in its unity by the spiritual men, without being divided and parceled out to the multitude, or, as he calls them, the
"fleshly faithful." It cannot be fragmented, split, or broken
down in any way, for nothing in it may be understood as history;
it is pure theology, typifying allegory for the two senses.

"Oculis legitur legentium, auribus sentitur audientium, ac
per hoc, ueluti quidam duo pisces, una eademque euangelistae
theologia accipitur, duobus sensibus conueniens" ("Readers
read it with their eyes; listeners hear it; one can thus understand how a single theological proposition works for two of our
senses: it is comparable to the two fish" *PL*, 348b; 366–67).

Even so sketchy an account of Eriugena's distinction between
the two allegories of exemplarity suggests why they could have
had so decisive an infuence on medieval discourse. Medieval
authors saw in this mode an occasion for fusing narrative,
"dire," with history, "faire," in a manner that produced a rewriting of events according to a religio-political agenda; the new
genre was called *historia* and became the most pervasive narrative form in the Middle Ages.[19] *Historia* stressed narrative rewriting of events, in which the "dire," understood as writing, revealed the hidden meaning of the "faire," that is of history. This
genre unabashedly privileged representation over fact, metaphysical truth over naturalistic observation.

Despite Eriugena's elaboration of the allegory of word, it was
not the exemplary mode of choice for the Middle Ages. *Historia*
privileged narrative in a manner more closely corresponding to
the medieval preference for evoking spiritual mysteries in secular and salvation history. Then, too, *historia* had classical precedent on its side since it was the carrier of the tradition of narrative that linked saying and doing as *ethos* and *nomos*. From a
Christian viewpoint, *historia* facilitated the microcosmic approach whereby the secular world of everyday life might be seen
as relating to the most exalted metaphysical conceptions of the
universe. The smallest incidents were thought capable of revealing divine purposes when properly interpreted. The poetic
subject, the consciousness revealing the grand design of *histo-*

ria, was thus a transcendent one, an *alter deus* or second god, not creating but discovering (*trobar, trouver, invenire*).

For the Middle ages, Dante was certainly the most spectacular practitioner of this mode, but he came to it with three centuries of tradition behind him. Dante realized the grand design of *historia* in a panorama that incorporated sacred and profane history in a cosmic demonstration of the consequences of joining doing and saying. Dante's maximalist version of *historia* has little in common with Montaigne's anecdotal approach to human conduct in the essay. But the differences should not obscure the fact that each plays out a version of the allegorical modes of exemplary discourse articulated by John the Scot: Dante, the allegory of *historia,* in which monumental writing encompasses moral vision; Montaigne, the allegory of example, in which seeing and saying, with minimal narrative, attempt to capture the enigma of doing.

Eriugena and Montaigne will finally part company in their ways of perceiving history as joined to discourse. Montaigne remains skeptical of discursive history. Seeing and hearing for Montaigne are critical rather than simply confirming modalities. Nevertheless, both authors share the view that saying *is* a form of doing and that doing, whether historical or personal and immediate, resists specular representation. What is left out of the saying is as much a part of the evaluative algorithm as what is included. Indeed, as we saw at the beginning of this essay, Montaigne's "example" is similar to Eriugena's "symbol": a speech-act grounded not on narration but rather on disnarration. The difference between the medieval avatars of John the Scot and Montaigne lies less in the initial premise of the allegory of saying and doing than in the optimism by which they approach the matter of a grandiose historical reconstruction for exemplary purposes. For Dante, history as a grand scheme could be exemplary precisely because of its status as mystery, as an enigma to be interrogated. For Montaigne, history is rather fragmented, symbolic, the confirmation of naturalistic observation that includes what does not happen as well as what does:

La consequence que nous voulons tirer de la resemblance des evenemens est mal seure, d'autant qu'ils sont toujours dissemblables: il n'est aucune qualité si universelle en cette image des choses que la diversité et varieté.

The inference that we try to draw from the resemblance of events is uncertain, because they are always dissimilar; there is no quality so universal in this aspect of things as diversity and variety. ("De l'experience," 1041b; *815*)

Each of these authors in his own way comes to grips with the allegory of saying and doing en route to defining a model of exemplarity he finds satisfying. In the rest of the paper, we shall see how each of these allegories may be illustrated by means of a politics of anger.

Montaigne: Anger as Example

Returning to our starting point, Montaigne's "De la colère," we recall that toward the end of the essay, he brings up the issue of whether it is better to repress anger altogether or use self-restraint in expressing it. In short, when is it permissible to indulge anger? Just as the question about *faire/dire* at the beginning of the essay opened up larger issues of literary representation, so this seemingly rhetorical query addresses another urgent literary matter: the nature of the subject in the text. Montaigne shows that the *essai* does not simply call into question old modes of representation, it postulates a new authorial subject as well by calling into question the authentic versus the counterfeit and true authority via self-knowledge versus weakness masked as authority. He contrasts a contingent individual judged according to principles of inner justice with the transcendent subject of Augustine and Dante. Augustine and patristic tradition displaced the authorial subject toward a universalist, transcendent model derived from scriptural authority. This is the poetic subject that undergirds the concept of the poet as *alter deus*, which makes possible the authoritative status of history predicated on the conjunction of saying and doing.

Montaigne critiques this metaphysical conception of a knowing subject by focusing on images of that subject in the heat of anger, a characteristic recognized as ambivalent even within classical and medieval theories. These theories naturalized the wrathful subject by examining the intention of the wrath. Dante, for example, like Homer, Virgil, and other classical predecessors, held that righteous anger was exempt from the customary condemnation of wrath. Any passions that displaced reason were generally proscribed in classical and patristic theories, but righteous anger could be exempt because the hero's anger served a just cause and was thus part of a rational scheme. Epic, the classical locus of doing and saying as *nomos* and *ethos* tended to be the main line of defense and illustration of the concept of righteous anger. Montaigne bases his critique of anger and the transcendent subject on a judicious contrast of citations from classical texts with his own observation and experience.

He does this in two contrasted movements, each introduced by a quotation from Virgil's *Aeneid*. Shifting the locus of the essay away from the classical period back to contemporary France, Montaigne adduces a man described ironically as at once "the most choleric man in France" and as "le plus patient homme que je cognoisse à brider sa cholere" ("the most patient man I know in curbing his anger," 696b; 543). This anger wracks the man with a violence and fury that Montaigne evokes by the first Virgilian metaphor to demonstrate the force of the violence to be restrained:

Magno veluti cum flamma sonore
Virgea suggeritur costis undantis aheni,
Exultántque aestu latices; furit intus aquaï
Fumidus atque alte spumis exuberat amnis;
Nec jam se capit unda; volat vapor ater ad auras.

So, when a fire of wood, loud crackling,
Is stoked up high beneath the belly of a boiling cauldron,
The water dances in the heat; within the cauldron the water
Seethes and fumes, bubbling, spitting up foam, till it cannot
Contain itself any more and a cloud of dense steam rises.[20]

But the outcome is not what the quotation and its Virgilian context lead us to expect. Virgil uses the metaphor to describe the anger that leads Turnus to declare war on King Latinus and ultimately on Aeneas. Montaigne uses it iconically as a measure of the anger that his oxymoronic angry/patient man contradicts through the effort of repression: the man's anger is so intense "qu'il faut qu'il se contraigne cruellement pour la moderer" ("that he has to constrain himself cruelly to moderate it," 696b; *543*). But then, in a double contradiction, Montaigne disavows the constraint, noting not the effort but its psychological over-head: *Je ne regarde pas tant ce qu'il faict que combien il luy couste à ne faire pas* ("I do not consider so much what he does as how much it costs him not to do worse," ibid.). The negative construction marks Montaigne's shift from narration to disnar-ration.[21] In a superb gesture of critical method, he intervenes at right angles to the rhetorical flow to comment not on what the narrative says but on what it doesn't say. By pointing to the omission, he indicates the negative implications of repression as another story that has not been told because society conven-tionally counseled curbing one's wrath except in battle—as Montaigne himself reminds us: "et c'est [la cholere] tousjours imperfection, mais plus excusable à un homme militaire: car, en cet exercice, il y a certes des parties qui ne s'en peuvent pas-ser ("and anger is always an imperfection, but more excusable in a military man, for in that profession there are certainly oc-casions that cannot do without it," 696a; *543*).

Compounding the disnarration, Montaigne cites another Latin tag to show that in restraining anger, "le plus patient homme de France" does not face his anger in a manner that ei-ther leads to or promotes self-knowledge. Montaigne's putative exemplary individual is less a model of constraint than a coun-terfeit sage, a stock figure, ridiculous as the boiling cauldron, whose error consists in speciously concealing what he genu-inely feels: "Omnia vitia in aperto leviora sunt; et tunc perni-ciosissima, cum simulata sanitate subsidunt" ("All vices openly displayed are lighter to bear, but terribly pernicious when hidden beneath a feigned health," Seneca *Epistolae*, LVI).

Montaigne uses the classical quotations in a double move-ment to render the example of "le plus patient homme que je cognoisse à brider sa cholere" more vivid while pointing out the inefficacy of the traditional approach to moral exemplarity via rhetorical devices not grounded on first-hand observation. He moves to destabilize the authority of the classical *exempla* while privileging the self as a source of pragmatic and truly reflective wisdom based on real-life experience. This movement will demonstrate the superiority of the autobiographical *essai*, based upon the example as he defines it, over pseudohistorical narrative exemplarity typified by Virgil's *Aeneid*.

Montaigne implements this corrective movement through the second quotation from the *Aeneid*, deployed as a transition into the final section of the essay, where we find his own philosophy of anger. Against the combined body of classical witnesses, metonymically represented here by Virgil and Aristotle, Montaigne will deny the efficacy of anger under *any* circumstances. The quotation, from *Aeneid*, XII, lines 103–6, comes from Virgil's description of the fury that grips Turnus when he arms for the final battle that will culminate in his death at Aeneas's hands:

> Mugitus veluti cum prima in praelia taurus
> Terrificos ciet atque irasci in cornua tentat,
> Arboris obnixus trunco, ventósque lacessit
> Ictibus, et sparsa ad pugnam proludit arena.

> So it is when a bull bellows out its first terrible
>   challenge to combat,
> And practices throwing all its fury into its horns
> By goring trunks of trees, butts at the air in anger,
> Paws and tosses the sand as a prelude of coming battle.

Montaigne does not include the two preceding lines describing Turnus's appearance that the metaphor enlarges: "He was wildly wrought up, so burning for battle that all his countenance / Seemed to shoot sparks, and darts of fire to come from his fierce eyes" (ll. 101–2). Virgil needs to distinguish between the dehumanizing, irrational anger of Turnus and the pious wrath of Aeneas, for the whole battle seeks to justify the efficacy of wrath when exercised in a worthy cause by a "pious" hero acting in accord with divine will. It is only under extreme provocation that Aenneas's rage is finally kindled, and then it leads him to implement a rational strategy against Turnus's army. At no time is Aeneas portrayed as dehumanized. Even in the final scene, when he kills Turnus, the angry Aeneas is shown by Virgil as motivated by pity and altruism:

Aeneas fastened his eyes on this relic, this sad reminder
Of all the pain Pallas' death had caused. Rage shook him. He looked
Frightening. He said: Do you hope to get off now, wearing the spoils
You took from my Pallas? It's he, it's Pallas who strikes this blow—
The victim shedding his murder's blood in retribution!
So saying, Aeneas angrily plunged his sword full into
Turnus' breast. The body went limp and cold. With a deep sigh
The unconsenting spirit fled to the shades below.

(*Aeneid*, XII, ll. 944–52)

Contrasting the *lame* (blade) that is the instrument of Aeneas's heroic anger to the *langue* (tongue)—"car je n'y employe
communement que la langue" ("for I ordinarily use nothing but
my tongue," 698b)—Montaigne, like Augustine before him, implicitly critiques Virgil's emotional and heroic aggrandizement
of passion. He reminds the reader that the spoken and written
word must be used strategically and rationally first of all to analyze emotion psychologically and philosophically. In place of a
narrative that leads inevitably to the justification of anger,
Montaigne authorizes a rhetoric of renunciation based upon re-
straint and calculation. He contextualizes anger differentially,
with respect to his precursors, by admitting it as a real psychological factor in human emotion, but one that is, finally, trivial
in its essence. The triviality of anger, Montaigne's most profound contribution to the literature, disjoins it from the transcendent pretentions accorded it by even those classical authors who opposed it.

Anger cannot be repressed, but it should only be vented in private or as a strategy for governance by contradiction. One may
indulge in anger over small things—always and only in word—
when people least expect it. But in larger matters, when it
would be most anticipated and justified, Montaigne restrains
his anger in a perverse but effective spirit of contradiction. His
description shows him preparing for the scenes of everyday life
as Turnus and Aeneas prepared themselves for battle:

Aux grandes occasions, cela me paye qu'elles sont si justes que chacun
s'attend d'en voir naistre *une raisonnable cholere; je me glorifie à
tromper leur attente;* je me bande et prepare contre contre celles cy,
elles me mettent en cervelle et menassent de m'emporter bien loing si
je les suivoy.

On big occasions I have this satisfaction, that they are so just that everyone expects to see a reasonable anger engendered; I glory in deceiving their expectation. I tense and prepare myself against them; they disturb my brain and threaten to carry me away very far if I followed them. (698b; 544)

Montaigne thus masters his subject matter as he does his subjective emotion by a rhetorical analysis that opens the received opinion of the classical and medieval *auctoritas* to the same skeptical pragmatism he applies to his own self. Anger is, finally, not literary, but a primitive emotional response productive of social and personal discord, an arm, as he says in contradicting Aristotle, that controls us, rather than being controlled by us. Whereas classical texts seek to narrate anger in positive or negative examples, Montaigne chooses to question that narrative tradition by pointing to the alternative narratives that have been repressed. The distance Montaigne places between the classical tradition and his own text, appropriately, is summed up in the emblem of self-governance that stands as symbolic of his politics of contradiction:

A mesure que l'aage me rend les humeurs plus aigres, j'estudie à m'y opposer, et feray, si je puis, que je seray dores en advant d'autant moins chagrin et dificile que j'auray plus d'excuse et d'inclination à l'estre, quoy que par cy devant je l'aye esté entre ceux qui le sont le moins.

As age makes my disposition sourer, I make an effort to oppose it, and will succeed if I can, in being all the less peevish and hard to please as I shall have more excuse and inclination to be so, although hitherto I have been among those who are least so. (698b; 545)

"De la colère" begins with praise of Plutarch's acumen in judging human actions (*faire*), and concludes with a discussion of Montaigne's own actions that illustrate the difficulty of making doing (*le faire*) consonant with saying (*le dire*), while circumscribing the limited range of possibilities where the two may coincide. In juxtaposing himself to Plutarch, Montaigne offers two models of exemplarity, the one dependent on a transcendent subject, the other on an individual questioning poetic voice. The first takes the epic canvas of *historia* as its purview, aggrandizing the status of hero as mimetic model for the society at large and the poet as second creator, *alter deus*, stage-managing the theater of exemplary behavior. This is the mimetic mode that we talked about earlier and that may be found, *mutatis mutandis*, in Virgil, medieval epics like the *Chanson de Roland*, and historiographers like Froissart and Joinville. What Montaigne admires in the medieval historians is their straightforward representation of their matter. As writers, Froissart, Commynes, Joinville, Eginhard are viewed favorably by Montaigne because he regards them not as historians but as unaffected performers of historical discourse. Thus of Philippe de Commynes, he says:

Vous y trouverez le langage doux et aggreable, d'une naifve simplicité; la narration pure, et en laquelle la bonne foy de l'autheur reluit evidemment, exempte de vanité parlant de soy, et d'affection et d'envie parlant d'autruy; ses discours et enhortemens accompaignez plus de bon zele et de verité que d'aucune exquise suffisance; et tout par tout de l'authorité et gravité, representant son homme de bon lieu et élevé aux grans affaires.

Here you will find the language pleasant and agreeable, of a natural simplicity; the narrative pure, and the author's good faith showing through it clearly, free from vanity in speaking of himself, and of partiality or envy in speaking of others; his ideas and exhortations accompanied more by good zeal and truth than by any exquisite capacity; and, throughout, authority and gravity, representing the man of good background and brought up in great affairs. ("Des livres," 399–400a; 305–6)[22]

Montaigne's praise of Commynes illustrates how the performative subject appeals to the senses, involving the reader in a narrative immersion, so to speak. It is that dimension of participatory reading that Montaigne critiques wryly in the passage from "Sur des vers de Virgile" quoted above: "Ce que j'y trouve à considerer, c'est qu'il la peinct un peu bien esmeue pour une Venus maritale" ("What I find worth considering here is that he portrays her as a little too passionate for a conjugal Venus," 827b; 645). *Historia* depends for its exemplary force on the reader's participatory involvement. It implies an authorial subject of omniscient dimension able to represent time and space as universal constructs linked across centuries and buttressing worldviews. The performative in this mode stems from its agenda to replay or reimagine metaphysical postulates.

Example as Pedagogical Symbolism

Against this authorial conception, Montaigne proposes a pedagogical subject. The personal presence of a skeptical intelligence in the text marks this mode of rational discourse, which we might call pedagogical symbolism. This mode favors the discontinuous anecdote, quotation, and personal comment. It actively avoids narrative and the representation of facts in favor of something akin to the allegory of saying (*allegoria dicti*):

Je ne fay point de doute qu'il ne m'advienne souvent de parler de choses qui sont mieus traictées ches les maistres du mestier, et plus veritablement. C'est icy purement l'essay de mes facultez naturelles, et nullement des acquises; . . . Qui sera en cherche de science, si la pesche où elle se loge: il n'est rien dequoy je face moins de profession. Ce sont icy mes fantasies, par lesquelles je ne tasche point à donner à connoistre les choses, mais moy: elles me seront à l'adventure connuez un jour, ou l'ont autrefois esté, selon que la fortune m'a peu porter sur les lieux où elles estoient esclaircies. Mais il ne m'en souvient plus.

I have no doubt that I often happen to speak of things that are better treated by the masters of the craft, and more truthfully. This is purely the essay of my natural faculties, and not at all of the acquired ones. . . . Whoever is in search of knowledge, let him fish for it where it dwells; there is nothing I profess less. These are my fancies, by which I try to give knowledge not of things, but of myself. The things will perhaps be known to me some day, or have been once, according as fortune may have brought me to the places where they were made clear. But I no longer remember them. (387a; 296).

The pedagogical subject uses the sparse, direct prose of the apothegm, the *faire-dire* or written equivalent of speech, as appropriate to philosophical reflection. He is less concerned with fact, content, historical matter, than with the manner of expressing inner reflections: *Qu'on ne s'attende pas aux matieres, mais à la façon que j'y donne* ("Let attention be paid not to the matter, but to the shape I give it," 387a; 296).[23] Montaigne refuses to play the creator, the *alter deus*, preferring to develop the skeptical or instructing subject who takes a metacritical attitude vis-à-vis the primary material rather than pretending to control it.[24]

Montaigne, finally, alludes repeatedly to the tradition and

practice of *historia* to signal his disnarration, writing out or over that version of exemplum. The performative subject of *historia*, he seems to argue, relies upon rhetorical sleight of hand to effect a rapprochement of doing and saying. Pedagogical symbolism permits the skeptical subject to bring *faire* and *dire* together in a critique based on personal experience and a recognition of the complexity of phenomena. Recognition of the multiplicity of observed events or behaviors forces pedagogical symbolism to renounce any attempt to circumscribe them by narrative. Instead, the essay presents the fragmented, personal experience; a meditation on the knowledge gleaned from insufficiency.

This conjugation of personal and classical *faire-dire* offers the key to his surprising relationship vis-à-vis the medieval tradition of *allegoria facti et dicti* and *allegoria dicti sed non facti*. Paradoxically, Montaigne both repudiates the medieval narrative tradition of *historia*, the bulwark of universal history as Dante and others understood it, and yet reaffirms a concept of example as historical symbol on which he founds a defense of religion as orthodox as Eriugena's or Dante's.[25] No matter how "scientific" or empirical Montaigne may be—empiricism leads him to reject outright the concept of historical narration that undergirds Dante's *Commedia*—discourse finally yields a symbolic confirmation of faith that works in much the same way as Eriugena's conception of the symbolic allegory of word: not by what is narrated, but by the interpretation of what is not told: "Parquoy qui juge par les apparences, juge par chose autre que le subject" "Therefore whoever judges by appearances judges by something other than the object," p. 583a; 454).

What matters in historical narrative—at once a vain pursuit and a pursuit of inestimable value[26]—is not the dates or events, not the narrative, but the example. And the example always resides beyond the literal discursive level. In terms of medieval exegesis, Montaigne situates the value of historical exemplarity at the allegorical and anagogic levels of meaning. But unlike medieval exegesis, predicated upon a conviction of universal truth, Montaigne's essay translates the performative narrative of *historia* (the "vain pursuit") into a pedagogical symbolism of exemplarity ("of inestimable value"); it does so by substituting subjective critical judgment or personal point of view (*nous, Michel de Montaigne*), for the misleading omniscient narrative perspective of *historia*.

Historical narrative, when viewed critically, teaches how to read obliquely:

> Mais que mon guide se souvienne où vise sa charge; et qu'il n'imprime pas tant à son disciple (c) la date de la ruine de Carthage que les meurs de Hannibal et de Scipion, ny tant (a) où mourut Marcellus, que pourquoy il fut indigne de son devoir qu'il mourut là. Qu'il ne luy aprenne pas tant les histoires, qu'à en juger. (c) C'est à mon gré, entre toutes, la matiere à laquelle nos esprits s'appliquent de plus diverse mesure.

> But let my guide remember the object of his task, and let him not impress on his pupil so much ᶜthe date of the destruction of Carthage as the characters of Hannibal and Scipio, nor so much ᵃwhere Marcellus died as why his death there showed him unworthy of his duty. Let him be taught not so much the histories as how to judge them. ᶜThat, in my opinion, is of all matters the one to which we apply our minds in the most varying degree. (155a, c; 115)

Judgment relies on reason. Montaigne's strategy in proposing an exemplary discourse stripped of narrative and the emotions aroused by it leads to a radical critique of sensory perception as a key element of the performative. Anger typifies the extreme example of judgment distorted by emotion. "Ce que nous voyons et oyons agitez de colere, nous ne l'oyons pas tel qu'il est" ("What we see and hear when moved by anger, we cannot hear as it really is," 580a). We can now better understand the objection to the performative function of anger in historical narrative as illustrated by the second Virgilian quotation from the last part of "De la colère":

> So it is when a bull bellows out its first terrible
> challenge to combat,
> And practices throwing all its fury into its horns
> By goring trunks of trees, butts at the air in anger,
> Paws and tosses the sand as a prelude of coming battle.

The performative would be simply trivial if merely confined to poetic histories. As Montaigne shows, however, it suggests or justifies actions in the real world. He uses anger to expose the uncritical judgment underlying political passions in his own time and country. The performative model of history licenses a somewhat fine distinction he seeks to make between theological anger and theological zeal. Religion had long sanctioned anger in a just cause; indeed Augustine's notion of a just war lay in his radical reevaluation of the spirituality of the Sermon on the Mount to show that "warfare now became necessary rather than inherently sinful."[27] "Motivated by a righteous wrath, the just warriors could kill with impunity even those who were morally innocent. Objective determination of personal guilt was not only unnecessary but irrelevant."[28] As any reader of the *Chanson de Roland* or other medieval epics knows, objective factuality gives way to rhetorical portrayal of righteous wrath as an important attribute of the Christian hero, the *miles Christi*, in the face of the iniquitous enemy.

In a passage revealing the mimetic connection he makes between narrative performance and actions in the world—a consistent point of the personal anecdotes in the *Essais*—Montaigne suggests that righteous wrath is simply personal anger writ large, and no justification for political acts. We see here an attempt to map pedagogical exemplarity on a scale beyond the personal, by arguing that performative narrative simply transposes a subjective ego into a transcendental one:

[L'un de noz historiens grecs] . . . dict aussi que les Factions des Princes sur le subject de la Theologie sont armées non de zele mais de cholere; que le zele tient de la divine raison et justice, se conduisant ordonnément et moderément; mais qu'il se change en haine et envie, et produit, au lieu du froment et du raison, de l'yvraye et des orties quand il est conduit d'une passion humaine.

One of our Greek historians . . . says also that the factions of princes in theological disputes are armed not with zeal but with anger; that zeal takes after divine reason and justice when it guides itself with order and moderation, but changes into envious hatred and produces tares instead of wheat and nettles instead of grapes when it is guided by human passion. ("Des prières," 307c; 233)

By locating history within the realm of sensory perception, where anger is symptomatic of extreme actions justified by sensory apprehension, Montaigne maneuvers the performative subject of historical narrative into a situation where it can no

longer be logically held to represent truth.[29] Since the true nature of the *faire* as event cannot be known, then the allegory of
word and deed cannot represent history accurately, a fact ignored by medieval avatars of Eriugena—although not by Eriugena himself. Montaigne's pedagogical symbolism, the form
the example takes in his *Essais*, attempts to bridge this aporia of
event-as-fact by a concept of symbolic language not dissimilar
to Eriugena's second mode of allegory, the *allegoria dicti* or allegory of word but not event. The purpose of this symbolic
mode, Eriugena said, was pedagogical: to report, for purposes of
edification, something that had not happened as though it had
happened. Referentiality matters less in this mode than pedagogical intention; free from the distraction of historical event,
language becomes the indivisible discourse of true spirituality.
One might also say that liberated from mimetic constraints,
language could transform itself into patterns of conjecturality,
words of imagined behavior. In short, linguistic metamorphosis
can illustrate positive moral traits.

   The world Montaigne imagines in his *Essais* beyond the imperfect one of mutability and sensory perception puts the failure of history and of historical language behind and points
instead toward a mystical realm of symbol, indeed of metamorphosis out of language, where the human abandons itself
to a higher power. This movement of elevation beyond the human correlates with Eriugena's notion of theosis—the mystical
meeting point where humanity and divinity momentarily
join.[30]

   At the end of the "Apologie de Raimond Sebond," Montaigne
adumbrates a philosophy of human ascent and divine descent
that marks yet another point of conjugation between him and
John the Scot. This unexpected movement in Montaigne opens
a window that makes such seemingly distant echoes more understandable. That Eriugena should have reached Dante by
diverse routes—most notably, through Honorius Augustodu-
niensis—is hardly remarkable. But Frances Yates has shown
that Eriugenian Neoplatonism was also a strong influence on
Raymond Lull, whose attempt "to base memory on Divine
Names which verge on Platonic Ideas in his conceptions of

them . . . is closer to the Renaissance than to the Middle Ages."[31] Elsewhere, she has shown that via Lull, Eriugena strongly influenced such important Renaissance thinkers as Montaigne's younger Italian contemporary, Giordano Bruno.[32] In many ways, Montaigne's use of names in the titles of his *Essais*, and the moral philosophy systematically deployed through those names and examples suggest the methodological construction of a world vision one associates with Renaissance arts of memory.

Returning to our subject, Montaigne's recursive loop back to mysticism grounds his pedagogical symbolism in a contradiction of which he is perfectly conscious: *cette conclusion si religieuse d'un homme payen* ("This all too religious conclusion of a pagan," "Apologie de Raimond Sebond," 588a). It enables him to avoid the negation of transcendence that his skepticism would otherwise entail by affirming, with an orthodoxy worthy of Eriugenian patristics, that not by stoic philosophy but by divine grace can man hope to exceed the human condition, and then only in the most exceptional cases:

Ny que l'homme se monte au dessus de soy et de l'humanité: car il ne peut voir que de ses yeux, ny saisir que de ses prises. Il s'eslevera si Dieu lui preste extraordinairement la main; il s'eslevera, abandonnant et renonçant à ses propres moyens, et se laissant hausser et soubslever par les moyens purement celestes. (c) C'est à nostre foy Chrestienne, non à sa vertu Stoïque de pretendre à cette divine et miraculeuse metamorphose.

Nor can man raise himself above himself and humanity; for he can see only with his own eyes, and seize only with his own grasp. He will rise, if God by exception lends him a hand; he will rise by abandoning and renouncing his own means, and letting himself be raised and uplifted by purely celestial means. c It is for our Christian faith, not for his Stoical virtue, to aspire to that divine and miraculous metamorphosis" (588–89; 457).

Dante's Politics of Historia: Anger

For Dante, *historia* was still predicated on the performative mode of the allegory of word and event. He believed in history and in the efficacy of narrating it for didactic purposes. He also believed in the justice of divine wrath, and in the efficacy of anger when used for a righteous cause. We find a striking confrontation of the pedagogical and performative approaches to exemplarity in two examples of Dante's theology of anger in *Inferno* and *Purgatorio*, examples constructed on situations strikingly parallel to those of Montaigne's examples discussed above.

In *Inferno*, XII, we find a classic example of the bestiality of rage in the image of the Minotaur guarding the passage to the seventh circle. Illustrative of Montaigne's contention that the inner repression of rage is worse than its open expression, Dante describes the Minotaur: "e quando vide noi, sé stesso morse, / sì come quei cui l'ira dentro fiacca" ("And when he saw us he bit himself, like one whom wrath rends inwardly").[33]

Like Montaigne, but for different reasons, Dante also seeks to demonstrate the inefficacy of anger as represented in classical texts, and particularly in Virgil's own *Aeneid*, for which Dante's *Commedia* stands less as a successor than a supplanter. Here in *Inferno*, XII, Dante offers us an image of an enraged bull that at once resembles and sharply differentiates itself from that described in Turnus's arming scene in *Aeneid*, XII (and I think we must accept the coincidence of the numbers, Book XII and Canto XII as a referential indicator):

> Qual è quel toro che si slaccia in quella
> ch'ha ricevuto già 'l colpo mortale,
> che gir non sa, ma qua e là saltella,
> Vid'io lo Minotauro far cotale.

And as a bull breaks loose in the moment when it has received the mortal blow, and cannot go, but plunges this way and that, so I saw the Minotaur do. (*Inferno*, XII, ll. 22–25)

Aeneid, II, lines 223–24, is the Virgilian subtext generally adduced for this passage. It describes the death of Laocoon caught in the coils of the sea serpents: "qualis mugitus, fugit cum saucius aram / taurus et incertam excussit cervice securim" ("A bellowing such as you hear when a wounded bull escapes from the altar, after it's shrugged off an ill-aimed blow at its neck"). In fact, the theological context of *Inferno*, XII, probably intends both passages as standing metonymically for the whole of Virgil's text and, indeed, for the classical tradition in general. The passage metaphorically delivers a death blow to classical views of anger—Turnus versus Aeneas, Juno versus Venus—and the mode of the texts that convey them. For as Virgil and Dante descend the slope away from the Minotaur, they walk over rocky debris that, Virgil says, had not yet fallen when he descended into Hell the first time just before the coming of Christ.

See how the performative mode manages to link historical event and biblical narrative—*factum et dictum*—in an assertion of Christian *historia*. Dante's performative subject differs from the skeptical and detached pedagogical one of Montaigne by its participation in and authorization of the elements of universal history it assembles: Holy Scripture, Virgil's *Aeneid*, historical event, eyewitness account. The performative subject surrounds itself with the testimony to a transhistorical written and lived moment encompassed by the imperious *vid'io*, "I saw": *Vid'io lo Minotauo far cotale*.

The debris is in fact the wreckage caused by Christ during the harrowing of hell. That wreckage must be seen performatively as attesting to the destruction of the power of the texts of the Old Alliance and of classical wisdom, henceforth seen as outmoded. Like Montaigne, Dante questions the efficacy of the classical *auctoritas*, at least that of Virgil. By way of increasing the performative authority of his own voice, Dante has Virgil himself make the association between anger, the monster, and the ruins of the edifice symbolic of the Old Regime:

> Così prendemmo via giù per lo scarco
> di quelle pietre, che spesso moviensi
> sotto i miei piedi per lo novo carco.
> Io gia pensando; e quei disse: "Tu pensi
> forse a questa ruina, ch'è guardata
> da quell'ira bestial ch'i'ora spensi."

So we took our way down over that rocky debris, which often moved under my feet with the new weight. I was going along thinking, and he said, "Perhaps you are thinking on this ruin, guarded by that bestial wrath which I quelled just now." (*Inferno*, XII, ll. 28–33)

The Virgil who quells the bestial wrath in Dante's Christian *commedia* performs an act of reversal and renunciation vis-à-vis his own *alta tragedìa*. Whereas the end of the *Aeneid* celebrates heroic anger with the dispatch of Turnus's "unconsenting soul" to hell, in this passage, Dante's Virgil describes a very different kind of descent into hell, and one that celebrates love in place of rage. For just prior to the pilgrims' arrival at Phlegathon, the river of blood in which boil those who suffered from "blind cupidity and mad rage," Virgil details Christ's *discensus*, the harrowing of hell. He does so in terms that make it the reversal of yet another classical doctrine, Empedocles' "theory of the alternate supremacy of hate and love as the cause of periodic destruction and construction in the scheme of the universe."[34]

Aristotle referred to this theory in his *Metaphysics*, and Saint Thomas commented on it in his gloss on Aristotle's text. Empedocles' theory, Thomas says, held that "there exists in the world a certain alternation of hate and friendship, in such a way that at one time love unites all things and afterward hate separates them. But as to the reason why this alternation takes place, so that at one time hate predominates and at another time love, he said nothing more than that it was naturally disposed to be so."[35] As a shrewd reader of the *Aeneid*, Dante recognized the applicability of Empedocles' doctrine to the thematics of Virgil's epic, from Juno's anger at the beginning to Aeneas's wrathfully vengeful killing of Turnus at the end, not forgetting Dido's self-destructive evolution from love to hate in the center. At the same time, the myth of Empedocles illustrated the interpretive indeterminacy of narrative history. In a wonderful example of disnarration, the Empedocles myth reported that the pre-Socratic philosopher had cast himself into the crater of the volcano of Mount Etna, leaving his sandals behind to mark his movement and to serve as a focus of speculation as to his motive. The sandals testified not to what *had* happened, but to how *little could be known* of what had happened.

The harrowing of hell physically imposed the evidences of a new metaphysics of immutable love on the ruins of these classical cultural artifacts, which now stood, like Empedocles' sandals, as a reminder of an effaced narrative:

> Ma certo poco pria, se ben discerno,
> che venisse colui che la gran preda

> levò a Dite del cerchio superno,
> da tutte parti l'alta valle feda
> tremò sì, ch'i'pensai che l'universo
> sentisse amor, per lo qual è chi creda
> più volte il mondo in caòsso converso;
> e in quel punto questa vecchia roccia,
> qui e altrove, tal fece riverso.

But certainly, if I reckon rightly, it was a little before He came who took from Dis the great spoil of the uppermost circle, that the deep foul valley trembled so on all sides that I thought the universe felt love, whereby, as some believe, the world has many times been turned to chaos; and at that moment this ancient rock, here and elsewhere, made such downfall. (*Inferno*, XII, ll. 37–45)

Dante makes of this passage a metaleptic proposition that converts the metonymy of classical learning into an allegory of the supremacy of New Testament theology; and he does so by figuratively reconstituting the rubble of Christ's *discensus*. This rubble serves as the material trace of event (*factum*) joined to the narrative (*dictum*) of that event to reveal the presence of a hidden historical intentionality and meaning. The loose rocks that provide such treacherous footing for the metaphysical weight of Dante pilgrim ("that rocky debris, which often moved under my feet with the new weight") are the shards of *questa vecchia roccia*, "that ancient rock," that was *riverso*, literally "overturned" in the sense of "flat on one's back." In his commentary, Charles Singleton points out that *vecchia* evokes the inscription over the gate of Hell at the beginning of Canto III, lines 5–8:[36]

> FECEMI LA DIVINA PODESTATE,
> LA SOMMA SAPIENZA E 'L PRIMO AMORE.
> DINANZI A ME NON FUOR COSE CREATE
> SE NON ETTERNE, E IO ETTERNO DURO.
>
> THE DIVINE POWER MADE ME,
> THE SUPREME WISDOM, AND THE PRIMAL LOVE.
> BEFORE ME NOTHING WAS CREATED
> IF NOT ETERNAL, AND ETERNAL I ENDURE.

Riverso rhymes with *converso*, "converted," and the *universo* that Virgil says felt love at Christ's *discensus*. By this metaleptic proposition, then, the context of the passage participates in the conversionary rhetoric of the *commedia* as a whole, which is itself a *riverso* or *converso* of Virgil's *alta tragedia*.

Like Montaigne, Dante seeks to contradict his classical *auctoritates*, but he does not do so in order to recover the space of his text for his own subjectivity. Instead, he differentiates between authorities in order to demonstrate the supremacy of the patristic model. In *Inferno*, he repeatedly bestializes humans in keeping with Boethius's theories. Thus in Canto VII, mud is the medium of punishment for the wrathful, as befits the Boethian image of the sowlike behavior of those who abandon themselves to the passions.

One must go to *Purgatorio*, XVI, to discover how the knot of anger may be dissolved in penance. There in a murky cloud of darkness, symbolic of the blindness that clouded the intellect of the penitents in life, Dante specifically links his politics of anger to literary and philosophical matters: the imagination and free will as agents of intention and meaning of historical event. In *Purgatorio*, XVI, he offers yet another reading lesson to show how heuristic allegory, responding to the patristic paradigm, can teach humans to subordinate passion to intellect via the exercise of free will. This lesson offers nothing more nor less than a prescription for overcoming the materiality of bodily discourse, the writing of anger into the text of the flesh. What distinguishes the souls in *Purgatorio*, XVI, from those in *Inferno* is their sign value. Unlike their counterparts in *Inferno*, they are complex as opposed to univocal signs. They have, in short, become analogies, in the Thomistic sense, capable of representing both the abandonment and the affirmation of intellect as free will.

In this canto, Dante brings anger as a passion down to the level of social pragmatics by invoking the abandonment of values in contemporary Europe. He casts Marco the Lombard as a spokesman for a pragmatics of free will, reminiscent of Augustine's *De Doctrina Christiana*, that ascribes current ills to an abandonment by the Church of its traditional role of moral leadership. The Church, by arrogating to itself the role of temporal and spiritual government, has exercised a fatal aggression on the divine order that decreed a separation between temporal and ecclesiastical governance:

> Soleva Roma, che 'l buon mondo feo
> due soli aver, che l'una e l'alta strada
> facean vedere, e del mondo e di Deo.

Rome, which made the world good, was wont to have two Suns, which made visible both the one road and the other, that of the world and that of God. (*Purgatorio*, XVI, ll. 106–8)

We should not miss the psychological subtlety of Dante's analysis here. He situates the social criticism in the context of dissolving the knot of anger, and he urges the necessity for proclaiming the Church as mired in the mud of the wrathful:

> Di oggimai che la Chiesa di Roma,
> per confondere in sé due reggimenti,
> cade nel fango, e sé brutta e la soma.

Tell henceforth that the Church of Rome, by confounding in itself two governments, falls in the mire and befouls both itself and its burden. (*Purgatorio*, XVI, ll. 127–29)

Dante ascribes the transgression of the Church to a failure of its contemporary leaders to understand that they are not the institution they represent, but only its servants. He shows that the offending prelates confuse their physical being with their ego, or self as consciousness, and that they then further confuse that image with the reality of history and the Church. In effect, they see the institution in their own image, an aggressive reversal in their minds of the reality whereby the Church, as a series of symbolic constructs (e.g., language, theology, philosophy, image, architecture, ritual), defined their roles and image, and not vice versa.

Dante's description of this "hostile takeover" of the Church by its leaders sounds convincing to us because it conforms so closely to what Jacques Lacan identified as a fundamental pattern of human aggression underlying the individual's relationship with its social context. Lacan argued that the role of the symbolic was to construct an individual ego identical not with the self but with the external images—parents, institutions, in short "the other"—with which the individual identifies in the unending effort of self-discovery. Commenting on Lacan's meditations on "Aggresivity in Psychoanalysis," Anika Lemaire writes:

The role of the symbolic is the social and cultural realization of man and the normalization of his sexual and aggressive instincts; but it therefore also has the effect of alienating him. It is here that the origin of human aggression is to be sought. Obliged to fashion himself with reference to and in rivalry with the other, obliged to wait for recognition from or judgement by the other, man is naturally inclined to a whole range of aggressive behaviour, from envy, morbid jealousy and real aggression to mortal negation of self or other.[37]

Anger for Dante, then, enacts the alienation of the subject from its being, which leads inevitably to aggression against the *frère ennemi*, whether at the level of social institutions or individual behavior. It is inevitably a transgression against the allegorical lesson of history because it severs the link between word and deed by substituting violence for a reasoned reflection on the place of the performative subject in the flux of history. Instead of using word and event to construct a version of the world in accord with the performative subject's beliefs, it uses aggression to clear a space for the subject at whatever cost. Within the context of Dante's theology, transgressive anger replays the second act of the Fall, the mortal negation of the self as double in Cain's killing of Abel.

Conclusion

If Dante illustrates here the vulnerability of the performative subject to authoritative abuse, he does not take the critical next step in his text to call the performative narrative itself into question, and with it the concept of historical truth. The fault, Dante implies, lies not with the narrative model itself, as with the abuse of it by ecclesiastical authorities. The whole point of his narrative progression from *Inferno* to *Paradiso* is to show the perfectability in his theology of history and the narrative that supports it. Even anger may be perfected in his schema when expressed by a Beatrice or other representative of the perfected Christian order. Throughout the *Commedia*, but particularly in *Paradiso*, Dante stresses the primacy of sight, especially spiritual in-sight, seeing with symbols. Dante relies heavily on perceptual images to convey the mystical vision of this *summa* of poetic *historia*. Like Montaigne, Dante shows that, in the last analysis, man can only transcend the human by a mystical metamorphosis out of language, but he does not arrive at this conclusion by means of the radical critique of the senses, leading to a disavowal of history, that engages Montaigne.

The performative for Montaigne founders on relativism, and particularly the impossibility of determining the intention or meaning of the *factum* that the *dictum* takes as its object in the performative narrative of *historia*. Even reason, for Montaigne, fails to establish historical intention and meaning satisfactorily. Montaigne's assessment of the abstract conjecturality of history as *factum* matches that of Eriugena himself. John the Scot's metaphor for the referential gap in language—the space between sign and referent—was the spring: he construed the distance between underground source and surface spring allegorically as nature's image of the concept of linguistic difference.

Montaigne's critique of performative *historia* leads to his evolving a concept of pedagogical symbolism underlying a nonnarrative example grounded in an empirical pragmatics. This mode rejects the certitude of historical truth as a guide for acts in the world in favor of practical observation of human behavior. By reformulating narrative into the discontinuous, empirical discourse of a new genre, the *essai*, Montaigne manages to distance himself from the medieval texts he disnarrates by maintaining their concerns while rejecting their forms. In so doing, he constructs a fresh kind of philosophical writing that exposes the aporias of performative *historia*.

Circe's Drink and Sorbonnic Wine:

Montaigne's Paradox of Experience

Je dis souvent que c'est pure sottise qui nous fait
courir apres les exemples estrangers et scholastiques.
(I often say that it is pure stupidity that makes us
run after foreign and scholarly examples.)
—Montaigne, "De l'expérience"

There is something second-rate about example.
It has bad press even among authors whose texts, like Michel de
Montaigne's, are constructed around countless classical and
modern examples. Having used example so copiously in his
work, Montaigne begins the concluding chapter of his *Essays*,
the text entitled "Of Experience" (ca. 1587), by a kind of negative apology of example. With a note of resignation, he reminds
his readers that experience, the source of examples, is only a
stopgap, a *pis aller* for rational knowledge:

Il n'est desir plus naturel que le desir de connoissance. Nous essayons
tous les moyens qui nous y peuvent mener. Quand la raison nous faut,
nous y employons l'experience

> *Per varios usus artem experientia fecit:*
> *Exemplo monstrante viam.*

There is no desire more natural than the desire for knowledge. We try
all the ways that can lead us to it. When reason fails us, we use experience—

> Experience, by example led,
> By varied trials art has bred. (1065; 815)[1]

The relationship between reason and experience indicates not
only a hierarchy in forms of knowledge but also a hierarchy in

discourse. A working definition of example—proposed merely as a preliminary guide into the complexity of "Of Experience"—might be that example is the link between a concept and a unit of experience that can be subsumed under that concept. Montaigne's terms point to the problems of establishing such a link, for "La raison a tant de formes, que nous ne sçavons à laquelle nous prendre; l'experience n'en a pas moins" ("Reason has so many shapes that we know not which to lay hold of; experience has no fewer," 1065; 815), and "La multiplication de nos inventions n'arrivera pas à la variation des exemples" ("Multiplication of our imaginary cases will never equal the variety of the real examples," 1066; 816). There is an unstable dichotomy between reason and experience in which the "fit" between the two domains is hampered by the variety and fluctuation on both sides. Attempts to abstract from experience to reach a generally applicable law are just as difficult as the attempt to move from a general law to find specific illustrative instances. For this reason, Montaigne describes example, in a celebrated passage, as the "lame" figure:

> Toutes choses se tiennent par quelque similitude, tout exemple cloche, et la relation qui se tire de l'experience est tousjours defaillante et imparfaicte; on joinct toutefois les comparaisons par quelque coin. Ainsi servent les loix, et s'assortissent ainsin à chacun de nos affaires, par quelque interpretation destournée, contrainte et biaise.

> All things hold together by some similarity; every example is lame, and the comparison that is drawn from experience is always faulty and imperfect; however, we fasten together our comparisons by some corner. Thus the laws serve, and thus adapt themselves to each of our affairs, by some round-about, forced, and biased interpretation. (1070; 819)

As a magistrate, Montaigne here specifically refers to the use of example as judicial precedent, cumulative historical instances linked on one side to the law, a product of reason, and on the other side to the ever-proliferating events, the cases that are brought to the court. A whole stratum of "Of experience" concerns the way language attempts to reduce the multiplicity of phenomena to a limited number of forms or laws. Montaigne asks: "Qu'ont gaigné nos legislateurs à choisir cent mille especes et faicts particuliers, et y attacher cent mille loix? Ce nombre n'a aucune proportion avec l'infinie diversité des actions humaines" ("What have our legislators gained by selecting a hundred thousand particular cases and actions, and applying a hundred thousand laws to them? This number bears no proportion to the infinite diversity of human actions," 1066; *815–16*). Commentators of this essay emphasize and reemphasize the problem of the "fit" of example to its generalization and the constant slippage that Montaigne both deplores and explores.[2]

Only a creative or "round-about, forced, and biased" (1070; *819*) reading of the law can make it applicable to the new cases presented to the court, for the jurist receives the laws and earlier interpretations from the past and tries to fit them to the present. Thus the conflict between reason and experience is also implicitly a conflict between the aspiration to a supratemporal order (the law, which accounts for the past and controls present and future) and a different knowledge that is fully engaged in the experience of passing time. These early pages of "Of Experience" emphasize the characteristic of example formation that most deeply fascinated Montaigne: the problem of resemblance between elements of experience. Into the already complicated matter of the fit between reason and experience (or between law and case), the author of the *Essays* introduces another issue—the relationship betwen one experience and another. The passage in which Montaigne considers the problem of judicial experience can serve as a basis to question all use of example, since the discourse of example supposes that a law can in some way subsume a large number of real (or even of imaginable) instances. If, however, the instances arrive at a sufficient level of difference from one another, the same general statement will no longer serve to include them. Thus reflection on the tense relationship between reason and experience that opens "Of Experience" yields to the even murkier investigation of the protean nature of experience itself.[3]

To outline this problem in somewhat different terms, we could say that example formation deals with two dimensions of integration: first, between statement and instance, and second, among instances. These relationships can be called vertical integration and horizontal integration, respectively. The problem of horizontal integration is the central problem to which Montaigne's essay addresses itself—how to determine the points at which similarity and difference among experiences trace a pattern. In the essay "Of the Inconsistency of Our Actions" (Book II, chap. 1), Montaigne evokes the problem of using the example of the emperor Nero, who is, in standard usage, the perfect example of cruelty. Rule and instance seem easily and firmly linked in this case. Yet on closer examintion of the accounts of Nero's life, Montaigne finds that Nero was not always cruel and therefore did not always fit the concept that his life is used to illustrate.[4] The example of Nero shows, therefore, how a problem in vertical integration arises from the instability in an attempt at horizontal integration of Nero's actions. From one action to another, from one moment to another, Nero's life was full of inconsistency. The failure in vertical integration can be traced to a lack of horizontal, experiential integration; Nero's actions are not sufficiently similar.

In order for experience to give us usable precedents—examples—we must somehow find a way to limit the constant diversification that experience brings. Should we again turn to reason for a purely conceptual guideline that will abstract from experience? If we do, we will discover a parallel multiplication of concepts: "d'un subject nous en faisons mille, et retombons, en multipliant et subdivisant, à l'infinité des atomes d'Epicurus" ("of one subject we make a thousand, and, multiplying and subdividing, fall back into Epicurus' infinity of atoms," 1067; 817). In opening "Of Experience" Montaigne seems to be exclusively preoccupied with the excess of difference as an obstacle to making useful examples. However, as the essay evolves, variety—that is, difference—turns out to be just as necessary as similarity in forming examples. In order for "instances," "cases," "experiences," or even "events" to precipitate themselves out of the continuum of life some distinction must be made between them. There must be a structuring element that permits one incident of experience to appear different from another; otherwise there would be no way to describe life in discrete statements.

All law would be illustrated and supported by reference to the same endless example, the totality of all perception.[5]

For Montaigne as writer similarity and difference are concepts controlling both the formation of examples and the choice of examples within a humanistic recovery of classical texts. To what extent are ancient examples—which, like laws, bear the impressive patina of age—different from recent examples from closer to home? How do examples from the experience of others differ from examples from the writer's own experience? The examples presented at the outset of the essay are third-person narrative examples. They are made up of experience perceived from the outside. In the course of the essay, Montaigne gives considerable attention to the structure of the first-person experience, much of which figures prominently in the essays to which "Of Experience" serves as conclusion. The problem of horizontal integration comes to the fore as Montaigne depicts the process of giving form to one's own experience, of imparting both conceptual and aesthetic structure to the stream of life. In moving from classical exempla to first-person experience, Montaigne shows how the necessary coexistence of difference and sameness is the crucial achievement of exemplary thinking in both classical and modern discourse.

Readers accustomed to Montaigne's oblique and seemingly digressive approach to the themes he announces at the outset of his essays will not be surprised that there is no single-minded and straightforward definition and analysis of example and exemplification in "Of Experience."[6] Although the essay begins with a strong statement of the relationship of example to inductive reasoning and to the foundation of all logic in the detection of similarity, the twenty thousand words or so cover a remarkable range of topics, from Montaigne's kidney stones and bowel movements to Socrates's military courage and the Spartan daughter of Leonidas (1100; 844). While Montaigne's initial challenge seems to be, "What can be learned from experience?" readers may find that the challenge takes the practical form, "What can be learned from 'Of Experience'?"

In responding to the latter question this article will work toward a fuller understanding of two opposed approaches to the description of experience, two forms of the horizontal integration that is so crucial to example making. Two tropes of Montaigne's will serve as markers as we reach a formulation that relates the problem of time—including the concept of history, a crucial matter to Renaissance humanists in general and to jurists in particular—to the problem of articulating experience along the borders of similarity and difference. These two figures, which will metonymically embody two different ways of ordering the flux of experience, are Circe's drink ("le breuvage de Circe") and the antithetical wine of the Sorbonne theologians. The first of these tropes allows Montaigne to focus on sameness through successive moments, while the second emphasizes diversity in successive moments.

To appreciate the way Montaigne mobilizes the concepts of similarity and difference from the beginning of the essay, consider the very first example in "Of Experience." Montaigne begins with an example-pair, within which the second example destroys the first:

Et les Grecs, et les Latins, et nous, pour le plus expres exemple de similitude, nous servons de celuy des oeufs. Toutesfois il s'est trouvé des hommes, et notamment un en Delphes, qui recognoissoit des marques de difference entre les oeufs, si qu'il n'en prenoit jamais l'un pour l'autre; et y ayant plusieurs poules, sçavoit juger de laquelle estoit l'oeuf.

Both the Greeks and the Latins, and we ourselves, use eggs for the most express example of similarity. However, there have been men, and notably one at Delphi, who recognized marks of difference between eggs, so that he never took one for another; and although there were many hens, he could tell which one the egg came from. (1065; 815)

One of these examples is the example of similarity: eggs. The example is formed by linking a concept—similarity—with physical objects—eggs. The other example concerns the ability to detect difference where sameness seems supreme. The man at Delphi is, again, the physical object linked to the concept "detection of difference." The Delphian undoes two connections at once. First, within the narrative in which he is a character, he finds the difference in the series of eggs and thus separates the eggs. Second, within the text of "Of Experience," the

Delphian is an example of how an apparently perfect and universally trusted example can be undone. The Delphian unhitches eggs from the concept of similarity by showing that each egg is in fact different. By unscrambling the eggs, so to speak, the Delphian has scrambled the example of similarity.

This example-pair sets forth the tension that runs throughout the essay. Experience seems to form examples strictly on the basis of resemblance. Threats to resemblance prevent examples from being formed, unhook the object or event from the concept (as examples *of*), and defeat experience in its claim to supplement reason as a means to knowledge. Yet the Delphian man, in the second phase of this introductory exemplification, shows that dissimilarity can also produce examples. Almost no one can tell one egg from another. The Delphian is extremely unlike other men. Yet this dissimilarity, far from disqualifying the Delphian from being an example, is his sole claim to status as an example. Both similarity and difference generate example, and indeed both qualities must coexist for an example to be recognizable. If the Delphian were not unusual, the anecdote about him would not be an impressive, memorable instance. His notable difference from other men makes him stand out, just as the sameness of eggs makes them stand out against other, more variable types of objects.

Montaigne takes his place alongside the Delphian and his wisdom of difference, arguing that no human effort—art, law, hermeneutics—can overcome the stronger force of proliferating difference: "La ressemblance ne faict pas tant un comme la difference faict autre. Nature s'est obligée à ne rien faire autre, qui ne fust dissemblable" ("Resemblance does not make things so much alike as difference makes them unlike. Nature has committed herself to make nothing separate that was not different," 1065; *815*). Oddly, although humans make laws and judgments to restrain diversity, these artifacts only increase diversity. Montaigne seems to shift between, on the one hand, a view of nature as one and undivided, philosophical hair-splitters and glossers notwithstanding ("il se sent par experience que tant d'interprétations dissipent la verité et la rompent"; "it is evident from experience that so many interpretations disperse the

truth and shatter it," 1067; *817*), and, on the other, a view of nature as always outrunning human attempts to limit its diversity. Yet implicitly it is this tension that produces example—the
movement toward verbally expressed law and the counter-
movement toward exception to that law:

Comme nul evenement et nulle forme ressemble entierement à une
autre, aussi ne differe nulle de l'autre entierement. Ingenieux meslange
de nature. Si nos faces n'estoient semblables, on ne sçauroit discerner
l'homme de la beste; si elles n'estoient dissemblables, on ne sçauroit
discerner l'homme de l'homme.

As no event and no shape is entirely like another, so none is entirely
different from another. An ingenious mixture on the part of nature. If
our faces were not similar, we could not distinguish man from beast; if
they were not dissimilar, we could not distinguish man from man.
(1070; *819*)

Similarity permits law to function, while dissimilarity is, with
regard to the law, an imperfection. In the background here is a
Platonic nostalgia for the Idea, always identical to itself, in contrast with the myriad of imperfect copies. Yet Montaigne takes
a position contrary to Platonic idealism, for he sees the law as
deriving from the multiplicity of the objects and events we encounter. Although the law attempts to describe and foresee experiences, seeking and valorizing similarity, law also provides a
measure that sharpens our sense of difference. Thus, from the
point of view of the legal mind, thinks Montaigne, similarity is
linked to perfection and difference reveals imperfection. Is that
imperfection in the law or in the object that the law fails to describe? For Montaigne, no doubt the former; yet for more con-
servatively or bureaucratically minded jurists, the imperfection
must seem to be in the nonconforming object. Example is the
point where law and experience meet, and hence Montaigne
places example between similarity and imperfection. Example,
to adhere strictly to Montaigne's image, limps (*cloche*). Is this
because it has two legs, one of which is always and necessarily
dissimilar from the other?

By apposition, Montaigne here comes as close as he ever does
to providing a definition of example: a comparison drawn from
experience. In doing this, Montaigne remains within the an-

nounced topic of the essay, yet at the same time he advances from the static view of example that is contained in the opening example of the eggs toward a dynamic, temporal view. The temporal nature of example—though often neglected—had been described long before Montaigne. In one of the earliest descriptions of this rhetorical figure, Aristotle's *Rhetoric* gives a clear case of how example (or *paradeigma*) works across time:

It would be an instance of the historical kind of example, if one were to say that it is necessary to make preparations against the Great King and not to allow him to subdue Egypt; for Darius did not cross over to Greece until he had obtained possession of Egypt; but as soon as he had done so, he did. Again, Xerxes did not attack us until he had obtained possession of that country, but when he had, he crossed over; consequently, if the present Great King shall do the same, he will cross over, wherefore it must not be allowed.[7]

Just like the Delphian egg-man of Montaigne's opening passage, Aristotle's audience is expected to recognize resemblance, yet the series is not synchronous but diachronic. The law or general statement manifested by this example cuts across time boundaries to recur at different periods. For Aristotle, examples are formed out of the historical record by detection of similarity against the great mass of dissimilar events. This view of example does not exalt past events as superior to present ones, does not create a mystique of antiquity, because to do so would run precisely against the usefulness of the figure, which functions only if the present resembles the past. If present capabilities and circumstances were different from those of antiquity, the ancient example would serve no purpose.

Montaigne does not write of example, as Aristotle does, to enable an orator to persuade the public. Instead the Renaissance thinker deals with individual choices and self-understanding. Yet the comparison of past to present and the process by which wit allies itself with memory to detect resemblance and difference are as crucial to Montaigne as to Aristotle:

A faute de memoire naturelle j'en forge de papier, et comme quelque nouveau symptome survient à mon mal, je l'escris. D'où il advient qu'à cette heure, estant quasi passé par toute sorte d'exemples, si quelque estonnement me menace, feuilletant ces petits brevets descousus comme des feuilles Sybillines, je ne faux plus de trouver où me consoler de quelque prognostique favorable en mon experience passée.

For lack of a natural memory I make one of paper, and as some new symptom occurs in my disease, I write it down. Whence it comes that at the present moment, when I have passed through virtually every sort of example,[8] if some grave stroke threatens me, by glancing through these little notes, disconnected like the Sibyl's leaves, I never fail to find grounds for comfort in some favorable prognostic from my past experience. (1092; 837–38)

Significantly, Montaigne's use of *exemple* occurs in a context emphasizing both succession and disconnection. Symptoms are written down because they are new, that is, because they *differ* from the previously prevailing condition. On the other hand, the note of this symptom becomes meaningful when a recurrence or *similarity* is perceived. Like the Sibyl's leaves, these notes are disconnected because example requires the uncoupling of an event or symptom from its immediate period so that it can be held up against similar occurrences in other periods.[9] This is the uncoupling movement that shifts from description to example. But this uncoupling—or unsewing, to use Montaigne's metaphor, "brevets decousus comme feuilles Sybillines" ("little notes, disconnected [*decousus*, unsewn, unstitched] like the Sibyl's leaves")—is a subtle and almost imperceptible process, that depends on forming similarities in order to perceive differences.

Here Montaigne recognizes the way example exists in, and proceeds from, time. Not the great historical time of public event that concerns the classical rhetorician, but the minute, inward events of a human life. Yet Montaigne's record of symptoms and the orator's appropriation of strategic cycles proceed from the same recognition that examples are made from the tension between similarity and difference. The event that illustrates a law or norm must both conform to one norm and depart from another. The example of the Great King takes an act that is unusual and breaks with custom, the Persian's presence in Egypt, and aligns it with similar exceptions to make a new rule. In other words, if the Great King usually were in Egypt or went to Egypt frequently, his presence there would not draw the attention of the Greeks or appear significant. Aristotle's example is the product of repeated disruptions of the normal residency of the Great King, a disruption that calls for a new law to cut across the previous one.

This dynamic of example also motivates Montaigne's notation of symptoms when they break with the background state, when a *new* symptom occurs. But these symptoms only become examples retrospectively, as the aging essayist begins to reconnect the fragments of his past into an account that is not chronicle or description but forecast and prognostic. Forming examples requires, therefore, attending to the sameness that is interrupted by difference, a sameness that does not even reveal itself as such until some contrast occurs to change the scale of perception and reduce the small changes of everyday experience into a stasis against which the bolder change can stand forth.

"Circe's drink" is the striking metaphor by which Montaigne conveys that force which forms habit with its enduring sameness: "C'est à la coustume de donner forme à nostre vie, telle qu'il lui plaist; elle peut tout en cela: c'est le breuvage de Circé, qui diversifie nostre nature comme bon luy semble" ("It is for habit to give form to our life, just as it pleases; it is all-powerful in that; it is Circe's drink, which varies our nature as it sees fit," 1080; *827*). Custom is the force that gives form across the boundaries of time but within geographic regions. Montaigne's comment on Circe's drink is the transition between his claim that he cannot be harmed by anything he has been accustomed to for a long time and his enumeration of national peculiarities. The Spanish cannot stomach French food; Germans become sick if they sleep on a mattress; the French object to the heat of stoves while the Germans abhor fireplaces. Custom thus provides temporal links within a nation while creating sharp differences at national boundaries. Circe, as incarnation of custom and duration, provides the sameness without which difference cannot appear, and Montaigne, as writer, takes Circe's side at least momentarily. His evocation of habit is strengthened by his insistence on the consistency of German taste. He does not write that *some* Germans, especially when they live far from the French border, avoid mattresses. In order to convey a traditional norm, the writer must emphasize sameness within each nation and accentuate the abrupt and even antithetical character of the contrasts from nation to nation that form this string of examples.

As one matrix of example, Circe assures diachronic sameness and synchronic difference. But this arrangement can be shuffled around to produce the opposite configuration in time: synchronic sameness and diachronic difference. Montaigne refers to another drink, the wine of the Sorbonne, to describe a sharp contrast within the same group from one moment to another:

Soit par gosserie, soit à certes, que le vin theologal et Sorbonique est passé en proverbe, et leurs festins, je trouve que c'est raison qu'ils en disnent d'autant plus commodéement et plaisamment qu'ils ont utilement et serieusement employé la matinée à l'exercice de leur escole. La conscience d'avoir bien dispensé les autres heures est un juste et savoureux condimant des tables.

Whether it is in jest or in earnest that the Sorbonne acquired its proverbial reputation for theological drinking and feasting, I think it right that the faculty should dine all the more comfortably and pleasantly for having used the morning profitably and seriously in the work of their school. The consciousness of having spent the other hours well is a proper and savory sauce for the dinner table. (1108; 851)

This sauce is the difference manifested in time between the morning and afternoon of the schoolmen, and while it can be considered a habit or custom, it is a habit that includes difference within itself. Unlike Circe's drink, which is a metaphor for the force generating a diversified sameness (diversified from class to class and nation to nation but never changing), the Sorbonnic wine is an example of a same diverseness, of a single group that includes a principle of contrast and does not need to be compared to a different group.

These two major organizing principles of contrast, Circe's drink and Sorbonnic wine, are the key to understanding Montaigne's evolution from the use of classical exemplary figures to the use of intimate details, which form the substance of the essays, particularly "Of Experience." Montaigne has perceived that the tension between sameness and difference that permits the discovery of a *pattern*—and hence the basis of example—exists almost everywhere. His evolution begins with his use of classical models in a way that is interchangeable with his use of medieval and modern ones. The context in which he mentions the Sorbonnic wine is part of a longer development that includes classical examples:

Quand je vois et Caesar et Alexandre, au plus espais de sa grande besongne, jouyr si plainement des plaisirs naturels et par consequent necessaires et justes, je ne dicts pas que ce soit relascher son ame, je dicts que c'est roidir, sousmetant par vigueur de courage à l'usage de la vie ordinaire ces violentes occupations et laborieuses pensées. Sages, s'ils eussent creu que c'estoit là leur ordinaire vacation, cette-cy l'extraordinaire.

When I see both Caesar and Alexander, in the thick of their great tasks, so fully enjoying natural and therefore necessary and just pleasures, I do not say that that is relaxing their souls, I say that it is toughening them, subordinating these violent occupations and laborious thoughts, by the vigor of their spirits, to the practice of everyday life: wise men, had they believed that this was their ordinary occupation, the other the extraordinary. (1108; 850)

Instead of presenting Caesar and Alexander as different from and more important than other human beings, Montaigne reverses the traditional exemplary value to present them as enjoying the same pleasures as other men. The difference that gives value to this example is the difference between Caesar and "Caesar"—that is, the external, static, conventional image of Caesar—and between Alexander and "Alexander." Like the theologians, these warriors include *within* their lives changes from one moment to another. The source of wisdom, which neither general fully appreciated, was the potential revaluation of the difference between their two occupations—one "glorious" and the other ordinary.

Montaigne deflates the status of these classical exemplary figures—as he does with similar figures in many other essays, most notably "That the Taste of Good and Evil Depends in Large Part on the Opinion We Have of Them" (Book I, chap. 14)—but he does so by use of an example. With this example he guides us away from the purely external appropriation of example toward an active process in which the boundary of exemplary difference is not located between us, ordinary mortals, and *them*, the high-ranking heroes. Although Montaigne is aware of the usefulness of external sources of example as provocation to self-awareness, he does not insist on this external aspect of example as strongly and as rigidly as did Machiavelli. The latter had argued, in *The Prince* and the *Discourses*, that historical phenomena could only be understood from "outside" history.[10] Like Machiavelli, Montaigne insists on the importance of a *break* or interruption in those phenomena we choose as examples.

The idea of breaking something recurs in "Of Experience" as a way of making something more fertile or of multiplying it. Often readers notice only the negative aspect to this breaking and multiplication, but there is a positive side as well.[11] The earth is broken for planting and cultivation—"la terre se rend fertile plus elle est esmiée et profondément remuée" ("the earth is made more fertile the more it is crumbled and deeply plowed," 1067; 816)—and quicksilver when broken becomes an uncountable number of droplets. This multiplication through division may confuse the seeker after a pure primordial nature—*Confusum est quidquid in pulverem sectum est*[12]—but multiplicity returns later in the chapter as a necessary step in self-discovery. The broken or disconnected notes, "unsewn like the Sibyl's leaves," permit Montaigne to unhook a symptom from the past, no longer perceived as a block but as cut up, divided into a fertile availability. The past crumbles to give the seeds of thought a place to grow.

Montaigne's *way* of dividing up phenomena into examples is an important contribution, based on a rediscovery of time as the core of example. For Montaigne the Sorbonnic wine really does correct Circe's drink of soporific custom. He learns to draw the line between certain types of successive experience within his own life rather than between his own life, as monolithic and consistent entity, and the lives of others. The discovery of the self through greater awareness of the other is surely a major step in the later *Essays*, as Patrick Henry has shown in a vigorous and persuasive study.[13] Discovery (and even formulation) of diversity in oneself is the long-term outcome of an internalization of the logic of example with which Montaigne wrestled throughout much of the *Essays*. Like the theologians who suffer through arduous disputations in the morning and then permit themselves a joyous and completely contrary experience in the afternoon, Montaigne is attentive to the alternations between comfort and pain in his own bout with kidney stones. As the theologians enjoy their wine more because of the contrast, so Montaigne prefers the acute, highly perceptible attacks of the stone to the languid, gradual phases of other maladies. Like Socrates, Montaigne rejoices "to consider the close alliance between pain and pleasure, how they are associated by a necessary link, so that they follow and engender each other in turn" (1093; *838*). The "link" (*estroitte alliance*) is the obverse of the *difference* between pain and pleasure, each of which is perceptible by virtue of the contrast. Moreover, pain and pleasure are distinguished within the flux of one's own experience in time, not by experiencing pleasure *next to* a person who is suffering. If you merely *see* a person in pain you cannot know what pain is. The simultaneous presence of contrasting states does not appear to Montaigne to bring knowledge as much as the internal successive experience that can be broken into a pattern. When Montaigne writes "I have passed through virtually every sort of example," he is wrestling with this difficult, paradoxical knowledge, which is both internal and yet distanced. In a way the enormity of pain can only be appreciated once the pain is passed; the significance of a symptom is manifested *later* by what follows. Therefore Montaigne's notes on his health give him a retrospective—and prospective—knowledge of himself at a temporal distance, yet within himself. Experience as source of examples binds the apparently hostile elements of sameness and difference by searching for difference within the perceiver.

The contrast between his own experience of kidney stone and the knowledge that others believed they could derive by observing him gave Montaigne a somewhat perverse amusement. The author describes how his mind helps him get past the acute torments of the stone:

Vous en plaict-il un exemple? Il dict que c'est pour mon mieux que j'ay la gravele. . . . Regarde ce chastiement; il est bien doux au pris d'autres, et d'une faveur paternelle. . . . La crainte et pitié que le peuple a de ce

mal te sert de matiere de gloire. . . . Il y a plaisir à ouyr dire de soy: Voylà
bien de la force, voylà bien de la patience. On te voit suer d'ahan, pallir,
rougir, trembler, vomir jusques au sang, souffrir des contractions et
convulsions estranges.

Would you like an example? It [my mind] tells me that it is for my own
good that I have the stone. . . . Consider this chastisement; it is very
gentle in comparison with others, and paternally tender. . . . The fear
and pity that people feel for this illness is a subject of vainglory for you.
. . . There is pleasure in hearing people say about you: There indeed is
strength, there indeed is fortitude! They see you sweat in agony, turn
pale, turn red, tremble, vomit your very blood, suffer strange contractions and convulsions. (1090–91; 836)[14]

Enjoying the scene he is making and the somewhat histrionic
pleasure of putting on a good face and making jokes in his visible agony, Montaigne is aware that onlookers can only guess
what he is really feeling. They could never give a true account
of the stone. The appeal to internal rather than external observation reaches its extreme in Montaigne's description of Plato's
version of the perfectly trustworthy doctor:

[P]our estre vray medecin, il seroit necessaire que celuy qui l'entre-
prendroit eust passé par toutes les maladies qu'il veut guarir et par tous
les accidens et circonstances dequoy il doit juger. C'est raison qu'ils
prennent la verole s'ils la veulent sçavoir penser. Vrayment je m'en fie-
rois à celuy là.

[T]o become a true doctor, the candidate must have passed through all
the illnesses that he wants to cure and all the accidents and circumstances that he is to diagnose. It is reasonable that he should catch the
pox if he wants to know how to treat it. Truly I should trust such a
man." (1079; 827)

The ideally experienced and disease-ridden doctor is contrasted
directly with those who only *describe* diseases like a town crier.
Descriptive knowledge of disease is based on perception that a
diseased person differs *from us*, just as the Frenchman under the
influence of Circe's drink of habit perceives the oddity of the
customs of the Germans and Spaniards living nearby. The ideal
doctor sees illnesses as different states of his own experience as
it reaches through time. Although Montaigne's detailed account of his own peculiarities and tastes as they evolved in the
course of his life—for instance, that he liked horseradish,

stopped liking it, and then liked it again—may seem far from
the extreme knowledge of the diseased doctor, these details are
examples generated by temporal contrast—the Sorbonnic
wine—and made available for the organizing work of language.

Having begun with an apparent condemnation of example because of its endless proliferation, Montaigne finishes by entering with pleasure and even fascination into the discovery of still
more minute differences, creating examples in which elements
of experience are joined with a plethora of concepts far more ex-
plosive than any of the laws referred to at the beginning of "Of
Experience." The essayist has moved from the skeptical observation of the twisting by which magistrates force a fit between
law and case, between precedent and current reality, to the joyous discovery of the production of concepts out of the disruptions of his own experience.

The conclusion of this final essay is devoted to the hope of enjoying a prosperous and healthy old age, seemingly a great departure from the consideration of judicial precedent that opens
"Of Experience." Yet there is, underneath the surface, a close
conceptual connection. At the beginning, diversity in experience is a source of anguish because Montaigne still writes from
the point of view of a magistrate attempting to fit all experience
into the mold of an abstract and timeless law. By the end, the
essayist has reversed his emphasis and turned toward the variation of experience as the source of both knowledge and pleasure.
Montaigne arrives at this conclusion by rehabilitating time—
particularly succession or diachrony—as a major feature of ex-
ample-making. Once succession is chosen as the major principle by which the world is divided into knowable units, then the
fragmentation that had appeared as a source of anguish in the
opening pages of "Of Experience" can be recovered and recognized as a positive and consoling resource. If Montaigne had
failed to do this, his examples would be timeless, fixed, and remote. When examples are both in the past and external to us,
they risk losing the tension, the fertility, and the unpredictability that generate our discourse. They also leave us like Montaigne's town crier calling for a lost dog he has never seen. Such
classical examples please us when we drink from Circe's cup,

but they cannot move us out of the path of habit to make us aware of the fertile disunity of ourselves. But we may, like the theologians, find a principle of contrast internal to the exemplary object. If we do so, shaking off the division between us and them (between modernity and antiquity, between Frenchman and German) we can revivify the example, detecting its fertile point of rupture and finding in it the pattern that can be stretched across the face of history.

The Discourse of the Example

An "Example,"
Chapter IV of the First Part of
'The Logic of Port-Royal'

> La théologie est une science, mais en même temps
> combien est-ce de sciences?
> (Theology is a science, but at the same time how
> many sciences?)
>
> —Pascal, *Pensées*

The fourth chapter of the first part of *The Art of Thinking*, or *The Logic of Port-Royal*, "Of Ideas of Things and of Ideas of Signs," offers to the reader, besides a definition of the notion of sign in general, a very interesting classification of signs.[1] The history of this chapter, which was introduced only in 1683 in the fifth edition, is well-known: it belongs to the latest series of additions that had begun with the 1664 second edition. These additions gave final shape to a work that was to determine, for over two centuries, with a clarity characterized by its consistency and its absence of mystery, a "standard" philosophy [*une philosophie "moyenne"*] of representation, of the idea, and of judgment, providing thus a founding charter to what history, in the Age of the Enlightenment and progress, was to call "ideology." However, it so happens that precisely the 1664 and 1683 additions have raised and will continue to raise questions in this text devoid of obscurity, interrogations that were to multiply as soon as this text, originally a handbook on logic with strong pedagogical intentions, became through these

Translated from the French by Anne Tomiche.

additions a treatise on moral philosophy, theology, and rhetoric.

In 1664, the additions seemed to respond to three different orders of concerns: moral, rhetorical, and logical. They are linked to one another in a coherent way by the resistance that opposes to the analysis of language the complexity of the thinking of which this language is supposed to be the faithful and transparent expression. In all the cases studied, whether rhetorical, logical, or grammatical, one notes a constant discrepancy between what is expressed and what is said, a hiatus between what is said and what is conceived, a gap between the term, the proposition, the discourse on the one hand and the concept, the judgment, and reasoning on the other: language abbreviates, forgets, erases, or masks what thinking elaborates. It is not a pure representation whose transparency would at the same time transmit and allow one to see the operations of pure thinking. Expressive forms, on whatever level, possess a certain autonomy. What kind? And what are its limits or its rules? The remarkable chapter 10 of the first part points to the external limits of this autonomy when it introduces, in regard to the confused and obscure idea, the acute moral analysis of self-representation: there are, in man, forces of opacity that, at the juncture of language and thought, compromise the natural and rational functioning of representation, its transparency. These are self-esteem, concupiscence, cupidity, and desire. Eloquence, ordinary language, the sophisms of discussion and conversation all belong to these forces, which work underneath pure discourse to turn it into an object of pleasure and an instrument of seduction.

In 1683 another set of supplementary texts appeared. A foreword to this edition, while specifying the circumstances, shows very clearly how the tensions, indeed the contradictions, characteristic of a cultural and historical field are assumed in the systematic unity of a text conscious of itself: "Various important additions have been made to this new edition of the Logic. These were occasioned by the objections made by the (Protestant) Ministers to certain observations it contained; it thus became necessary to explain and defend the parts they had endeavored to attack." Indeed, polemics with the Protestants, which was one of the main aspects of the strategy of Port-Royal in those days of religious peace [*Paix de l'Eglise*], provided the opportunity for these additions; but, however far from being adventitious, these additions undoubtedly relate directly to the very heart of the Port-Royalists' cognitive, ethical, and spiritual practice and theory. Arnauld and Nicole were aware of this but they never problematized the relation between the contingent historical pretext and the discovery of fundamental theoretical elements:

These explanations will clearly show that reason and faith are in perfect harmony, as streams from the same source, and that we cannot move far away from the one without departing also from the other. But although theological disputes have thus given rise to these additions, they are neither less appropriate nor less natural to logic; and they might have been made, even though there had never been any Ministers in the world, who had attempted to obscure the truths of our faith with false subtleties.

What, then, are these texts, both occasional and essential? They are all concerned with problems of language properly speaking. The first of these texts, chapter 4 of the first part, defines the idea of sign and provides a classification of it. Another is chapter 15, which studies the ideas that the mind adds to those that are expressly signified; especially when there is a discrepancy between signification and reference, the mind adds, without expressing them, more distinct ideas: "This happens especially in the case of the demonstrative pronouns, when, instead of the proper name, we use the neuter 'this,' *hoc*." The four chapters added to the second part are no exception to the unity of inspiration in these texts: chapters 1 and 2 deal with the relation between words and propositions and with the definition of the verb; they come straight out of Arnauld's *General Grammar*. Chapters 12 and 14 are devoted to confused subjects that are equivalent to two subjects, on the one hand, and to propositions in which the names of things are given to signs, on the other. In both chapters the problem tackled is a problem of language. In chapter 12, the problem dealt with is a problem of facts: ordinary language does not distinguish between things that bear some resemblance to each other and things that succeed one another in the same place. In chapter 14, the problem dealt with is a problem of right: when does one have the right to speak figuratively? What is the status in discourse of the tropes of word substitutions? As one can see, the coherence of the texts added in 1683 thus involves the problem of language which thereby comes to the forefront of the *Logic* and is organized around two axes. One, the semiotic axis, is oriented toward the structure of the sign: what is, in the sign itself, the relation between signification and reference when, in the text itself, such a distinction is still implicit? The other, the semantic axis, concerns the relation between the word and the proposition: what is a verb, as an act of assertion, as a concatenation of representations, but also as the articulation of Being [*l'Etre*] into beings [*étants*]?

Now, another unity links all these texts in a coherent way, a unity that is, however, not manifested by the logical and philosophical grammatical discourse in the different stages of articulation and development of the argument. Rather, it is manifested by another discourse, perfectly contemporaneous with the first, but fragmentary, discontinuous, constituted by autonomous signifying units, working on the first text as a subtext that would be woven with it but whose threads would appear only locally on the surface. This is the discourse of the "examples," and there is one privileged example that organizes, in a recurrent way, the whole network at the three levels: that of the concept or the term, that of the judgment or the sentence, and that of reasoning or discourse. This example is the theological dogma of Transubstantiation, which the Reformation called into question, the mystery of faith presented and summarized in a statement of language: "This is my body."

This general structure of the 1683 additions can also be found in the first addition, the fourth chapter of the first part, "Of Ideas of Things and of Ideas of Signs." In this text, the Port-Royalists formulate for the first time an argumentative strategy that consists in fusing the two streams of reason and faith and in solidly binding theology to logic, through the play of "the discourse of example." Hence, by entrusting logic (and reason) to reasoned and continuous discourse, and theology (and faith) to the illustrative, incidental, and adventitious discourse of the example, they intend to show the inclusion of the "theological" within the "logical," which they had asserted in their Foreword. Moreover, as part of their polemic with the "Ministers," they intend to show that religious heresy is only a particular kind of rational mistake. However, in doing so, they encourage a symmetrical and inverse reading: the theological model—a model supported in an insidious and fragmentary way by the discourse-of-examples, and especially the discourse that allows the construction of the consecrating statement as understood in the Catholic sense—namely, a model that opens a way to the understanding of how the sign functions as representation in the act of asserting things by the subject of the enunciation, that is, in the judgment (and the proposition in which the judgment is articulated) and in the general discourse through which the social community of speaking subjects institutes itself. One must add that this remarkable "theoretical" gain was probably achieved at the risk of compromising the general and rational theory of sign-representation by the surreptitious and "mysterious" theology of the sacramental sign, and more precisely of the eucharistic sign, and, reciprocally, at the risk of compromising the latter by the former.

The chapter opens with a general definition of the idea of a sign. It is a double definition since the sign is at the same time an *operation* through which the mind (that is, the subject) views any object only as a representative of any other object, and the *product of this operation*, hence this very object as a mere representative. This object is given the name of "sign," and a representation corresponds to this sign (of a sign), precisely the idea of a sign. The examples of signs privileged by the logicians to illustrate their general definition—this point is remarkable and has indeed already been remarked upon—are a certain kind of icon: "It is in this way that we commonly regard maps and paintings." Of ideas of things, as opposed to ideas of signs, the logicians give two examples: the earth and the sun. Of ideas of signs the examples are maps (which provide the scholar with the representation of the earth) and paintings (that is, representations that allow one to see, in their absence, the things to which the sun gives light)—two examples that thus echo

Poussin's definition of painting, formulated about twenty years earlier: "C'est une imitation faite avec lignes et couleurs en quelque superficie [le tableau] de tout ce qui se voit dessous le soleil, sa fin est la délectation" ("It is an imitation, made with lines and colors on whatever surface [the canvas], of everything that can be seen under the sun, and its end is delight").[2] Reformulating this definition, the logicians insist again on the double aspect of the sign, its being at the same time an "object" and an "operation"; and *the "object" is inseparable from its functioning, as the example might indeed be from discourse.* The object is the product of its functioning—this is the first definition of the sign, as the example is of discourse. And the object produces its functioning—this is its second definition. Thus, "the sign contains two ideas, one of the thing that represents, the other of the thing represented, and its nature consists in exciting the second by means of the first." What second discourse does the example produce? How does the example represent? What is it a representation of? In this case, the model of the sign is fertile. The nature of the sign—representation consists indeed in this "excitation," this transport of the mind from one pole (the representative) of the relation of representation to the other (the represented): the nature of the sign is this "metaphor" of the subject of an idea to another in the same idea. The example functions like a sign, and a sign is only thinkable in its functioning, as functioning. And if the privileged example, the paradigm for the sign, is the icon (the map or the painting), then the example is the icon of discourse and it is inside discourse. It functions as a map or a painting: it is an icon-sign of the discourse in which it is immersed, an icon that this discourse produces as it functions as discourse.

The logicians then offer three divisions of signs according to three criteria. First, the *epistemic criterion of certainty and probability*: some signs are certain and some are probable, and they need to be distinguished from one another, otherwise an effect may rashly be attributed to a cause when it might be the effect of another cause. Second, the *criterion of continuity and discontinuity*: some signs are connected with the things they signify and some signs are separated from them, and this classification leads to four maxims to which we shall come back. And finally, the *criterion of the natural and the institutional*: some signs do not depend on the fancies of men, and some others exist only by convention and do not have any relation with the thing they represent—thus words in relation to thoughts. The signs of language only appear in the last lines of this important chapter devoted to the ideas of signs, a chapter that opened with the examples, prevalent for the logicians of Port-Royal, of maps and paintings. And maps and paintings will reappear in the form of the map of Italy and the portrait of Caesar or of Alexander in chapter 14 of the second part, a chapter announced by the last line of chapter 4: "We shall explain, when dealing with propositions, an important truth concerning these kinds of signs (natural, institutional), namely that we are able, on some occasions, to affirm the things signified."

However, another network of articulation underlies the three divisions of the signs, a network formed by the examples, which, as a whole, is then subject to a *double coherence*. The *first* and obvious one is the coherence of the three binary typologies that the examples are meant to illustrate: the certain and the probable; the connected and the separated; the natural and the institutional. This coherence results from the production of the example by the discourse, as an example specifying, in its concrete particularity, the generality of the category or of the process of functioning. The *other* coherence, although more discrete, is no less operative: it concerns the *theological model of the Eucharist*. The sacramental sign appears in three places in the network. First, as the only example of signs separated from things—thus the sacrifices of the Ancient Law, which are signs of the offering of Jesus Christ, were separated from what they represented; Jesus Christ who is the signified of the signs is no other than the eucharistic Christ, whose sacramental institution is both the representation and the reiteration of the sacrifice. Second, as the final example of the third maxim,[3] developing the transformed category of the hidden and the revealed. Third, as an example illustrating the fourth maxim, the ultimate stage in the transformation of the couple of presence and absence in the notion of pure representation as double impression. As an example, and regardless of the differences in its textual presentation, the sacramental sign belongs to the same signifying isotopy: it orients the series of examples that precede and follow it, it gives the series its sense [*sens*]—its direction and signification—and puts the examples into perspective. If one considers the sacramental "sign" as a model or a paradigm of the sign in general, as an "exemplary" example of the sign, then one notices two characteristics: it is located on the internal borders of the taxonomy produced by the rational and logical discourse, and its surreptitious effect is to blur the distinctiveness of these borders.

The first example brings to light the maximum distance between the sign and the thing of which the sign is the representation, since this distance is at the same time the distance of history and the distance of the symbol: the separation between the sign and the thing is not only one between the figuring element [*le figurant*] belonging to the Old Testament and the Evangelical figured element [*le figuré*], but also the symbolic gap between the historical event of Jesus' death and its ritual and communal reiteration in the eucharistic sacrifice within the institution of the Church. With the figure of the sacrifice, the conjunction achieved in sacrament is separated in the dimension of sacred history. The signifier, which is a figure of the Old Testament, signifies or represents a signified that is a historical event transcribed in the New Testament. Thus, this factual reality is not only situated after the figure of the sacrifice, according to the order of temporal succession, but is also its model and its accomplishment in the axiological sense of the term: Jesus Christ immolated is the perfect sacrificial victim, and the sheep and bulls offered as sacrifice by the Jews are its figures.

This reality, which is second according to historical time and first according to religious value, thus defines the prophetic dimension of exegetical discourse since, in a sense, the cause of the effect comes after the effect that produces it analogically. This reversal is not without importance for the general structure of the sign, for in this case the duality of the order of cause and the order of sense allows the relation of substitution char-

acteristic of representation to "function," as we have seen, according to its two orientations: from the signifier to the signified that it produces and upon which it prevails, this being the
diachronic temporal order; and from the signified to the signifier that it erases, this being the achronic semantic order. Hence
the sacrifice of Jesus Christ is the "latest" of the sacrifices to
God; it is the ultimate term of a temporal series. But this term
is the principle of intelligibility of the series, its primary and
originary sense [sens, direction and meaning]. The signifier thus
has a function simultaneously in the "large syntagm" of the sacred history of the chosen people and of the Church, and in the
"large paradigm" of Christian Catholic theology. It is an ambiguous signifier, which defines the hermenuetic situation in the
distance opened by history and which theology cancels by reversing its sense [sens], and which, in its definition, reproduces
the ambiguity of the term "sense" [sens] since it is a temporal
direction and a relation of intelligibility.

Since the same thing may be at the same time both a thing and a sign,
it may obscure, as a thing, that which it reveals as a sign. Thus the
warm ashes hide the fire as a thing and reveal it as a sign. Thus the
forms assumed by Angels hide them as things and reveal them as signs.
Thus, the eucharistic symbols hide the Body of Jesus Christ as a thing,
while they reveal it as a symbol.

This second example thus initiates the conjunction of the signifier and the signified in the sacramental institution. With it
the text moves from exegesis to sacrament, from reading at a
certain distance to the perception of the sign in its immediate
efficacy. It is indeed a matter of a perception since we encounter, embedded in the same material reality (bread and wine),
both the thing and the signifier. We also have, here again, the
duality of the figuring element [figurant] and the figured element [figuré], but within the sacrament itself, and the second
example concerns here the internal split of the signifier in thing
and symbol. For, in a sense, there is only bread and wine, and, in
another sense, there is the flesh and blood of Jesus Christ. Indeed, the Ministers' mistake concerns this point, just as the Judaic mistake concerned the previous point. The latter had been

a mistake regarding the judgment about temporal diachrony and about distribution, a mistake regarding the syntagm of historical discourse, of signifiers and signifieds. The former mistake will be one regarding the judgment about the synchrony of the sacramental sign and about the organization of the signifier in the very structure of the sign.

For bread and wine are things that, as things, hide what they reveal as symbol (or sign), the body of Jesus Christ. Bread and wine function indeed as the "symbolic" signifier of the divine body, as the third example will show. At this point, an unthinkable idea emerges, which language seems to manifest by a "forgetting" of its phonic reality but which the Eucharist will actualize, namely, the idea that the "ideal" sign would be that of a dematerialized reality, of a "spiritual thing" that would present in a visible way the invisible in the representation—the idea that the perfect signifier would be simultaneously visible and material in order to convey the signified, and invisible and immaterial in order not to put an obstacle in its way.

The second and third examples are the "dialectic" moments of this paradoxical constitution. In a first step, the thing keeps its full materiality to overshadow the signified but overshadows it as a thing and not as a signifier: a signified without a signifier, it cannot reveal itself for lack of a sign. Thus on the one hand, it is invisible. On the other hand, we have within sight a simple thing, totally visible, full, and entire. The second step is that of a signifier that is only signifier, whose entire function is to cancel itself in the presence of the signified it represents; all that remains is the thing-form of the signifier, a transparent form defined only by the emergence in it of the signified: a signifier without signified, or a signifier whose signified only appears in its signifying representation.

In a third step, the first two steps are superimposed in the unity—split and reunited—of the presence of the eucharistic symbols as representatives and things, as revealing-overshadowing. With the eucharistic symbols or the forms assumed by Angels, the thing is totally signifying and it is totally thing. In its manifestation, "consecrated" bread is similar to ordinary bread. However, the thing becomes this supplement, in order to signify visibly, as sign, the body of Jesus Christ.

Here, the mistake of the Ministers will be to make bread a symbol-thing that does not hide anything but metaphorically figures the body of Jesus Christ, the nourishment of souls; a signifier whose signified, within the dualism of a spiritual symbolics, remains at a distance. The sign is not connected with the thing but separated from it by the space of the figure and of the symbol. For, not having understood or acknowledged the complex dialectic of the sign, they are condemned to theological erring. It thus makes sense that the introduction of the chapter on the idea of a sign in the *Logic* provides, in the perspective of a polemical charity, the opportunity to return to authentic theological discourse. Thus, "these explanations clearly show that reason and faith are in perfect harmony, as streams from the same source."

Since the nature of the sign consists in exciting in the senses, by means of the idea of the thing signifying, that of the thing signified, that so long as that effect remains—that is to say, so long as that double idea is excited—the sign remains, even though the thing in its proper nature is destroyed. Thus it does not matter whether the colors of the rainbow, which God has taken as a sign that he would stop destroying the human race, be true and real, provided our senses always receive the same impression, and that they are enabled by this impression to conceive God's promise. And, in the same way, it does not matter whether the bread of the Eucharist remains in its proper nature, provided it always excites in our senses the image of that bread which enables us to conceive of the way in which the body of Jesus Christ is the nourishment of our souls, and how the faithful are united to each other.

With the third example, Arnauld and Nicole take a new step in the enunciation of the theological discourse concerning the Eucharist. The structure of the sign in its most general possibility has allowed one to think simultaneously the thing and the sign, the thing as a pure signifier, the signifier as a material thing. With the third example, this substantiality is dissolved, the thing itself "is destroyed in its proper nature," and all that remains is the sensible quality through which the thing manifests itself to the senses, a sensible quality that is the signifier of natural reality as a signified and that it signifies as a representation to the mind. But it would be a serious mistake to think—as the Ministers conveniently argue—that representation would be the same as similarity and that to speak of a relation of meaning as visible would be to indicate a relation of copy to model, "seized" by a mimetic reproduction. In the Eucharist, our senses clearly show us roundness and whiteness. But only common minds, locked up in their sensualist or scholastic prejudices and ignoring the rational principles of the discourse of physics, will think that behind roundness and whiteness, perceptible qualities, there is the substantial reality of bread as a round and white substance in all respects similar to the perceived qualities. The dogma of the Eucharist is coherent with the principles of Cartesian physics. By making the sensible quality of a representative sign that is not similar to the substance, the new physics could welcome without any difficulty the "theologomenon" thanks to this disjunction, once faith had acknowledged that there was a change of substance not in correlation with a change of qualities.

However, while the substance of bread is destroyed in its proper nature, the third example's specific function is to save the very form of the signifier, the appearance of bread in the sensible qualities that form its image in the soul. This signifier is not a dead envelope meant to cover up the change of substances, but it must still manifest both these substances one after the other. On the other hand, this permanence of the signifier on the surface of the substances that it communicates in a visible way has its signified, which is double: to make us "conceive of the way in which the body of Jesus-Christ is the nourishment of our souls, and how the faithful are united to each other." Here again the signified is separated from the signifier since the stress is placed on its symbolic function. But it is also engaged in the signifier itself by an actualized metaphor, opposite to the metaphorical de-actualization performed by the Protestants, since the bread is actually eaten, in common, by the faithful, while the body of Jesus Christ is a nourishment for the souls and the meal in which it is consumed is a spiritual communion within the institution of the Church.

The third example thus relies on principles of physics to legitimate the change of substance that coexists with the permanence of the sensible qualities which signifies them, but, first and above all, it aims at the signifying function of the eucharistic bread. It then produces a new split, this time not between the thing and the signifier in the structure of the sign, but in the signifier itself, between the signifier as the body of Jesus Christ in the appearance of bread and the signifier as the bread, the image in the mind, the representation of the communal spiritual nourishment.

To conclude, let us only note that the theological example of the eucharistic sign *performs* for the "discourse" of logic (and of grammar) what the eucharistic sign *does* for the sign in its general structure. Not only does it give to the series of examples its sense, its direction, and its end by instituting among them, based on its own signifying isotopy, a complex coherence that belongs to a figurative or exegetical order; but further, destroying the semantic substance of discourse in its very nature, its logico-grammatical "property," the theological example turns the series into a *figure*, the figure of a discourse on theology—a discourse *about* God and a discourse *of* God—and of one of theology's founding truths. However, it does so without ever enunciating this discourse as such and without ever ceasing to enunciate itself as a "discourse of examples," that is, as the discourse articulating the particular cases of application of the logical and grammatical models.

In other words, this complex relation of the discourse of the "theological" example to the discourse of science reveals its strategic function, namely, to be its productive link without ever appearing as such, in the same way that "eucharistic symbols hide the body of Jesus-Christ as a thing, while they reveal it as a symbol," or in the same way that "the bread of Eucharist can be destroyed in its very nature provided it always excites in our senses the image of that bread which enables us to conceive of the way in which the body of Jesus Christ is the nourishment of our souls."

The discourse of the example *appropriates* the discourse of generalizing formalities in which it is grafted while giving it its strongest power over the particulars that these forms, categories, models, and so on aim to construct as an object of knowledge. But the *figures* that it draws in the text in which it is inscribed *disappropriate* it in the same movement, displace it toward an alterity, an other-of-the-text that each example, regardless of the rigor and the precision of its construction as a "simple illustration" of the model, constantly opens in the text in which it is produced. Thus, the "example" of the eucharistic sign in the general model of the sign constructed by the Port-Royalists introduces, in a rational and reasonable (Cartesian) philosophy of representation, of judgment, and of reasoning, the pragmatic power of the sacramental theology, which calls into question, through the mystery of the language-body, the most secured foundations of a thinking of the idea and of the sign.

PART II

Exemplarity in Literature

Fables of Responsibility

> A decision can only come to pass beyond the
> calculable program that would destroy all
> responsibility by transforming it into a program-
> mable effect of determined causes. There can be
> no moral or political responsibility without this
> trial and this passage by way of the undecidable.
> Even if a decision seems to take only a second
> and not to be preceded by any deliberation, it is
> structured by this *experience of the undecidable*.
> —Jacques Derrida, *Limited Inc.*

"Twenty-six hundred years ago Aesop said: It is
not always safe to imitate a bad example."[1]

What would we humans do without bad examples—without
the example of the bad example, and without our regular inoc-
ulation by and against it? Responsibility begins in the bad example: one could even say that the only good example, the only
one worthy of the imitation, interiorization, and identification
that the example calls for, is the bad example. The subject is
only installed in its stance of responsibility and security after
the passage through the bad example, after the security failure
that teaches the fragility of identity and the defense against the
other. And yet there could be no experience of difference, no
change, and no relation to the other without the adventure of
the comparison and its failure—precisely because it is not always safe.

What is at stake in the fable is the interpretation and practice of
responsibility, the exposure of the subject to the call and the
name with which it is constituted and which puts it in question. The Aesopian fable, from Socrates' dream in the *Phaedo* to
Zora Neale Hurston's mules and men and Francis Ponge's "Fa-

ble," has at once taken responsibility for granted and put it at risk, a structuring difficulty that goes some way in accounting for the peculiar persistence of the fable even in those texts that have put the most rigorous questions to traditional theories of responsibility.[2]

The fable is offered for example, but for the kind of example that asks to happen in an act of something like imitation or identification, in the rhetorical event of a comparison. The title given by Alexander Gelley to the original incarnation of the collective project that has culminated in this volume, "Exemplary Tales: Narrative Examples and Moral Meanings," provides a generous starting point here. In its repeated coordination of the rhetorical (example) with the narrative, and hence of trope with temporality, and then its destination in the ethical and semantic values generated by such textual complications, it suggests a certain hesitation in or over the text—its figures and their deployment—which might at least delay the final establishment of those values. The promise of the "and," which guides us through text to value, whether ethical or semantic, is also a threat: the threat of example's excess, its iteration in the title and the text.

When the examples are fables of responsibility, aimed at producing and securing the morality of, precisely, meanings and of the subject who means, can they finally be submitted to the logic of an evaluative destination with such thoroughness that they will efface themselves in the accomplishment of their mission? Or might the example, the fable, remain, and if it does— which cannot be taken for granted, anymore than the converse—what remains of moral meaning, of responsibility for example, along with it? When the very rhetorical mechanism of the fable, the rule of comparison and a certain identification, is in its turn named and put into question by the example that depends on it for its operation and its coherence, what exactly is being exemplified?

This question cannot be evaded when, toward the end of the section lettered "r" in *Limited Inc.*, Jacques Derrida raises the possibility of an inability to assume the place of the other, to know what the other calls for, a structural inability that he associates with the ambivalence marking everything given in response to a desire and even perhaps every response as such. The names he offers for this inability include "undecidability" and "the unconscious," and *Limited Inc.* is among other things an analysis of the necessity to take the unconscious and the other into account in any consideration of the ethics and politics of responsibility. But even before the frequently quoted concluding passage that proposes "something like a relation [*comme un rapport*]" between "the notion of responsibility manipulated by the psychiatric expert (representing the law and politico-linguistic conventions, in the service of the state and its police) and the exclusion of parasitism" in speech act theory,[3] Derrida suggests that a certain policing of the subject and its identity is already required by conventional theories of responsibility, and that the unconscious and undecidability name possible disruptions of this control. The theoretical maneuver is important, and fifteen years later is still largely unassimilated by contemporary political and literary theory, but of even greater interest here is the mode of its enunciation and the literary vehicle entrusted with its exemplification. Derrida asks "What is the unity or identity of the speaker? Is he responsible for speech acts dictated by his unconscious?" and offers a number of hypotheses about his "own" unconscious. He concludes with a fable:

All that simply to suggest, briefly, that it is sufficient to introduce, into the manger of speech acts, a few wolves of the type "undecidability" ... or of the type "unconscious" ... for the shepherd to lose track of his sheep [*il suffit d'introduire dans le bergerie des* speech acts *quelque loups du type 'indécidabilité' ... pour que le pasteur ne puisse plus compter ses moutons*]: one is no longer certain where to find the identity of the "speaker" or the "hearer," ... where to find the identity of an intention. (*LI*, 143; 75)

The fable of the shepherd, his manger of sheep, and the wolves named "unconscious" and "undecidability" draws of course on the Aesopian story of the wolf in sheep's clothing, the predator that dissimulates itself by simulating its prey and that provides the permanent example of the ruses of infiltration and tactical deception, of stealth and parasitism precisely. As the nineteenth-century scholar Joseph Jacobs "retells" the fable from William Caxton's *Aesop* of 1484:

A wolf found great difficulty in getting at the sheep owing to the vigilance of the shepherd and the dogs. But one day it found the skin of a sheep that had been flayed and thrown aside, so it put it on over its own pelt and strolled down among the sheep. The Lamb that belonged to the sheep, whose skin the Wolf was wearing, began to follow the Wolf in Sheep's clothing; so, leading the Lamb a little apart, he soon made a meal of her, and for some time he succeeded in deceiving the sheep, and enjoying hearty meals.
Appearances are deceptive.[4]

Responsibility in the Aesopian fable begins with this: self-evidence, self-consciousness, the identity of the speaker, and the free binary choice (wolf or sheep, appearance or reality).[5] And in Aesop the fable names the simulation—the borrowing, comparison, or simile (wolf as sheep)—as the very definition and signature of the predator. La Fontaine's version ("Le Loup devenu Berger"), which has the wolf imitating the shepherd instead of the sheep and finally giving itself away when unable to counterfeit his voice, makes this principle of identity as the unmasking of appearance explicit: "Toujours par quelque endroit fourbes se laissent prendre. Quiconque est loup agisse en loup: c'est le plus certain de beaucoup" (in Marianne Moore's translation: "A counterfeit's sure to be exposed to the light. A wolf is a wolf in every pulse; no use pretending something else").[6] Both versions teach eternal vigilance, the exclusion of the parasite, and the law of the closing of the gate and the identification of subjects, as the task of responsibility. The fable of the threat of the wolf as deep-black installs a certain regime of responsibility—border controls, identity checks, and rules against concealment of essence—as the space of ethics and politics, the regulation of the play of forces through the control of self-presentation. The classical and Aesopian theory of the responsible subject is constructed against the threat of this predator, designed to produce the conditions for the counting and accounting of agents. It is the sheep who demand that the wolves expose themselves as wolves, as such and not as sheep.

Derrida's fable, though, adds at least one more turn to the sequence of simulations by reinscribing this most traditional story of responsibility as the fable of its own undoing. In its insistence on the effects of a "structural unconscious" at odds with "the ethical and teleological discourse of consciousness," what is at stake is an effort "to make appear (and to leap) the security barrier which, *at the interior of the system*, . . . condemns the unconscious as one condemns or bars access to a forbidden place" (*LI* 139–40; 73). But this opening is not simply stated as a theorem that intervenes from some outside to protest the systematic exclusion of "appearance," "deceit," or the unconscious. The fable of responsibility is not exposed as a theoretical error to be rectified by a higher-order discourse. Rather, the breaching of the barrier happens in the very place that was to have been secured, from some other "interior of the system." "[I]t is sufficient to introduce, into the manger of speech acts, a few wolves of the type 'undecidability' . . . or of the type 'unconscious' . . . for the shepherd to lose track of his sheep." *The wolf of undecidability imitates, that is, not only the sheep but also the earlier wolves, and so the fable itself plays the part of the wolf in fable's clothing.* With the introduction of this wolf, in this sentence itself, the first fable (appearance is deception, identities must be verified, the sheep must be accounted for, a wolf is a wolf) is infiltrated by the very thing it sought to exclude, and in precisely the mode against which it had warned. The measured and accountable space of the first fable, the oriented manger, is replicated by another fable that actively disorients it, that redeploys the same elements so as to lose track or lose count of them. A fable, yes, but a counterfeit, even a simulacrum of a fable: the unconscious of the fable. The parasite here simulates the host designed to resist it. The fable of losing count, that is to say, produces within the body of the fable the very situation it describes—it states just the threat—the loss of control and the difficult decision—that it practices. And it performs what it describes. As Derrida has said of another text, called "Fable," its inventiveness "results from the single act of enunciation that performs *and* describes, operates *and* states. Here the conjunction 'and' does not link two different activities. The constative statement is the performative itself since it points out nothing that is prior or foreign to itself. Its performance consists in the "constation" of the constative—and nothing else."[7]

Derrida argues that the fable thus exemplifies Paul de Man's characterization of undecidability as an infinite and intolerable acceleration: the oscillation is that defined by the unstable circulation between the mode of the fable and its undoing in its "own" terms. The fable here is at once ironic and allegorical, in the fullest sense which he gave to these terms, linked as they are in "their discovery of a truly temporal predicament" (P, 28; 329). The experience of that predicament defines another responsibility, and the moral of the story undergoes a sharp mutation. *Fabula docet*: "This is only another reason why, at the 'origin' of every speech act, there are only societies which are (more or less) anonymous with limited responsibility or liability, a multitude of instances, if not of 'subjects,' of meanings highly vulnerable to parasitism—all phenomena that the 'conscious ego' of the speaker or the hearer . . . is incapable of incorporating as such" (LI, 143; 75–76). The fable is doubly difficult: not only does it practice the very tactics of stealth and simulation excluded by the ethical and teleological discourse of consciousness (the dominant theory of responsibility), which is to say of fable, in order to reinscribe the form of the fable against itself, but the theory of responsibility it articulates anew begins from the very impossibility of that exclusion. What could responsibility mean without the risk of exposure to chance, without vulnerability to parasitism, without the opening of the conscious ego by what it cannot contain—without the indiscernible wolf. Without them, there would be nothing of responsibility but the choice between yes and no, this or that, nothing but the application of a rule of decision and of a program. No responsibility without undecidability, without the unconscious and its parasites, and no fable, no example, without the risk of a certain simulation. In real life, as in fable: "as if . . . the simulation of real life were not part of real life!" (LI, 167; 90).

If at the origin of the fable there has always been a vexed relation between literature and philosophy, sheep and wolf, slave and master, then it must be emphasized that the relation has been a question of the responsibility of the example. Hegel, for one, found the relation rather artificially articulated, the fable a little *too* exemplary: "Aesop himself is said to have been a misshapen humpbacked slave; . . . his notions are only witty [*witzig*], without any energy of spirit or depth of insight and substantive vision, without poetry and philosophy [*ohne Poesie und Philosophie*]. His views and doctrines prove indeed to be ingenious and clever, but there remains only, as it were, a subtle investigation of trifles."[8] Like the first wolf in sheep's clothing, hidden in order to be discovered as an example, lost track of in order to be recounted at a higher level, the fable according to Hegel simply mines its material for its exemplarity:

Instead of creating free shapes out of a free spirit, this investigation only sees some other applicable side in purely given and available materials, the specific instincts and impulses of animals, petty daily events; this is because Aesop does not dare to recite his doctrines openly but can only make them understood hidden as it were in a riddle which at the same time is always being solved. In the slave, prose begins, and so this entire genre is prosaic too.[9]

What Hegel marks as prose or wit, "without" either poetry or philosophy, can be rewritten as the intervention of a rhetorical dimension of language between literature and philosophy.

At least that is the strategy in the earliest known *Life of Aesop*, probably written by a Greek-speaking Egyptian in the first century A.D. but apparently dating in the main to at least the fourth or fifth century B.C., where the story of the fable is again told, if this time somewhat more irreverently, as the story of literature's (ir)responsibility to philosophy.[10] The central narrative of the *Life* begins when Xanthus the philosopher decides to buy a slave, goes with his students to the slave market, and encounters the disfigured Phrygian Aesop (recently granted the power of speech after assisting a priestess of Isis and hence become too difficult for his previous master to handle). Their first exchange is exemplary, as the philosopher interrogates the slave in order to determine whether "he knows anything," receives equivocal replies, and finishes by asking, "Do you want me to buy you?" Aesop responds by specifying the rhetorical situation of the question and its implied reversal of the relation of instruction and example, thus outlining the conditions of the philosopher's responsibility: "What do you mean? Do you think that you already own me as an adviser so that you can get advice from me about myself? If you want to buy me, buy me. If you don't, move on. I don't care what you do. . . . No one is putting you under bond to buy me. You're entirely free to make your own choice. If you want to take me, pay the price." (A, 43).

Xanthus completes the transaction and pays the price, and the story that follows narrates the difficulty of knowing in advance what the price will turn out to be. Over its course the relation of master to slave, philosophy to literature, is reversed and undone, rearticulated as the predicament (and its exploitation) of responding in a language not one's own, in language both literal and figurative. Aesop, at once *witzig* and responsible, does what he is told—which can always mean more than one thing. "Aesop said: . . . I wasn't supposed to do anything more than I was told. If I slipped up on my instructions, I was going to be answerable at the cost of a beating." (A, 51). The free choice of the free man, the philosopher as master, is shown to depend on a language that always passes through the other, making "what do you mean?" a question often asked and just as often answered, usually more than once. Its inevitable appearance in language renders the unity and intention of the philosopher permanently questionable. If the philosopher gives orders and lessons, Aesop, enslaved and obligated to respond, determines to "give the philosopher a lesson in how to give orders." The general form of Aesop's response is to exploit the difference that always opens between the presumed literality of an order or an intention and the inevitably figural appearance it assumes. Every encounter thus becomes a philosophical lesson for the philosopher, in the form of a fable: "Aesop said 'You shouldn't have laid down the law for me so literally, and I would have served you properly. But don't feel sorry about it, master. The way you stated the rule for me will turn out to your advantage, for it will teach you not to make mistakes in the classroom. Statements that go too far in either inclusion or exclusion are no small errors'" (A, 53). Of course, one can only do more—or less—than one is told. The general lesson of all these bad examples (and the philosopher is his own best bad example) is that statements, precisely because they are statements, dictated by nothing reducible to the unity of an intention or the identity of a conscious ego, can only ever go too far. Language, language as the rhetoric of instruction and persuasion, only takes to the extent that it mistakes, especially when it gives and takes for example. But there is no slave revolt in morality here: what the *Life of Aesop* undoes most compellingly is any stability that might ground the hierarchichal subordination of literature to philosophy as master to slave—and vice versa.

"If the relation that unites and divides philosophy and literature is a relation of *master to slave* (and one of them in fact fears for its life), what discourse can be undertaken about philosophy which would not already be that of philosophy itself, that is to say that which always prohibits in advance . . . formulating a different type of question about it?" With this question, Philippe Lacoue-Labarthe (in a 1969 essay called "La Fable") proposed the fable as a name for the mutual implication and asymmetrical interference of literature and philosophy. If in the years since then this interrogation has been much maligned, misunderstood, and abused, it is clear that for Lacoue-Labarthe the term "fable" required precisely the effort that today remains largely untried: the suspension of the self-evidence of the categories "literature" and "philosophy" in order to use each to put the identity of the other into question.[11]

The governing opposition of any consideration of this relation must be the one we have already encountered in the fable: appearance and reality. Reading the extraordinary sixth moment of Nietzsche's "How the True World Finally Became a Fable (History of an Error)"—"with [the abolition of] the true world we have also abolished the world of appearances!"—Lacoue-Labarthe follows Nietzsche's midday thought of a kind of fiction (*incipit Zarathustra*) that would not simply oppose (the deceit of) appearance to (the truth of) reality, since in this sixth step "appearance is nothing other than the product of reality. [To think fiction] is precisely to think without resorting to this opposition, *outside* [hors] this opposition: to think the world as fable. Is it possible?" (F, 16). To reach this exterior, the moment of the shortest shadow and the end of the longest error, requires in its turn thinking fable as language. *Fabula* (narration or account), derived as it is from the Latin root *fari* (to speak) and linked to the Greek *phanai* (to speak or to say), finally implies nothing other than language as such. The Littré defines *fable* simply as "ce que l'on dit, ce que l'on raconte" ("what is said, what is told"). *Fabula* thus translates at once *logos*, true discourse, and *mythos*, fictive or fabricated discourse, not by subsuming them under some abstract generality of language but by referring them both to a more originary difference:

The identity [between appearance and truth] that Nietzsche suspects does not in fact hide an identification of a deeply dialectical nature, where *logos* is the truth of *mythos* (as true speech), but where *mythos* authenticates the ontological originarity of *logos*, its purity prior to the split and the opposition between the two. *Mythos* and *logos* are exactly the same thing, but the one is not more true (or more false, deceptive, fictive, etc.) than the other, neither true nor false; the one and the other are the *same* fable. The world has actually become fable. What is said of it, thus (*fabula, fari*). (F, 19)

Fable—"a saying [*dire*] pure and simple" (F, 20)—thus renders secondary, impertinent, and irrelevant the division of language into true and false, *mythos* and *logos*. And in erasing the difference betwen the deception of appearances and the truth of reality, in undoing the opposition as an error, Nietzsche's fable retraces the error of "the occultation of [another] difference, but one which is not the *originary* difference between the truth and its other. . . . History of an error: history of a language, history of language insofar as it has been desired and wanted as a literal language, at the very moment when it proceeded essentially and necessarily by figure(s)" (F, 21). This desire, the philosopher's desire as well as that of the traditional fable, is here frustrated by the fable itself, which tells the story of the desire as the history of an error. An error *of* language: "the fable is the language about which (and within which) these differences, which aren't ones, no longer have currency: literal and figurative, transparence and transference, reality and simulacrum, presence and representation, *mythos* and *logos*, logic and poetry, philosophy and literature, etc." (F, 21–22). Which means that fable is not exterior to philosophy, nor contained by it; it reinscribes the division between philosophy and literature as the language on which they both rely but which opens them up, from "within" to an other over which they finally have little control. Each plays the wolf of undecidability to the sheep of the other, at once allegory and irony of the other in a superimposition and an oscillation that breaks the mirror of reflection and opens it to the alterity of an ungoverned figuration.

According to the entry under "fable" in the *Dictionnaire Le Grand Robert* there is a psychological examination called the "test des fables," defined as a "[p]rojective test or trial consisting of ten fables in which the hero is placed in a situation that requires a choice. In order to interpret the *test des fables*, the hypothesis is made that the child identifies itself with the hero of the fable." This test is the test of the fable as such, the adventure of an identification that can only occur in the comparison that a fable demands. The governing rule of the fable as an exemplary tale, as a certain experience or a trial, has always been Horace's dictum in the *Satires*, "with a change of names, the fable is told about you [*mutato nomine de te fabula narratur*]."[12] The fable is an address or a call to the other, a direct address to a second person singular (*te*), even if it proceeds by the indirection of a change of names and the detour of a thematization. In doing so, it opens a difficult responsibility: it superimposes the relation of an address to the other in its singularity and in its anonymity (responsibility for the other) onto the traditional predicament of an articulation between the order of knowledge or cognition and that of action, ethico-political or otherwise, between what La Fontaine called the body and soul of the fable, the narrative and its moral (responsibility for oneself). The fable does not bear this burden simply on those occasions when the story told exemplifies that *savoir faire*, the self-consciousness of knowing what or how (not) to do, by which the Western philosophical tradition has come to define responsibility. Rather it bears the burden in its very structure, in the peculiar mode of enunciation, an address to an other, which makes it a fable and which immediately reinterprets the category of responsibility.

The motto "mutato nomine de te fabula narratur" functions as a kind of moral for the fable as such, a densely layered summary of its difficulty. Before anything else, the fable is simply told or recounted, "that which is said" (*fabula narratur*), but in the mode of a strangely insistent passivity and anonymity, even an automatism. Subjectless, it appeals, issues the call of a narration from an undetermined location: something like a saying pure and simple, it appeals to the other, aimless and heedless of its origin.

If, in telling, the fable issues a call or an appeal, that address is structured as an appellation, even an interpellation, but with a twist: the apostrophe calls the other by a different name. We are addressed in the fable under what can only be a pseudonym, in the intimate (and properly ethical) singularity of the *tu-toi* but stripped of a proper name. The rhetorical strategy of reading the fable consists in undoing that mutation, and in the experience of having it come undone for "you." The Horatian mechanism, again impersonal, of the *mutato nomine* suggests a transsubjective movement in which names are changed, exchanged, substituted, and simulated: a tropological movement, not exactly a system of metaphor or metonymy, in which the exchanges are governed by a logic of resemblance or contiguity, but rather a somewhat more disorderly motion—call it, with a nod to the sheep and to the other, mutonymy.

And the other is, among others, you. The fable, before and after all else, poses the questions of address, of apostrophe, and of reading. The fable at once thematizes and calls, is addressed to (about *and* for, subject matter *and* destination) the second-person singular—in general. The rhetoric of fables does not limit itself to tropes as such, to nouns exchanged symmetrically for one another, but opens or posits, without substitution or exchange, its reader (you) and the difficulty of its reading.

It is here that the question of responsibility can be posed with the greatest rigor. The address to the other—to the other as at once the you who reads and the you who might be lured into an identification, into the risk or the experience of an imitation or a comparison, a mutation—must be somehow as open as it is focused; a public address with a singular destination. In this structure it exemplifies, as it were, the responsibility that Maurice Blanchot calls "disastrous."[13] In the fable, the other appeals to me:

> It is the other who exposes me to "unity," making me believe in an irreplaceable singularity, as if I must not fail him, even while withdrawing me from what would make me unique: I am not indispensable; in me anyone at all [n'importe qui] is called by the other—anyone at all as the one who owes him aid—the un-unique, always the substitute. The other is himself always other, lending himself, however, to unity; he is neither this one nor that one, and nonetheless it is to him that, each time, I owe everything, including the loss of myself.
>
> The responsibility with which I am charged is not mine, and because of it I am no longer me. (D, 28; 13)

We are, in the term Blanchot adopts from Levinas, the "hostage" of the fable; at once directly addressed and nameless, except as "you." Nonindispensable and without dispensation, "the irreplaceable one who is not in his own place," "the nonconsenting [and] unchosen guarantee of a promise that he hasn't made" (D, 35; 18).

There is no rule for behavior in this situation; the call or appeal of the other, the cry for help, withdraws from me any self-consciousness, any transparency, with which I might have been able to govern my actions. Which is to say, it renders me responsible. As Derrida has recently argued in L'autre cap (The other healing):

> [M]orality, politics, responsibility, if there are any, will only ever have begun with the experience of the aporia. When the path is given, when a knowledge opens up the way in advance, the decision is already made, it might as well be said that there is none to make: irresponsibility, good conscience, one applies a program. Perhaps, and this would be the objection, one never escapes the program. In that case, one must acknowledge this and stop talking with authority about moral or political responsibility. The condition of possibility of this thing, responsibility, is a certain experience of the possibility of the impossible: the trial of the aporia from which one may invent the only possible invention, the impossible invention.[14]

Responsibility, like the fable that teaches it, must be an invention or it is nothing at all.

*

The second section of Nietzsche's *On the Genealogy of Morals* opens with an etymological consideration of the moral concept "responsibility," *Verantwortlichkeit*. "To breed an animal which can promise—is this not the paradoxical task that nature has set itself in the case of man? . . . To be able to stand security for his own future [*für sich als Zukunft gutsagen*: to make good his word as future, for himself] is what a promisor does. This is precisely the long story of how responsibility came to be."[15] Responsibility names the capacity to respond, to answer—which is to say, to be able to give and give back, to keep, one's word, to promise and to promise to answer. For Nietzsche, the ability to make and keep one's promises means being (able to be) held accountable not simply by another but, already in advance, by and for oneself: to act in anticipation of the call to answer to the other for one's actions, in other words, to answer to oneself in the place of the other. The responsible animal can account for the way in which it keeps, or fails to keep, its promises—and it must do this to and for *itself*. On Nietzsche's reading, this animal comes from a fable.

That lambs dislike of great birds of prey does not seem strange: only it provides no ground for reproaching these birds of prey for bearing off little lambs. And if the lambs say among themselves: "these birds of prey are evil; and whoever is as little as possible like a bird of prey, but rather its opposite, a lamb—would he not be good?" [*Diese Raubvögel sind böse; und wer so wenig als möglich ein Raubvogel ist, vielmehr deren Gegenstück, ein Lamm—sollte der nicht gut sein?*] . . . [T]he birds of prey might view it a little ironically [*spottisch*] and perhaps say: "*we* don't dislike them at all, these good little lambs; we even love them: nothing is more tasty than a tender lamb." (*G, 33; 44–45*)

But if the fable does not seem strange to begin with, it has a strange moral: the lambs triumph in gaining the ability, and then the right, to hold the birds of prey responsible for doing what they do, being what they are. In fact, the fable itself enacts the victory, does the trick. Nietzsche explains the moral—morality itself—as resulting from the exploitation of a purely linguistic resource and approaches the story as *at once* a fabulous narrative about language and how it gets turned—with animals playing its roles—into an ethical and epistemological system, *and* the medium itself of the exploitation, the putting to use or the abuse of a linguistic possibility. Thus the fable not only enacts but also reveals the invention of responsibility, does and undoes the trick. Nietzsche analyzes it as follows: "only thanks to the seduction of language, . . . which understands and misunderstands all effects as conditioned by an effector, by a 'subject,'" do the birds first appear to have had a choice in their action, to have made a decision about the lambs. The interpretation or institution of the birds as *subjects*, as choosing, willing agents, depends on a fiction, a fable: "'the doer' is simply fictioned onto [*hinzugedichtet*] the deed." Language makes action without a subject impossible, allowing what Nietzsche calls "popular morality" to "separate strength from expressions of strength, as if there were a neutral substratum behind the strong man, which was free to express strength or not to do so." This linguistic necessity, a grammatical position and nothing else, is "exploited" into the claim that "the strong man is *free* to be weak, the bird of prey free to be a lamb—thus is gained the right to make the bird of prey *accountable* for being a bird of prey [*dem Raubvogel es zuzurechnen, Raubvogel zu sein*]" (*G*, 35–36; 45).

The rest of Nietzsche's analysis, which pursues the genealogy of responsibility through the promise, memory and forgetting, debt, and writing, need not be pursued any farther here, as long as the moral of his fable of the birds and the lambs is underlined.[16] First, it *is* a fable, and the promising animal is a creature of fable. Second, the fable narrates a story about language—about the grammatical subject, promising (*versprechen*) and keeping one's word (*gutsagen*), and answering—and the peculiar way it makes responsibility possible: responsibility is an exploitation of a verbal possibility, nothing more, but nothing less. Third, the fable does not simply tell about language: it *is* the very language that prosaically fictions the merely grammatical subject into the acting, responsible, human subject, thanks to the tropological operation we might call not anthropomorphism but zoomorphism. But the fable puts the reliability of that rhetorical expansion into question precisely to the extent that it performs it. The operation is as suspect as it is inevitable.

However difficult, this version of the fable remains relatively simple. It bears comparison with the fable of the eagle and the raven, an Aesopian standard that opens the sixth part of William Caxton's *Aesop: Life and Fables,* or the *Book of the Subtyl Histories and Fables of Esope* (1484):

The fyrst fable is of the Egle and of the rauen.

No One ought to take on hym self to doo a thynge / whiche is peryllous withoute he fele hym self strong ynough to doo hit / As reherceth this Fable / Of an Egle / whiche fleynge took a lambe / wherof the Rauen hadde grete enuye wherfor upon another tyme as the sayd rauen sawe a grete herd of sheep / by his grete enuy & pryde & by his grete oultrage descended on them / and by suche fachon and manere smote a wether that his clowes abode to the fleece of hit / In soo moche that he coude not flee awey / The sheepherd thenne came and brake and toke his wynges from hym / And after bare hym to his children to playe them with / And demaunded of hym / what byrd he was / And the Rauen ansuerd to hym / I supposed to haue ben an Egle / And by my ouerwenynge I wende to haue take a lambe / as the egle dyd / But now I knowe wel that I am a Rauen / wherfor the feble ought in no wyse to compare hym self to the stronge / For somtyme when he supposeth to doo more than he may / he falleth in to grete dishonour / as hit appiereth by this present Fable / Of a Rauen / whiche supposed to haue ben as stronge as the egle.[17]

Paraphrased, the fable tells the story of the raven, which, having once watched with envy as a flying eagle snatched a lamb from the flock and carried it off, later attempts a similar feat. But a raven is not an eagle, and "his clowes abode to the fleece" of the lamb: his prey becomes his trap. Captured by the shepherd, his wings are broken and taken from him, and he is given to the shepherd's children as a plaything. An interrogation follows, or rather, an identity check. The shepherd "demaund[s] of hym what byrd he was," and the raven answers by retelling the fable itself as a narrative of a false supposition and its correction: "I supposed to haue ben an Egle / And by my ouerwenynge I wende to haue take a lambe / as the egle dyd / But now I knowe wel that I am a Rauen." Thus the moral warns against mistaken comparisons or self-confusions, in strikingly Nietzschean terms: "the feble ought in no wyse to compare hym self to the stronge."

Now, while this fable is obviously not one among others, as its relation to the *Genealogy of Morals* makes clear, it does in fact exemplify a general pattern or determined configuration in fables: the triple coincidence of a choice, a confusion of identities or names, and a response (the wolf in sheep's clothing exposed).[18] Here, the fable weaves this configuration into a thought of responsibility, or responsibilities. Its destination, reading backwards from its conclusion, is the establishment of the raven as an (ir)responsible agent, one that—because it *is*, is an "I," has a name and a choice about its action, because it could have done otherwise—can be called to respond for itself (to render itself and the reason for its action) and can be shown its error and its fault. Its errancy consists precisely in wandering away from its name—or more radically, in not knowing or not even having its own name—and thus mis-taking itself for another (name). The lesson of responsibility can thus be formulated: act in accord with the fate prescribed for you by your name, "in no wyse compare." As Caxton puts it elsewhere: "none ought to fayne hym self other than suche as he is." [19]

So, if the raven *was* confused a first time, we trust that "now," in the fable's word, with its error corrected it can act responsibly. If it forgot its name, forgot who it was, once, that is all in the past, *now*. Now it knows it is the responsible agent it always has already been but didn't know until just now. The fable narrates the raven's narration of the temporalized passage from being to knowledge, the making explicit or the speaking of being as knowledge, from an unspoken *I am* to the cognitive utterance "now I knowe wel that I am a Rauen." The raven's is the history of an error—corrected. In this case, the raven errs in comparing itself with, and then taking itself to be, an eagle. It takes the other's name, takes it seriously. The comparison or simile—"*as* the egle dyd"—operates as the hinge of the error, the rhetorical mechanism of feigning or dissimulation that the fable aims to ward off by exposing. And here the process, the trial or the test of the fable, works to undo the aberrant name, to restore the proper name to the proper bird, to allow the raven to say "I" and with the self-assertion reconnect the name and the thing—or perhaps to connect them for the first time. (We will return in a moment to the *perhaps* of this first time.) The establishment of the responsible agent, the raven as subject, thus coincides with the rectification of the tropological error against which the conclusion warns. Don't change your name, in other words. Or, know your name, and what it means, you can do. The fable narrates the passage from error to knowledge and installs—as its moral, as moral—the subject that can link its "I" with its name in a cognitive proposition. And with the ability to say "I am . . . ," which always hides behind it an "I promise (that I can)," enters the active or ethical order. The aberrant tropological substitution ("I *supposed* to haue ben an Egle") and its undoing ("now I *knowe* wel that I am a Rauen") together secure the institution of responsibility with a powerful dialectical negativity: the subject, the linkage of the I with the name, is found on the far side of its loss, tested so as to be guaranteed. This critical system (error, correction, I = name) thus fixes the link between the order of cognition (whether false supposition or true knowledge) and that of action ("I wende to haue take a lambe, *as the egle dyd*, but . . . ")—because I know what I am, I know what I can and cannot do, and will act accordingly in the future. I, *raven*, promise: to be a raven.

The fable of responsibility can be read, then, as a story about language and its dangers, a demystification of its pretended power. A raven may be *like* an eagle, but it *is not* an eagle. It would have us understand that only the names, the words "raven" and "eagle," not the creatures themselves, can be transposed or substituted. The raven's response ("the shepherd—demaunded of hym what byrd he was and the Rauen ansuered to hym") corrects its prior linguistic mistake and reestablishes the proper proper name with the proper "I." It is thanks to that link between I and name, and on the basis of the error's earlier erasure, that cognition and action, knowing and doing, articulate themselves: know your name and do what it says. Responsibility is nothing other than the response to the name by which one is called: "now I knowe wel that I am a Rauen."

Now, earlier we encountered the question of whether we are to read the raven's summary self-assertion ("I am a Rauen") as a *restoration* of a lost or confused proper name to its proper owner, as a *recognition* in the strict sense of a second or recovered cognition, as a *reconnection* of an only momentarily unhinged articulation, as the *result* over time of an I coming into its own name "now" out of a momentary misnaming "then"—or, rather differently, we read this auto-appellation and its now as a more irruptive explosion of a singular, new, unprecedented, strictly literal or starkly verbal "I," and of a now without then. This suggestion forces itself on a reader mindful of an excess, a certain rhetorical slippage or overhang, in the responsive narrative that the bird gives the shepherd. "I supposed to haue ben an Egle, and by my ouerwenynge [overweening]"—excess of comparison, envy—"I wende to haue take a lambe as the egle dyd, but now I knowe wel that I am a Rauen." Simply put, the questionable aspect of this passage, this passage from supposition to knowledge, is whether *supposing* and *knowing* belong to one and the same homogeneous system, such that the latter can effectively erase the former without left*over* or excess. If supposition means dissimulation as disguise or false knowledge, or even as guess or surmise or premise, then new knowledge known well will surely unmask error's true face and make possible its reconfiguration. But if in "supposition" we read the more ungovernable and unrecoverable force of positing, of position or imposition, then we may find a more active operation of disruption at work. The first narrative—the recovery of the knowledge of the proper name on the basis of its (temporary) ignorance—is only possible thanks to a different and strangely prior forgetting, this time of the arbitrary initial donation of the name, the *saying* by which what the fable calls "the sayd rauen" gets its name. If the fable is to be read as the story of an undoing, then the second substitution of proper ("raven") for improper ("eagle") names ought to reverse, symmetrically, an initial aberrant substitution of improper for proper. But the fable raises the possibility that the second turn, rather than erasing the initial error, only adds another one. Because the bird began *without a name*, by losing a name it didn't yet have.

This other fable narrates the invention or the institution of the name, the response that precedes its call and posits it after the fact. The bird begins the fable without (knowing) its name, covers the gap by comparing "itself" to another by borrowing the other's name (a supposed-eagle), learns the hard way of its figural error and pays the penalty in its disfiguration (a wingless not-eagle). Then it attempts to recover from this loss by taking—or better, assuming—a name it never had ("now I knowe wel that I am a Rauen") but is left with nothing other than this name since it is "no longer" a raven but merely a child's plaything, (is) no longer the raven it never was. Which means that the first figure ("eagle" for "raven") was no substitution but an arbitrary imposition, a sup-position, as there was no name ("eagle" for "——"), only a covering over of the blank that marks an *initial deferral* of the name. So the chiasmus that ought to reverse, symmetrically, the substitution of eagle for raven founders on an initial excess of comparison. Or lack of name. Too much eagle and not enough raven, never enough raven. The raven is only ever "the sayd rauen," and that is the whole difficulty of the thing. Still, difficulty or no, the imposition is as necessary as it is groundless. How could one not confuse oneself with a name? But the fable tells the story, this time, of a non-symmetrical movement from nameless bird to birdless name, the generation of the pure name that is the precondition for the invention of the "I." This I is just as disfigured as the so-called raven, a plaything for children, just as empty and robbed of its properties, and this doubled blank provides the equivalence that makes the utterance "I am a Rauen" possible. With difficulty, and at the price of its intelligibility.

This asymmetry on the level of tropes and their narration opens onto a second-order asymmetry of reading, and puts our understanding of the fable into question. Which is to say, it opens the question of a responsibility, ours, which would not take its own possibility for granted: a difficult, even abyssal, responsibility, all the more demanding for its difficulty. To put it simply, you are responsible for reading the fable, but the fable refuses to be read. The moral—be responsible, which is to say, don't compare yourself with what you're not, heed the call of your own name and resist the seduction of a false supposition, a mistaken comparison—requires, in order that it be understood and taken seriously, that it be ignored. You, reader, are asked to compare yourself with the raven, to assume its name and follow its example, in order to learn not to compare yourself with what you're not. The apostrophe of reading (which is the signature of the fable as a genre, the moral as address to the reader) is just as aberrant as the simile of the fable. You are not a raven, not even like a raven, and don't think you are. But in order to learn not to make this figural error, you must compare yourself to the raven with its disfigured self-knowledge. *Mutato nomine de te fabula narratur.* You must (not) compare, by changing your name. And a change in names is what got the raven into the trap in the first place. In no ways compare: no one ought to feign himself as other than he is. The fable is a trap, and you are an animal: its address cannot be avoided. The fable is structured as a double bind: to heed its call you must ignore its call, you must make the mistake the fable denounces. In order to read, you must not read. And you cannot choose not to read.

But what is reading if not a response in this impossibility?

In the classic version of the fable of the wolf in sheep's clothing, translated in Handford's Penguin *Aesop* as "A Case of Mistaken Identity," the wolf of undecidability finally falls victim to another sort of error, a mistake of chance that reinstalls the identity of the responsible subject in its demise. The moral defines the seriousness of the subject, over against a certain "play," as a matter of life and death: "Assuming a character that does not belong to one can involve one in serious trouble. Such playacting has cost many a man his life." Another bad example, that is to say, and another change of names to be undone. But the fable of the wolf in sheep's clothing tells the story of an accident:

A wolf thought that by disguising himself he could get plenty to eat. Putting on a sheepskin to trick the shepherd, he joined the flock at grass without being discovered. At nightfall the shepherd shut him with the sheep in the fold and made fast all round by blocking the entrance. Then, feeling hungry, he picked up his knife and slaughtered an animal for his supper. It happened to be the wolf.[20]

The moral of La Fontaine's "Corbeau Voulant Imiter l'Aigle" (Crow wanting to imitate eagle) says it another way: *L'exemple est un dangereux leurre* ("The example is a dangerous snare").

ALEXANDER GELLEY

The Pragmatics of Exemplary Narrative

La fable, modèle praxique incertain.
—Louis Marin,
Le Récit est un piège

From the point of view of a formalist approach to narrative—of a narratology—the idea of exemplary narrative is paradoxical. The postulate of narratology is of a narrative specificity, of a pure state of narrative whose integrity and autonomy serves as the basis for more complex, mixed forms. Formalist theories have characterized this pure state in various ways. Thus the Russian Formalists' distinction between *fabula* and *suzhet* postulates as *fabula* a kind of proto-sequence of action that represents the source for particularized narrations; these latter constitute the *suzhet*, the specification of a narrative substance. Gérard Genette's idea of a "frontier" between narrative and discourse offers another way of conceiving such a pure state of narrative. In a well-known essay, Genette proposes a series of hypothetical divisions or boundaries that would allow one "to recognize in a negative sense, as it were, the limits of narrative."[1] He is perfectly aware of the fact that such a notion of boundaries represents nothing but a construct designed to account for the necessary crossings and interpenetration between fundamental elements of the text.[2] What is most relevant for our discussion is the boundary Genette draws between *récit* and *discours*, narrative and speech. He demonstrates that while in practice each mode is mixed with the other, the relation of the two is by no means symmetrical: speech or discourse quite readily absorbs elements of narrative within it; narrative,

In memory of Louis Marin

on the other hand, treats discursive intrusions (such as narrator's commentary) as a kind of "cyst," an alien element: "The purity of narrative, one would say, is more manifest than that of speech."[3]

The topic of this paper involves another kind of incursion into the purity of narrative, namely, the function of exemplification, the use of narrative to teach, to illustrate, to persuade. It is true that the functional application of narrative, its turn to pragmatic ends, is so ingrained in our literary tradition as to seem innate to the form. But this fact by no means contravenes the formal specificity of narrative. What we want to examine in this paper, then, is another "frontier" of narrative, another of those crossings where narrative compacts with a function that, in a formal sense, is distinct but in practice is regularly attached to it.

Susan Suleiman's study of exemplary narrative provides a useful analysis of the pattern under discussion, an analysis that throws into relief what I have termed the specificity or purity of the narrative element.[4] She distinguished three strands in every parabolic—and, more generally, "exemplary"—narrative: the story itself, an interpretation, and a generalization in the form of a lesson or injunction. Further, the relation of these strands "can be defined as a chain of implications: the story implies ('calls for') the interpretation, which in turn implies—but is also implied by—the concluding injunction" (p. 32). This structure of implication, as she points out, involves a hierarchy of control or determination, where a fundament—the most general and thus most comprehensive level—controls those above it. Thus the injunction, though implied by the interpretation, nonetheless governs it logically, and the interpretation in turn governs the narrative. Often one or two of these may be omitted and remain implicit. But the narrative, although hierarchically the last, can never be omitted since it cannot be deduced from the others, though they may well be (and often are) deduced from it.

Much of Suleiman's discussion involves considerations of just what motivates the pattern of implication. In what sense and under what conditions does a story "call for" an interpreta-

tion? It becomes evident in her analysis of certain New Testament parables that one cannot identify formal indices in the
narrative that point to a specific interpretation. This can only
be derived from an "intertextual context," a set of other texts
posited independently of the story. Suleiman concludes, citing
a definition of exemplum provided by Barthes: "[T]here is no
such thing as a story that 'expressly entails *a* meaning.' If a story
is to be read as having a single specific meaning, it must either
be interpreted in a consistent and unambiguous way by the
teller, *or* it must exist within a context that invests it with intentionality" (p. 43). Suleiman thus provides us with another
version of the boundary that defines narrative but at the same
time reveals its habitual intercalation with extranarrative
forms of discourse.

There is nothing surprising in all this. Already in Aristotle example is classified as a function within a pragmatic order,
namely, rhetoric, the art of juridical and political discourse.[5] Example, alongside enthymeme, is considered a technique of argumentative persuasion, *probatio*: enthymeme—a kind of abbreviated syllogism or folk logic—works by way of deduction,
whereas exemplum works by induction, and more specifically,
by means of analogy. In order to illustrate forms of rhetorical argumentation, Aristotle typically draws on instances from history or mythology that are presented so as to fit into an inductive series and lead to an unambiguous conclusion. But such a
procedure proves to be inadequate when the instances utilized
in an argument reach a certain amplitude and complexity. This
is evident with the New Testament parables, where, as Suleiman points out, the possibility of "indirect communication," of
a figural meaning, undermines the rhetorical model of exemplary demonstration.

Under very different circumstances a similar pattern may be
seen in the emergence of Renaissance narrative forms, such as
the novella. In the medieval fable the narrative sequence is un-
equivocally oriented toward an apothegm, a *sententia*, the
moral point.[6] Now in Renaissance narrative the expansion often went well beyond the limits implicit in the older didactic
forms, without, however, altogether obliterating the basic prag-

matic (moral) orientation. Thus we find in the novella (e.g., Boc-caccio) a problematization of the exemplum whereby the narrative element stands in an oblique relation to the moral kernel that it was meant to illustrate. The exemplum becomes over-determined: its applicability in moral or social terms is tested. A field of applicability, a pragmatic context, remains but is now incorporated into the narrative frame rather than oriented out-ward to an extranarrative context.

Complications of this kind call for a reconsideration of Sulei-man's model of exemplary narrative. This model is, of course, no more than an abstract schema, and we would expect it to be realized in a variety of ways according to historical and institu-tional variables. Suleiman herself juxtaposes two contrary ex-planations of the New Testament parables: the traditional "ped-agogical impulse" that operates in terms of a normal model of communication, and another that is predicated on secrecy, on enigma, one where "the slippage between the story and its au-thoritative (authorial) interpretation allows for the entry of other, divergent meanings" (p. 35).[7] But her analysis treats the latter alternative as exceptional.

What needs to be stressed is that insofar as an authoritative interpretation is required for validating the linkage between the narrative and the injunction, the inductive pattern that Sulei-man proposes—and that is based on the Aristotelian model—is put out of play. In her model the interpretation derives logically from the narrative and leads to the formulation of a rule of ac-tion or behavior, the pragmatic level, the injunction. But if the interpretation is already determined by an "authoritative" in-stance, it is at the other end, the level of injunction, that we should look for a source of the interpretation, of whatever "meaning" is to be imputed to the story. We recall that Sulei-man pointed out that while two strands of the system, the inter-pretation and the injunction, have a kind of logical priority or position of control, they can operate offstage, as it were, implic-itly and indirectly. By contrast, the narrative element needs al-ways to be present—it cannot remain implicit. Our argument has shown, however, that this element is, in a sense, *without meaning*. Or, to put it another way, the meaning of the narrative arises only as a function of all the elements of the structure. Thus it would seem that the two less overt but more determinant factors in the system, the interpretation and the injunction (in Suleiman's terminology), bear closer consideration.

"Injunction"—the prescriptive or hortatory gesture that caps exemplary narrative—may well apply in the strict sense to the sermon or other didactic forms, but what about texts where this function is conspicuously framed or dramatized? Can one still speak of a performative element when injunction is mediated by narrative frames or modalized by a genre structure?[8] In the model that we have been examining, from what does injunction proceed? Is it a necessary consequence of the "interpretation," or does it derive from an agency that only apparently depends on the logic of example, of the narrative demonstration? Another way of stating this problem is to ask, at whom is injunction aimed? And whom does it reach? There are no self-evident answers, I think. But it may help to look at a literary instance of fable that brings directly into play the status of the addressee, the target of the lesson or injunction.

In the fables of La Fontaine the didactic form of exemplary narrative functions as a schema or stereotype that gives rise to multiple permutations. La Fontaine wrote for a clearly delimited society in which the reach of every allusion, every persuasive tactic could be calibrated. The narrative element, the diegesis, is never primary but always subordinate to a strategy that is oriented first of all to the possible effects of the discourse on a diverse readership. In "The Power of Fable" ("Le Pouvoir des fables") we track the addressee through a series of displacements, displacements that bring about shifts not only in the narrative scene (that is, in the identity and relation of the agents producing the narrative, the addressor and addressee) but also in the narrative substance, in the story itself. The *pouvoir*, the force of fable, of fabulation, is examined by exemplification rather than analytically. The relay of narrative scenes is such that each appears to proceed naturally from another, but with each shift the stakes of the story alter significantly. It requires agility on the part of the reader to follow the tracks of the story, to know *what story*, at any given moment, is at issue.

Le Pouvoir des fables
A Monsieur de Barillon

La qualité d'ambassadeur
Peut-elle s'abaisser à des contes vulgaires?
Vous puis-je offrir mes vers et leurs grâces légères?
S'ils osent quelquefois prendre un air de grandeur
Seront-ils point traités par vous de téméraires?
    Vous avez bien d'autres affaires
    A démêler que les débats
    Du lapin et de la belette,
    Lisez-les, ne les lisez pas;
    Mais empêchez qu'on ne nous mette
    Toute l'Europe sur les bras.
    Que de mille endroits de la terre
    Il nous vienne des ennemis,
    J'y consens; mais que l'Angleterre
Veuille que nos deux rois se lassent d'être amis,
    J'ai peine à digérer la chose.
N'est-il point encor temps que Louis se repose?
Quel autre Hercule enfin ne se trouverait las
De combattre cette hydre? et faut-il qu'elle oppose
Une nouvelle tête aux efforts de son bras?
    Si votre esprit plein de souplesse,
    Par éloquence et par adresse,
Peut adoucir les coeurs et détourner ce coup,
Je vous sacrifierais cent moutons: c'est beaucoup
    Pour un habitant du Parnasse;
    Cependant faites-moi la grâce
    De prendre en don ce peu d'encens;
    Prenez en gré mes voeux ardents,
Et le récit en vers qu'ici je vous dédie.
Son sujet vous convient, je n'en dirai pas plus:
    Sur les éloges que l'envie
    Doit avouer qui vous sont dus,
    Vous ne voulez pas qu'on appuie.

Dans Athène autrefois, peuple vain et léger,
Un orateur, voyant sa patrie en danger,
Courut à la tribune; et d'un art tyrannique,
Voulant forcer les coeurs dans une république,
Il parla fortement sur le commun salut.
On ne l'écoutait pas. L'orateur recourut
    A ces figures violentes
Qui savent exciter les âmes les plus lentes:
Il fit parler les morts, tonna, dit ce qu'il put.
Le vent emporta tout, personne ne s'émut;

L'animal aux têtes frivoles,
Étant fait à ces traits, ne daignait l'écouter;
Tous regardaient ailleurs; il en vit s'arrêter
A des combats d'enfants, et point à ses paroles.
Que fit le harangueur? Il prit un autre tour.
"Cérès, commença-t-il, faisait voyage un jour
    Avec l'anguille et l'hirondelle;
Un fleuve les arrête; et l'anguille en nageant,
    Comme l'hirondelle en volant,
Le traversa bientôt." L'assemblée à l'instant
Cria tout d'une voix: "Et Cérès, que fit-elle?
    —Ce qu'elle fit? Un prompt courroux
    L'anima d'abord contre vous.
Quoi! de contes d'enfants son peuple s'embarrasse!
    Et du péril qui le menace
Lui seul entre les Grecs il néglige l'effet!
Que ne demandez-vous ce que Philippe fait?"
    A ce reproche l'assemblée,
    Par l'apologue réveillée,
    Se donne entière à l'orateur:
    Un trait de fable en eut l'honneur.

Nous sommes tous d'Athène en ce point, et moi-même,
Au moment que je fais cette moralité,
    Si *Peau d'âne* m'était conté,
    J'y prendrais un plaisir extrême.
Le monde est vieux, dit-on: je le crois; cependant
Il le faut amuser encor comme un enfant.

The Power of Fable
To M. de Barillon

Can Ambassadorial status stoop to hear common storytelling? Am I permitted to offer you my verses with their light-hearted graces? If now and then they dare you as overweening? You have many other matters to sort out than the debates of the Rabbit and the Weasel: read them, don't read them; but do prevent the whole of Europe from being set about our heels. That from a thousand places on earth enemies should come to us, I can accept; but that England should wish our two Kings to weary of being friends, is a thing I do find hard to digest. Is it not yet time for Louis to take some rest? Is there another Hercules, after all, who would not weary from combatting this Hydra? And must it raise yet another head against the efforts of this arm? If by eloquence and skill your versatile wit can soften hearts and turn away this blow, I shall sacrifice to you a hundred sheep; that's a lot for an inhabitant of Parnassus. But please do graciously receive the gift of this small quantity of incense. Kindly accept my ardent wishes, and the tale in verse I am hereby dedicating to you. Its subject is an apposite one for you; that's all I shall say: you prefer people not to be heavy-handed in the Praise that envy itself must admit is your due.

In Athens of yore, a frivolous and light-hearted people, an Orator seeing his country in danger hastened to the Tribune; and with tyrannical art attempting to force hearts in a republic, he spoke strongly on the common weal. They did not listen: the Orator had recourse to the kind of violent figures that are capable of arousing the slowest souls, he had the dead speak, he thundered, said what he could, but his words were wafted away on the wind; no one was stirred by them. The animal with the many empty heads, beings accustomed to these devices, did not deign to listen. They were all looking somewhere else: the attention of some, he saw, was fixed on some street-urchins fighting, and not on his words. What did the tub-thumper do? He tried another tack. "Ceres," he began, "was travelling one day with the Eel and the Swallow. A river stops them; and the Eel soon swam, the Swallow soon flew across." Immediately the gathering cried out in a single voice: "And what did *Ceres* do?"—"What did she do? Her quick anger straightway arouses her ire against you. What, her people bother themselves with children's stories! And they alone of all the Greeks neglect the consequences of the peril that threatens them! Why not ask what Philip is doing?" At this reproach the gathering, brought to its senses by the Fable, now gives itself over completely to the Orator: the honor of this was due to a piece of Fiction. We're all Athenians on that score; and I myself as I write this moral, were I to be told the tale of Donkey Skin, would take extreme pleasure in it; it's an old, old world, they say; and so I believe, but it still has to be amused like a child.[9]

The fable dramatizes a double power of fabulation: to sway an audience and to argue a cause. This is the didactic aim of animal fables, appropriate for the masses—"L'animal aux têtes frivoles" ("The animal with the many empty heads")—though a sophisticate like the dedicatee, the ambassador, might somehow be exempt—"Lisez-les, ne les lisez pas" ("read them, don't read them"). Yet even the crowd, although accustomed to this kind of fare, will often resist. It will consume the bait yet remain unaffected by the substance, the lesson. It's only when the bait, the narrative line, is snatched away in mid-course—*Et Cérès, que fit-elle?* ("And what did *Ceres* do?")—that the crowd submits to the speaker and becomes attentive to his message. But is the ambassador really exempt from the seduction of the fable of Demosthenes, the Athenian orator? The preamble suggests that he is—"La qualité d'ambassadeur / Peut-elle s'abaisser à des contes vulgaires?" ("Can Ambassadorial status stoop to hear common storytelling?")—but the flattery is so effusive that it can go either way, and in the conclusion he too is included among the gullible narratees of fiction.

In the lengthy preamble the ambassador is enjoined to operate in his official mission—involving an immediate political crisis between France and England—in terms of persuasive address:

> Si votre esprit plein de souplesse,
> Par éloquence et par adresse,
> Peut adoucir les coeurs et détourner ce coup . . .

If by eloquence and skill your versatile wit can soften hearts and turn away this blow . . .

In that sense the ensuing fable, the anecdote about the Athenian orator, is a kind of demonstration that La Fontaine offers to a peer, a fellow rhetorician, who will know how to put the story to good use. And yet the point of the story, or rather the point of the demonstration (for we never get the whole story of the eel, the swallow and Ceres) is that the story has no point. It serves merely as bait. It arrests the wayward attention of the crowd. But the point intended by the Athenian orator, the injunction proper that calls on the Athenians to awaken to the danger posed by Philip of Macedon, is enunciated in no indirect fashion. Here the lesson may be seen to carry over directly to the addressee of the frame discourse, M. de Barillon, though with a reverse directive: just as Demosthenes resorts to a fable to arouse the Athenians to defend themselves, so M. de Barillon should engage his rhetorical arts to prevent a war.

There is still the epilogue to consider: "Nous sommes tous d'Athène en ce point" ("We're all Athenians on that score"). Perhaps the speaker is only maintaining the mode of courtesy, of exaggerated self-abasement of the preamble: he too, like any member of the vulgar audience, is liable to swallow the bait of fables, quite regardless of any *moralité*, of a serious message. At the same time, in universalizing the phenomenon, he is able to include the ambassador among those who are caught: "Le monde est vieux, dit-on: je le crois; cependant / Il le faut amuser encor comme un enfant" ("it's an old, old world, they say; and so I believe, but it still has to be amused like a child.") The question about Ceres—*Et Cérès, que fit-elle?*—though neatly nested in a double frame, radiates out and hooks, in some fashion, all the auditors—the Athenian crowd, the ambassador, the narrator, and—let us not omit this—us too, the readership that constitutes yet another frame, another level of addressee. The *pointe*—the thrust, the catch, the puncture—hits more than a single target. The force of the fable lies not so much in any explicit lesson or injunction as in its ability to vary the targets in an expanding series. In another of the *Fables* La Fontaine writes:

> L'exemple est un dangereux leurre:
> Tous les mangeurs de gens ne sont pas grand seigneurs;
> Où le Guêpe a passé le Moucheron demeure.
>
> The example can be a dangerous bait:
> Those who would be man-eaters may not be such
>   great personages;
> Where the wasp slips through the flea gets caught.
>
> (Book II, no. 16)

In what sense may we say that the fable works like a trap, turning the addressee into a target? I am here alluding to Louis Marin's *Le Récit est un piège* (Narrative is a trap), which includes an interpretation of "The Power of Fable." Marin demonstrates that in a political context like that of the court of Louis XIV, in which every transaction implies a test of strength and status, the poet, the *habitant de Parnasse*, although he may appear to cede the power game to the statesman, is capable of demonstrating, in the very act of rendering homage, a power that even the politically powerful cannot elude. The ambassador has been enticed through flattery, through the promise of pleasure, to listen to a story. But what it finally teaches him is the limitation of his own power. Marin writes:

The power of fables—to tell a story is to offer to whoever listens to me the imaginary satisfaction of a desire, the benefaction of a pleasure. What is this desire? That of knowledge, desire of theory, desire of truth. But that knowledge, that theory, that truth is never uttered in the accomplishment of narrative since it is imaginary. . . . Thus the desire within that desire: that the possible world be the real world; but the poet takes good care not to indicate to the ambassador a path in this aporia.[10]

Narrative becomes the instrumentality of a desire that only it itself can assuage: in the process it arouses another desire, that "the possible world be the real world," a desire that even the most powerful cannot be assured of realizing. Marin's analysis is valuable in showing a continuity in the play of power between the fictive and the extrafictive. Fiction, narrative, *fable* involves, in his view, "an uncertain model of praxis."[11]

La Fontaine's "The Power of Fable" seems especially revealing in this respect because, within brief compass, it demonstrates how a framing device sets into motion a switching operation that scatters the addressee function and makes it available for multiple and varied messages. In a restricted fable structure the *you*, the target of the message or lesson, is presumed to be a general or universal subject. The reader can feel safely out of the way. But when this structure is transgressed, when the addressee becomes subject to a systematic rerouting, and derouting, operation, the premise of fictionality—namely, that the reader can always elude the address, the *you* of the text—collapses. This switching operation, what Jean-François Lyotard has analyzed under the concept of *commutation*,[12] would, of course, affect not only the addressee function but also the other "posts" or stations in a narrative circuit (in Lyotard's sense): the addressor, the referent, the meaning. In light of our discussion of La Fontaine's fable, it is the addressor-addressee (or narrator-narratee) dynamic that regulates the force of injunction, and it is on this issue that we must focus our analysis.

The criticism of Paul de Man, like that of Marin, has often focused on the dissimulations or deviancy of rhetorical logic, and he too provides us with an analysis of exemplary narrative that is designed to test its logical pretensions. In Heinrich von Kleist's short dialogue "Über das Marionettentheater" (On the marionette theater) de Man sees "a particular version, at the level of narrative" of a more general paradox. Whenever an example is invoked as support for a general proposition, what is claimed implicitly is that its validity, its "exemplarity," will be self-evident. But just how is this validation realized? If by way of the example, then it can hardly serve as conclusive support for the general proposition, since the example would be taken primarily on its own terms, as an isolate, singular instance. If, on the other hand, the validation is to be achieved at the level of the generality, this would require an act of stipulation or imposition, which, of course, exceeds the logical framework, since the general proposition has not yet been authenticated. "Can any example ever truly fit a general proposition?" de Man asks;

Is not its particularity, to which it owes the illusion of its intelligibility, necessarily a betrayal of the general truth it is supposed to support and convey? . . . Instead of inscribing the particular in the general, which is the purpose of any cognition, [with the example] one has reversed the process and replaced the understanding of a proposition by the perception of a particular, forgetting that the possibility of such a transaction is precisely the burden of the proposition in the first place.[13]

De Man's formulation here is stated in terms of philosophical discourse, while the argument of the essay from which this is taken deals with a narrative text. But de Man would insist that his demonstration is by no means impaired by this crossing of genres. The issue of validation or legitimation ("inscribing the particular in the general") involves a fundamental rhetorical strategy that is operative both in philosophical and in literary texts. Thus examples in a narrative work, even when they are not explicitly linked to a rule or principle, may still serve to invoke a rule and orient the text toward a level of generality. What de Man terms the "forgetting" of "the possibility of such a transaction"—that is, of situating a particular in the function of a general—signifies for him the ruse of example as a rhetorical device.

However, the faultiness of the logic doesn't signify that the strategy won't work; in fact, de Man notes, "every reader will attempt, and probably succeed, in making the anecdote fit the argument." What should be recognized, he argues, is that it works not because of its logical consistency but—and here his position converges with that of Suleiman—because of a structure that is attuned to the context of reception. But to understand what is at work we need to abandon Suleiman's neat, tripartite model, with its implication of a sequential, orderly progression. The "interpretation," the second and mediating level, according to Suleiman, is supposed to motivate the injunction. But interpretation turns out to be less the product of a narrative rationale than of an extranarrative imposition.

Kleist's "Marionettentheater" is cast in the form of a dialogue between the first-person narrator and Herr C, a dancer of some prominence. Herr C puts forward the paradoxical proposition that wooden puppets are capable of displaying a greater degree of charm, of natural grace (*Anmut, natürliche Grazie*) than humans, a proposition that is extended in the course of the colloquy to the general principle that consciousness (*Bewußtsein*) radically inhibits the manifestation of grace and beauty in man, an inhibition that can be lifted only by means of a transcendence of consciousness—whether momentary, through instinctive reflex movement, or infinite, through the recovery of paradisic innocence. Three anecdotal instances, told alternately by the interlocutors, serve to develop this proposition. At the conclusion the narrator, although somewhat dazed (confused, *zerstreut*), is fully persuaded.

De Man argues that while Kleist stages a dialogue that is apparently a benign scene of instruction, a free dialogic exchange designed to clarify an initial premise, the means by which persuasion is realized is anything but dialogic or free. There is a marked discrepancy between rule and practice, between the principle that Herr C wants to demonstrate and his way of doing it. The premise at issue, we recall, involves the recovery of grace (both in the sense of personal charm, beauty, *Anmut*, and of divine grace, recovered innocence). The exemplary anecdotes themselves, however, stress a formalization of consciousness to the point of radical deformation in the service of an absolute, but mechanical, ideal of grace (the puppets) or of brute animal instinct (the bear). When K, the narrator, acknowledges at the end of the dialogue that he is *ein wenig zerstreut* ("somewhat distracted") he only confirms what has been evident all along: that he has been at the mercy of Herr C's personality and that the point of the examples, far from being self-evident, derived from Herr C's domineering, skillful manipulation of the discourse.

It is relevant here to look at the larger argument in de Man's essay, that is, the issue of pedagogy and especially the conjunction of the pedagogic with the aesthetic. The prime target of the essay, you may recall, is Schiller as author of *Letters on the Aesthetic Education of Mankind*, and it had begun with a quotation from a letter by Schiller in which he projects the model of a perfect aesthetic society by an image of a group of dancers executing intricate but harmoniously ordered patterns of a dance. Related to this is Schiller's reading of Kant's *Critique of Judgment*, and his influential but, in de Man's view, drastically reductive appropriation of Kant's thorny epistemological arguments for a much simpler and cruder position, what de Man terms an ideology of the aesthetic, a conception of the aesthetic as a training ground for good citizenship. All this is implicit in the way Schiller views the ensemble of dancers: the beauty of their patterns reflecting the reconciliation of skill and spontaneity, discipline and freedom.

Now without entering further into this large subject, namely, the misreadings of Kant's *Critique of Judgment* (a subject that de Man treats in a number of essays), let me try very briefly to focus the issue of pedagogy in relation to our discussion. In the "Marionettentheater," as we have seen, Kleist exposes a glaring discrepancy between the ostensible principle or truth factor at issue—namely, the wished-for recovery of grace, of spontaneity, both physical and spiritual—and the series of demonstrations that are provided, namely, the several anecdotes recounted by the interlocutors and, no less significantly, the relation of the interlocutors to each other. The methods of instruction or persuasion are authoritarian, coercive, and calculated, whereas the content or topic of the instruction involves unselfconscious immediacy and unsought grace.

Whether this is a risk of all teaching situations or simply a consequence of this instance as staged by Kleist is not directly addressed by de Man, but one may conclude that he suggests the former. What is at issue in his argument is not simply that the force of examples depends more on the way they're presented, on the skill or authority of a speaker (teacher), than on any meaning or truth they may embody. It is, more insidiously, that any mode of instruction or injunction—the calculated effort to impose a truth for the betterment of the addressee—will, whether it succeeds or not, tend to undermine the truth factor itself. Truth wants to be taught, but is it then still truth?

The question may be related to what Lyotard has termed "l'hétérogénéité de la phrase éthique avec la phrase cognitive" ("the heterogeneity between ethical phrase and cognitive phrase"). He continues: "This limitation is not due to some finitude of human beings. It results from the absence of a homogeneous language. An 'abyss' (KUK, Introduction) separates every descriptive phrase, including the critical metalanguage of the deduction, from the prescriptive phrase. The latter, when taken as the referent of the former, must elude its grasp."[14] This is part of a wide-ranging argument in *The Differend*, an argument that makes fundamental separations among various phrase regimens (*régimes de phrases*, such as the prescriptive, the constative, the exclamatory) as well as among genres of discourse (such as the tragic or the technical; see pp. 128–29). Lyotard's aim is to guard against any automatic bridge or linkage (what Suleiman terms implication) between, say, a thesis or principle and the call for its application or actualization, the injunction.

When Suleiman writes that the injunction is addressed to an auditor who had already "correctly interpreted the story," does not this "correct interpretation" already assume an incorporation of the level of injunction? But how? In what sense might injunction be encoded at the level of interpretation? We can begin to explore this issue by looking at the level of interpretation in Suleiman's model—the articulation or thematization of principles, rules, "truths" that the narrative is presumed to exemplify. This level is often directly identified in a text. The La Fontaine fable, we recall, singled out the moral, *moralité*—a term that characterizes both the form—pithy, authoritative, conclusive—and the content—a rule for right action or behavior. Maxims, apothegms, constitute reservoirs of moral teaching. They may be considered abbreviated exempla, generalities to be supplemented by illustrative instances.

The coupling of an example with a rule or maxim (of a particular with a general) may be problematic in regard to both elements, the example and the rule. In the traditional parable structure the rule or maxim is relatively clear, whether explicitly stated or not. Difficulties of interpretation here generally arise with the narrative: does it illustrate the rule? how? But the difficulty on the other side is of a different kind. The "truth" or rule may be *too* clear and simple. Maxims, let us remember, are commonplaces, part of the doxa. They are easily grasped, but their relevance may be so general as to apply to everything and nothing. One has the impression sometimes that this very vagueness is used as a bait, holding out the illusion of some meaning, some truth as the payoff for the narrative. "All happy families are alike, but an unhappy family is unhappy after its own fashion." Everybody knows this opening sentence of *Anna Karenina*. There is perhaps something comforting in reading this at the beginning of an 800-page novel. We have something secure in hand even as we start. But do we ever recur to this pronouncement and look in it for a key to the subtleties that emerge in the course of the narrative?

There are certain Kafka stories that are constructed so as to highlight a maxim, an articulated truth factor, in such a way that its linkage to the narrative becomes both inescapable and enigmatic. In "The Penal Colony" ("Die Strafkolonie") the machine designed to execute the judgment is, let us recall, a writing instrument that inscribes rules or maxims on the body of the victim—the rules being those that the victim is supposed to have broken. Let me evoke briefly the goal of this machine: to inscribe the law on the body of an individual in such a way that, in the course of protracted torture and at the height of his agony, he finally comprehends the *meaning* of the inscription. But to grasp this meaning, in what the officer describes as a climactic moment of spiritual revelation, requires the victim's acquiescence, his positive assent to the mutilation of his body. The law, in each case, consists in pithy injunctions. The story gives us two instances: *Ehre deinen Vorgesetzten!* ("Honor thy superiors!") and *Sei gerecht!* ("Be just!") Kafka's fable may be read as a gruesome literalization of the underlying principle of all authoritarian pedagogy: to win the assent of the pupil, to make the pupil complicit in the process of formation, of *Bildung*, however vacuous the lesson, however destructive the process of learning. Let us note also that the machine in this tale is a theater of inscription designed, among other things, to articulate words of wisdom, maxims of right action. The act of punishment, the drawn-out ritual of mutilation, serves, in a sense, only as a means of establishing an appropriate setting or surface (that is, both aura and writing surface) for the words of truth, the authoritative injunctions to be inscribed on the back of the victim. Not unlike the marble slabs on which the media artist Jenny Holzer has inscribed enigmatic homilies, the writing surface itself in "The Penal Colony" becomes a more potent agency of signification than any message inscribed on it.

With "The Penal Colony" I have, of course, chosen an extreme case, so let me turn to a more typical and muted utilization of maxims and sayings in a narrative work. Goethe was an inveterate coiner of maxims and sayings. He was also a shrewd practitioner and, to some extent, an innovator of the novella form. The traditional coupling of narrative and moralism in this form is something that Geothe took fully into account, though he seldom applied it in a conventional manner. But one can't help but notice a certain imbalance on this level in his writing practice, especially in his later work. The abundance, to the point of excess, of his production of maxims, apothegms, and epigrams stands in curious relation to the economy and polish of his narrative art. One of his problems as a writer appears to have been a need to find a place for his wise sayings, a place, that is, that would preserve them but at the same time demonstrate their use, their potential application. The oft-remarked distancing tone, the urbane irony, of his narrative persona in the fiction gave him some opportunity to incorporate extradiegetic commentary without breaking the flow of the narrative and without commiting the persona too far. But even so, there remained large blocks of generalities that had to be stocked with minimal or even no narrative support. (I am thinking of "From Makarie's Archive" in *Wilhelm Meister's Years of Travel* ["Aus Makariens Archiv," *Wilhelm Meisters Wanderjahre*], Bk. III, and of *Max-*

ims and Reflections [Maximen und Reflexionen].) Here maxims reveal their derivation from a doxa, a storehouse of commonplaces which have no determinate place. From this perspective we can appreciate some of the strategies that Goethe undertook to utilize such material.

In *The Elective Affinities (Die Wahlverwandtschaften)* a novel constructed in some respects as a very tight, inevitable tragic action, Goethe includes all kinds of ancillary materials. One of these is the notebook of Ottilie, the tragic heroine, a notebook that is for the most part a kind of commonplace book in which she copies out a great variety of moral, social, and aesthetic reflections. Naturally, every interpreter has tried to apply one or another of these to the powerful and enigmatic principal narrative, but where you have some dozens of possibilities, there will be little agreement about the choice. In introducing Ottilie's notebook, the narrator makes a remark that, in spite of its reflective urbanity, can be taken as a kind of challenge to the reader:

We have heard of a singular practice of the English marine. All of the cordage of the royal navy, from the heaviest to the thinnest, is spun in such a manner that a red thread goes through the whole, which one cannot pull out without undoing everything, and whereby even the smallest pieces may be identified as belonging to the crown.

Similarly a thread of consideration and affection that links and marks the whole goes through Ottilie's diary. These notations, reflections, expanded sayings, and whatever else appears there thus become proper to the writer and significant for her. This is evident even in any individual passage we have selected and communicated.[15]

The reader is thus put in the position of having not only to deduce the relevance of a moral, its possible applicability to the narrative, but to select the moral itself. Given the multiplicity and diversity of choices the author makes available, this must prove a vain task. Yet what is noteworthy here is that a character within the fiction is constituted on the model of an exemplifying practice. The enigma of Ottilie, of this fragile, otherworldly, opaque creature, is, in one sense at least, quite readily figured by the red thread—not by what *hangs* on it, that is, not by the semantic and conceptual material it brings together—

but simply by its function, namely, to generate a serial form that is determined in purely textual (and not psychological, spiritual, etc.) terms. The "character" Ottilie, then, is spelled out in the *drift*[16] of the reflections she collects in her diary; that is, the seriality of a sequence traces a vector, points to a meaning, that is nowhere explicitly articulated.

In "The Penal Colony", we recall, the maxim or truth factor is articulated as a fusion of truth and prescription. The prescriptive force, in fact, is so strong that it absorbs the truth factor and we are left with a rule so rigid and absolute that it destroys the addressee. In *The Elective Affinities*, on the contrary, the truth factor—the maxims and reflections that distill the operative ethical norms—is so diffuse and so tenuously affixed to the action and its agents that the prescriptive force seems almost wholly absent.

The kind of functional model that Suleiman projects illustrates a meshing, an interaction based on a reductive conception of the constituent elements. Maxims, apothegms, mottoes offer a direct presentation of normative precepts, but they are not automatically linked to a prescriptive mode, that is, to a legitimated form of injunction. The gap between the level of precepts, of articulated truths, and that of injunction cannot be accounted for in terms of a closed narratological model like Suleiman's. But this model has helped us specify how a performative potential challenges any structural model.

Here one might turn to the third element of Suleiman's model, the narrative proper, but it is difficult, for reasons we have discussed, to view this level as parallel to the other two. If it stands by itself it requires, in Suleiman's terms, something like a "correct interpretation" in order to demonstrate its exemplarity. In other words, the receptor, the addressee, must supply what is missing, must discern just what in the narrative might privilege one interpretation and not another. To explore this kind of form we would need to look at works in which the exemplarity of narrative units is itself an issue.

Is this not precisely what the frame structure involves—a way of turning narrative into an interpretive modality, of en-dowing narrative with a second-order function? Its primary sub-ject matter, then, is no longer the diegesis, the action or situa-tion it recounts, but the status of the narratives it enframes. The question then becomes: What frames a story? And what would a poetics of frames look like?

Parabolic Exemplarity

The Example of Nietzsche's Thus Spoke Zarathustra

Nietzsche in Basel studied the deep pool
Of these discolorations, mastering
The moving and moving of their forms
In the much-mottled motion of blank time.
—Wallace Stevens,
"Description without Place"

What is at stake when I say, "Take, for example, the parables in *Thus Spoke Zarathustra*?" The alogic of example is the following: On the one hand, to say something is an example is to imply that it is only one of many possible examples. This minimizes the importance of its distinctive features. I take, for example, *Thus Spoke Zarathustra* out of many texts that might have illustrated my point just as well. This is the logic or tropologic of synecdoche: part for whole. I choose one part of what I implicitly claim is a homogeneous whole. Any other part of this whole could have stood for the whole. One handful of grain is as good as any other to show the quality of a sack of wheat. On the other hand, the fact that I choose this one example singles it out for special attention. My choice implies that it is especially or even uniquely exemplary. The fact that I choose this one out of so many justifies close attention to its minutest details. No choice of an example is innocent. Each carries with it a whole set of perhaps question-begging assumptions. A good part of conceptual argument in philosophy or theory is carried by the unsaid in the example. Moreover, an exemplary example must repeat in miniature the structure of the whole. This fractal miniaturizing obeys a quite different tropological law from the one that governs synecdoche. Now the part

is like the whole not by being a random segment of a homogeneous totality, everywhere like itself, but by repeating on a
small scale the large-scale pattern of the whole. The exemplary
part is now seen as at once a unique unrepeatable feature of a
heterogeneous whole and a cunning exact repetition in small of
the large. How can both synecdoche and fractal miniaturizing
simultaneously govern the work of examples?

A parable offers an opportunity to investigate this paradox
further. A parable is an exemplary little story functioning to
make clear some conceptual point. The apparent casualness of
the choice and the discrepancy between the story and its parabolic meaning imply that many other little stories, an indefi-
nite number, would have done as well. On the other hand, the
conceptual point tends to become, historically, so tied to the little story that they form an inseparable couple. If you want to
know how to get to the kingdom of heaven, listen to the parable
of the sower in Matthew. I have said the example repeats the
whole in miniature. Parable exhibits this feature of exemplarity
in a special way. Parables, as biblical scholars have recognized,
tend always to be about the efficacy of parables. They are parables of parable. This is frequently the case with secular parables
too.

If parables are exemplary of the functioning of examples, it
may be that all examples are not just exemplary examples but
examples of example.[1] An aporetic turning back of example on
itself is a distinguishing feature of the working of examples generally. This might mean that far from advancing the conceptual
argument they are meant to illustrate, examples tend to bring
the argument to a stop by introducing the problematic *mise-en-
abîme* of example. In the case of fractals, the miniature version
of the whole is made of parts each of which is in its turn a miniature of this first example and of the larger whole. Examples
and parables may work the same way. Each example calls forth
another example, each parable another parable of that parable,
and so on ad infinitum. The parable within a parable in *Thus
Spoke Zarathustra* exemplifies that. It would follow from this
that an example, it may be, is not a cognitive clarification but a
certain extremely problematic kind of speech act or performa-

tive. It legislates or constitutes, but what it does is to disrupt the cognitive clarity of the argument it was meant to clarify.

Anyone who has tried to come to terms with *Zarathustra* will know what the problems are. *Zarathustra* is generally considered to be one of Nietzsche's most important works, perhaps even the most important of all. It is the centerpiece, included in its entirety, of Walter Kaufmann's widely used *Viking Portable Nietzsche*. Nevertheless, it can hardly be said to be the center of attention in recent important studies of Nietzsche.[2] Nietzsche called it "A Book for All and None." This may mean that it is, as Kaufmann says, "by far Nietzsche's most popular book," while at the same time never actually being read.[3] What would it mean to read *Thus Spoke Zarathustra*?

Zarathustra is quite unlike any other work by Nietzsche. Here Nietzsche's main "ideas"—the death of God, the eternal return, the overman, the revaluation of all values, the great noon—are "presented" —(if that is the right way to put it) not discursively, conceptually, and aphoristically, in the first person, as in most of Nietzsche's work, but in dramatized, narrative form. *Zarathustra* has a protagonist, an elaborate setting, and a rudimentary story involving various personages and animals, as well as journeys across a landscape of solitary mountains, inhabited plains, seashore, and sea. Moreover, the style of *Zarathustra* is, to say the least, heightened, portentous, melodramatic. Zarathustra preaches in a loud voice. Here the Dionysiac is practiced, not just described. The irony and light touch that Nietzsche prized in Mozart or Stendhal and that leavens even his own *Ecce Homo* seems for the most part absent here. Finally, if the large-scale structure of *Zarathustra* is narrative rather than aphoristic or argumentative, the local grain or texture of the style is not just pervasively figurative. That would be too little to say. Much of the time Nietzsche presents figures without the clear and distinct concepts they appear to be in aid of presenting. The reader is given the figurative without the literal, as if what Zarathustra has to say can only be said in figure. These local figures are often, though by no means always, drawn from the large-scale topographical setting of the narrative. One example is the last sentence of the sixth section of "On Old and

New Tablets," from the Third Part: "Those who are going under [*die Untergehenden*] I love with my whole love: for they cross over [*gehn hinüber*]" (*Z*, 447; 312). What in the world does that mean? The sentence uses "figuratively" the geographical terminology of the "literal" setting. How can this mode of expression be justified as a way of presenting what everyone agrees are Nietzsche's central concepts, the eternal return, the death of God, the overman, the great noon, and so on? Is the mode of presentation necessary, the only way Nietzsche could say what he had to say, or are these stylistic features a way of dressing up in dramatic and ornately figurative form what could just as well have been said in a straightforward logical, argumentative, conceptual way?

In order to answer these questions, it will be necessary to exemplify in a little more detail what the problems are in trying to read *Thus Spoke Zarathustra*. The third part of *Zarathustra* begins with a section called "The Wanderer." The first three parts of *Zarathustra* were initially published separately, so one might imagine someone who had picked up part three in a bookstore and was sitting down in all innocence to begin to read. The first sentences are straighforward scene setting. They might have appeared in a novel: "It was about midnight when Zarathustra started across the ridge of the island so that he might reach the other coast by early morning; for there he wanted to embark. There he would find a good roadstead where foreign ships too liked to anchor, and they often took along people who wanted to cross the sea from the blessed isles" (*Z*, 403; 264). So far so good. The reader feels perfectly at home, except for the place name "the blessed isles," which sounds a little odd. A few sentences later, however, when the reader enters into Zarathustra's meditations as he climbs the mountain to reach the harbor on the other side of the island, she enters another world of discourse:

And one further thing I know: I stand before my final peak [*meinem letzten Gipfel*] now and before that which has been saved up for me the longest. Alas, now I must face my hardest path! Alas, I have begun my loneliest walk! But whoever is of my kind cannot escape such an hour—the hour which says to him:

"Only now are you going your way to greatness! Peak and abyss—

they are now joined together. [*Gipfel und Abgrund—das ist jetzt in eins beschlossen!*]"

   . . .

"And if you now lack all ladders, then you must know how to climb on your own head [*so mußt du verstehen, noch auf deinen eigenen Kopf zu steigen*]: how else would you want to climb upward? On your own head and away over your own heart!"

   . . .

"But you, O Zarathustra, wanted to see the ground and background of all things [*wolltest aller Dinge Grund schaun und Hintergrund*]; hence you must climb over yourself [*so mußt du schon über dich selber steigen*]—upward, up until even your stars are *under* you!"

   . . .

Alas, destiny and sea! To you I must now go *down!* [*Ach, Schicksal und See! Zu euch muß ich nun* hinabsteigen!] Before my highest mountain I stand and before my longest wandering; to that end I must first go down deeper than ever I descended—deeper into pain than ever I descended, down into its blackest flood.

   . . .

Whence come the highest mountains? I once asked. Then I learned that they came out of the sea. The evidence is written in their rocks and in the walls of their peaks. It is out of the deepest depth that the highest must come to its height. [*Aus dem Tiefsten muß das Höchste zu seiner Höhe kommen.*] (*Z*, 403–5; 264–66)

Something strange has happened to the language here. The topographical elements of the setting—mountains, night sky, and sea—have become the vehicle for expressing something else, but that something else is not expressed in conceptual terms. Rather, it is expressed exclusively in terms drawn from the landscape: "Alas, destiny and sea! To you I must now go *down!* . . . It is out of the deepest depth that the highest must come to its height." Nor is this strange mode of expression intermittent in *Thus Spoke Zarathustra*. It is the pervasive and almost universal level of discourse. Reading *Zarathustra* right depends on getting right what it means to use language in this way. "The Wanderer," for example, is followed by "On the Vision and the Riddle" ("Vom Gesicht und Rätsel"), one of the most important sections in the whole of *Zarathustra*. Here the eternal return is most powerfully affirmed. But it is affirmed not in conceptual terms but precisely in "vision and riddle," in the form of a story Zarathustra tells to those on shipboard as they sail away from the blessed isles. It is the story of a vision, or rather of a vision within a vision, both of which are told in the same circumstantial, topographical terms that are used in the first sentence of part three, cited above. First Zarathustra tells the sailors the story of how he climbed a wild mountain path with a dwarf on his back, the "spirit of gravity," and then expounded to the dwarf the meaning of a gateway they reach in their climb: "From this gateway, Moment [*Augenblick*], a long, eternal lane leads *backward*; behind us lies an eternity. Must not whatever *can* walk have walked on this lane before? Must not whatever *can* happen have happened, have been done, have passed by before? . . . —must not all of us have been there before? And return and walk in that other lane, out there, before us, in this long dreadful lane—must we not eternally return?" (*Z*, 408–9; 270). Then within that vision, as Zarathustra tells it to the sailors, another vision displaces the first, a parable of the first parable, the vision of the shepherd with the snake in his mouth and throat who is transfigured when he finds the courage to bite off the head of the snake: "No longer shepherd, no longer human—one changed, radiant, *laughing!*" (*Z*, 410; 272). A moment before, Zarathustra gives four names for the story he tells. It was a vision, a riddle, a foreseeing, and a parable: "You who are glad of riddles! Guess me this riddle that I saw then, interpret me the vision [*das Gesicht*] of the loneliest. For it was a vision and a foreseeing [*ein Vorhersehn*]. *What* did I see then in a parable [*im Gleichnisse*]?" (*Z*, 410; 271–72).

The stylistic texture of all of *Zarathustra* remains more or less like this, even when what is presented is not explicitly vision and riddle. Almost any passage would serve as example. I cite one passage from much later in part three, from the second section of "On Old and New Tablets":

My wise longing [*Sehnsucht*] cried and laughed thus out of me—born in the mountains, verily, a wild wisdom—my great broad-winged longing [*meine große flügelbrausende Sehnsucht*]! And often it swept me away and up and far, in the middle of my laughter; and I flew, quivering, an arrow, through sun-drunken delight, away into distant futures which no dream had yet seen, into hotter souths than artists ever dreamed of, where gods in their dances are ashamed of all clothes—to speak in parables and to limp and stammer like poets; and verily, I am ashamed that I must still be a poet [*daß ich nämlich in Gleichnisse rede, und gleich Dichtern hinke und stammle: und wahrlich, ich schäme mich, daß ich noch Dichter sein muß!*—]. (Z, 444; 309)

These passages contain a terminological clue that will make it possible to name the mode of discourse of *Zarathustra* and so have a hypothetical way to read it all. Zarathustra says he has been speaking in parables. What does this mean? The word "parable" is the only rhetorical term that appears repeatedly in *Zarathustra*. It is used here and there to name what sort of thing the book itself is. The word "parable" does not appear in the early lectures on rhetoric. It was not part of the ancient taxonomy of tropes. The trope of "allegory" is, however, defined, as is "riddle." The definition of allegory is cited from Quintilian: "Allegoria (inversio) . . . aliud verbis, aliud sensu ostendit" ("Allegory [inversion] . . . presents one thing in words and another in meaning."[4] The riddle (*das Rätsel*), is "a very obscure allegory" (*eine ganz dunkle Allegorie*). It is, says Quintilian, "not permitted in a speech" ("ist in der Rede unstatthaft").[5] Though the term "fable" (*Fabel*) does not appear in the lectures, it does appear just at the beginning of "On Truth and Lies" as the proper term to define the initial story of the clever but ephemeral animals that appeared on a star in a remote corner of the universe and "invented knowledge [*das Erkennen erfanden*]."[6] What is the difference between an allegory, a fable, and a parable? Why does Nietzsche in *Zarathustra* define what he is doing as parable rather than as allegory?

One answer is clear enough. In a multitude of ways *Thus Spoke Zarathustra* is modeled on the gospels. It tells the story of a wandering preacher who teaches a new doctrine, often by way of parables. One section of part three is called "Upon the Mount of Olives." Another is called "On Old and New Tablets." Many passages are more or less explicitly reversals of what Jesus taught, as when Zarathustra "the godless," says "Do love your neighbor as yourself, but first be such as *love themselves*—loving with a great love, loving with a great contempt" (Z, 421; 284). The publication of part four of *Zarathustra* was held up after the onset of Nietzsche's insanity by the fear that it would be confiscated for blasphemy. That did not happen, perhaps because no one read it. In any case, "parable" is a key word in the gospels (*Gleichnis* in Luther's translation): "And he spake many things to them in parable" (Matthew 13:3). Nietzsche's (or Zarathustra's) use of the term "parable" is part of the parodic reversal of the gospels in *Zarathustra*. What, then, is a parable, and how do Zarathustra's parables differ from Christ's?[7]

A parable is a little, realistic story that has a hidden meaning. It means something other than what it says. The figurative meaning, according to the etymology of "parable," is "thrown beside" the literal meaning. As the German word *Gleichnis* implies, the figurative meaning is presented in a "likeness" or "image." *Gleichnis* means "image, simile, metaphor, figure of speech; allegory, parable" (*Cassell's German Dictionary*). Parable differs from allegory not only in the biblical resonance of the former term and the more classical resonance of the latter (in spite of the fact that both are derived from Greek words), but in the fact that a parable is a short, realistic story embedded in another argument or narrative, whereas a long text may be allegorical from one end to the other. This is true whether we are thinking of Dante's definition of Christian allegory or of Paul de Man's contention that all texts are allegories of their own unreadability.[8]

The difference between Christ's parables and Zarathustra's is easy to state. Christ's parables all have to do with the kingdom of heaven and how to get there. As I have already said, the biblical parables have to do with their own working. An effective parable is a performative use of language. When it works, when it is presented to those who have eyes to see and ears to hear and understand, the parable is a way to get from here to there. A parable is a way to cross over to the kingdom of heaven. Moreover, though the parables of Jesus were probably originally presented as enigmatic little stories—riddles without a "solution," the corresponding spiritual truths—as the parables exist now in the gospels the literal meaning is explicitly given. Jesus' explication of the parable of the sower is a good example: "But he that received seed into the good ground is he that heareth the word, and understandeth it; which also beareth fruit, and bringeth forth, some an hundredfold, some sixty, some thirty" (Matthew 13:23). The parables of Jesus are told by the Word, the Logos,

since Christ is the Word. Their meaning is governed by the
Word. This Word can be stated conceptually as well as in parabolic form. The Word is the ground and guarantee of all words,
whether conceptual or parabolic. It may be reached by those
who hear the word and understand it. For them words are transparent windows opening to the Word.

Why then does Jesus speak to the people in parables? Jesus
gives the answer to the disciples, who ask just that question:
"Because it is given to you to know the mysteries of the kingdom of heaven, but to them it is not given. For whosoever hath,
to him shall be given, and he shall have more abundance: but
whosoever hath not, from him shall be taken away even that he
hath. Therefore speak I to them in parables: because they seeing
see not; and hearing they hear not, neither do they understand"
(Matthew 13:11–13). The paradox of Jesus's parables is that they
are addressed to ears that will not understand them. If you can
understand them you do not need them. If you need them you
will not understand them.

The parables of Zarathustra are radically different from the
parables of Jesus. They are different because Nietzsche's theory
of language and his conception of the human epistemological
situation is radically different from the New Testament one.
The phrases at the end of the passage quoted above from "On
Old and New Tablets" tell the reader what that theory of language and that situation are: "—to speak in parables and to limp
and stammer like poets; and verily, I am ashamed that I must
still be a poet!" (Z, 444; 309). As Freud says by way of the citation from al-Hariri at the end of *Beyond the Pleasure Principle,*
"What we cannot reach flying, we must reach limping [*erhin-
ken*]. . . . The Book says, it is no sin to limp. [*Die Schrift sagt, es
ist keine Sünde zu hinken.*]"[9] In what comes just before the
identification of speaking in parables, on the one hand, and
limping and stammering like poets, on the other, Zarathustra
has described a flight of his "wise longing" into a visionary future "where gods in their dances are ashamed of all clothes."
The gods need no clothes and are ashamed of them. Zarathustra, though he is ashamed of it, must clothe what he says in the
covering of parabolic language. To do this is to limp rather than

to dance and to stammer rather than to speak clearly. To stammer is to speak a language that cannot be understood because the material or bodily dimension of language—sounds and the effort of tongue, lips, palate, and throat—gets in the way of comprehensible meaning. Instead of perspicuous speech, repetitive and almost incomprehensible sounds are produced. Of Zarathustra's language and the language of *Thus Spoke Zarathustra* it can be said, to borrow phrases from *The Birth of Tragedy*, that it is "almost undecided as to whether it will communicate or conceal, as if stammering in a foreign tongue."[10] Or, rather, Zarathustra has no choice but to stammer. He must, willynilly, cover what he says in the garments of parable because no naked language exists for what he is trying to say. Here is another reversal of biblical precedent. When Adam and Eve ate the apple of knowledge they saw that they were naked, were ashamed of it, and covered their nakedness with fig leaves. Zarathustra, reversing this, is ashamed that he cannot go naked. Even, or perhaps especially, his vision of those "hotter souths than artists ever dreamed of, where gods in their dances are ashamed of all clothes" must be expressed in the shameful garments of parable. The passage is an example of what it talks about. Rather than defining parable it gives more parabolic or figurative definitions of it: limping, stammering like poets, wearing clothes when you ought to dance naked.

Unlike Jesus' parable of the sower, where the answer to the riddle is clearly given in literal language, the distinction between figurative and literal language clearly marked, Zarathustra's language attempts to lift itself, so to speak, by its own bootstraps, or to climb on its own head. It is parable about parable rather than parabolic expression of some available literal language. It must be this because for Zarathustra, as for Nietzsche in the early lectures on rhetoric and in "On Truth and Lies," no literal language exists. The ideas about language of the early writings on rhetoric are still the underlying presuppositions of *Thus Spoke Zarathustra*. Zarathustra (or *Zarathustra*) speaks in parables from one end of the book to the other, but it is a curious kind of parabolic language, which cannot be translated into its conceptual or literal meaning.

The traditional rhetorical name for this kind of language is "catachresis." Catachresis is the bringing in of a term from another realm to cover or clothe a gap in language. Nietzsche's example in "Description of Ancient Rhetoric" is the use of *lapidare* to describe the throwing of clods or potsherds: "while *lapidare* has the obvious meaning of 'to stone,' there is no special word to describe the throwing of clods or potsherds. Hence abuse or *katachresis* of words becomes necessary."[11] When Nietzsche says, "Those who are going under I love with my whole love: for they cross over," he means just that and only that. It is an error to think that the proper reading of this sentence would translate it into some conceptual language for which it is the parabolic expression. *Zarathustra* is throughout parables without proper meaning.

I have spoken of such language as an impossible self-suspension whereby Nietzsche's parabolic language sustains itself on itself rather than by its decipherable reference to the ideas it presents parabolically. A parabolic figure for this appears repeatedly in *Zarathustra*: the reversible image of a vehicle that becomes itself carried by what it carries. Zarathustra carries the dwarf, spirit of gravity, up the mountain, but his own lightness and laughter rise above that heaviness and, so to speak, ride on it. When Zarathustra climbs the mountain at the beginning of the third part, he says, "You must know how to climb on your own head." Zarathustra's most important definition of parable, in "The Return Home," depends on just this reversal of rider and mount, of tenor and vehicle, to use familiar twentieth-century terms for the literal meaning and its metaphorical expression. The terms are appropriate, since metaphor means, etymologically, "carried to another place," "transferred." But in Nietzsche's figures carrier becomes carried and vice versa. As Zarathustra's "*home*, solitude" says to him in "The Return Home": "Here [meaning here in your home solitude] all things come caressingly to your discourse [*Rede*] and flatter you, for they want to ride on your back. On every parable you ride to every truth. [*Auf jedem Gleichnis reitest du hier zu jeder Wahrheit.*] (*Z*, 432; 295). When Zarathustra is at home, all things are easily turned into language. Things are carried by words. In being turned into words they become parable. Parables are the vehicles of things, by the series of displacements Nietzsche describes in the early rhetorical writings, each displacement further from the unknowable thing in itself: from nerve excitation to subjective image to word-sound. The passage, in its personification of things as caressing, fawning animals that want to be carried on Zarathustra's back, is an example of what it names. In this figure the unknown and unknowable things are turned into a little parable, like the fable of the man who ended by carrying his own donkey. Then the relation of rider and beast of burden reverses again. The things turned into parabolic words become the beast of burden on which Zarathustra rides: "On every parable you ride to every truth." What those "truths" are we know. They are the mobile army of metaphors, metonymies, and anthropomorphisms that constitute the parables. They are truths that cannot be extricated from the figures used to express them, for example, the topographical notations that form the narrative armature of *Thus Spoke Zarathustra*. Zarathustra remains constrained to speak in parables and to limp and stammer like poets even when he is naming as accurately as possible the nature of those parables.

Nietzsche in *Thus Spoke Zarathustra* remains true to the theory of language he proposed in his early writings. But to say he remains true to his early theory of language is not enough. Those ideas about language cannot be detached from the epistemological presuppositions that underlie them. A theory of rhetoric, for example, Aristotle's, Quintilian's or Nietzsche's, can never be detached from the epistemological and ontological presuppositions that underlie it. Aristotle's theory of tropes cannot be separated from his confidence in our ability to know the essence of things through our senses. Nietzsche moves without transition from language about our imprisonment in "nerve excitations" to language about the linguistic displacements of metaphor. To accept a theory of tropes is implicitly also to accept its epistemological or even physiological ground. In the case of *Thus Spoke Zarathustra*, the topographical language does not name the scenic background within which a dramatic action or a conceptual argument unfolds. That language remains in the foreground as a primary vehicle of meaning. It says something that can be said in no other way.

I began by proposing a more or less general theory of example. I promised to exemplify this with the parables in *Thus Spoke Zarathustra*. The investigation of the example has led me to a different place and to a different proposition, namely a recognition that even though anyone at any time is constrained by the alogic of exemplarity, the working of example in a given case cannot be separated from the epistemological, linguistic, and metaphysical presuppositions of the one who says "for example . . . " This coming out at a different place exemplifies my claim that an example always disrupts and alters the conceptual argument it is adduced to support.

"The Beauty of Failure"

Kafka and Benjamin on the Task of Transmission and Translation

Kafka's short pieces have been frequently characterized as parables[1] and, just as frequently, this term has been contested, modified, or rejected as inappropriate. What is at stake in this terminological discussion is the exemplary function of the traditional parable and its transcendental-theological weight. Although, as Walter Benjamin reminds us, the exemplary task is undercut in Kafka's "parable" by their ostensible rhetoric of failure, Kafka's texts do not merely dramatize the inaccessibility of truth but precisely call into question the very notion of exemplarity with its theological and epistemological horizon. Yet, if Kafka's parables do not just renounce their exemplary function, if they do not leave us only with negative knowledge, then we need to ask about the implications of the rhetoric of failure deployed so frequently both in Kafka's texts and in Kafka criticism. I would like to suggest that Kafka's strategic use of failure as a response to the traditional tasks of the parable is intertwined with a critique of the often opposite tendencies of modern aesthetics: the autonomy of the work of art and nostalgia for linguistic community. By preserving a paradoxical sense of obligation, such failure contests not only the autonomy of the work of art—or what Benjamin calls "a negative theology" of pure art deprived of any social function—but also a reductive understanding of the social function in terms of a nostalgic longing for the immanence of the common being.

Yet, before we try to account for the effects of Kafka's peculiar mimicry of parabolic form, we should discuss briefly the exemplary function of the traditional parable. The parable is usually situated between the exemplary tale or the transparent allegory intended to illustrate the general truth of the doctrine on the one hand, and the enigmatic riddle on the other.[2] In the Judeo-Christian tradition, the parable is a traditional tool of exegesis of the Scriptures, or a means to reveal a moral or spiritual truth.[3] Midrash, for example, offers several parables on parables illustrating this hermeneutical function: a parable is like a man cutting a path through a thicket of reeds; it is like a handle with which an unwieldy chest or a jug of boiling water can be carried; it functions as rope with which cold and sweet water can be brought from a well.[4] As all these passages imply, the parable carves a way to the understanding of truth, it functions as a "tool" without which some spiritual or moral insight would not be brought to light. Parables, like other exemplary forms of literature, are not intended to speak of and for themselves but are implicitly or explicitly organized around the binary structure in which the particular discloses or illustrates the truth.

In biblical hermeneutics, the issue of exemplarity has been a perennial problem, posing difficulties about the proper interpretation of parables. Because the exemplary character of the parable is by no means evident, it can be grasped only through an elaborate process of interpretation. According to the peculiar "theory" of parables in Mark, chapter 4, for example, teaching in parables illuminates but at the same time delays understanding: "Unto you it is given to know the mysteries of the kingdom of God: but unto them that are without, all these things are done in parables: That seeing they may see and not perceive; and hearing they may hear, and not understand" (Mark 4:11–12). Yet this interminable postponement is neutralized by the spatial split of audience: parables perpetuate the division between those who comprehend and those who fail to do so, between those who can read the spiritual sense and those who stumble on the parable's intentional unreadability.[5] As Jean Starobinski remarks in his interpretation of Mark 4, the teaching in parables preserves a "nonreception of the message," by creating "a cleavage between those who understand" and those who are kept outside understanding.[6] On religious grounds, such a deferral of understanding can be recuperated by some form of eschatology, whereas in the secular text the delay assumes a form of unreachable futurity.[7] However, even when a parable, like Mark 4, dramatizes a delay in understanding, it nonetheless orients the text toward a general truth, toward a promised revelation, even if this revelation remains hidden or postponed.

"On Parables":
Exemplarity, Transmissibility, Figuration

The relation between the linguistic structure and enigmatic revelation is of particular importance in Kafka's parables. Although placing Kafka in the context of parable is a familiar critical gesture (see Benjamin, Frank Kermode, and J. Hillis Miller among others), Kafka's interpreters feel obliged to provide certain (usually negative) qualifications because of the transcendental/theological weight that the traditional term implies. Theodor Adorno, for instance, argues that Kafka's parables signify not "through expression but its repudiation"; Wilhelm Emrich claims that they empty out the classical notion of the universal; and Heinz Politzer suggests that they are organized around a paradox.[8] Certainly, Emrich's and Politzer's approaches complicate or even deflate the content of the "transcendental," or the "universal," in Kafka's works, but their analyses leave the binary structure (example/general truth) intact.

Politzer's interpretation is "exemplary" in this respect. According to his reading, Kafka's parables reveal the impossibility of translating the transcendental into ordinary language. This impossibility, this negative revelation of truth, constitutes a paradox at the core of the parable:

Such a paradox will be generated wherever *the natural* and *the supernatural* meet, that is, when a message which is inaccessible to ordinary verbalization is to be *translated* into the vernacular of reasonable and generally intelligible communication. . . . Circling around this nucleus, they maintain a suspense originating in the never defined *relation their actual plots maintain with their backgrounds*.[9]

What is symptomatic about this approach is that the crisis of exemplarity—or what Politzer calls a paradox of exemplarity—is articulated in terms of an aborted transmission. The loss or the inaccessibility of truth in Kafka's parables is expressed in the figure of a failed translation. Yet Politzer's emphasis on the *failure* of translation in Kafka's texts still preserves the notion of truth that is not only inaccessible to but also independent of "ordinary" language. This truth cannot be known but it leaves an imprint on the text by fragmenting and splintering its language. Although Politzer is very perceptive of "clefts, cracks, and crevices" in Kafka's parables, these incongruities, according to him, merely reveal "the depth behind the realistic detail" and imply a negative relation to the transcendental.[10] Therefore, instead of illustrating the transcendental, the parable bears the evidence of the "incompatible meeting," of the antithetical relation between the quotidian language and the esoteric truth. Consequently, in Politzer's reading, skepticism about ordinary language remains in complicity with the affirmation of truth "inaccessible to ordinary verbalization." With the emphasis on the inaccessible transcendental or on the emptiness of traditional exemplary forms, this strain of Kafka criticism in fact perpetuates both the notion of linguistic skepticism and the concept of truth distinct and separate from the process of signification.

It is all the more surprising that Benjamin, one of the first Kafka critics, accounts for Kafka's resistance toward the transcendental without either resorting to a negative revelation of truth or simply accepting the idea of the "immanence of the text."[11] In his 1934 essay, "Franz Kafka: On the Tenth Anniversary of His Death," and four years later in his programmatic letter to Gershom Scholem (included in the English edition of "Illuminations" as "Some Reflections on Kafka"),[12] Benjamin likewise situates Kafka's prose in the tradition of Hasidic parables, and points to its deficiency in illustrating moral or spiritual truth. Although Benjamin too admits that the negative characterization of Kafka's parables is probably more rewarding, at the same time he warns us that this deficiency of Kafka's texts can be easily misread.[13] In his 1934 essay, Benjamin diagnoses this misreading in terms of either a "supernatural" or a "natural" interpretation: "There are two ways to miss the point of Kafka's works. One is to interpret them naturally, the other is the supernatural interpretation. Both the psychoanalytic and the theological interpretations equally miss the essential points" (*I*, 127). Needless to say, Politzer's reading is a fine example of the theological misreading of the deficiency of Kafka's parables. Four years later, Benjamin finds even his own reading of Kafka too apologetic. This time Benjamin sees the deficiency of Kafka's parables explicitly as their failure to transmit truth and argues that in order to "do justice to the figure of Kafka," it is essential to confront the significance of this failure without apologies.

As Benjamin points out, Kafka, of course, is not the first modern writer to face the loss of truth and the disintegration of tradition. Skepticism about truth and language can be said to describe the condition of modernity in general. Yet, whereas other writers "cling" to the loss of truth (by expressing this loss in the form of paradox, empty universal, or linguistic skepticism, we might add), Kafka entirely redefines the significance of this loss: "It is this consistency of truth that has been lost. Kafka was far from being the first to face this situation. . . . Kafka's real genius was that he tried something entirely new: he sacrificed truth for the sake of clinging to its transmissibility, its haggadic element" (*I*, 143–44). In this brief but remarkable insight, Benjamin stakes his understanding of Kafka's writings and of Kafka's modernity (the sense in which Kafka "tried something entirely new") on his reinterpretation of the very old concept of failure.[14] Reading "failure" in Kafka's parables in a way directly opposite to Politzer (and to the majority of Kafka criticism), Benjamin argues that Kafka's focus on the circulation or linguistic transport of meaning eventually aims to destroy the metaphysical concept of truth separate from the mechanism of signification. Consequently, what Kafka's "failure" exposes is not the inaccessibility of truth but the fact that the very idea of truth is one of the effects produced by language. It is this shift from truth to transmission, from illustration to transformation, that destabilizes the relation of exemplification: for Kafka an exemplary message loses its consistency and exists only as "rumor" or "decay of wisdom."

The surprising "sacrifice" of truth that transmissibility per-

forms requires more attention, because traditionally, we are accustomed to think of transmission as the preservation of truth
rather than its destruction. Benjamin suggests, however, that
transmissibility is not a counterpart of illustration or a faithful
preservation of truth but a linguistic movement that actively
trans-forms and de-forms the meaning of the text. Since transmissibility is a process of deformation, it leaves Kafka's interpreters in a position of "pupils who have lost the Holy Writ."
Consequently instead of taking the law as providing guidance
on the journey of interpretation, Kafka takes the journey itself
as providing its own law. This is at least the way Benjamin reads
Kafka's *das Gesetz der Fahrt* ("law of the journey"): a route of
unexpected reversals and distortions that derange causal connections between origins and destinations, wishes and fulfill-
ments, annunciation of messages and their reception (*I*, 139).[15]
Without a guiding law or a destination, this movement of Kafka's parables is, however, still tied to a sense of obligation. It requires "attentive listening" to the "indistinct sounds" even
though these sounds can no longer be recuperated into knowledge or meaning. Because of this attentiveness—which is perhaps only an openness to the past that can no longer be recuperated or to the future that cannot yet be seen—Benjamin stakes
transmissibility against oblivion.

According to Benjamin, the law of this wandering is best expressed in Kafka's reversal of the Sancho Panza story, entitled
"The Truth About Sancho Panza" ("Die Wahrheit über Sancho
Panza"). After reading chivalric romances, Sancho separates
himself from and then sends ahead his tormenting demon,
which becomes forever diverted from its "preordained object."
Sancho, a philosophical fool who manages to transform the tradition of the chivalric romances and in the meantime to get rid
of "the burden from his back," follows his demon "perhaps out
of a sense of responsibility" but derives a healthy entertain-
ment from such unconstrained wandering. As the story emphasizes, it is an experience of reading that unexpectedly trans-
forms the relationship between the demon and Sancho Panza.
Instead of truth, reading offers both a sense of responsibility and

a sense of relief—relief that comes, paradoxically, from a loss of a "preordained object."

Quite a different figuration of detachment from the origin of truth can be found in a very short text entitled "Couriers" ("Kuriere"). Yet here, too, such detachment functions as the condition of transmissibility. In this text, couriers, representative of the whole class of Kafka messengers, endlessly repeat messages that have become meaningless because no one wants to play the king dispatching information. The king functions here as a figure of authority and origin, the one who commands the messenger to repeat his message to the people. The authority of this figure is a guarantee of the consistency of both the message and its transmission. This disregard for the absolute source of meaning may cause the messages to become meaningless, but it does not remove the couriers' obligation of transmission: "They (the couriers) would like to put an end to this miserable life of theirs but they dare not because of their oath of service."[16] In other words, the work and obligation of transmission continues even though it empties out the point of its origin in the process.

With the king missing from the game from the outset, the couriers—the figures of transmissibility *par excellence*—not only repeat but also produce the messages they carry. Furthermore, they themselves invent the role of the missing king in the first place—it is a part of their game. Since the text evokes the opposition between the king and the couriers, between the origin of truth and its transmission, only to destroy it, the inaccessible origin does not bespeak the failure of transmission but is, in fact, one of its effects. This predicament of Kafka's couriers may exemplify just what "transmissibility in the absence of truth," in Benjamin's sense, signifies. One additional point should be stressed here: if the couriers' game evokes a sense of anxiety and even despair, Sancho's story is an example of a joyful playfulness. These two parables are, therefore, symptomatic of ambivalent responses in Kafka's texts to the "sacrifice of truth for the sake of transmissibility."

Benjamin's focus on transmission in Kafka's parables is by no means accidental—it is one of the main concerns in his own writing.[17] Whether it is art collecting, translation, reproduction, or the citationality of history, Benjamin offers a minute analysis of the effects of transmission. Therefore, in order to understand more precisely how transmissibility dislocates the structure of exemplarity, it is essential to refer to Benjamin's two famous essays "The Task of the Translator" ("Die Aufgabe des Übersetzers," 1923) and "The Work of Art in the Age of Mechanical Reproduction" ("Das Kunstwerk im Zeitalter seiner technischen Reproduzierbarkeit," 1936). These essays not only analyze two different kinds of "transmissibility" but deploy diametrically opposed rhetoric: the problem of translation apparently calls for a rhetoric of organicism and kinship between languages, whereas reproduction of the work of art deploys a rhetoric of mechanization. Yet despite the difference in their approaches, both texts focus upon a certain kind of iterability that drastically changes the meaning of the original, its structure, and its relation to history.[18]

"The sacrifice of truth for the sake of transmissibility" in fact quite accurately describes what happens with the meaning of the original in the process of translation. Not surprisingly, one of the main questions Paul de Man asks about "The Task of the Translator" concerns the function of failure in Benjamin's essay: "the question then becomes why this failure with regard to an original text, to an original poet, is for Benjamin *exemplary*."[19] Inadvertently echoing Benjamin's reading of Kafka, de Man likewise suggests that in order "to do justice to the figure" of Benjamin and his relationship to modernity, one needs to do justice to his peculiar understanding of failure. In both readings (in Benjamin's reading of Kafka and in de Man's of Benjamin), the question of failure, insofar as it is one of the main effects of transmissibility, is intertwined with a redefinition of both language and modernity. In particular, this strategic use of failure allows for a departure from the notion of modernity as a critical overcoming of the past.[20]

From the outset Benjamin insists that translation should not aim to restore the meaning or the "poetic" quality of the original. In fact what the process of translation reveals is that meaning or message is not essential even in the original: "Ihr Wesent-

liches ist nicht Mitteilung, nicht Aussage" ("Its essential quality is not statement or the imparting of information," *I*, 69).
Therefore, "any translation which intends to perform a transmitting function cannot transmit anything but information—
hence *something inessential*" (*I*, 69, emphasis added). If translatability manifests the special significance of the original, how
are we to understand this manifestation, which renders the
original's meaning as "something inessential"? Such a striking
conclusion is possible because Benjamin departs from the traditional theory of translation based on the likeness between
languages and replaces it with a notion of their kinship based on
complementarity: "translation thus ultimately serves the purpose of expressing the central reciprocal relationship between
languages" (*I*, 72). The task of the translation, then, is not to reproduce the meaning of the original but to complement its intentions and, thus, to mark the temporality of its historical existence.

In the context of his theory of translation, Benjamin articulates transmissibility not as a reproduction or preservation of
truth but rather as a temporal and disruptive process of supplementation, which radically transforms the relation between
language and meaning. If in the original, language and signification appear to be as closely related as are the fruit and its skin,
in translation meaning is only "loosely" attached to its language, which in its excess resembles "ample folds" of the royal
robe. This destruction of the "natural" bond between meaning
and language, which eventually proves language "unsuited to
its content, overpowering and alien," is the main effect of translatability.[21] As the contrast between the figures of the fruit and
the royal robe implies, the supplementary work of transmission
not only reveals the excess of language but also changes the entire conception of language: no longer natural, language assumes the character of the social artifice.

Such a linguistic transformation has far-reaching consequences for modern aesthetics. Resembling the effects of the
Baroque allegory, translation utterly destroys the conception of
the organicist unity of the work of art—in anticipation of Benjamin's argument in "The Work of Art in the Age of Mechanical

Reproduction," we can say that translation destroys the *aura* of the original. In translation the work does not even remotely resemble the organic unity of the fruit and the skin, but instead appears as a fragment of pure language, as a broken part of the vessel.[22] However, since translatability, according to Benjamin, is always already an essential quality of the original, translation cannot disrupt the original unity of meaning or the organic wholeness of the original merely from the outside; instead it supplements or intensifies the "intentions" already inherent in the original work of art.

Yet the effects of "failure" or "sacrifice of truth" performed by translation cannot be confined only to the realm of aesthetics. The process of translation not only disrupts the unity of the original, not only shatters the natural bond between language and meaning, but also destroys a certain nostalgic notion of the linguistic community. Thus, even in this early essay, Benjamin's focus on the excess of language does not lead to aestheticism but examines, if only tacitly, its social implications. Benjamin argues that translation can manifest the kinship between the languages only when it inscribes their foreignness and incompleteness within its own language. A good translation, therefore, allows its own native tongue to turn into a foreign one.[23] That is why the task of the poet and that of the translator are very different: whereas the poet is still concerned with the "immediacy" of meaning, the translator transforms his native language in its totality and therefore shifts the weight from the subjective to the collective conditions of enunciation. Repeating in an uncanny way the terms of Benjamin's interpretation of Kafka, de Man reads this transformation of the native tongue as the "errancy of language": "this movement of the original is a wandering, an *errance*, a kind of permanent exile if you wish, but is not really an exile, for there is no homeland."[24] De Man does not pursue this topic further, yet his focus on the condition of "permanent exile" calls attention to the crucial issue raised in Benjamin's essay: the effects of translation on the linguistic community. Although Benjamin insists that translation should not concern itself directly with questions of communication, audience, or readers, the act of translation, by inscribing difference into the native language, questions the very ethos of the common and the shared and eventually destroys the immanence of the common being. With its emphasis on differential, fragmentary, and the inorganic character of languages, Benjamin's theory of translation can be seen as the antithesis of the community based on the natural and intimate common bonds. As an antidote to the modernist nostalgia for the being in common, translation becomes a safeguard of sorts against the complicity of this nostalgia with fascism.[25] Consequently, translation questions not only the organicist concept of the work of art but also the organicist notion of a unified linguistic community—community of speech without difference or artifice. If translation can be seen as a form of criticism, then this criticism undoes the aestheticization of linguistic community—or what Benjamin calls, in "The Work of Art in the Age of Mechanical Reproduction," the aestheticization of politics.

Benjamin argues that translation interrupts the linguistic immanence of a given community because it liberates the effects of pure language from the "weight" of the particular meaning: "It is the task of the translator . . . to liberate the language *imprisoned in a work in his re-creation of that work*" (*I*, 80, emphasis added).[26] Again the essay resorts to a metaphor to describe the effects of such liberation. As a circle touched by a tangent, translation "touches the original lightly and only at the infinitely small point of the sense," in order to pursue "its own course according to the laws of fidelity in the freedom of linguistic flux" ("so berührt die Übersetzung flüchtig und nur in dem unendlich kleinen Punkte des Sinnes das Original, um nach dem Gesetze der Treue in der Freiheit der Sprachbewegung ihre eigenste Bahn zu verfolgen," (*I*, 80).[27] This last metaphor is also the most startling depiction of what Benjamin means by "the sacrifice of truth for the sake of transmissibility." As in his analysis of Kafka's parables, here too Benjamin stresses the "law of the journey," that is, the trajectory, the path (*die Bahn*) and the movement of language (*Sprachbewegung*), and not the origin or destination, not *Punkte des Sinnes*. Yet it is precisely this transformation of specific languages, the expansion of linguistic norms and conventions in the direction of pure lan-

guage, that constitutes both the task and the threat of translation—silence and the loss of meaning in the "bottomless depth
of language": "Hölderlin's translations in particular are subject
to the enormous danger inherent in all translations (and transmissibility as such, we might add): the gates of a language thus
expanded and modified may slam shut and enclose the translator with silence" (*I*, 81, emphasis added). The beauty of Kafka's parables, like the beauty of Hölderlin's translations, both of
which Benjamin so admires, lies in a similar estrangement and
extension of language beyond the shared linguistic norms and
the commonality of linguistic criteria.

A similar dissolution of the context and disintegration of
meaning is performed by the other kind of transmissibility—
what Benjamin calls mechanical reproduction. Like translation, mechanical reproduction detaches an object from its
unique place and time within the tradition and substitutes for
its unique existence, for its authenticity, a plurality of copies
that can function in a multiplicity of new historical situations.
Although this transposition of contexts reactivates the reproduced object, retaining thus the minimum of its identity, at the
same time it shatters the "authenticity," or the *aura*, of the
work of art as well as the consistency of tradition (*I*, 221). Like
translation, reproduction does not affect the stability of the
work of art merely from the outside, especially in the case of
new art, for example film and photography, that is already "designed for reproducibility." Consequently, the process of reproduction not only does not preserve the integrity of the original
but entails a radical revision of the traditional aesthetic categories such as authenticity, the organic concept of the *work* of art,
and the disinterested contemplation of art. When Benjamin
compares classical painting with film, photography, or Dada poetry, he points out that the concept of totality and unity of the
work of art gives way to the assemblage of multiple fragments.

Although transmissibility questions the very concepts of origin, authenticity, and truth, this does not mean that the significance of the work of art collapses either into linguistic skepticism or into aestheticism. On the contrary, as Benjamin makes
clear, the disintegration of the aura destroys the aesthetic dis-

tance, that is, the separateness or the autonomy of the work of art, and therefore opens up a possibility for the politicization of art. And yet, because of the radical fragmentation and heterogeneity of the reproduced art, its meaning cannot be absorbed or contemplated in the process of reception. Because reproducibility causes dispersion of meaning, Benjamin relates reception of the work of art to the shock effect. Consequently, even though reproduction destroys separateness or the distance of the work of art, this does not entail an assimilation of art into social praxis but rather a disintegration of the cultural and social context in which the work of art is received.[28] It is this disruption of social and linguistic immanence that opens a possibility of critical revision of both aesthetics and social praxis.

Both kinds of transmissibility—translation or mechanical reproduction—have a similar shattering effect on the consistency of tradition and truth: they perform a fragmentation of meaning by displacing the work of art from its linguistic or historical context. Whereas the relation of exemplification implies the stability of the context or system in which an example is imbedded (the dependence of an example on a general truth or idea), transmissibility dissolves such stability by displacing the work of art into a foreign location. By insisting on a disjunction between transmissibility and truth, Benjamin, in spite of the rhetoric of kinship, puts into question both the primacy of origin and the continuity of derivation.[29] Still, this loss of the consistency of truth, and the subsequent loss of the unity and integrity of meaning, is linked, for Benjamin, both to the sense of obligation and to the possibility of critical intervention.

Benjamin's theory of translation not only illuminates but perhaps is in turn informed by Kafka's parables. Can we say that Kafka's works already include their own intralinear translation? (In his "The Task of the Translator," Benjamin suggests that most of the great works of art do so.) Such a statement of course cannot mean that Kafka's parables lay special claim to completeness but rather that they initiate the process of violent transformation, which brackets the norms of the common language and questions the mastery of the native speakers. Benjamin's emphasis on the estrangement of the familiar language, on the shattering of the myth of the mother tongue and of the nostalgia for a community, describes in fact not only Benjamin's own complicated relationship to German culture but also Kafka's. As Kafka writes in a well-known letter to Max Brod, this multilingual situation of Jewish writers, writing in German and living in Prague, results in "three impossibilities":

They existed among three impossibilities, which I just happen to call linguistic impossibilities. . . . These are: The impossibility of not writing, the impossibility of writing German, the impossibility of writing differently. One might also add a fourth impossibility, the impossibility of writing. . . . Thus what resulted was a literature impossible in all respects, a gypsy literature which had stolen the German child out of its cradle.[30]

Finding himself a stranger in every language, Kafka literally writes under the exigency of translation, which makes the traditional concept of literature "impossible in all respects."

Such "gypsy" writing, which violates linguistic norms of propriety and property, reconceptualizes the notion of literary language and its relationship to truth and to linguistic community. The characteristic movement of Kafka's parables and their problematic destination is perhaps most explicitly addressed in two very famous texts, "On Parables" ("Von den Gleichnissen") and "My Destination" ("Das Ziel"). The first text, "On Parables,"[31] is structured around the opposition between the wise, who speak their wisdom only in parables, and the "many," who complain that such words of wisdom are without use in everyday life. The dispute concerns two different concepts of language: The many insist that language should have a clear referential status, and that it should remain "closely" embedded in community and social praxis. The words of the wise on the other hand disrupt this closeness and familiarity by performing the act of crossing over to "something unknown to us," to "some fabulous yonder." Parables may be the words of wisdom, but useless and deadly wisdom because they do not bring the truth closer (*näher*) to us, to our life. On the contrary, parables separate language from the immediacy of the here and now, from life, and from the expression of the singular or collective subject. Contrary to the expectations of the anonymous listen-

ers, the parabolic language questions the unproblematic relation between literary language, everyday practice and the familiarity of the communal bonds. Consequently, parables do not
intend to "translate" truth into an ordinary language, but rather
estrange the familiar language so that the stability of linguistic
and communal norms can no longer be taken for granted:

> When the sage says: "Go over," [*Gehe hinüber*], he does not mean that
> we should cross to some actual place [*die andere Seite*, literally, an-
> other side] . . . ; he means some fabulous yonder [*sagenhaftes Drüben*],
> something unknown to us, something too that he cannot designate
> more precisely [*das auch von ihm nicht näher zu bezeichnen ist*, liter-
> ally, more closely] and therefore cannot help us *here* in the very least.
> (*PP*, 10–11, emphasis mine).

This complaint of the "many" might arise from an unexpected difference between the parables and the traditional examples, which precisely are supposed to make the truth immediately intuitable, to make it appear in the proximity of our understanding. As Kant writes in the preface to the *Critique of
Practical Reason*, examples do not introduce anything new to
our knowledge, but they have the important pedagogical role of
manifesting the truth in the immediacy of the here and now.
However, the particular transfer operating in Kafka's parables
takes us away from knowing, from progressing to a precise destination, or from any sense of destination at all. Disrupting the
closure of linguistic norms, the act of crossing performed by
parables merely displaces us from what is familiar and does not
promise in return any specific location where the movement of
the parable would come to rest. Instead of the proximity of
truth, it increases the distance between the words and their
meaning—even the sage cannot indicate the direction of the
parable "more closely." Since this movement severs language
from "the life we have," the adverb *hinüber* indicates the direction of death, which—like the silence in Hölderlin's translations or the emblem of the skull in baroque allegory—is the ultimate loss of signification. Perhaps it is the anticipation of
death as the only limit to the restless displacement from the
present site that unsettles the process of demarcation and con-
textual grounding. The movement of the parable, its perpetual

"going over," undermines proper (*eigentlich*) meaning, the stability of the linguistic norms, and the possession of truth in everyday life. Because of the transgression of every determining site, not only are parables unable to "help" us *here* in our daily life, but this loss of referential meaning is not compensated by any promise of transcendental wisdom.

This relentless crossing that the parable performs does not leave the initial distinction between the parable and reality (*Wirklichkeit*) intact. The reality in Kafka's text is associated with the set of values based on life, property, pragmatic knowledge, practical results (*das Ergebnis*), and the immediacy of here and now. In the context of such values, parables appear to disclose only negative wisdom: they "merely say that the incomprehensible is incomprehensible" and therefore seem to be deprived of any social relevance. Although it is tempting to read Kafka's figuration of the parabolic language as a manifestation of the complete dissociation of the work of art from the social praxis, such reading would in fact contain the effects of disruption and limit them to the level of aesthetics. However, the transgressive power of the parables does not allow them either to rest in the negative knowledge of skepticism or to confine that negativity to aesthetic alone. As the ending of the text shows, any clear sense of distinction between reality and the parable, between the aesthetic and social praxis, disappears. The desire to separate the disturbing effects of the parable from reality becomes a matter of gambling, which may bring a gain for the sake of reality, but always a loss in the parable.

So what happens when we follow the parables? The interpreters themselves become "incomprehensible" parables, propelled away from their own self-presence and self-understanding. Consequently, the parable questions not only social but also subjective knowledge: "Würdet ihr den Gleichnissen folgen, dann wäret ihr selbst Gleichnisse geworden und damit schon der täglichen Mühe frei" ("If you only followed the parables you yourselves would become parables and with that rid of all your daily cares," *PP*, 10–11). This problematic destination (*das Ziel*) of Kafka's parables and their enigmatic promise of freedom is elucidated in a very short text, "My Destination" (*Das Ziel*), whose main character can be read as one who follows the parables. It is a story of a master who prepares for a "truly long journey." However, the only destination that he wants to reach is to be out-of-reach, always Away-From-Here: " 'Weg-von-hier,' das ist mein Ziel." In a very peculiar twist of the familiar causal relations, destination is described only in terms of a displacement from the present site, or a disruption of immanence. Such retranslation of the most familiar terms collapses the very distinction between the departure and destination, mastery and servitude, bcause language also departs from its own categories and criteria. Ironically, the parable undermines any teleological fulfillment, such as destination, aim, or possession, within the very rhetoric of teleology that sets its narrative in motion.

This division between those who are concerned with life and those who follow the parables operates in other Kafka stories. In contrast with the characters who want to be admitted and reach their destination, the figures of the drifters—the absentminded window gazers, meditators without an object to meditate on—constantly risk losing the ground under their feet:

I stand on the end platform of the tram and am completely unsure of my footing in this world, in this town, in my family. Not even casually could I indicate any claims that I might rightly advance in any direction. I have not even any defence to offer for standing on this platform, . . . letting myself be carried along by this tram.[32]

"Unsure of their footing in the world," these figures are frequently called writers. Dramatizing a lack of fulfillment and an absence of specific destination, the examples of art in Kafka's parables precisely undermine the ground "under our feet." The performance of Kafkan artists, like the trapeze artist or the hunger artist, strives for a perpetual suspension rather than a permanent grounding. Although they seem to represent extreme aestheticism, these figures of artists disrupt and question the very boundary between performance and ordinary life, between literary and common language.

The movement of transmissibility, which parables perform when they do not say what they mean, when they disrupt sociolinguistic norms and the sense of proper meaning, is associated with the movement of figurative language. Benjamin him-

self considers transmissibility to be an irreducible feature of poetic language: Kafka "did fail in his grandiose attempt to
convert poetry into doctrine, to turn it into a parable and restore
to it that stability . . . which, in the face of *reason*, seemed to
him to be the only appropriate thing for it" (*I*, 129, emphasis
added). Precisely because of this failure, or at least what appears
as failure in the face of reason, Kafka's texts accomplish something opposite: they turn the language of reason and doctrine
into the figurative, literary language of poetry.

Although the crossing of the parable has been compared to
the metaphorical transfer,[33] let us point to the important difference between Kafka's parables and classical definition of metaphor based on resemblance. Indeed, the word "parable" in German, *das Gleichnis*—coming from *gleich*, "similar, like," but
also "equal"—would suggest that such metaphorical transfer
operates on the basis of analogy, similitude, or likeness. This etymology emphasizes resemblance and correspondence, which
allows for the metaphoric substitution of properties. However,
what Kafka describes in *Gleichnis* does not operate on the basis
of resemblance; "going across" fails to bridge two poles of metaphorical exchange just as it fails to connect the point of departure with the point of destination. It is an impossible crossing
that disrupts the links of similarity or claims to continuity. In
an endless departure from any stable site, the movement of
Gleichnis cannot rest in a crystallization of a complete figure.
In Kafka's writing, there is always an extra turn that disrupts
the likeness that is the basis of metaphorical crossing. The frequently recurring figures of crossing in Kafka's parables (en-
trances, doors, bridges, gates, joints, and graves) dramatize this
unpredictable turning of figurative language. The stability of
metaphorical transfer is disrupted by turning of the figure upon
itself. Not surprisingly, metaphors in Kafka's parables extend or
violate the boundaries of linguistic norms, which secure the social exchange and communication in discursive community.
The story "The Bridge" ("Die Brücke") presents but one of the
many examples of such a fateful metaphoric turn, interrupting
the traffic of social exchange: "A bridge to turn around! I had not
yet turned quite around when I already began to fall, I fell and in

a moment I was torn and transpierced by the sharp rocks which had always gazed up at me so peacefully from rushing water" (*CS*, 412).

The Pit of Babel: Translation as the Limit of Formalism and of Linguistic Community

It is not surprising that Kafka should reach to the most exemplary story on language, transmission, and translation—the biblical text of the Tower of Babel. In the wake of the Babelian confusion of tongues, Kafka's parables investigate the effects of translation on the formation of linguistic community and on modern aesthetics. Kafka's revision of the biblical story juxtaposes two opposite tendencies in language. On the one hand, Kafka explores the ways in which a structural or architectonic aspect of language can both presuppose the unity of the common speech and secure an expression of the communal essence. As the monument of construction and signification, the Tower of Babel already assumes, or at least anticipates, the unity of the native tongue and the unity of community. This complicity between construction and communal speech in Kafka's parables questions not only the possibility of pure formalism separated from social praxis but also the natural unity of linguistic community free from conventionality and artifice. On the other hand, the failure of such a monumental task of exemplary construction points to the necessity of translation. Since translation reveals differences, dispersion, and heterogeneity already at work in the native language, it functions as the limit of both formalism and communal unity.

But we should first consider the "original" biblical text whose twists and tropes inform both Kafka's parables and Benjamin's "The Task of the Translator." From the very beginning the biblical narrative makes explicit the exemplary social function of the tower, which is supposed not only to reach the sky but also to express the name of the builders.[34] The undertaking of this gigantic architectural project is possible in the first place because of the unity of the communal speech: "the whole earth was of one language and one speech" (Genesis 11:1). This reciprocal unity of language and community, a precondition for the coherence of the architectural structure, is very forcefully expressed in a Hebrew idiom: "speaking with the same lip" (Hirsch, 204). "Speaking with the same lip" suggests not only the phonetic sameness of speech but also transparency of language, which, by precluding all misunderstanding, secures social wholeness. To return to Benjamin's aphorism at this point, "speaking with the same lip" would give us both the access to truth and the guarantee of its transmissibility. The divine intervention confirms this terrifying power of human language: "Behold, the people is one, and they have all one language; and this they begin to do: and now nothing will be restrained from them, which they have imagined to do" (Genesis 11:6). Such prelapsarian language poses no resistance to the project of exemplary construction.

However, what is already suspicious about the primordial and seemingly unmediated unity of language and community is the people's anxiety about making a name for themselves and their fear of dispersion, both in a geographical and in a linguistic sense. The unity of language makes the construction of the tower possible, but at the same time it calls for its protection against dispersion. The preservation of this language as well as the fulfillment of the edifying task depends on the successful completion of the tower with its top in the sky. The tower then not merely demonstrates the power of human language ("nothing will be restrained from them") but already functions as a protective complement. A certain defect in the "speech with the same lip" calls for the mediation of the architectural project in order to express the name of the people and secure its transmission through the links of genealogical continuity. The unity of "speech with the same lip" is therefore not unmediated but relies on construction/figuration as a means of both expression and preservation. This state of language reflects the double bind of the exemplary narrative itself, in which the moral relies on the mediation of both the redundant narrative and incomplete figural language.

The advent of translation, a result of divine intervention, dissolves the desired unity of the community into the multiplicity of tongues, after which neither the completion of the tower nor the exemplary expression of the name for the generations to come is possible. In his essay "Des Tours de Babel" (The Tower of Babel), Derrida suggests that this biblical "origin" of translation not only points to the multiplicity of tongues but also the limits of the structural stability of language:

The "tower of Babel" does not merely figure the irreducible multiplicity of tongues; it exhibits an incompletion, the impossibility of finishing, of totalizing, of saturating, of completing something on the order of edification, architectural construction, system and architectonics. What the multiplicity of idioms actually limits is not only a "true" translation, a transparent and adequate interexpression, it is also a structural order, a coherence of construct. There is then (let us translate) something like an internal limit to formalization, an incompleteness of the constructure.[35]

This incompletness—this interminable postponement of closure that Derrida underscores in his reading—has to be interpreted not only in the formalist but also in the social sense. With an ironic twist of the builders' intentions, God's punishment does not erase the possibility of expression altogether but merely perpetuates the inglorious name for the tower and the builders. Confusion, scattering, reversal are part of this naming act, which is already a retranslation of the name that the builders intended for themselves: "Therefore is the name of it called Babel; because the Lord did there confound the language of all earth: and thence did the Lord scatter them abroad upon the face of the earth" (Genesis 11:9). This double aspect of God's act (destruction and reinscription of the intended meaning) raises the question about the significance and the consequences of the divine punishment. In his *A Commentary on the Book of Genesis*, Umberto Cassuto gives the literal translation of the phrase "they shall not understand" as "they shall not hear" (Cassuto, 247). Thus, God not only confuses people's tongues and lips but also their ears. The destruction of "speaking with the same lip" also destroys a possibility of hearing with the same "ear"—that is, a faithful reception, repetition, translation of the message. Consequently, this dispersion of linguistic unity in turn undercuts the unmediated unity of the discursive community. To use Stanley Cavell's terminology, the figure of the Tower of Babel precisely destroys the primordial *attunement* of the speakers, their agreement in judgments, their capacity to share the same language.

This confusion of hearing might provide some explanation of the problematic ending of the biblical text. Apparently, the story elucidates the meaning by giving an etymological explication of the name "Babel." Yet the fulfillment of this etiological task is based on mishearing and mistranslation, on the confusion of two different words through phonic similarity. Almost all biblical commentators warn us not to take this etymology literally: "This explanation of . . . Babel . . . is of course etymologically irrelevant; it was popularly invented, for Babel means 'gate of God' " (Rad, 145). The biblical text, we are told, derives its etymology from the Hebrew "balal," whereas the derivation "proper" comes from the Mesopotamian word "Bab-ili"—gate of God (Cassuto, 229). Thus the whole etiological purpose of the narrative is based on a linguistic confusion, a turn of translation that allows for the obliteration of a primary sense and the reinscription of a derogatory meaning. And it is not one act of mistranslation among others, but the most devastating one, since it confuses the transcendental foundation of meaning—the gate of God, which the tower hopes to reach—with scattering and confusion. Marking the incompleteness of figuration and the dispersion of communal unity, the advent of translation replaces the intended signification and in effect "guarantees" the improper etymology of the proper name. Thus the linguistic and architectonic structure is incomplete on both sides: it cannot provide the safe transmission of the transcendental message, but it does not reach the state of total obliteration either. It remains an emblem of translation, threatening with confusion and unexpected reversals of meaning.

As in the biblical text, the architectonic edifices in Kafka's parables are intertwined with the transmission of obscure messages and precarious ideas "in their magnitude" (PP, 37–39).[36] In his many reinterpretations of the biblical story, Kafka explicitly emphasizes the parallel between the unfinished construction, confused language, and dispersed community. Emblematic of the space between the gate of God and babbling, the

Tower of Babel hovers over all of Kafka's fiction in the form of its castles, temples, and burrows but is most explicitly evoked in several short texts like "The Tower of Babel," "The Pit of Babel," "The City's Coat of Arms," and "The Great Wall and the Tower of Babel."

Kafka develops the figure of the tower in terms of the basic oppositions implied in the biblical story: ascent/descent, exemplification of truth/confusion, tower/pit, building/digging, communal unity/dispersion. The shortest, almost aphoristic piece, "The Tower of Babel," juxtaposes the spiritual ascent with the failure of the building: "if it had been possible to build the Tower of Babel without ascending it, the work would have been permitted" (*PP*, 35). In the most laconic form, this commentary points out that the project of construction predicated upon ideas of unity, completeness, and internal harmony is inevitably subordinated to some metaphysical aim. What is at stake is not the actual skills of building but the desire of ascent attached to them. What does it mean to ascend the Tower of Babel? To reach the gate of God—to gain the higher realm of wisdom—or to re-create the original unity of the community? Whatever we mean by this "fabulous yonder" (*PP*, 11), ascending to the top also echoes a familiar hermeneutical task of reaching the peak of understanding and truth. Constructions like the Tower of Babel would always tempt us with a disclosure of the ultimate truth, and it is primarily for that reason that their completion is perpetually postponed in Kafka's parables.

Is there any way of escaping from the construction/ascension pattern, from the structure promising the disclosure of truth and the unity of the community? Although many of Kafka's texts elaborate such "routes of escape," we will focus on his two parables "The Pit of Babel" and "The City's Coat of Arms."[37] Announcing "that some progress must be made," the anonymous worker in the first of those texts proposes digging a subterranean passage, the pit, instead of building the tower:

What are you building?—I want to dig a subterranean passage [*Gang*]. Some progress must be made. My station [*Standort*] up there is much too high.
We are digging the pit of Babel. (*PP*, 35)

The pattern is no longer an ascent but a descent, an immersion in the formlessness of earth, which suggests a complete resignation from any revelation of truth. In this transmission of the biblical text, the central metaphor of construction is deliberately confused with digging and endless lateral extension: the word "building" (*bauen*) in the question is replaced by "digging" (*graben*) in the answer. This improper substitution is already a result of a wrong hearing, an unpredictable turn of figuration. Digging as a form of "progress" implies then a radical departure from the ideas of structural unity and coherence associated with architectural metaphors and especially from the promise of "ascent" or disclosure of truth that invariably accompanies them. By contrast, Kafka's anonymous digger is not motivated by any desire of ascent but complains that his standpoint "up there is much too high." No longer bound to express a name or to signify, his work is an attempt to escape from "up there." In search of alternatives to "exemplary" constructions, the pits and burrows in Kafka's parables suggest a deliberate "progression" of the text into darkness and obscurity.

The substitution of the word "digging" for "building" and of "pit"/"passage" for "the tower" conveys the idea of the formation of a different text, no longer submitted to the ideal of unity, coherent organization, and exemplary expression. A similar transformation of the function of the structure in "The Burrow" has been analyzed by Henry Sussman: "[t]he construction consists in the hollowing, not protrusion, in addition of complication, not assertion, in the expansion of darkness, not illumination. The construction is already deconstruction to the same extent that it has been constructed."[38] In the context of the explicit reference to the biblical narrative, such a text intensifies the effects of translation. It not only reverses the author's intentions and thereby destroys the legibility of the text but also removes the ground of social and linguistic unification. With its shift from the singular to collective enunciation, the summative comment of the conversation—"we are digging the pit of Babel" (*PP*, 35)—implies a total collapse of the exemplary structure and the impending communal dispersion. Instead of crystallizing one governing figure, the text deepens an abyss that prevents the saturation of exemplary meaning.

Such failure of the "art of building" and the loss of the "primacy of idea" is explicitly thematized in "The City's Coat of Arms" ("Das Stadtwappen"). This parable accounts for the constant deferral of the building of the Tower of Babel as the result of the workers' deep mistrust in their present skills, which might not be sufficient for materializing "the idea of . . . the tower that will reach to heaven." What paralyses the generation of builders is then a sense of an unbridgeable gap between the unmediated idea and the discontinuous and imperfect process of mediation/expression. This sense of a gap produces fear that the next generation might "find the work of their predecessors bad, and tear down what has been built so as to begin anew" (PP, 37–39). Thus the work of mediation, even when it is called progress, is ironically interconnected with destruction: tearing down, ruining, indeed hollowing out the previous construction. The very progress in the skills of building is what threatens both the continuity of construction and the genealogical continuity between the generations of workers. This fear of transmissibility—that the next generation will not continue the work of the previous one, but will realize the "idea" in a different way—is what makes the builders hesitate even to lay the foundations.

Such reasoning, which tries to find a compromise between the stability of the idea and the incompleteness of the construction, deferring the task of fulfillment always to the next generation, results in yet another paralyzing impasse. The apparent flaw lies in the workers' assumption that the essential thing is the very idea of building and that everything else is secondary: "The idea, once seized in its magnitude, can never vanish again" (PP, 37). This general opinion asserts the primacy of thought, truth, and the immediate contemplation of an exemplary idea. However, the defect in what seems to be merely secondary—the limitation of both the material and linguistic resources—not only reverses this hierarchy but eventually destroys the irresistible idea itself: "To this must be added that the second or third generation had already recognized the senselessness of building a heaven-reaching tower [*die Sinnlosigkeit des Himmelsturmbaus*]" (*PP*, 38–39). In this way, the divine punishment in the biblical text does not even need to occur because all its consequences are already to be found in the nature of construction itself.

In the course of the parable, the art of building becomes a figure of textuality—for example, "art of building" requires "roads" of communication, "digging" means also "engraving," workers are at the same time interpreters—which "tears apart" the totalizing exemplary purpose of the text. It seems that even the workers are aware of this linguistic danger, because in their effort to minimize confusion and multiplicity of tongues, they give much thought to "guides" and "interpreters" who should secure the reliable "roads of communication" (*PP*, 37). What is at stake then in the linguistic impasse brought about by the failure of the exemplary task? In the biblical text, when the roads of communication are destroyed by the advent of translation, the construction of the tower is abandoned. In Kafka's text, however, mere reflection on the temporality of transmissibility already undermines the stability of the transcendental idea and thus leads to the impossibility of even starting the construction—"such thoughts paralyzed people's powers" (*PP*, 39).

This paralysis thematized in Kafka's text raises again a question whether it is possible to build, write, interpret when we already know "that the incomprehensible is incomprehensible" (*PP*, 11). Walter Benjamin argues, however, that this failure of the transcendental purpose is not an impasse but a liberating force in Kafka's prose: "To do justice to the figure of Kafka in its purity and its peculiar beauty one must never lose sight of one thing: it is the purity and beauty of failure. . . . One is tempted to say: once he was certain of eventual failure, everything worked out for him *en route* as in a dream" (*I*, 144–45). Thus, the failure that Benjamin discusses is not a sign of skepticism in Kafka's texts but rather is transformed into a strange condition of creativity and social exchange. Kafka's parable not only narrates the failure of the tower but also shows how this failure unpredictably gives rise to a "bastard child": a city whose inhabitants produce new sages and new songs. As in "The Pit of

Babel," the impasse of the exemplary construction unexpectedly breeds an alternative route, a mere sidetracking at first,
which then takes the place of the original project. By the time
the builders have recognized the senselessness of the tower,
they find themselves already deeply involved in the unplanned
city. The city is a completely different type of construction and
presupposes a different understanding of the community: de-
centered, heterogeneous, built without any governing idea. It
arises out of endless confusion, disputes and wars between various nationalities, already caught in the predicament of translation. It does not possess any fixed boundaries or structure, but
its monstrous growth is fueled precisely by the development of
the skills of construction and destruction occasioned by the
conflict between generations and nationalities. It spreads by ac-
commodating the multiplicity of tongues and the war of de-
sires. Such monstrous growth is a further "proof" for the leaders
that in the absence of the communal unity the construction of
the tower should be deferred.

Mirroring the predicament of the builders of the city, Kafka's
own interpretation of the biblical text reflects the possibilities
and risks of intertextuality. As "The City's Coat of Arms" implies, each generation of workers/interpreters, driven by "irresistible desire" to complete the structure, will eventually "tear
apart" what has already been built. When completion or supplementation of the previous text is indistinguishable from its destruction, then the process of transmissibility implied in Kafka's parables subverts the stability of transcendental ideas both
in their own discourse and in the texts that serve them as ante-
cedents.

"The Ground Under Our Feet": "The Great Wall of China"

Transmissibility, which allows us to account for the movement of Kafka's language transgressing the determining contexts and the bounds of linguistic norms (always Away-From-
Here), prevents the crystallization of a unified meaning. Such a
transgressive movement of language questions the possibility

of the common ground, of some underlying although frequently hidden foundation that would anchor the text in order to preserve the integrity and stability of its meaning. All the more interesting in this connection are stories like "The Great Wall of China" ("Beim Bau der Chinesischen Mauer"), in which the metaphor of the foundation, of the common ground, is very prominent. Kafka's parables explore the figure of the ground in a double sense: in the epistemological sense as the foundation of truth (*Wahrheitsgrund*) and in the social sense as the unity of the community sustained by its common ways of speaking (the ground under *our* feet). The attempt to restore the lost "true Word" to the community in "Investigations of a Dog" ("Forschungen eines Hundes"), for example, turns around the double notion of a ground (the ground of science on the one hand and the "foundation of universal dog nature" and existence on the other), though both kinds of investigations bring about violence and monstrosity. As Cavell argues, these two ways of grounding the meaning of the text reflect also two different senses of the exemplary task: in the first case this task can be understood as a revelation of truth, in the second as a restoration of the representative speech.[39] By looking more closely at parables like "Prometheus" and "The Great Wall of China," we are going to ask the question whether the dissolution of the epistemological foundation can be compensated for by the unity of the community. In other words, can transmissibility be regulated by the community "speaking with the same lip"? Can the linguistic unity of the community restore a possibility of exemplary stories?

Kafka's "Prometheus" focuses on the effects of transmissibility with respect to the epistemological rather than the social ground of truth. It raises the question about the ground of its own linguistic performance, which is especially evident in the recurrence of the word "ground" (*Grund*) in German compounds such as *grundlos* and *Wahrheitsgrund* (*PP*, 82). This story, like every Kafka parable, tries to explain "the inexplicable," but instead of providing an exemplary message, it wearily multiplies the versions of itself. Thus, not only does Kafka retell here the myth handed down by tradition, but the narration itself proceeds by progressively turning away from each successive variation. This movement of supplementation and dissolution empties out previous crystallizations of myth and furthermore points out that the wearisomeness of such repetition eventually collapses the legend into the inexplicable.

Kafka's retelling of the myth of Prometheus brings into focus two kinds of transmission. As a messenger who steals, Prometheus is a figure of an improper and discontinuous transmission. In contrast, the outcome of the Greek myth thematizes what a proper repetition might be in the figure of the endlessly renewable punishment. Yet it is precisely the possibility of perpetual repetition (repetition that does not affect the integrity of meaning) that the turns of Kafka's parable undermine: "Nach der vierten *wurde* man des *grundlos Gewordenen* müde. Die Götter *wurden* müde, die Adler *wurden* müde, die Wunde schloss sich müde" ("According to the fourth, every one grew weary of the meaningless affair. The Gods grew weary, the eagles grew weary, the wound closed wearily," *PP*, 82–83, emphasis mine). The movement of becoming and turning into (*werden*)—the peculiar unfolding of the parable—performs the ungrounding of truth, the dissolution of the common site sustaining all the variations of myth. The parable turns into *grundlos Gewordenen*—a groundless affair (literally, groundless outcome). The parable may derive from a substratum of truth (*Wahrheitsgrund*), but in its progressive turns it has "in turn to end in the inexplicable." The German *grundlos* can mean both "boundless" and "groundless" or "unfounded." Both of these connotations—lack of determining boundaries and lack of foundation—point to the two aspects of transmission: it is precisely because of the opening up of the determining frames that we can no longer find the secure foundation of truth in Kafka's text.

Yet, as the parable "The Great Wall of China" shows, this dissolution of the epistemological ground of truth sustains a desire for the other kind of grounding and for a different kind of myth—for the unity of the community reflected in the common ways of speaking. From the outset we are told that the wall cannot fulfill its function either as the foundation of a new

Tower of Babel or as the secure boundary of the empire because the continuous construction is replaced by a piecemeal work, which leaves many gaps open for penetration from the outside. Piecemeal construction (*Teilbau*) is characterized by the heterogeneous collage of fragments, unexpected transfers and shifts in the composition, problematic junctions, and necessary gaps, all of which forever postpone totalization and closure of the work. The story is an investigation into the necessity of such a construction, which for all practical purposes is only "a makeshift, and therefore inexpedient" (*CS*, 240).

The sequence of the parables investigates the disturbing social uses of such an "inexpedient" construction. It also reveals how the common ways of talking are created and sustained in the first place. Rather than serving as a protection against "the wild hordes" of the enemies, the wall with its discontinuous structure perpetuates the threat of external invasion. And it is this imaginary threat of penetration from the outside that provides the most expedient means to neutralize alterity inside the community: to exclude everything that is foreign, contaminating, or unsettling to its linguistic unity. The porous wall consolidates the community of speech in more pervasive ways than the work of any closure would be able to accomplish: it binds the people together by making them define themselves against the threat of the other—the foreigners, who are in turn marked as locusts or wild beasts, that is, as those who are deprived of community, speech, and humanity. Thus, the unification of the sociolinguistic space simultaneously demarcates its outside as dangerous, inarticulate, and destructive. Because the wall by itself does not provide a rigid distinction between the native and the foreign, it points out that only the united people—those who have overcome "the confines of the narrow circulation of one body" for the sake of the collective body of the nation—can preserve this difference: "Unity! Unity! Shoulder to shoulder, a ring of brothers, a current of blood no longer confined within the narrow circulation of one body, but sweetly rolling and yet ever returning throughout the endless leagues of China" (*CS*, 238). The metaphor of the collective body conveys the sense of a uniform social space that rests on the unmediated common ways of "speaking with the same lip" rather than on social institutions or conventions. The transmission of messages within such a community is like the continuous and uninterrupted flow of blood within the body—it only furnishes a further proof of its organic unity. It is as if these common ways of speaking or standing are supposed to give the community the very ground on which its feet can rest.

Although the wall with its piecemeal construction cannot secure this sociolinguistic unity against external contamination, the very weakness in its construction (the discontinuities and gaps, and the shifts in the direction of building) proves "to be one of the greatest unifying influences among our people; indeed, if one may dare to use the expression, the very ground on which we live." And the fact that this "fundamental" (the one that becomes the fundament) weakness is not available to further interpretation implies that the unity of the community would have to be presupposed—or, to use Stanley Cavell's word, acknowledged—rather than proved.[40] What is at stake in those dreams of the community is not only the understanding of truth but also the possibility of dwelling, or rather, *footing*, in the world:

All the more remarkable is it that this very weakness should seem to be one of the greatest unifying influences among our people; indeed, if one may dare to use the expression, the very ground on which we live. To set about establishing a fundamental defect here would mean undermining not only our consciences, but, what is far worse, our feet. (CS, 247–48)

The great wall can provide such stable "footing" by locating difference and alterity on the outside and also by sustaining a perpetual threat of their violent penetration into the inside. What the course of the parable insists on, however, is that the fatal alterity infects the body of the community always already from within. The "stupendous" work of closure reveals that the inside of the empire is so heterogenous and unsurveyable that it cannot be subsumed under one body. The sheer vastness of the empire cannot be embraced or traversed: "So vast is our land that no fable could do justice to its vastness, the heavens can scarcely span it." With the eclipse of the uniform sociolinguistic space, the circulation of messages between the emperor and the distant subjects no longer flows "like blood within the body," but is characterized by interruptions and spatiotemporal reversals, which undermine the stable poles of the sender, message, and receiver. As one of the parables proclaims, the emperor sends his message on his deathbed, but his message cannot traverse freely even within the imperial palace because of the collapse of the communal unity:

> But the multitudes are so vast; their numbers have no end. . . . But instead how vainly does he wear out his strength; still he is only making his way through the chambers of the innermost palace; never will he get to the end of them; . . . and if he succeeded in that nothing would be gained; the courts would still have to be crossed; and after the courts, the second outer palace; and once more the stairs and the courts; and once more another palace; and so on for thousands of years. (CS, 244)

What this passage implies is that the figure of the one discursive body is both composed of and disrupted by the dregs and the formless sediments of the city. By exposing a fatal alterity inhabiting the common body this paralysis of circulation disarticulates the vision of the unified social space. Furthermore, the unsettling power of transmission endlessly postpones the moment when the people could embrace the "palpable living reality to their breasts," for it confuses the living with the dead, the luminous presence with the ghost. Taking the risk of undermining "our feet," the parable suggests that the very idea of the community as one living body is only a "figure fortuitously exalted from an urn already crumbled to dust" (CS, 245). As translation shatters the aura of the work of art, so too Kafka's parables deprive ordinary communal speech of its life and fragment the organic unity of the common body. By returning the social body to its grave, Kafka's text once again leaves us with a sense of failure. Yet this failure not only destroys the possibility of grounding the exemplary meaning of the text in the common ways of speaking but also exposes a violence inherent in that kind of grounding. Thus, for Kafka as for Benjamin, it is precisely the beauty of failure that disrupts the aestheticization of politics and enables in turn the politicization of aesthetics.

*

Intending to articulate what is "entirely new" in Kafka's parables, Benjamin theorizes transmissibility in the context of the
possibilities and limitations of modernity. Kafka's relation to
modernity cannot be grasped, however, when his texts are interpreted in terms of skepticism, the lost truth, or the inaccessible transcendental; as Benjamin notes, many writers before
Kafka have faced and accommodated themselves to such metaphysical predicaments. Benjamin's insight into the process of
transmissibility in Kafka's texts offers a way out of this impasse. For Benjamin, what is transmitted is not the "consistency of truth" but the essential possibility of its refiguration.
As he writes, "Kafka's writings are by their nature parables. But
it is their misery and their beauty that they had to become *more*
than parables" (*I*, 144). As if accepting the bet presented in "On
Parables," Benjamin thus interprets the deficiency of Kafka's
parables, their apparent testimony to the loss of truth as a "predicament" of the modern age, as a gain, and links this surplus to
a peculiar obligation. Although it destroys the consistency of
truth and tradition, this obligation of "transmissibility" questions the notion of modernity both as a critical overcoming of
the past and as a project to provide criteria for itself out of its
own present situation.[41] By disrupting both linguistic and social
immanence, the obligation of transmission orients the text to
an unreachable past, the truth of which can no longer be recuperated in the present, and thus it opens a future without a calculable destination. No longer tied to the recuperation of truth,
this sense of obligation nonetheless enables Kafka to make a
critical intervention into aestheticism without succumbing to
the modern nostalgia for the lost community.[42] Thus, although
Kafka's parables often stress a destructive character of transmissibility, its "tearing apart" of the inherited systems and traditions, they also present it as a liberating process, and, Benjamin adds, as hope.

PART III

Exemplarity in Philosophy

IRENE E. HARVEY

Exemplarity and the Origins of Legislation

"Ah! Sien grazie ai Numi!"
("Ah! Praised by the Gods!")
Radames[1]
—Giuseppe Verdi, *Aida*

Plato claimed, in contrasting the example of the 'slave-doctor' with that of the 'free-doctor,' that all laws should have a double structure.[2] This duplicity entails an element of coercion or of threat on the one hand and an element of persuasion on the other. The slave-doctor *dictates* his remedies, diagnosis, and prognosis to the slave; the free-doctor's technique entails learning about the patient in order to better persuade him or her to follow the doctor's advice. Revising this double doctor example, Plato later claims that these two elements are not both laws. Rather the slave-doctor's technique can be seen as law *proper*, whereas the free-doctor's can serve as the example for the *preamble* to the law. The preamble, like a *prelude* in music, introduces the law, preparing the listener to hear it in a certain way. Indeed, it frames audibility itself as it relates to a willingness or unwillingness to act. The preamble thus serves as a *pre-text* such that the law will not simply be heard but the legislator, in announcing the law, will be convincing and thereby able to establish his pronouncements *as law*.

The role of exemplarity in establishing the differences between the pre-text or preamble and the law proper was thus central in Plato long before it became so once again for Rousseau. Indeed, Plato's notion of the legislator can itself be seen as a pre-text, as an Exemplar and an example for Rousseau's claims considered as law. This structure would allow us to see Rousseau himself as a legislator and his texts, in particular *The Social*

Contract, as his announcements of law—indeed, the law of the law.[3] It is a short step from this point of view to seeing Rousseau's texts as a critique of law, in the Kantian sense; that is, as revealing or at least examining the conditions of the possibility of law. The latter perspective, attained via these multiple pretexts, is the one I will trace here. The role of exemplarity in turn will be shown to be more than a pre-text; indeed, I will show that it is capable of reframing the notion of pre-text (and hence, pretext) itself as a constitutive and presupposed, though unthematized, structure of exemplarity.

My particular focus will be the three intellectual forebears chosen explicitly by Rousseau as the Exemplars and examples of the legislator. These three forefathers are also denied the rights of paternity by Rousseau, and by this denial he denies as well the constitutive, formative, indeed progenitive nature of exemplarity. His reading of, or pre-text for, these examples thus situates them within his discourse as mere examples, yet also outside of his discourse as Exemplars or models upon which he bases his own claims for the Legislator. We must therefore examine this double relation, parallel to Plato's two types of doctors, so as to reveal Rousseau's double reading and double framing not only of the capacities, criteria, and character needed in a legislator but also of the legislator's task, responsibility, and limits.

The three forebears who authorize the notion of the Legislator for Rousseau are (in this order of appearance and importance, as we shall show later): Moses, Lycurgus, and Numa. Lawgivers and legislators all, historical or legendary figures whom Rousseau *implants* within his discourse *as examples*. It is precisely this *as-structure* that inhabits exemplarity itself, which we shall proceed to examine.

The issue of the authority of the legislator is thus raised at the same instant as that of the authority of the examples chosen, and the choice itself of particular examples. The unthematized necessity of these choices will be shown to be no accident for Rousseau's project or for exemplarity in general. His concealment of the choice by exposing it as his claim that they are "accidental" will be investigated in the light of this usage as strategic and rhetorical rather than extrinsic, external, and reducible. The constitutive links between the exemplifier and exemplified will again be explored here.

Finally, I will consider the example of examples—the frame of the frame or the pre-text of the pre-text concerning the legislator in particular. This model of models is a fiction created by Rousseau to serve his own ends, but in the name of a truth, under the guise of truth, and explicitly articulated as a double relation. That is to say, the notion of "Moses" cuts at least two ways for Rousseau since "Moses" is the example of examples insofar as his laws have endured the test of time, are still in effect, and remain powerful despite all types of opposition placed by history in the path of Jewish law as a way of life. On the one hand, Rousseau criticizes "Moses" with respect to the performance of miracles (Moses' pre-text) as a method of offering evidence for the divine authority of his discourse. On the other hand, Rousseau insists that the Legislator must have recourse to the rhetorical ploy of this reliance on an *apparent* divine origin for the laws. The *vulgar* will not understand, follow, or be receptive to the legislation without a pre-text. This tangle of displacements can be thematized via the issue of exemplarity insofar as Rousseau uses "Moses" as an example rather than Moses and insofar as the example that actually frames the issue is claimed to be merely a supplement, mere illustration for clarification, and thus external to the discourse. But this so-called supplement will emerge here as the foundation of Rousseau's text, as well as the origin of the origin of legislation, though he can never be acknowledged as such. In short, the improper will be shown to ground the proper such that a certain illegitimacy, lie, vice, sin, immorality and illegality not only is unavoidable in the constitution of law but founds the possibility of the reverse. But these structures of exemplarity are prior to the distinction given above: rather than being subject to them, exemplarity instead makes them possible. We shall thus begin with Rousseau's location of the examples concerning the origins of legislation and his rhetorical ploy concerning the rhetorical ploys of the Legislator himself.

Preconditions of Legislation

Rousseau's approach to his own examples of legislators is anything but direct. They are neither introduced to us as models, or Exemplars, nor mentioned in what might be called the "preamble" concerning the law of the law. Rather, he sets up preconditions that are necessary if not sufficient conditions for the possibility of *effective* legislation. That is to say, the origins of legislation, according to Rousseau, entail a certain readiness of the people, a ripeness, he calls it, a certain genius that arises in this historical vortex, and a variety of social, political, military, economic, and religious circumstances that come together to form the context for the possibility of legislation. In addition, the wisdom of the legislator-to-be must be manifest in a particular understanding of "the people" and in turn an understanding of his own role, as lawgiver, such that he will be (1) comprehended and (2) listened to and obeyed by them. Prior to examining the role of exemplarity here, we must begin with an examination of Rousseau's own claims concerning the preconditions of legislation. In turn, the role of Moses, Lycurgus, and Numa as constitutive, albeit behind the scenes at this point, will emerge explicitly as a result of this "pre-text" of pre-texts.

The Context of Readiness for Legislation

Rousseau was often concerned to follow the example of Montesquieu concerning the limits of applicability of any general principles to a particular historical, cultural, or geographical setting.[4] Nonetheless, a set of preconditions is listed by Rousseau concerning the conditions of the possibility of legislation in general. To begin with, "the people," not yet a people as such, not yet a true sovereign power, perhaps still in slavery, still under the yoke of a dictator or in a state of anarchy of some sort: this "people" should nonetheless "already be connected by some common origin" (*SC*, 95), by interest or convention. But ideally they should not have a set of customs or superstitions that are already well-entrenched or immutable. In other words, the unity of the people is more of a legacy and hence a prophecy than an actuality. It is this proto-unity, a hidden unity, a sleeping unity, that the legislator will come to awaken, realize, and make its conditions of manifestation possible.

Further, the community should not have "carried the yoke of law" (*SC*, 95) as yet. We have a people here on the verge of liberty, morality, and virtue who have never known them. It is a "people" at the point of its political puberty, or at the moment of discovery of itself, indeed, at the moment of discovery of its "maturity," its political ripeness for law. In short, the legislator will lead "the people" to recognize itself as such—to eat of the tree of knowledge, of law; to awaken to the knowledge of good and evil. The legislator is thus at once the liberator of the people, their savior, and also their downfall, their serpentine seducer. This double motif will arise again shortly with respect to the rhetoric of the legislator.

Concerning the stability of this "people," Rousseau insists that they should ideally not be at war, not on the verge of a sudden conquest or invasion; in short, they should not be fighting with their neighbors but should have the capacity to do so and to win, should a battle arise. This latent military capacity provides for a certain independence, a certain stability, and thus for the possibility for economic self-sufficiency as well. To provide all the basic necessities of life, for and by means of each other, and to be economically and militarily independent of other nations and states, is thus one of the preconditions for political independence and the establishment of law. In turn it is clear that the limits of laws are also established by this context such that the legislator-to-be will have an effect on only one people; for Rousseau, there is no legislator in general, though the legislator need not be a homegrown or hometown boy. Indeed, he can be and in many senses should be an outsider in relation to the community. But this position is nontransferable; the laws for one people cannot and should not be the laws for another.

The size of the proto-people, already demarcated by a common origin, a shared land, common defense, and economic cooperation, should be large enough to provide all of the above internally but small enough so that "each member can be known by all" (*SC*, 95). In short, it is not the example of the Roman Empire that Rousseau cites here concerning the readiness for laws, but rather that of Sparta prior to and during the emergence of Lycurgus. It is also the example of the Israelites, enslaved in the land of Egypt, waiting for Moses, in some sense at least.

Given the above conditions, Rousseau insists that there must arise, for legislation to be enacted, for the State to be founded, for a people to be created, and, hence, for true sovereignty to be possible, an extraordinary man of great wisdom—unique in abilities, in foresight and with a particular understanding of the people and his role in their destiny.

Characteristics of the Legislator

First, it is necessary to understand why the legislator must be a man, according to Rousseau, and could not (ought not) be a woman. He does not flatly proclaim this, but all that he says of women makes his position quite clear on the matter. Sophie, as the proto-type of woman, as formulated via the "fiction" of *Emile*, as destined to be Emile's wife, the mother of Emile's children, is destined by nature to serve man.[5] A woman's bio-social constitution, despite in some ways being an "empire over man," (*E*, 371) fundamentally limits her political participation. She determines nothing; she is determined. Her role is submission—free submission—to the law of man; indeed, to man's law. We should recall that this act is the very meaning of freedom for Rousseau in general; man is free insofar as he submits to the law. The law offers this reward or consequence insofar as it is the embodiment of the General Will; the General Will is just insofar as it is true to itself and pronounces only the good of the whole, the public good, public interest rather than private. The latter is the root of corruption and vice. Thus to the extent that woman rejects man's law she is the origin of vice and corruption and, potentially, the downfall of the State.

In turn, Rousseau determines that a woman's proper place is determined by nature, by biology, understood as both capacities and incapacities particular to woman—to be in the home, to be a wife/servant to man, and mother/servant to his children. She does not educate, she nurtures; she does not learn, she acquires habits; she does not reason, she acts; she does not discuss, she pleads; she does not complain, she cries. In short, women remain paradoxically prepubescent yet also the source of sexuality itself. The issue here, however, is simply that women are excluded *a priori* by "the nature of things," (*E*, 394), from the political role of legislator. It is not a woman's place to lead men but to follow them.

The man, then, who would be legislator must be capable of recognizing all of the above: the preconditions of ripeness of a people to become a people. The legislator as midwife is not an accidental motif here, despite the prohibition of women from this domain.

Nothing can authorize the legislator since he is essentially outside of constitutional legitimacy and propriety (*SC*, 85). As the origin and founder of the State, the "inventor of the machine," not its technician, as Rousseau claims, the legislator has no peer, no equal, no confidante and can have no authorization but what he creates in the eyes of the people. We shall return to this, but suffice it to say for the moment that the legislator knows (and he must know to be a legislator) that he acts without example, without precedent; and in order to create, he creates *ex nihilo* and without authority—unlawfully founding the law. And this of necessity.

What he must do, Rousseau says, is "dare to undertake to give institutions to a nation" (*SC*, 85), and hence, he ought to feel himself capable of changing human nature. The character of the legislator thus entails a certain audacity, a certain leap into the future, a wager, a risk, and a judgment. He is expected to "transform every individual," to "deprive man of his natural powers in order to endow him with some that are alien to him" (*SC*, 85). He must make man dependent on others for his survival. The status of this very particular man must be analysed here. He takes the burden of freeing humanity—a nation, at least—upon his shoulders. He must see himself as capable of changing human nature. He himself is not changed by this, yet he is already the product of his own action. What this mirroring entails is that the legislator must see himself on the one hand as unique and outside of humanity, and on the other as just another man who is subject to laws prior to the enactment of laws as such. The issue here must be: which laws is the legislator subject to?

Laws of reason? Laws of nature? Divine law? Clearly the legislator is not subject to societal laws, is not part of the constitution, as Rousseau says, does not rule as such, but makes ruling
itself possible. In this sense he is outside of the laws. Thus it
would seem that he is only subject to the law of nature, which
is force, not persuasion, not reason. It is the law of the strongest.
The legislator is, however, not authorized, by Rousseau, to use
force. He is not a slave-doctor but a free-doctor: he must persuade the people, not force them (SC, 87). The legislator should
not be mistaken for a usurper of power. Thus the people must
be living in peace rather than war, Rousseau claims, so that
they will not be victimized by one who would masquerade as a
legislator. The question still remains as to which laws, if any,
the legislator must be subject to, or predisposed toward, in order
to be a legislator and in order to legislate effectively. These laws,
neither societal nor natural, must be seen as divine, Rousseau
will claim, and the "as" of their appearance will be our focus of
analysis shortly. But first, the legislator must also have an understanding of "the people", their limits of understanding, their
needs; and he must know how to reach them with his laws so
that the laws will not emerge stillborn, or be "scattered before
swine."

Understanding "the People" as "the Vulgar"

Rousseau has no illusions concerning the natural inequalities
and differences of capabilities between one man and another.
Natural talent and its unequal distribution among a population
leads us away from *amour de soi* and toward *amour propre* with
all the latter's ensuing problems and vices. Thus it is not surprising that the legislator has no equals, no peers, and presumably no rivals—at least, no true rivals. Nonetheless, ideally, the
people should not be led by anyone other than themselves; they
ought, as free, to be the authors of their own laws (SC, 83). In
fact, however, "the people" prior to the establishment of law
should be recognized by us and the legislator as "a blind multitude, which often knows not what it wishes because it rarely
knows what is good for it" (SC, 83). The people, Rousseau
claims, "always desire the good," and this is their strength and

the fundamental hope for humanity, but (and this is the problem that grounds the need and legislation of the legislator) "they do not always discern [the good]" (*SC*, 83). Hence, an abyss is opened up here concerning the people's knowledge of their own good and their desire. Their desire canot be faulted and should not be altered; it is this that allows the legislator to legislate, to be heard, and to have something (of value) to say (to the people). But the reason the legislator is needed and is indispensable is that only he can lead the people to recognize what they know already but do not realize. The legislator thus helps the people to remember, as Plato would put it, what they already know. The legislator in this light appears as an educator in the sense of the Socratic pedagogue in the *Meno*. He asks leading questions, with a hidden agenda in mind, and brings the people to recognize what they will see as "their own wisdom" via that of the legislator. In this sense, the legislator is the one who will *show* the people the path that they are *already* seeking. Thus the social, economic, cultural, and military preconditions surface again as the network of forces that have led the people to seek in the first place. They are in need of legislation and the legislator and in some respects at least they recognize this need.

But, the legislator in seeing all of this must realize that "the people" "must be made to see objects as they are" (*SC*, 94). The legislator is the bearer of truth, the one who unveils the realities of things as they are; yet it is also the legislator who "changes human nature" (*SC*, 85), who creates *ex nihilo*, who "invents the machine." Rousseau's reliance on a rhetorical or magical motif is thus already surfacing here. It is not simply a restorative recognition that is at stake, but a double relation of repetition and difference such that the legislator is not seeking to redeem the people but to give them life for the first time. He will be the father of the people, not their savior. Indeed, once he creates them, he will have no power. His task will be completed and his responsibilities fulfilled.

While "making the people see objects as they are," he is at the same time creating the people and the objects by radically transforming both in the process. The legislator must go beyond "the real," Rousseau argues. One should recall that the above project is already beyond actuality as such but we must move beyond this beyond. The legislator must sometimes make the people see into the future. He must foretell, foresee, and indeed prophesy on the strength of a vision that he cannot and dare not share with them or with anyone. This is the Covenant of the legislator with himself. Rousseau insists that the legislator must also "make the people see objects as they ought to appear" (SC, 94). But how should things appear? What sort of fiction is thus promoted by Rousseau as a *modus operandi* for the legislator? Furthermore, how does the legislator know this? "He is a genius" (SC, 85) is Rousseau's quick and ready response. Even if we grant the wisdom of the legislator, how can he tell the people of such dreams, how can he convince them he is not mad but wise, how can he translate this unreality into a pragmatic program of laws the people will obey? He cannot, Rousseau tells us (SC, 85). Indeed, this stage is the one where Rousseau's examples rise to rescue his notion of the legislator. It is precisely at this point that the "legislator" must rely on something other than himself in order to carry the day and found the state. What is at stake is a rhetorical ploy by which the authority of the legislator can be established beyond question in the eyes of his people, and by which his determination not only of how things "truly are" (presumably not the appearances that the people already have) but also of how they "ought to appear" (clearly at the very least a fictional account of the real) will be accepted and acceptable. The crux of the matter is how the legislator now manipulates all the dimensions introduced thus far in order to "give the laws" to the people in fact. This announcement, made at the right time and place and to the right people, must be performed by the legislator such that his proclamations will be *seen as* and *taken as* laws. They cannot be laws as such but must appear as they ought to be—from the legislator's standpoint, at least. This *as-structure* as a rhetorical ploy must now be examined.

The Rhetorical Ploy

"Always to reason is the mania of small minds. Strong souls have quite another language. It is with this language that one persuades and makes others act" (E, 321). The task of the legislator, as the expression and the condition of the possibility of the expression of the General Will, is fundamentally fourfold. He must create political laws, whereby the State acts upon itself; civil laws, whereby relations between members of a State are regulated; and criminal laws, which are concerned with the disobedient members of the State; and finally he must create what Rousseau calls "public opinion." In fact this latter creation is presupposed not only by the former three, but also by the possibility of the audibility of the legislator as such. Assuming that the preconditions listed above for the emergence of effective legislation have been met, Rousseau insists that the legislator must employ a number of rhetorical ploys in order to pronounce and thereby establish the laws as laws for the people as a people.

As we know, the legislator and the people do not fundamentally speak the same language—not even, or at least not yet, the language of reason. Despite Rousseau's defense of reason in the name of the reformation against Catholic authority, he does not argue for reason or logic to be employed in the foundation of the State or in the strategy of enacting or announcing the laws. Instead, the legislator must appeal to the passions, on the one hand, and divine authority, on the other (another sort of passion, to be sure).

Paradoxically, the passion the legislator must excite is that of "love of country"; indeed, of a country that does not yet exist but that is supposedly desired. One should recall that the desire of "the people" is always for the good and thus always true, but they lack the knowledge of procedure, the method or path by which to reach the good. Hence, the need for the legislator both to lead them to the path and to be the path himself. An additional paradox arises, however, concerning the love of country that the legislator is addressing. The first precept of the laws should be to "love the laws," which are still to come. Thus, love of law is the precondition for the love of law. In turn, Rousseau must reveal a way to establish the love of law that does not presuppose itself. His recourse and ultimate resource is another love, also presupposed, which is fundamentally political. This is a sacred love; indeed, a love of the sacred. Given a religious body of proto-citizens here, the legislator can claim to be relying on God's will, God's desire, and hence to be proclaiming not his own laws but those of God Himself. It is this reliance as a resource, as a rhetorical ploy, that must now be addressed.

Divine Authority

Rousseau openly admits that this supposed divine authority is an appearance and that the legislator himself should keep the truth about this to himself. This secret, which is his alone, is the secret origin of the laws and the possibility of law itself. It is, in short, more than Plato's Noble Lie, though it bears a certain rhetorical kinship with the latter.

In *The Social Contract*, Rousseau explains this tactic in the following way:

And as the lawgiver can for these reasons employ neither force nor argument, he must have recourse to an authority of another order, one which can compel without violence and persuade without convincing.

It is this which has obliged the founders of nations throughout history to appeal to divine intervention and to attribute their wisdom to the Gods; for then the people, feeling subject to the laws of the states as they are to those of nature, and detecting the same hand in the creation of both man and the nation, obey freely and bear with docility the yoke of the public welfare.

A sublime reason, which soars above the heads of the common people, produces those rules which the lawgiver puts into the mouth of the immortals, thus compelling by divine authority persons who cannot be moved by human prudence. (*SC*, 87)

The issue here in the foundation of the foundation of the law is precisely, Who speaks? Who writes? Who authorizes or what authorizes the legislator, who cannot be recognized as such except after the fact, to legislate? Insofar as the legislator cannot rely legitimately on force without becoming a corruption of himself, a usurper of power, or on reason without assuming a parity of intellect with the masses that will remain an ineffective and solitary dream or result in the persecution and/or ostracism of the would-be legislator, he must displace and deny his own authority. It is precisely this displacement—"these are not my laws" (but yours and God's); "it is not I that is speaking" (but the General Will and God); "it is not I that signs" (but you and God)—that is to be used to create the possibility of "the people's" acceptance of his proclamations as law. Thus the legislator explicitly claims to have no authority beyond that of the average member and, hence, of every other member of the State-to-be; yet he must also claim that he alone has been chosen to give or deliver (not create) the laws to the people. He portrays himself as God's messenger, who is somehow closer to God than anyone else yet who is not his own man. He is not free to accept or reject this role—he has no choice in the matter. In short, his persona is one of self-sacrifice, having no signature, no voice of his own. He is the personification of the General Will prior to its establishment. He is, in short, a fiction—a living fiction—who writes his own script yet forges the divine signature in order to make his fiction seem credible and real. What the legislator is not expected to create but must rely on and presuppose in all of this is the love of God and of His Will, His Laws, and His Pronouncements to the people. This love is what will serve the legislator for his own ends, in the name of God and in the name of the people.

Should the people doubt the authority of the legislator, they would be simultaneously doubting their own faith, their own love of God—a blasphemous act. But should the people doubt the signature of the legislator as that of the divine source, then the legislator is revealed as the fraud he truly is. The key issue thus becomes the theatricality of the legislator insofar as the people never find out the true origin of the laws. If need be, the legislator should employ a final disappearing act, following Lycurgus's example, in order to sustain the fiction as real.

Rousseau himself relies on a number of not-so-divine authorities in order to develop this notion of the originator of law and the "divine speech" of the legislator. He turns to examples, historical and legendary, of other legislators who have employed such means effectively to found their respective nations via their respective gods. Far from being truly anonymous, speechless, or illiterate, these examples stand out in the Western tradition precisely because they did sign their laws in the very act of denying the same. The role of exemplarity here in the multiple displacements of authority, from the legislator, from Rousseau (as author and legislator), will be shown to be precisely the framework by which authority is in fact not displaced at all. The device of displacement will be shown to be constitutive of authority, in fact, if not in appearance.

The Authority of "Divine Authority"

The resource and resort of Rousseau for his notion of the legislator is paradoxically not a divine source, at least not directly. Rousseau himself is notably not claiming to be "the voice of God," though he often does claim to speak for or through "the voice of Nature," and the latter is certainly a ventriloquism of God Himself (for Rousseau especially). Nonetheless, at this juncture the issue becomes a question of the origin of the notion of "legislator," which is not simply a question of nature or God. It is rather an issue of exemplarity located within historiography, legendary stories, and textuality itself. Let us turn then to the legislators of the "legislator," first according to Rousseau, who somewhat less than openly admits to this reliance on historical precedents as examples for his "own" theory.

In *The Social Contract*, the examples of legislative authority are in fact rather obliquely mentioned, as if they were mere illustrations of the theory, indeed of the principles that have already been outlined. In refusing to accept "worthless authority" (*SC*, 87) as the basis of the legislator's actions, Rousseau suggests another foundation via Moses and "the child of Ishmael" whose legislative acts have stood the test of time: "Worthless authority may set up transitory bonds, but only wisdom makes lasting ones. The Law of the Hebrews, which still lives, and that of the child of Ishmael which had ruled half the world for ten centuries, still proclaim today the greatness of the men who first enunciated them" (*SC*, 87). What is to be admired here, by these examples, is the permanence established; indeed, the establishment of permanence single-handedly by these respective legislators of each "system of laws." In addition, the signature that has stood the test of time is in each case that of wisdom itself. That these laws are not the foundations of actual States as such but of religion is not addressed by Rousseau. His

aim in highlighting these examples here is to read them as ex-
emplifiers of endurance, of true legislators insofar as the law endures. His other examples, however, do not exemplify this but
instead reveal quite the contrary.

In his work concerning the government of Poland, Rousseau
uses three examples of legislators from the ancients "who de-
serve particular attention." These are, in order, Moses, Lycurgus, and Numa.[6] The question for us will be, what status and
functions do these examples have and what role do they play in
Rousseau's discourse, in his theory of the legislator in general,
and in the relation between these two? In addition, one must
ask: what are the relations between these three examples, what
does their order of appearance itself expose, how do they inter-
act with each other as examples? Furthermore, how are they
read by Rousseau? How does he create a "Moses," a "Lycurgus,"
and a "Numa"? How do the examples betray what they are supposed to exemplify or reproduce? Are they in fact productive
and creative rather than reproductive? Are they pre-text that
only appears in the guise of a postscript, seeming to come after
the fact as accidental appendages to the theory, but are in fact
its progenitors, its unacknowledged city fathers? In short, how
is exemplarity here operating in relation to the signature, as a
result of Rousseau's acknowledgment of the rhetorical ploy
needed by the legislator? Ultimately, the question will be: Is
Rousseau an example of himself? Is he both the sovereign and
the subject of his own discourse? If so, how does exemplarity
play on both sides of the tracks such that it is made to *appear* to
operate in some ways, whereas *in fact* it is operating in quite
other ways?

Let us begin then with Moses and the transformation of
Moses into "Moses," that is to say, into the example of Moses.
This entails seeing Moses *as* an example, and thus the quotation marks could be doubled, if not multiplied indefinitely in
light of the multiple mediations at stake here.

The example of Moses appears explicitly in Rousseau's work
"On the Government of Poland" (*OC III*, 956–59), in conjunction with Lycurgus and Numa; in his "Political Fragments"

(*OC III*, 499), concerning the uniqueness of his laws in relation to those of Solon, Numa, and Lycurgus; and again in *The Social Contract* (*SC*, 87–88), as the Jewish lawgiver whose wisdom is evident in the permanence of his laws. In short, "Moses" appears again and again in Rousseau's discourse on legislation and becomes the key example in this discourse. Let us first examine "Moses" as one of three apparently equally important examples of the legislators of ancient times, as opposed to the "makers of law" of modern times.

Rousseau offers us, in "On the Government of Poland," a portrayal of Moses with which he seeks to exemplify the "spirit of ancient institutions" (*OC III*, 956). Thus "Moses" is already an example in at least three senses of the term: as an example of "ancient legislators," as an example of the spirit of ancient institutions, and as an example of the notion of a legislator as such, as we shall see.

Moses' accomplishments relevant to this role of exemplarity include the following in this context. First, Moses created a political body and a free people out of an errant group of fugitives and slaves without arts, without talents, without arms, without courage, who had no land or property of their own. And second, Moses gave them morals and inalienable customs such as other nations had; he created rites and particular ceremonies, a sense of paternity and unity among the people and gave them an identity that separated them from their neighbors (*OC III*, 957). Thus Moses "transformed human nature": he freed a people; he established an identity, laws, customs, and morality where previously there were none. Moses, therefore, created a State, established the possibility of the social contract and, hence, of sovereignty and the exercise of the General Will for the Hebrews. Moses' rhetorical appeal to divine authority and his performance of miracles to provide evidence for that authority are notably not the issue for Rousseau here.

The role of Moses as an example at this juncture is thus selective and establishes a certain highlighting of some of Moses' accomplishments while neglecting others. This strategy is in evidence in all exemplarity formations. To see Moses *as* an example is thus to create a "Moses" whereby an economy of visibility and invisibility is established. "Moses" is to be seen as "an ancient legislator," as an example of the spirit of ancient institutions, only insofar as the particular accomplishments noted above are in focus. These traits are the issue, not his miracles, not his reluctance to be chosen by God, not his debates with Pharaoh, his delegation of power to Aaron, his fury on descending from Mt. Sinai with the tablets, his smashing of the laws, and so forth. Those acts are indeed exemplary, but not of what Rousseau aims to focus upon. They might in fact conflict with the notion of the legislator that Rousseau wishes to portray. Indeed, the Moses of the Bible[7] is not the Moses that Rousseau is referring to here. He is creating a "Moses" in order then to refer to him; we could call Rousseau's "Moses" anything since it is only by a homonym on the one hand and a catachresis on the other that he uses the name "Moses."

In "*Political Fragments*" Moses arises again but not as one of three apparently equally important examples. Here he is instead the unique example that stands apart from other examples of legislators (*OC III*, 499). This transformation moves Moses into a field by himself: he becomes an example of himself, indeed an Exemplar rather than an example. An Exemplar, as model, is constituted in order to set up an ideal, or a telos, or perhaps a lost origin such that this case of the Exemplar is a limit case. It is a solitary position and usually one that cannot be reached. The example, on the contrary, is one of many possible examples, and its uniqueness is subordinated to its substitutability. The example could equally well be replaced by another like itself, whereas the Exemplar, by its very structure, must lay claim to a uniqueness that overturns all similarity or analogy. The paradoxes here are multiple, but let us examine them through the lens of "Moses" and our issues of legislation and its origins.

The rhetoric that establishes the difference between an Exemplar and a mere substitutable example can be seen in Rousseau's text when he distinguishes "Moses" from Solon, Numa, and Lycurgus. In his earlier text, we should recall, Rousseau offers us a list of seemingly equally privileged mere examples of legislators. These mere examples were, however, also Exemplars insofar as they serve to guide Rousseau's own discourse concerning the government of Poland, but the issue here is that "Moses" is used in two different ways according to two different structures of exemplarity. Under the title "On Jews," in "Political Fragments" (*OC III*, 499), "Moses" is offered as the source of "a surprising and truly unique spectacle." This event is precisely the fact that Jewish law, far from having expired with Moses, has endured for over three thousand years and has done so despite the Jews' lack of a common land or country, despite their transformation and mixing with "innumerable strangers," their dispersion throughout the world, their subjugation and persecution. The law of "Moses" nonetheless survives, Rousseau tells us, and the Jews, as the example of "Moses" here and vice versa, have conserved their customs, their laws, their morals, their patriotic love, and their initial social unification. "Moses" stands above all other legislators in this regard, and in particular above Solon, Numa, and Lycurgus, whose laws, though more recent than those of "Moses," have all without exception disappeared.

Thus "Moses" is more than a mere example here; indeed he becomes the legislator of legislators, in principle if not in fact. So it would appear at least. But again, what has "Moses" left us? What is the legacy of his legislation: laws, customs, morals, love of country, and a social bond. It is worthy of note here that Israel, as a Jewish state, had evidently not been founded in Rousseau's time, nor was it his concern in his discourse. Rather, despite the absence of property, of a land, a country, the *nation* of the Jews survives, and with them, the law of "Moses." That is a legislator.

Rousseau's desire for the permanence of the law—for its immutability and transcendence of all earthly forces that would disrupt, destroy, or weaken it—is clearly in evidence here. But this is not the last word on "Moses." Once again, "Moses" here, as in *The Social Contract*, is an example of the creation of something that endures and that ideally would unite a people through the generations. In short, "Moses'" law has become *sacred*, and not political at all. Thus the Jews had no State, no sovereignty, no political expression of a General Will. Rather, this law, despite its cultural aspects, is fundamentally a religious law insofar as "Moses" is its father. The task of the legislator then is a sacred one, or at least this is one of the lessons one could take from the notion of "Moses" as the Exemplar of the legislator.

On the other hand, one could read "Moses" here as a failure, and a greater failure than his apparent counterparts. The laws of Solon, Lycurgus, and Numa were all secular, though divinely sanctioned via a number of rhetorical structures of legitimation. "Moses," however, not only gave the laws to his people to form a people, not only gave them morals, customs, and so forth, but also gave them a new vision of God. He is the messenger of a God who is seeking to be reborn. This rebirth is what is at stake in the example of "Moses," and the uniqueness of this case turns "Moses" into a bad example, not the best, not the model to follow, but the model to be avoided. The State, though founded via the love of the sacred, is not fundamentally reducible to that. Rather the transformation of human nature effected by the legislator entails the displacement of this love of the sacred for the love of country. "Moses" is not a good example of this, despite or perhaps because of the survival of his laws. Rousseau claims again and again that all States must die; no form of government and no people will endure forever. Rather, it is the nature of political organizations to be essentially finite (SC, 135). Corruption and decay are intrinsic to the political process. States are born and States die. Legislation is by its very nature suitable at best to one people at one time; it cannot keep up with the transformations of the people and will thus inevitably lead to the downfall of the State. Such was the case with Solon, Lycurgus, and Numa (OC III, 957)—for their laws and their States.[8] Such was not the case with "Moses." Thus one must ask: of what service is the example of "Moses" to Rousseau's exposition concerning the origins of legislation? Is he a good example, a bad example, an Exemplar? Is the function of the "Moses" example to be evidence of the historical actuality of Rousseau's principles, or to offer a contrasting particular to that which Rousseau is truly suggesting, or to be an Idea in the Kantian sense, or an inversion of the same? This question can

only be answered via the issue of miracles and magic and the relation of "Moses" to Pharaoh. We shall return to this, but first
let us turn to the case of Lycurgus, as the second in the series of
examples named by Rousseau under the title "spirit of ancient
institutions."

Lycurgus undertook to create a people already degraded by servitude and by the vices that those conditions had created. He
imposed a yoke of chains such as no other people had ever experienced, Rousseau claims, but in doing so he united them and
gave them an identity. He showed them their country in their
laws, in their games, their domesticity, their passions, and their
festivals. He left them no time to be alone, and by this continual
constraint instilled in them a great love of country. This love
was the strongest and most distinctive passion among the Spartans, the one that lifted them "above humanity." Sparta was
only a village, Rousseau admits, but the constitution created by
its laws made it a force before which the Persian Empire trembled. Such at least is the "Lycurgus" that Rousseau seems concerned with here (OC III, 957).

One should notice first the rhetorical structure that marks
"Lycurgus" as not only a mere example but also an Exemplar,
and with him, the example of Sparta as unique. First, the yoke
of chains is unlike any other ever imposed on a people. The
uniqueness of "Lycurgus's" constraints is thus established. He
instilled a love of country that was the strongest and most distinctive passion of the Spartans. Thus the effect of his laws is
also unique—among the Spartans, in their character, as compared with all other passions (also controlled by "Lycurgus's"
laws), the love of country becomes the Exemplar of passion as
such.

The "Lycurgus" example, therefore, as a mere example of an
ancient legislator, nonetheless is the source of the Exemplars
that Sparta and the Spartans alone provide. The Spartan love of
country is unlike that of any other people—stronger and more
pervasive in every aspect of life. "Lycurgus's" laws thus control
the passions in an extreme way, an exemplary way, for Rousseau, and offer us an extreme case of the passion of law as being

the law of passions. That "Lycurgus" obtained his authority from a divine source and that he eventually had to leave Sparta for his laws to survive is not however mentioned here by Rousseau. Apparently, the source of this passion for law is not exemplary, not the model, and not relevant to the issue at hand. Yet, Lycurgus's reliance on the rhetorical ploy of divine authority and hence divine authorization is precisely parallel to the notion that Rousseau articulates for his legislator. Such an evident "contagion"—formative or accidental?—seems strangely omitted here when Rousseau is openly discussing the exemplary roles of these legislators. Is Rousseau concealing something, or has he forgotten this other paternal relation he inherits from Lycurgus? Even more strange is that both "Moses" and "Lycurgus," named and described in tandem in "On the Government of Poland," omit this connection. Is this a rhetorical ploy? What else unites this series of examples? Or what do "Moses" and "Lycurgus" have in common such that they can be seen as examples of the "same thing": as ancient legislators and as the "spirit" (singular for Rousseau) of ancient institutions? Perhaps the answer lies in the third and final example here, that of Numa.

Despite the generally understood role of Romulus in the founding of Rome,[9] Rousseau claims that "Numa was the true founder of Rome" (*OC III*, 957). All that Romulus did was unite the brigands of the area, and this in a way that could not have endured. Numa, on the other hand, gave this unification a solidity, a stability that could survive. He created an indissoluble body, a political body; he transformed the brigands into citizens less by his laws, Rousseau claims, than by his institutions (*OC III*, 957). The latter served to attach one member to the other and render the city a sacred place via a variety of rites and superstitions. Thus "Numa" is to be seen as one who also took the raw material of humanity and formed it into a living body of political consequence. Surprisingly, the power of "Numa" as exemplified here is evidenced more by his institutions than by his laws, nonetheless the legislator cannot establish institutions except by laws. Thus the issue of the creation of laws is also central here despite Rousseau's apparent attempt to displace the focus. Again, the issue here that is strangely omitted is the authority upon which "Numa" acts, that source of his power which in turn makes his proclamations as law into law, rather than empty or idle speech.

We must begin with an examination of Rousseau's own account of these choices of Exemplars or examples of legislators as he enumerates the characteristics that all three share. He insists that "the same spirit" (*OC III*, 958) guided all the ancient legislators. ("All" here presumably refers to all, yet also the three named legislators serving as examples of all through synecdoche. This motif of exemplarity arises often in Rousseau's texts, in particular those concerning theology and education.)

The unifying ground that in turn legitimizes Rousseau's choice of these three examples includes the following, according to Rousseau. All sought a means of attaching the citizens to their respective countries and to each other. They found these means in particular customs, religious ceremonies that by their nature were always exclusive and national. They also found them in the games that brought citizens together, in exercises that strengthened them physically. Finally, they encouraged theater, which united the people by reminding them of a common history, common ancestors, shared pains, virtues, victories, and morals. All of this becomes exemplary and provides a source for emulation, admiration, and unity. For instance, Homer's poetry and the tragedies of Aeschylus, Sophocles, and Euripides all have served such functions (*OC III*, 958).

These methods of unifying the people into a people in each case were effective and lawful, and were the institutions through which the legislator managed to instill and reinforce a tremendous love of country, unification of the citizenry, and a common bond that sanctified the State as such. In short, the private interest was transformed in each case into a public interest. In each case the natural order of self over community was inverted and virtue was born, both as a possibility and as a fact.

Thus Rousseau has established a common bond between his

examples via the rule of law he has laid down for us here, so that through this string of initially seemingly unrelated examples a type of institution is created. They have, Rousseau tells us, the same spirit, and it is this that unites them. In turn, Rousseau, in his use of these three brigands, has made them by means of exemplarity into citizens, playing the same games, founding the same institutions, performing the same rites and rituals, bonded together such that they form a State of legislators. So at least does the situation of exemplarity appear here. Of necessity, however, things are not that simple, not that united, and not that lawful, as we shall see.

We must therefore reread Rousseau's example and seek other common bonds that, though unmentioned by Rousseau, unite them. But as closer scrutiny will show, these bonds in no way unite them according to a public interest, a moral and virtuous interest, but rather unite them according to a law that cannot be acknowledged as such. The leading thread for this analysis will be found in the sequence itself of the three examples, how they create and re-create each other, how the origins of these legislators in fact clash and do not, except by an act of violence or theatricality, offer us a synthetic or unified view of "the spirit" or the "body" of the legislator. In turn we must consider Rousseau's own discounting of precisely these examples.

Discounting the Examples: Intra-Exemplary Structures

Any man can engrave tables of stone, or bribe an oracle, or pretend to secret intercourse with some divinity, or train a bird to speak in his ear, or find some clumsy means to impose on the people. He who is acquainted with such means only will perchance be able to assemble a crowd of foolish persons; but he will never found an empire, and his extravagant work will speedily perish with him. (*SC*, 87)

In this striking claim, we find Rousseau disclaiming the ancestry of his own theory of the legislator. Neither Moses (who engraved the tables of stone), nor Solon or Lycurgus (who bribed oracles), nor Numa (who claimed secret intercourse with a divinity), nor Socrates (who trained a bird to speak in his ear) has any rights to the status of Exemplar for Rousseau's legislator. In this disclaimer, we also find the indictment that none of these men or their "clumsy" methods of assembling "foolish" crowds could ever found an empire. Furthermore, their "extravagant work" will certainly perish with them.

The paradox could not be more surprising since in the next statement "Moses" is again invoked as having founded Jewish law, which "survives to this day." In addition, Solon, Lycurgus, and Numa have all been invoked in other contexts, where Rousseau has valorized their methods of establishing laws and institutions, by which great States were founded: Rome, Sparta and Athens, in particular. The question for us must be: what is signified by this discounting of precisely the examples upon which Rousseau relies? Does it signify? What "other law" is being appealed to here? What ruse of legislation is Rousseau himself employing such that he cannot acknowledge the very origins of his own theory? Why must he deny his own fathers here? Is this a manifestation of a law of exemplarity? We will answer in the affirmative to the latter question and must now proceed to illustrate precisely how we arrive at such a conclusion about Rousseau's text.

We should recall that establishing the origins of legislation entails the use of a rhetorical ploy that situates the origin of the law outside and prior to the legislator. This ploy claims that it is not I, the legislator, who signs the law; rather the law is the work of the gods, indeed the people's gods. This rhetorical ploy was employed by each of the three legislators that Rousseau cites as primary examples. Moses insists to Pharaoh and to the Israelites that his entire project of attempting to free the latter from slavery to the former was God's idea.[10] He is following a divine commandment, he says, and thus others too must listen. Such is the ruse upon which his authority stands, from Rousseau's point of view at least. Likewise, Lycurgus invokes the gods of his people via the oracle in order to ratify his laws and his lawmaking. They authorize and legitimize not only Lycurgus's role as legislator but also his particular legislation as such. Xenophon describes this event of authorization in the following way:

But of all the many beautiful devices contrived by Lycurgus to kindle a willing obedience to the laws in the hearts of the citizens, none, to my mind, was happier or more excellent than his decision not to deliver his code to the people at large until, attended by the most powerful members of the polis, he had betaken himself to Delphi and there inquired of the god whether it were better for Sparta and conducive to her interests to obey the laws which he framed. Not until the divine answer came—"Better will it be in every way"—did he deliver them, laying it down as a last ordinance that to refuse obedience to a code which had the sanction of the Pythian God himself was not only illegal, but impious.[11]

Thus we have testimony of the rhetorical ploy used effectively to establish the laws of Sparta and, in a certain respect, Sparta itself. Rousseau, strangely enough, makes no reference to this rather perfect example of his own theory of the rhetorical ploy necessary as the first act of the legislator.

In Solon's case too, according to Plutarch's text—which Rousseau knew rather intimately and recommended as required reading for the adolescent Emile—an oracle enters the scene in order to sanction his leadership and his legislation. The legend has it, Plutarch tells us, that the oracle said the following words to Solon: "Seat yourself now amidships, for you are the pilot of Athens. Grasp the helm fast in your hands; you have many allies in your city."[12] Thus Solon becomes the lawgiver of Athens and is respected, obeyed, and admired as such.

Numa as well had the knack of introducing a divine source for his own authority and as the origin of his laws and institutions. His rhetorical ploy was slightly more imaginative than those of the others in that he claimed, according to Livy (also a familiar source for Rousseau) that he was "in the habit of meeting the goddess Egeria by night, and that it was her authority which guided him in the establishment of such rites as were most acceptable to the gods and in the appointment of priests to serve each particular deity."[13] Livy even acknowledges this to be a rhetorical ploy rather than a statement of fact when he says that Numa aimed to "inspire them with the fear of the gods." Further, according to Livy, "[s]uch a sentiment was unlikely to reach them unless he first prepared them by inventing some sort of marvellous tale; he pretended therefore."[14] Clearly Numa's tactic was a ruse; clearly he managed to fool the Romans into believing such a tale; and clearly he exploited their belief

in gaining their acceptance of the form and content of his legislation. They willingly obeyed him and his laws since the Goddess herself was their mother and author. She had signed the
laws via intercourse with Numa. Prior to this affair, Numa had
become the legislator of Rome by means of the gods' sanction as
well, though Egeria forms a useful supplement to the initial divine ruse.

In view of all the detail available to Rousseau concerning the
similar rhetorical ploys invoking divine authority used by these
four legislative examples, the issue for us is, why does he fail to
even mention this connection? The fact is, he does not fail to
mention it at all. He openly denies its relevance! As I showed
above with the opening citation, Rousseau overtly denies any
connection between his concept of the legislator and the examples of Moses, Lycurgus, Numa, and Solon when it comes to authorization by divine authorities. The fact of the matter is that
the legislators' rhetorical ploy is not only a hidden law of exemplarity linking all four examples to the "theory of the legislator as such," albeit without being announced by Rousseau,
but this ruse is also the hidden law of the choice of these examples themselves. Although Rousseau claims they show the
spirit of ancient institutions and thus defends his choice of examples, this other, unacknowledged law concerning another
shared and constitutive element (in the framing of Rousseau's
notion of the legislator) is anything but unitary. We have, however, uncovered the law of these examples insofar as this element, more than the rest since it is the element of origin and
paternity, is the ultimate ground of the possibility of the legislator as such. This "law" illustrates the hidden principle governing the choice of these particular examples—why these
rather than others—but it also illustrates paradoxically what
Rousseau cannot acknowledge, namely, the rhetorical ploy operating within his own text, the ploy that authorizes not only
his examples but also the clandestine relation between his notion of legislation and his examples of legislation. His discounting of these examples aims to cover precisely this relation, but
in the act of concealment Rousseau paradoxically reveals the

inverse of his position. There are enough clues to warrant our inversion of his inversion in order to reveal these laws.

The nature of this law of exemplarity is anything but simple, as I mentioned above. First, let us consider precisely how the recourse to divine authority as a ruse is produced. Moses acts the part of the reluctant messenger. It was not his idea to be God's chosen liberator/legislator, and he initially balks at God's request: "But who am I?" (Exodus 3:11). Further he claims he will not know what to say to the Israelites, let alone to Pharaoh. In addition, he implies that the Israelites (not to mention Pharaoh) will never believe him (Exodus 3:13–14). And so the story goes. What is at stake here, in appearance at least, is not a wise extraordinary would-be legislator but an innocent, average, reluctant puppet for what is truly a divine ploy rather than a rhetorical ploy. (Rousseau's position on this inverts the traditional interpretation of Moses since "Moses" is to be placed in the service of legislators—in the company of Lycurgus, Numa, and Solon.) The truth of the origins of "Moses'" legislation would not be that God actually came to him in the burning bush and spoke but rather that "Moses" managed to use these rhetorical ploys in order to persuade the Israelites as well as Pharaoh that he was acting on divine authority rather than according to his own will.

Concerning the case of Lycurgus and Solon, the gods appealed to, rhetorically at least, speak through the oracle at Delphi—the traditional place for the voice of the gods to be heard. That their gods are multiple and Greek makes no difference to the role of exemplarity here. These historical factors, so relevant to the effectiveness of the legislation, can be excluded in the creation of the notion of the legislator as such, and they are. So, too, the Jewish God for "Moses" becomes irrelevant for Rousseau.

Finally, Numa's appeal was to his own and his people's gods as well: the Roman gods. He did not fornicate with a Greek goddess but a Roman one—otherwise his rhetorical ploy would certainly have been ineffective with the Romans.

Thus the law of the examples here, what governs Rousseau's choice of them and governs their connection is also what distinguishes them and does not cohere. There is no concept of god that can entail the Hebrew, the Greek, and the Roman pantheons and thrones. There is no single rhetorical ploy that is or would have been effective in all cases. Thus what is at stake here is itself a rhetorical ploy such that a certain "Moses," a certain "Lycurgus," "Numa," and "Solon" are employed in order to father together—despite their differences—the notion of the legislator as such. In addition, this paternity created by the structure of exemplarity must in turn be denied (via Rousseau's rhetorical ploy in turning to the "nature of things" as God's work concerning authority and legitimacy) in order that the "principle itself" of legislation and all that this entails can be presented as independent of any actual legislator or legislation in fact, in history, or indeed in legend.

The additional relations between these examples induces a certain double vision: what is revealed as irrelevant in fact conceals something, something that not only has greater relevance than first supposed but indeed amounts to a law organizing the relations between the examples themselves. This entails the ordering of the list of examples offered to us.[15] In every case, Rousseau names "Moses" first, then usually "Lycurgus," then "Solon" or "Numa." This privileging of "Moses" as the first in the set is more than a mere accident. "Moses" is in fact the law of the series; he is not just another member—he legislates the legislator. What is at stake here is Rousseau's understanding of Moses in another context that at least seems to have no relation to politics: the context of religion, in which Moses is compared to Christ and the issue of the status of miracles is raised (OC III, 732–34). In his response to criticisms of both The Social Contract and Emile, Rousseau aims to clarify his position on the value of miracles as Exemplars, including their value as evidence of divine power and authority.

How are we to interpret Moses' performance, Rousseau asks, especially when it appears that Christ also performed miracles analogous to those of Moses? Hence, the judgment of one will carry over via the contagion of one example by another and their apparent reversibility. Let us turn now to Moses as a miracle worker in the early days in Egypt, demonstrating his divine connection and thus his own lack of authority which would thereby be inverted and establish precisely the opposite. In addition, we must examine the role of Pharaoh's magicians as they mirror Moses in his miraculous acts. Notably, Rousseau discusses the magicians in *Emile* (*E*, 172–75), emphasizing their need to hide the law of their performance in order that the performance will appear to be what it is: magic. So too, the educator, Rousseau admits, and so too, I will suggest, the legislator.

The Critique: Moses and the Magicians

In Rousseau's third letter "written from the mountain" as a response to the critics of both *Emile* and *The Social Contract*, he seeks to clarify his position concerning the status of miracles (*OC III*, 727–54.) What, if anything, can they be legitimately seen *as examples* of? His accusers insist that *Emile*, through the guise of "a profession of faith of the Savoyard Priest," argues against the veracity and, indeed, the possibility of divinely orchestrated miracles. Hence Rousseau can be seen as impious, and in fact he was accused, as was Socrates, of impiety as well as sedition. The ensuing banning of his writings was thus defended as a safeguard to the well-being of the State—of several States. Rousseau's defense, which could be called an apology (*OC III*, 710), again following Socrates,[16] seeks to reveal not only that his critics have misunderstood him but that they have inverted his claims. Thus the defense seeks to show Rousseau to be more pious, more rational, and more patriotic than his accusers. As is well-known, this defense worked neither for Socrates nor for Rousseau.

However, the issue here for us is not the judicial aspect of Rousseau's debate but the philosophical treatment he offers concerning the multiple roles of "Moses" in his discourse. That "Moses" is contrasted with Christ and then with the magicians (*OC III*, 744–47) will serve to locate the various formulations of this central figure in the constitution of Rousseau's notion of the legislator. So we must make the detour via these multiple "Moseses" and the issue first of miracles and second of magic, in order to return to "the legislator as such" in the light of these possible frameworks for viewing his origins. Let us begin then with Rousseau's defense of his piety via the guise of a critique of the possibility of miracles.

Moses and Christ

Rousseau suggests, as is his usual tactic in his own defense, that a good definition of terminology could present a productive beginning for any debate. To this end, he proposes a list of criteria or qualifications that should characterize anyone claiming to be an *Envoye de Dieu*, or messenger of God. These include the following, which pertain notably to Moses and Christ: (1) the nature of the doctrine espoused—its utility, beauty, saintliness, truth, and profundity; (2) the ones chosen—their saintliness, their truth, their purity of morals and virtues; and (3) the emanation of divine power that interrupts or changes the course of nature by the will of the one who examines it (*OC III*, 728–29). We should recall that the legislator can also be characterized as a messenger of God by virtue of precisely these traits, though Rousseau does not explicitly name him here. The paradoxes involving the saintliness of the doctrine and of the one chosen—saintliness that is supposedly recognizable in advance, allowing a judgment of whether a person is a messenger of God or an imposter—are exposed here, though not addressed as such by Rousseau, with one exception.

This paradox concerns miracles, those emanations of divine power that interrupt or alter the course of nature. Often Rousseau states that using miracles as proofs or indeed as examples of God's authorization of the would-be messenger is an act of metalepsis (reversing the cause and the effect). Just as Augustine insisted that one requires faith in order to understand and thus that belief precedes reason and the methodology of evidence,[17] so Rousseau insists that using miracles as proof of the divine mission of a would-be messenger is simply an inversion of the progress attained by the Reformation. In this regard, Rousseau can indeed be seen as a rationalist; he accepts nothing that has not passed through the trial of reason, regarded as an individual source of authority and veracity. He uses Descartes's methodology, following the example of the *Meditations*, under the guise of the Savoyard Priest's "Profession of Faith" (*OC III*, 721). Rousseau insists that miracles, if they exist, must be held up to the scrutiny of reason and cannot be taken on faith. What can and must be taken on faith is that Christ was in fact who he appeared to be. The exemplary nature of his action was, for Rousseau, proof enough that Christ was of divine origin and authority. His miracles are another issue, and so are those of Moses. Rousseau says, "Rather than the establishing of faith being the object of Jesus' miracles, instead one must have it already in order that the miracles can be performed" (*OC III*, 734). Furthermore, Rousseau claims that his faith in Christ depends in no way on the miracles He performed, *if* that is what they were. On the contrary, he says, "if they [Christians] believe in Jesus because of his miracles, for my part, I believe in spite of his miracles, and I believe that my faith is stronger than theirs" (*OC III*, 735). At this point he begins to turn the tables on his accusers and question their faith since it seems to rely on the "performance of miracles," which Rousseau will now begin to examine.

He claims that miracles are not necessarily signs or examples of God's power and authority speaking through someone since they are not infallible signs. One can be fooled by a trickster, Rousseau observes and hence, the perception of a miracle is the first matter at issue here. How can one know for sure that what one perceives is indeed the truth? Are we not deceived by our senses, however clear and distinct? Furthermore, Rousseau adds to this Cartesian picture the issue of the passions. In the beginning we feel, he says, and our feelings govern our perceptions and in turn our knowledge. So it is to the passions that the legislator too is to appeal in order to effectively persuade "the public."

Again Rousseau begins his discussion with a definition, offering the following as defining criteria of miracles, which he will proceed to analyze: a miracle is (1) an immediate act of divine power; (2) a perceptible change in the order of nature; and (3) a real and visible exception to the laws of nature (*OC III*, 736–37). All of these characteristics can be summarized by the third one, which in fact grounds the others. Insofar as an action violates the laws of nature, its source must be a divine power, and it can be recognized only as a perceptible change in the order of nature. The issue is thus an epistemological one: how can we know a miracle when we see one? The ultimate criterion is that it *violates* the laws of nature. This in turn presupposes, Rousseau argues, that we know all the laws of nature in order that we can know that *one* of them has been violated by this would-be miracle. Do we know all these laws? Will we ever know them? Have we ever known them? All three questions must be answered in the negative; therefore, it follows as a matter of logic that we can *never* absolutely and with certainty recognize a miracle when we see one. The issue ultimately is human fallibility, and insofar as infallibility cannot be assured, miracles cannot be accepted as such.

With this analysis in hand, Rousseau returns to the issue of Christ and reaffirms his faith and conviction in Him despite the performance of what His followers called miracles. Maybe He did perform them, maybe He did not, says Rousseau to his critics, but this is not the proper criterion for piety nor for the acceptance of Christ as the son of God. If his critics think it is (and he knows that they do), that is too bad for them. And he thereby seals his fate, as did Socrates.

Moses used miracles in order to show, by example, that he was under divine orders to do what he was doing. Rousseau's analysis of Moses in the light of his condemnation of miracles thus indicts this would-be messenger of God. Miracles offer no reliable evidence of anything. That Moses used them as proof places him under suspicion, according to Rousseau, and this lifts Christ above the earlier lawgiver since Christ did not need to resort to such a performance as a testimony of his authority. In short, it may have been a ruse when Moses performed miracles, but most likely was not when Christ did (*OC III*, 734–35, 731).

At this point, Rousseau begins to blame the Jews (*OC III*, 733) for demanding such a performance as evidence. That they did not realize the fallibility of human knowledge of miracles leads therefore to the questioning of the veracity of Jewish law—despite its endurance for over three thousand years. He meekly defends the Jews' demand as well, however, insofar as "they wanted a Messiah who would appear to them and be totally miraculous" (*OC III*, 733), but in the name of "true faith" Rousseau sides ultimately with Christ as the real prophet of mankind. Fundamentally, Rousseau insists that Christ's divine authority shows itself in his speech, in predication (*OC III*, 730). That Christ debated with his critics, and won the arguments, offers proof for Rousseau that he was not a trickster, though he may have been a good rhetorician. Moses is seen as a divine messenger only by virtue of his miracles and is thus on shaky ground under the criteria for a bona fide divine messenger.

In addition, Rousseau analyses Moses' competition with the magicians prior to the inscription of the law on the tablets indicting that performance as the pre-text for the reception of the law and in turn further indicting the status of Moses. All of this must seem at least paradoxical, if not troubling, with respect to the role of "Moses" as the Exemplar for the legislator as such. Now it would seem that the status of Moses is in question not only in view of the authenticity of his miracles in relation to Christ's but also in view of his attempt to distinguish his "magic" from that of the Egyptian magicians, who were quick to repeat most of the "miracles" that Moses performed. An examination of this convergence of miracles and magic will lead us to yet another vision of Moses as an example of examples of the legislator.

Moses as a Magician

Having registered his suspicion concerning the validity of miracles as examples and therfore as evidence for divine authority, Rousseau turns again to Moses as he relates to the magicians of Pharaoh. To begin the discussion of this issue, Rousseau makes a distinction between what might be called "true miracles" and "false miracles" (*OC III*, 744). False miracles in this context are events that are indeed truly miraculous but that are used to support a "false doctrine." In other words, the use of miracles as a means to an end is not at issue here (though he has discounted the exemplarity of miracles as such above, including those of Jesus) but rather the end for which those miracles are performed. Such at least is the pre-text set up by Rousseau in order to examine the problem of distinguishing magic from miracles; indeed, to question whether this is possible at all. Rousseau says: "Thus how does one distinguish the ones from the others, and what can verify a miracle, if whoever sees it cannot discern by any assured mark taken from the thing itself if it is a work of God or that of the Devil? It would be necessary to have a second miracle to certify the first" (OC III, 745).

Thus graphic consequences arise for Rousseau concerning the problem of Moses' confrontation with the magicians. That Moses enters into a contest with them at all opens him to the charge implied above that he may in fact be performing tricks rather than miracles—that is, working for the devil rather than God. If there is no intrinsic mark in the event itself that distinguishes a true miracle—performed by God via Moses—from false miracles, presumably performed by a demon through the magicians, what conclusions can we (or Rousseau) draw concerning the authority of Moses? As Rousseau says: "The same authority that attests to miracles attests also to magic, and this authority again proves that the appearance of magic differs in no respect from that of miracle" (OC III, 745).

What is under fire here in comparing Moses and the magicians and their indistinguishable performances, all of which appear to "transgress the laws of nature," is the status of Moses as a divine messenger of God. In the initial phase of the Exodus account of Moses' confrontation with Pharaoh and his battle with the magicians, for every miracle Moses performs as evidence or as an example of his divine authority, the magicians counter with an identical performance of magic that they do not attribute to divine authority, or at least not to Moses' God. Thus Moses' divine examples are indistinguishable from the magicians' examples of magic tricks. Consequently, Moses' authority is placed in question in the eyes of Pharaoh, though of course, in the end, Pharaoh succumbs to Moses' demand that he let the Israelites go, but only as a result, Rousseau insists, of Moses' having outdone the magicians. He wins the battle by performing better magic, not by the performance of miracles over magic. The rhetorical ploy itself is never confirmed, and can never be confirmed once Moses plays into the hands of the magicians by trying to outdo them, trick for trick. That Aaron is the actual mediator in this process alters little, according to Rousseau, since he simply represents another displacement in the process that attributes the authority ultimately to God.

The preamble to the final act is worthy of recall here since it is the turning point in the battle between Moses and the magicians. In Exodus 8:18, we are told: "The magicians tried to produce maggots in the same way by their spells, but they failed. 'It is the finger of God,' said the magicians to Pharaoh, but Pharaoh remained obstinate." Since this trick, which outdoes the magicians, is not enough for Pharaoh, Moses via Aaron via God introduces "swarms of flies," which sweep over the Egyptians but avoid the Hebrews, as an example of the distinction God makes between his Chosen People and others. Pharaoh, we are told, still is not convinced, because God does not want him to be—as we are later informed when God Himself confesses His rhetorical ploy to Moses in order that he can display His divine powers before the Hebrews as He did before Pharaoh. Thus God extends the time of Moses' performances for the benefit of the Hebrews in the name of rhetoric. In the end, we are told, "the magicians were no match for Moses because of the boils, which attacked them and all the Egyptians" (Exodus 9:12). But Pharaoh refuses to accept Moses' demands yet. Pharaoh does eventually claim to be convinced, but this too is a rhetorical ploy aimed at making Moses cease his mischievous behavior, which is wreaking havoc in Egypt (Exodus 9:27). The last act of devastation is of course the "one last plague" whereby the Lord kills every first-born of man and beast during what will be called Passover. Following this disaster, Pharaoh tells, indeed orders Moses and his people to leave, and they do.

Is Pharaoh truly convinced that Moses speaks for God? No—we are told that he admits Moses' authority at least once only to persuade Moses to stop the devastation. Are the Israelites convinced? No—given that they doubt the veracity of Moses' divine claims once they are out of Egypt and begin to encounter adversity along the route to the promised land. Again Moses is forced to perform "miracles" that have the appearance of the Lord's blessing and powers.

All of this is prior to Moses' reception of the laws as such and his original acts of legislation for the Israelites. All of this is, in short, a pre-text, a preamble that will teach us and presumably the Israelites how to read Moses. Rousseau's position on this story is unequivocal since he situates the heart of the matter in the mirror image articulated initially in the contest of tricks between Moses and the magicians. At best, Rousseau admits, "one can thus use true signs in the service of false doctrine; a sign itself proves nothing" (*OC III*, 746). Thus the magicians can be seen as having performed miracles, though in the service of a demon rather than God. A somewhat ironic gesture to be sure on Rousseau's part, but not unusual in his discourse. What he ultimately claims in this regard is that owing to the indistinguishability of the performances in the early stages, nothing can be proven by these acts as such. The performance of miracles is thus inadmissible as evidence for Moses' divine authority not only for the reasons noted above concerning miracles as such but also now for the reasons given in relation to magic. Rousseau says, "And if one admits magic with miracles one has no sure rule, nothing precise or clear to distinguish the ones from the others: hence, miracles prove nothing." (*OC III*, 747).

The issue again appears to be that of certain and infallible criteria to distinguish miracles from magic, criteria that Rousseau illustrates are not possible in principle. That Moses eventually won out proves nothing for Rousseau, except the minimal claim that Moses was certainly a better magician than the official court magicians. Upon this his authority rests, since this and this alone we can say with certainty. That this magic was in fact a divine act rather than a human one is not defensible since there is no evidence—no mark that distinguishes Moses' acts from those of the magicians.

Furthermore, Rousseau claims: "I well know that those persons in a hurry will return to the doctrine: but they forget thereby that if the doctrine is established, the miracle is superfluous and that if it is not then the miracle proves nothing" (*OC*

III, 747). It is worth noting that Rousseau does not refer to the end results of the contest, nor does he need to since his point here is not to make him into a magician but to illustrate the lack of definitive proof of his divine connection. That Moses claimed to have the latter is not in question by Rousseau, but what this claim in fact means is in question.

In effect, Rousseau's reading of Moses, his creation of "Moses," is characterized not only by raising doubts about the meaning of what he said he was doing, but also by establishing his fundamentally secular status. Rousseau reveals here that Moses has no claim to divine authority, in fact, though he does need to rely on this claim (and his magic as its sign) in order to convince Pharaoh and the Israelites. The problem is that in the end the Israelites are not convinced by his miracles, and neither is Pharaoh. Thus miracles and magic as a rhetorical tactic (and this applies to God also, we should recall) can be dispensed with. Moses' power ultimately comes from the laws that he offers with wisdom to his people, not from the performance of miracles.

It is no accident that Rousseau has created a vision of "Moses" that seems to mirror his vision of the legislator. This coincidence, unearthed on our detour into the issue of miracles, is part of what might be termed the "cunning of exemplarity." In framing the frame of the legislator, in framing Moses as "Moses," Rousseau has offered a pre-text through which to understand the origins of legislation, albeit clandestinely. We should recall that "Moses" is introduced in relation to the legislator as both a mere example and as an Exemplar that inverts and subverts its own exemplary status. "Moses'" success in legislating, the fact that his laws and his people endure to this day, is also his failure, from Rousseau's standpoint. His success is theological, not fundamentally political. But Rousseau insists that the task of the legislator is not fundamentally a religious or theological one (*SC*, 85, 186). The would-be legislator, in order to give initial weight and rhetorical power to his claims, needs to use religion for political ends. That "Moses" ended up using politics for religious ends can in no way be a model ultimately for the "legislator as such." This rupture be-

tween the exemplifier and the exemplified will be examined
shortly, but first we must return to Rousseau's notion of the legislator in the light of this new vision of "Moses" as a magician.

The Legislator (Moses) and Exemplarity

Having taken the detour through Rousseau's vision of
"Moses" as more than a simple example, one among others, of
an ancient legislator, I will now return to his notion of the legislator as such and the origins of legislation. The relations between this notion of a legislator as such—his task; his historical, social, economic, and military context; his qualities; his
understanding of the "people"; and his methodology—are not
simply copied from the visions of "Moses" as lawgiver, on the
one hand, and as magician, on the other. We must now examine
these relations as they illustrate in context multiple *structures
of exemplarity* at work, albeit in a somewhat unacknowledged
way, within Rousseau's texts as a whole.

The Choice of Examples

Derrida once claimed concerning his own texts, "the choice
of an example can never be justified absolutely."[18] Yet in analys-
ing Kant's examples, he revealed a hidden logic operating that
would indeed show that the choice of examples is never arbitrary.[19] Is this a contradiction, and how do such claims relate to
Rousseau's choice of "the chosen": "Moses"? First, Derrida's
claims concerning his own and others' examples do not offer a
conflicting or double standard on the status of examples.
Rather, I suggest, the lack of a complete justification must be
seen as "justification" within the argument made thematically
in the text. That is to say, "Moses" as more than a mere substitutable example cannot be justified by Rousseau insofar as the
notion of the legislator as such is claimed to be independent of
and untainted by any particular empirical or historical case of
legislators. The discourse, according to Rousseau, is concerned
with the legislator in principle, and the principles of legislation,
not with a historical representative of those principles (SC, 49).
Thus the weight of the argument falls on the principles, not on

the "necessarily" accidental examples offered as a mere post-script, as detachable from and extrinsic to the issue itself. In other words, the empirical case cannot be offered as a founda-tion for the notion in principle or we no longer have a notion in principle; the latter becomes a mere (illegitimate) extension of the empirical case: an inflation to the level of principle from the level of actuality. An inflation that, in short, cannot be justified. However, that the examples offer us evidence of something more than this accidental and detachable appendage is what Derrida reveals in his analysis of Kant. That examples are not arbitrary or interchangeable but rather integral to the constitu-tion of the "as such" as such is what is at stake here. That they cannot be acknowledged in this way is also clear. Thus we are dealing here with a necessarily clandestine structure that none-theless exhibits a number of lawful properties; indeed, it reveals itself textually in the very *rhetoric of concealment*. The denials of essential relevance, the disclaimers of internal attachment, the claims to substitutability or to a potentially infinite series always betray their opposites. In this case, "Moses" and the se-ries of examples offer such evidence of these other laws operat-ing within Rousseau's text.

Furthermore, that "Moses" becomes the example of exam-ples gives us a clue as to the law of the series of examples and the rather intimate connection between "Moses" and the legis-lator. That "Moses" is constitutive of or at least operative as a framework for the constitution of the "as such" of the legislator must also be denied by Rousseau. But this denial, albeit implicit in the framing of his argument, reveals again that some other values have been imputed to "Moses." Indeed, one finds that "Moses" surfaces again and again in a variety of Rousseau's texts, in a variety of guises, for a number of ostensible purposes. This obsession with "Moses" has been documented above, but we must now turn to the structures of exemplarity in operation there.

The Hermeneutics of Exemplarity

That Rousseau reads "Moses" in a certain way, indeed creates a "Moses" via his reading, has been suggested in a multitude of ways above. The issue becomes, therefore, how is this reading, this creation, possible? According to what is Rousseau's reading of "Moses" as "Moses" as an Example (of a variety of issues) framed? What frames the pre-text here? Is "Moses" the pre-text for the legislator as such? Is the legislator as such the frame of "Moses"?

Let us begin with the hermeneutic tradition of simplicity, coherence, and narrativity.[20] That a text has meaning can be shown, according to this tradition, by synthesizing the parts into a coherent whole. "Totality" and narrativity organize a reading such that wholeness, even as an Idea in the Kantian sense, serves as the origin and telos for the ensuing strategies of reading. Given such a framework, what would a hermenuetics of exemplarity entail? That "x" is seen *as* an example already presupposes a framework of interpretation that contextualizes x as "x." In other words, the claim that "x" is to be seen as an example presupposes a structure of *intentionality* such that the example, once constituted, must therein be seen as an example *of something*. It refers to something outside of itself that has already been named, or promises to be named. Thus the constitution of "x" as an example is not only a reading of x: the constitution of "Moses" is more than a number of readings of aspects of Moses that are brought together to form a new man in no way analogous to Moses. Thus "Moses" is not in an exemplary relation to Moses, though the former is hermeneutically related to the latter.

Insofar as exemplarity operates within a horizon of intentionality (textual intentionality, one might call it), however, the example is not to be seen or read as such.[21] It points beyond itself, indeed disappears totally, in the service of what it exemplifies. Here we have a dynamic that parallels though it is not reducible to the structure of the sign, as both an empirical and an ideal object.[22] Its telos and its essence have been traditionally to disappear in the face of what it represents. To offer itself up for sacrifice, to become invisible, while presenting and saving what it represents, refers to, or means. Likewise, the example seems to offer itself to be sacrificed completely such that the surrounding text, the frame of the example, can return to itself via the examples and recognize itself via the reader. The traditional motif of the detour—as essentially unnecessary but empirically, paradoxically useful—returns here through one of the structures of exemplarity. The problem is that this apparent explanation for what occurs between the exemplifier and the exemplified does not in fact articulate what is occurring.

That the example apparently depends for its meaning on the surrounding text—which both introduces it "as an example" and terminates its effect, surrounding it after the fact and limiting its domain—is not in question here. Both of these frameworks ostensibly control the work of the example and constrain its locale and its power to operate strictly within the limits set out by the frame. The example, it would seem, has no power of its own but borrows its effectiveness precisely from this framing. An example, in this respect, never stands alone, is never an example as such, but rather always exhibits its own incompleteness and dependence. Such is the rhetoric of exemplarity at least. The "other logic" operating here is that the apparent dependence of the example on its frame in fact operates the other way around, the more so in cases where the example is minimized, disclaimed, and denied. The Exemplar admits of this relation, whereas the mere example never does and never can since it is invariably claimed to be accidental and dependent, rather than essential and constitutive of the frame itself.

Let us turn back now to our "example" of these structures: the relations articulated between "Moses" and the legislator. We are not claiming that "Moses" frames the notion of the legislator for Rousseau, but rather that something more complex is in operation here. First, Rousseau creates a "Moses," but the question remains, what frames this creation? Does the legislator as such organize Rousseau's vision of "Moses," allowing it to be created from a selective economizing of Moses? Or is it the other way around? We suggest: neither. Rather there is a double hermeneutic operating here between the mere example and the Exemplar; and also between this relation and the legislator as such. This double hermeneutic involves not simply that one side frames such that the other is framed, but rather that a mutual enframing occurs such that neither side is constituted in advance. In a continual oscillation, each informs and frames the reading and constitution of the other. Neither side comes first; the two are equally primordial. The legislator as such only mirrors "Moses" after the fact, and vice versa. That is, the work of exemplarity operates in such a way as to vibrate between exemplifier and exemplified, the conceptual fluidity of each contaminating the other, enframing the other, constituting the other in the same act in which it constitutes itself.[23] What this means is that exemplarity fundamentally is not a conceptual framework but makes conceptual frameworks as such possible. It is not empirical any more than it is purely intelligible. Rather, exemplarity negotiates this rupture before it is a rupture, and sustains that separation after the rupture is constituted; namely, in the domain of philosophy as such. Exemplarity makes the "as such" possible and impossible at the same time.

In this context, structures of exemplarity in their many guises—offering the "empirical case" as evidence, as precedent, as analogue, as inversion, and so forth—have been shown to organize Rousseau's text in a way that makes his argument, on the thematic level, possible. Derrida, too, has aimed to reveal "another logic," that of the supplement, which operates clandestinely in Rousseau's discourse, and I do not dispute his findings. Rather, I am suggesting here that the "other logic" revealed by Derrida is not the only clandestine operation at work in textuality. There are many, and he has located only one—not the central, key or essential one, at that. What this entails is that the structures of exemplarity as constitutive for philosophy, in Rousseau's case in particular, and potentially for philosophy as such, relativize the would-be usurpation of all intratextual, intradiscursive "other logics" by *differance*. The latter operation cannot usurp the structures of exemplarity without itself turning into an *Ur-Begriff*, or a ground for all other grounds. It is this movement of usurpation in Derrida's claims for *differance* that I reject here—nothing more and nothing less.

The structures of exemplarity suggested above are neither dependent upon nor organized by the logic of supplementarity[24] or of *differance* or of parergonality, though there is a relation. At the very least, I insist that these structures of exemplarity do not cohere and form Exemplarity as such; they do not synthesize into one concept moving in one direction with one telos and one arche; nor do they simply exemplify *differance*. In addition, I suggest that exemplarity and *differance* can and do in fact both inhabit that same "other side" of philosophical textuality, and, potentially, textuality as such. Their relation in more precise terms will be the subject of a larger work. My intention in the above analysis of Rousseau was simply to begin to exhibit the clandestine nature of the structures of exemplarity in general. In turn I must acknowledge that my hidden agenda has been to read Rousseau's text through the lens of exemplarity such that the guiding thread of the legislator as such would be revealed in its oscillating constitution with "Moses," as itself oscillating in a constitutive way to reveal those same structures. Thus the structures have emerged here as structures of the connection between the legislator and "Moses"; they have not been simply presupposed as the framework of claims then imposed on a victim.

Again we find the slave-doctor in discourse with the free-doctor, the pre-text talking with the law. It is the pre-text that must lie, not the law, according to Plato;[25] it is the free-doctor who uses the rhetorical ploy to persuade his patients. Thus freedom is constituted, and thus the origin of the laws cannot be law itself, cannot be the "itself" or the "as such," but rather rests upon a mutual constitution of a legislator and his people, such that neither exists in advance of "the moment of legislation." This first act, however, is not to give the laws but to establish the authority of the legislator as the immanent lawgiver. Thus the legislator uses the pre-text, the lie, in order to establish himself as the example of himself, to make his acts to come exemplary and therefore legitimate. Thus exemplarity operates not only at the origins of legislation but prior to those origins; it makes them possible. Exemplarity in this sense makes the rhetoric of exemplarity itself possible. Can we ask where exemplarity comes from? Is it an originless origin, a clandestine unlawful origin, or an orphan of anonymous origin? To ask the question of origins is to ask the question of exemplarity, but this is not to answer any of the above. The origins of exemplarity can thus be seen only in effect, only after the fact, which is true of all clandestine textual operations. The nature of such structures is to conceal themselves as such in the very acts of productivity, creation, and constitution. Only in the constituted, the produced, the created can the traces of precisely how something became what it is be located. This is true of *differance*, just as it is true of exemplarity. It is, in short, a type of creation *ex nihilo*, and necessarily so.

Rousseau's last word on the subject might well be the following: "I contented myself with being a magician because I was modest; but if I had had the ambition of becoming a Prophet, what would have prevented me from becoming one?" (*OC III*, 738)

DAVID LLOYD

Kant's Examples

At the conclusion of "The Methodology of Taste," the closing section of the first part of *The Critique of Judgment*, Kant evokes as an exemplary moment a cultural situation resembling that which a series of cultural thinkers, notably Georg Lukács and Mikhail Bakhtin, will conceive to be the moment of epic:

There was an age and there were nations in which the active impulse towards a social life *regulated by laws*—what converts a people into a permanent community—grappled with the huge difficulties presented by the trying problem of bringing freedom (and therefore equality also) into union with constraining force (more that of respect and dutiful submission than of fear). And such must have been the age, and such the nation, that first discovered the art of reciprocal communication of ideas between the more cultured and ruder sections of the community, and how to bridge the difference between the amplitude and refinement of the former and the natural simplicity and originality of the latter—in this way hitting upon that mean between higher culture and the modest worth of nature, that forms for taste also, as a sense common to all mankind, that true standard which no rules can supply.
Hardly will a later age dispense with those models.[1]

It is a moment of appealing utopianism in a heretofore rigorously theoretical work, a moment whose appeal can scarcely have been negligible in the disintegrating post-feudal condition of late-eighteenth-century Germany. It can be taken as a document for a historic compromise between an intellectually powerful bourgeoisie with a comparatively underdeveloped economic base and a traditionally powerful but declining aristoc-

In memory of Joel Fineman

racy confronting the spectre of bourgeois revolution. As such, this passage may appear as a blueprint, if not *the* blueprint, for defining the political function of aesthetic culture.[2] For this idealized representation of cultural harmony marks the turn of a "disinterested" aesthetic to serving an interest that is not merely *moral*—for the explicit function of judgment is indeed to mediate from sense and understanding to ethics and reason— but also political. The universal claims of aesthetic culture, the postulation of aesthetic judgment *as if* it were valid for all men, are most political precisely where they claim to be least so, representing, in the very denial of interest, the bourgeois interest in forging a sphere of purely formal equality and identity for all mankind, irrespective of cultural or economic distinctions. The aesthetic sphere is held to transcend all such "contingent" differences, and, with less paradox than might at first seem, it is in the turn to this domain as the *beyond* of political interest that the formal terms of bourgeois ideology are constituted. As we shall see, any reflection upon the aesthetic therefore entails a reflection upon the constitutive elements of bourgeois ideology, and that particularly in relation to the pedagogical formation of the subject.[3]

The concern of this essay, then, is with the fate of aesthetic disinterest when it falls back, as it must, on a pedagogical imperative in order to realize the very conditions of its possibility. To formulate the relation schematically, if judgment mediates between understanding and reason, it is pedagogy that constitutes the bridge between morality and politics. Understanding politics as a mode of freedom effective in the sphere of nature, one can easily grasp how politics itself should require the aesthetic sphere to enable the interaction of what are, for Kant, otherwise entirely discrete spheres. Any pedagogy formed according to aesthetic reflection will therefore be constitutive of the very possibility of politics itself. Central to the analysis of these relations here will be some questions as to the status of the *exemplary* (with which we can scarcely dispense) in the aesthetic and in the pedagogical spheres, which will be akin to logically adjacent questions of representation in the political sphere.

Kant's cultural ideal is not merely ideal; it has the status of an example (*Muster*). As an exemplary moment—and there are others in the third *Critique*—it draws up into a transcendental analysis questions that are inevitably historical.[4] This is not merely a matter of Kant's adducing a historical example by way of illustrating a possible cultural synthesis. That he should do so, and that he should choose, at the end of a century that foregrounded the Roman model to the point of inspiring revolution in both 1776 and 1789, what is apparently a Greek model, are doubtless in themselves interesting details of intellectual history.[5] But the very problem we find in establishing with any certainty that it is indeed the Greek model that Kant has here in mind is indicative of a far more profound, and in this context profoundly problematic, historicization of the aesthetic by way of examples that are as indispensable to the aesthetic itself as they are to "later ages." Our difficulty arises from the fact that Kant's exemplary moment is a formalization of a specific cultural moment that, to use his own terms, derives a concept from a manifold of (historical) phenomena. The concept in question is clearly regulative rather than constitutive: we could not construct such a culture for ourselves, but its supposed prior existence nonetheless regulates our judgment according to the idea of an exemplary union of freedom and constraint. The aesthetic judgment involved here demands the formalization of the specific example (*Beispiel*) in order that it may become exemplary (*musterhaft*) and the singular instance may gain universal validity.

Universal validity is achieved in such a manner by an aesthetic judgment that, in this as in other instances, the formal qualities apparently attributed to the object (namely, the reconciliation of freedom and constraint, the individual and the collective) are in the first instance properties of the judgment itself:

[B]y the name *sensus communis* is to be understood the idea of a *public* sense, i.e., a critical faculty which in its reflective act takes account (*a priori*) of the mode of representation of every one else, in order, *as it were*, to weigh its judgment with the collective reason of mankind, and thereby avoid the illusion arising from subjective and personal conditions which could readily be taken for objective, an illusion that would

exert a prejudicial influence upon its judgment. . . . This . . . is effected
by so far as possible letting go of the element of matter, i.e., sensation,
in our general state of representative activity, and confining attention
to the formal peculiarities of our representation or general state of representative activity. (*CJ*, 151, sec. 40)

The "common" or "public" sense involved here appears as at
one and the same time the foundation for and the product of the
mode of judgment that recurrently produces and depends upon
the identity of the individual subject with mankind in general.
The insistence of such a circularity at the foundation of aesthetic judgment enforces a formal historicization of the aesthetic that is inextricable from its dependence on the exemplary.

To elaborate this point: it would be possible to conceive of the
relationship between the individual subject and mankind in
general as a spatial figure, the subject set then over against the
humanity from which it is differentiated. Such a spatial figure
would perhaps highlight the geography of relations of domination and would certainly accentuate questions of interest. Indeed, such a figure has a certain self-evidence, a self-evidence
that crystallizes in moments of struggle in the fundamentally
antirepresentational forms of barricades and guerrilla warfare.[6]
Kant's example, however, saves representation precisely by en-
dowing a geography of differences with a temporal disposition,
effective at more than one level. In the first place, the example
(*Beispiel* or *Muster*), as an aesthetic presentation that will become the means to the formation of a concept of *glückliche Ver-
einigung* ("happy union"), is suspended between its own age
and a later one (*das Zeitalter . . . ein späteres Zeitalter*). For the
first, being to itself an unreflective totality, this cultural solution cannot be exemplary; for the later age, the example becomes the mark of a certain inadequacy or falling away from an
exemplary original. But in this suspension, the presentation of
the exemplary moment becomes its representation as representative, not of itself, but of an ideal to which even the example
itself must be seen as inadequate. If a later age continues to depend upon an earlier example to conceive of a possible union between constraint and freedom, culture and nature, its very
movement away from nature ("weil es der Natur immer weni-

ger nahe sein wird"), in the *historical* process that differentiates "universal communication" from "the narrow life of the lower animals," necessitates the independence of judgment from the very examples with which it hardly can dispense.

This paradoxical demand is rooted in the first place in the problem of a common sense that is at once the *a priori* foundation of taste *and* its product. The common sense that is the foundation of taste, precisely as a *sense,* cannot be deduced transcendentally or be supplied by universal rule: its exercise as its manifestation depends upon prior examples. But the danger of this dependence is that it threatens to produce dependence in the very subject whose relation to judgment should be one of "free conformity to law." (Without this relation of the individual to humanity in general, we could not even speak of "common sense," for without autonomous subjects there could be no communication through which the universality of common sense could be realized.) At the same time, the common sense that is a universal human property and foundation of the aesthetic, to which appeal is always made in the processes of aesthetic judgment, is in the first place a latency, which must be drawn out and made manifest by the force of examples. The example, a formalization of the particular such that it comes to represent a universal idea, is indispensable to the production of the common sense on which assent to its exemplary or representative status is based. It is the sine qua non of a pedagogy that must produce in its subjects that common sense from which it derives its legitimacy.

An exemplary pedagogy, by virtue of its dependence on examples, must accordingly always entail a formally historical formation of its subjects. This formal historicity is evident at several levels:

1. The exemplary status of the examples called upon in pedagogical practice is predicated on a formalization that is historical, dependent at once on a lapse and an idealizing projection.

2. Only temporally is the common sense latent in each and every human subject realized or developed.

3. The subject of pedagogy is always belated with regard to the examples that are held up for judgment.

4. The subject of pedagogy always falls short of the examples that are projected.

5. The pedagogue is always exemplary for the student, that is, at once precedent and projected as a model.

We will elaborate each one of these propositions in turn.

1. We have already seen, in relation to an example, how the example contains a historical structure, predicated on a historically necessary lapse from what looks like the natural immediacy of a historical culture to itself and projected forward as exemplary of what must be reproduced, artificially or by way of pedagogical formalization, in a future state. Further analysis, by means of a further formalization, will show that the historical character of this example is not an accidental result of the general claims being made but is intrinsic to the structure of the example as such. For an example is always an example for the judgment, and in order to have the general validity or universal communicability of the exemplary (i.e., of that to which the assent of other judgments may be at least formally demanded), the example must be judged for its formal and not for its material or accidental qualities (*CJ*, 151). In the first place, then, comes the presentation of a sensuous manifold, relatively accidental in its internal relations, and only in the second place its representation for the judgment, "letting go of the element of matter" and "confining our attention to the formal peculiarities of our representation or general state of representative activity" (*CJ*, 151). Insofar as it serves as an example, therefore, any object of judgment, whether an apparently atemporal form such as a Grecian urn or an apparently historical matter such as Greek culture, necessarily involves a temporal structure in the movement from presentation to representation, from *Beispiel* to *Muster* (*bleibende Beispiele*) and finally to *Begriff* (cf. *KU*, 300).

2. The exemplarity of the example in its temporal structure is not a characteristic of the object itself (indeed, as we have seen in the example of Greek culture, it cannot be exemplary to or for itself) but must be referred to the "general state of representative activity" of the judging subject. The temporality of the example for this subject is already a function of an exem-

plary temporality in each act of judgment. If we consider only the form of the act of judgment, abstracted from its specific material instance, it becomes exemplary of *any* act of judgment as a universally valid representation of common sense, and that precisely by virtue of the temporal movement from the material to the formal that is definitive of such a judgment. But the act of judgment, formally considered, is simultaneously exemplary of the relation between judgment and the production of common sense, since the repetition of acts of judgment in their formality itself constitutes the sphere of common sense both within each individual and as a public sphere. This entails an analogous formalization, whereby each act of judgment becomes exemplary by rising above "subjective and personal conditions" and by being weighed against the *possible* rather than the actual judgments of others. The formalization within each judgment is therefore exemplary of a necessary formalization of all judgment that is constitutive of the public sphere of common sense. It is not difficult to show that, for Kant, the process described here is formally identical with that which the human race undergoes in the movement from the primitive immediacy of gratification characteristic of "the savage" to the interest in "universal communication" characteristic of civilization.[7]

3. It is to this process of formalization that an exemplary pedagogy is directed, assuming as its metahistorical poles a prior immediacy from which the example lapses (or rises: theology is never far off here)[8] and a projected universal communicability that is at once its goal and its product. On the one hand, it depends on examples, without which it could not produce a *concept* of its end and without which, more importantly, it would become a systematic or "mechanical" rather than an exemplary pedagogy: that is, it would operate by way of determinate concepts upon the understanding rather than by evoking the free play of the subjective judgment. On the other hand, dependence upon examples remains a constant threat to what is to be produced, namely, a free relation of the subject to itself and to others, that is, a *free* conformity to law. There is, at first, the purely empirical problem that the subject of pedagogy has the example held up before him or her, that he or she comes always after the

fact and depends upon the example for edification. That is, however, merely a way of expressing the more critical point that,
precisely because it is a mode of *sense*, common sense cannot
be manifested or produced in the absence of examples. Which is
to say that in a certain sense what is most original to human
being, the foundation of judgment and of communication, if not
indeed of reason itself, is not autonomous but actually dependent upon its objects.[9] The sphere of common sense, properly
one that establishes the identity and equality of all judging human subjects as possible by way of formalization, can only be
produced or reproduced by way of the constant insistence of its
instantiations. The power of the example over the student is accordingly itself a formal and not merely incidental characteristic of aesthetic pedagogy. It is not merely that dependence on
examples—"the go-carts of the judgment"[10]—hampers the independence of the mind emerging from tutelage insofar as the
student mistakes the example for the rule, thereby fixating on
the particular matter rather than the general form. That dependence is moreover a necessary formal consequence of the intrinsic historicity of examples themselves, "with which a later age
can scarcely dispense."

4. The dependence of the belated student upon historical examples is matched by the student's inadequacy with regard to
the exemplary as projected ideal, and again in consequence of
the formal *historicity* of the exemplary. The necessary contingent inadequacy of the student to the ideal projected by pedagogy—a function, so to speak, of lacking age, experience, erudi-
tion or whatever, as well as of institutional positioning—is here
no more than the expression of a systematic incapacity. Only by
the achievement of an entire independence from examples, as
the matter of or for judgment, could the judging subject attain
to the pure formality of the ideal. But even supposing the example were given of an exemplary pedagogy, such indeed as
Kant describes here, in which examples continually give way to
a process of formalization that seeks to dispense with them, the
ideal remains strictly inconceivable without an instance—even
a minimal one—of exemplification that is finally irreducible as
what has to have been formalized.

5. One result of this twofold shortcoming of the student is the inexpungeable melancholy of the pedagogical scene, even, if not especially, in its ironic mode. A certain theological residue taints even the most secular accounts of liberal education both with the idea of a fall from the self-immediacy of that which becomes exemplary but is not that for itself and with the anxiety of an unattainable redemption. But the allure of a melancholy aura should not prevent recognition of the intimate relation between precisely such a model of enlightened education, directed at developing the autonomy of the students by way of an always projective displacement of "truth," and the institutions of pedagogy themselves, with their humane hierarchies of power that the geography of every classroom reproduces and reinforces beneath the temporal scheme it frames.[11] We will return to locate the logical ground of this relation in the universal claims made by liberal or aesthetic education, as by critical philosophy generally, concentrating here on the exemplary status of the pedagogue as presented by Kant.

The demand made by Kant upon the master is that he should be at once exemplary and the site of examples: "Der Meister muß es *vormachen* was und wie es der Schüler zu Stande bringen soll" ("The master must illustrate what the pupil is to achieve, and how achievement is to be attained") (sec. 60).[12] The act of exemplification is here at once spatial and temporal: if the master can stand before the students in his role as exemplar, it is only because he has done before what they in their turn must do after his example. If the master's standing in the classroom represents spatially a punctual gathering of disparate and ill-informed subjectivities to the light of the exemplary, it represents yet more importantly a temporal relation, in which the exemplary master is at once prior and projected, instance (*Beispiel*) and model (*Muster*). Needless to say, the exemplary status of the pedagogue has nothing to do with character; it is an effect of the historical structure of exemplification as it informs what is precisely a *liberal* education. The incidental, material, and spatial presence of the master, a *Beispiel* whose singularity becomes indifferent, is assumed in his transformation along temporal lines into a *Muster* that is, as is any truly exemplary example, projected toward an ideal.

One might say, according to the logic of the example outlined above, that it is intrinsic to the function of the exemplary pedagogue to disappoint. Following both this logic and that of the liberal education that Kant here sketches, it becomes clear that the "perfect" pedagogue, insofar as such a prodigy is conceivable, would be as imperfect an example as would be the pedantic pedagogue whose practice is limited to the inculcation of rules and regulations by rote. For it is the force of the example to fall short of the ideal toward which it gestures, just as it is the proper procedure of the pedagogue to point out this shortcoming of the example with regard to the ideal:

> Only by exciting the pupil's imagination to conformity with a given concept, by pointing out how the expression falls short of the idea to which, as aesthetic, the concept itself fails to attain, and by means of severe criticism, is it possible to prevent his promptly looking upon the examples [*Beispiele*] set before him as the prototypes of excellence, and as models [*Muster*] for him to imitate, without submission to any higher standard or to his own critical judgement. This would result in genius being stifled, and, with it, also the freedom of the imagination in its very conformity to law—a freedom without which a fine art is not possible, nor even as much as a correct taste of one's own for estimating it. (*CJ*, 226, sec. 60)

This passage, which amounts to a sketch of the procedures of a liberal as well as a specifically artistic education, is deeply informed by a structure of disappointment, or of un-deception, *Ent-täuschung*. In the realm of the aesthetic, every concept must be revealed to be a deception, since it is only the *formal* possibility of being subsumed under a concept that the example should represent. The free play of the understanding and the imagination would otherwise be stifled, and with that the possibility of the reconciled and reconciling work of the genius. Accordingly, in the relationship between the master and the students as in that between the concept and the judgment, all that the master exemplifies (*vormacht*) must disappoint if his pedagogy is to be exemplary. The students' disappointment in the master, itself a crucial moment in aesthetic education, is the fulfillment of a process of exemplification whose goal is to produce autonomy of judgment in the student.

Clearly, of course, the exemplary standing of the pedagogue is formally unaffected by the disappointment of the students. Rather, that exemplary status is reinforced by a transition in the students' relation to the example from concentration on its material or conceptual instantiation of apparent rules of procedure to the process by which *aesthetic* judgments are to be made. The pedagogue now exemplifies the process of enlightenment that is initiated by the perception of the perpetual and determinate inadequacy of the example to the ideal. It would be correct to say that the exemplary standing of the pedagogue is, in consequence, an ineradicable effect of structure merely, were it not for the fact that the material presence of the master is a crucial moment in the temporality of exemplification. In accordance with the historical structure of any example, it is the spatial presentation of the pedagogue, the there-beforeness of the master in all his materiality, that must be overcome or displaced by a temporal representation that is founded in the fact of the master's absolute priority—his always having been there before—but that is then deferred into the perpetual inadequacy of the model to the ideal. We can see that in this movement from presence to deferral, the structure of the example is retained, such that the disappointment discovered in the inadequacy of the pedagogue gives way to an exemplariness founded in a process of projection that the master now comes to represent to the students.

There is consequently no escape from the insistence of the exemplary within this model pedagogy. Or rather, there is one, but only for the genius, a concept that in a very real sense is required within the third *Critique* to create a rupture, in the form of exemplary freedom, in the otherwise dismal continuities of exemplary repetition. The concept of the genius in the Third Critique has been frequently enough discussed elsewhere to need little elaboration here.[13] Suffice it to say that the principal problem for Kant is to account for a productivity that is apparently at once rule-bound and free, that achieves, in other words, what is elsewhere impossible, a following of examples combined with independence of them: "It [the rule] cannot be one set down in a formula and serving as a precept—for then the judgement upon the beautiful would be determinable according to concepts. Rather must the rule be gathered from the performance, i.e., from the product, which others may use to put their own talent to the test, so as to let it serve as a model [*Muster*], not for *imitation* [*Nachmachung*], but for *following* [*Nachahmung*]" (*CJ*, 171, sec. 47; *KU*, 245).[14] "The possibility of this is difficult to explain," Kant goes on, and at least part of the difficulty is to explain the possibility of a following of examples that has nothing to do with learning. The opposition of genius to learning is absolute, since "learning is nothing but imitation" (*CJ*, 169, sec. 40). For the genius, the example (here, *Beispiel*) is no more than a minimal stimulus to production according to natural gifts that are original to him and that work *auf ähnliche Art* ("on similar lines") to those of the previous genius (*CJ*, 170, sec. 47). The genius stands outside the repetitions of an exemplary pedagogy, since his skills can be neither communicated nor learnt and since the originality of the genius is not progressive but returns always to the same ground in nature. Paradoxically for aesthetics, the repetition proper to genius is one that cannot *develop* and for precisely that reason leaves the freedom of the subject intact.

For all that, genius remains exemplary: it is the "exemplary originality [*musterhafte Originalität*] of the natural endowments of an individual in the *free* employment of his cognitive faculties" (*CJ*, 181, sec. 49; *KU*, 255). Exemplary for the subsequent genius only in the accidental or contingent sense implied above, the genius produces for humanity at large exemplary products for the judgment of *taste*. Unlike genius, taste is a progressive faculty and intimately associated with pedagogy. Indeed, as we have seen, the progressive formation of taste is *inseparable* from an exemplary pedagogy. The problem that arises here is that although the concept of genius indicates an example of human freedom independent of imitation, it provides no solution to producing that freedom in the sphere of pedagogy. Not that this would be a problem, were it not that what defines genius is effectively that to which the formation of taste is intended to bring the subject, namely, the perfect reconciliation of freedom and constraint. (This accounts, of course, for the ease with which the conditions for the possibility of a "correct taste" are subsumed within those for the possibility of a "fine art" at all; *CJ*, 226, sec. 60).

The discussion of genius thus recapitulates in many respects the discussion of taste that precedes it. In other, equally important respects, it is incompatible with the terms established for the development of taste. To reiterate, the concepts both of *development* and of *autonomy* are inseparable from the concept of taste. Thus, in section 32, Kant writes of the young poet: "It is only in aftertime, when his judgement has been sharpened by exercise, that of his own free will and accord he deserts his former judgements—behaving in just the same way as with those of his judgements which depend wholly on reason. Taste lays claim simply to autonomy. To make the judgements of others the determining ground of one's own would be heteronomy" (*CJ*, 137, sec. 32). Though the young poet can by no means be coerced to conform to the judgment of others, nonetheless in the independent development of his taste, he comes to conform. The possibility, indeed from a certain standpoint the inevitability, of this process derives from a formal identity in the mode of aesthetic judgment in all subjects that permits the claim to universality of a judgment of taste "just as if it were objective" (*CJ*, 136, sec. 32).[15] The process of judgment occurs consequently in a fashion that seems to make no firm distinction between that process as it takes place in the genius and the process as it occurs in the mere person of taste:

Following which has reference to a precedent, and not imitation, is the proper expression for all influence which the products of an exemplary [*exemplarischen*] *author* may exert upon others—and this means no more than going to the same sources for a creative work [*aus denselben Quellen schöpfen*] as those to which he went for his creations, and learning from one's predecessor no more than the mode of availing oneself of such sources. Taste, just because its judgements cannot be determined by concepts or precepts, is among all faculties and talents the very one that stands most in need of examples [*Beispiele*] of what has in the course of culture maintained itself longest in esteem [*in Beifall*]. Thus it avoids an early lapse into crudity, and a return to the rudeness of its earliest efforts. (*CJ*, 138–39, sec. 32)

It is the process of *development* that again distinguishes two faculties—genius and taste—which are otherwise apparently identical in their processes, both demanding originality and autonomy, both needing to return to exemplary instances for procedures, not for rules.[16] Genius constitutes an ex-ceptional example, by definition unpredictable in the mode of its productions, which in turn only make the transition from instance to model by way of aesthetic judgment. Where the products of genius, and indeed, initially, the objects of aesthetic judgment in general, are conceived of as *Beispiele*, it is taste that identifies their exemplary (*musterhaft*) quality. It is not hard to be convinced of the regularity of this conceptual patterning in the third *Critique*: time and again, the term *Beispiel* is employed of objects that are in the process of being or that have yet to be taken up into the judgments of taste or that are, for the subsequent genius, mere initiating instances to be followed, not imitated. *Muster*, together with its adverbial derivative, *musterhaft* (or, less often, *exemplarisch*), on the contrary, is reserved for what is projected as exemplary in the stronger sense of a model for the estimation of all attainments or judgments. Insofar as *Beispiele* become exemplary, *musterhaft*, a developmental logic is intrinsic here; insofar as a development is implied from the casual intuition to a universal claim, what is narrated is the critical move from private judgment to "universal communicability." The analysis of aesthetic judgment as a faculty is thus governed by its implication in the form of universal history, for which the insistence of the exemplary is indispensable, just as the aesthetic judgment itself both produces and estimates progress toward universal communicability on the basis of examples, *Beispiele*, which through it become *Muster*:

But in the universal communicability of the sensation (of delight or aversion)—a communicability, too, that exists apart from any concept—in the accord, so far as possible, of all ages and nations as to this feeling in the representation of certain objects, we have the empirical criterion, weak indeed and scarce sufficient to raise a presumption, of the derivation of a taste, thus confirmed by examples [*Beispiele*], from grounds deep-seated and shared alike by all men, underlying their agreement in estimating the forms under which objects are given to them.

For this reason some products of taste are looked on as *exemplary* [*exemplarisch*]. (*CJ*, 75, sec. 17)

The problem that recurs here for taste, a problem by definition absent in the case of productive genius, is how to guarantee the *autonomy* of judgments of taste under the condition of their constitutive dependence on examples. The argument that follows anticipates that made much later (in section 60), though with specific reference to taste rather than to genius:

For this reason some products of taste are looked on as *exemplary* [*exemplarisch*]—not meaning thereby that by imitating others taste may be acquired. For taste must be an original faculty; whereas one who imitates a model [*Muster*], while showing skill commensurate with his success, only displays taste as himself a critic of this model [*zeigt, sofern er es trifft, zwar Geschicklichkeit, aber nur Geschmack, sofern er dieses Muster selbst beurteilen kann*]. Hence it follows that the highest model [*das höchste Muster*], the archetype [*Urbild*] of taste, is a mere idea, which each person must beget in his own consciousness, and according to which he must form his estimate of everything that is an Object of taste, or that is an example [*Beispiel*] of critical taste, and even of universal taste itself. (*CJ*, 75–76; sec. 17)

The archetype of taste must be autonomously begotten, or, rather *hervorgebracht* ("brought forth") by each judging subject as the "highest example," the example of examples by which all other examples, as mere *Beispiele*, are at first to be estimated. Clearly its attainment of the status of *idea*, however, would demand the impossible condition that the example lose its exemplificatory status, crucial to which is its material instantiation in a representation of whatever kind. Even the highest of examples must fall short of the *idea*—which is, as Kant goes on to remark, "a concept of reason," that is, not susceptible of representation—and be redefined as an *ideal*, "the representation of an individual existence as adequate to an idea": "Hence this archetype of taste—which rests, indeed, upon reason's indeterminate idea of a maximum, but is not, however, capable of being represented by means of concepts, but only in an individual presentation—may more appropriately be called the ideal of the beautiful. While not having this ideal in our possession, we still strive to beget it within us [doch in uns hervorzubringen streben]" (CJ, 76). What appears at first as the unproblematic begetting in each and every individual of an idea that would guarantee the subject's critical autonomy becomes, by the very logic of the example and of the faculty proper to the aesthetic, namely, the imagination, a striving after an unattainable possession. For no example can escape the condition of being given in a presentation even where its exemplary representation is projected toward the ideal to which no presentation could be adequate, nor can the activity of (aesthetic) judgment take place without having such examples be presented to it. The ideal is accordingly strictly and essentially unattainable, not for the contingent reason that mankind or its artists are not yet adequately cultivated, but according to the logic of the aesthetic itself.[17]

This logic of the aesthetic, predicated on the insistence of exemplary material, however residual or minimal it may become, places the ideal irrevocably out of reach. At the same time, it is the demand, equally intrinsic to the aesthetic, that judgments of taste be made autonomously that leads, a little paradoxically, to the limits to be posed on the autonomy of the aesthetic sphere itself. For the necessity to pose an "ideal of beauty" as the only guarantee of the autonomy of each subject's judgment of taste entails a movement from the purely aesthetic to the moral. Where an *ideal* is posited for any object, an underlying end must be determinable for that object. In consequence, "[o]nly what has in itself the end of its real existence, only *man* that is able himself to determine his ends by reason . . . admits . . . of an ideal of *beauty*" (CJ, 77).[18] This figure of *man* is at once the ground and the end of the aesthetic; like common sense, it is the basis on which the universality of the aesthetic can be posited and the end that moral reflection finds in the examples of taste. Encapsulated in section 17, "The Ideal of Beauty," is the narrative that everywhere shapes the *Critique*, a narrative that moves from matter to form, from sense to commonalty, from example to idea, from beauty to morality. It is also, crucially, the narrative within which the "normal idea," which allows of cultural and geographical differences in perception and judg-

ment (cf. *CJ*, 78), is superseded by the rational idea whose proximal attainment is governed by a singular and ethical temporality. Within this narrative the importance of judgments of taste
is to negotiate developmentally the circular movement from
common *sense* to *common* sense and to do so by way of examples. This narrative is contained already in the historical character of the example and in the aesthetic disposition of the judging subject, in both cases proposing to mediate between the necessary difference of the particular and the equally necessary
universality of communicability (*Mittelbarkeit*).

We have already seen how the historical structure of the example as such causes a perpetual deferral within the pedagogical scene, given that the ideal the example represents[19] is always beyond attainment. Now, since we see in section 17 that
in order for the aesthetic to lead to the autonomy of the judging
subject it must connect with the moral through the positing of
an *ideal*, we can state that the process of this pedagogy must be
ironic. For it entails the subject's formal reflection upon the
conditions of any particular judgment about an (exemplary) object as a condition at once for the judgment of the object's adequacy to the ideal and of the subject's formal capacity as critic,
that is, as autonomous rather than dependent on the example.
The formal reflection upon the particular reflection has an
ironic narrative structure insofar as the secondary reflection always "knows more" than that prior one upon which it reflects,
if only by virtue of its generalization. This is to say that irony is
always of a temporal or narrative nature and requires a developmental economy that is always at someone's expense.

To describe irony in these terms is of course immediately to
take issue with what at present is probably the single most influential argument concerning the nature of irony, namely, Paul
de Man's essay "The Rhetoric of Temporality."[20] In Part 2 of that
essay, de Man emphasizes what are for him two crucial features
of irony: the simultaneity of its split consciousness, appearing
"as an instantaneous process that takes place rapidly, suddenly,
in one single moment" (*BI*, 225), and its radical antagonism not
only to historical thinking but also to the "reconciliation of the

self with the world by means of art" (*BI*, 219), which is the burden of several versions of aesthetic history. To an extent, and despite the necessity it involves him in of skirting the problem raised by Lukács's (and, indeed, Bakhtin's) identification of the novel with an ironic consciousness, de Man's characterization of irony is persuasive.[21] It is insufficient, however, precisely insofar as it ignores the developmental schema that structures the formal temporality of irony, regardless of whether its duration is the instantaneous apperception of a split consciousness or the extended narrative time of the novel. For as in the case of the exemplary, the recognition of a perpetual *inadequacy* is precisely what regulates the pedagogical effect of an ironic aesthetic in a continuous "striving to attain" that, as indeed de Man puts it, appears as "an endless process that leads to no synthesis" (*BI*, 220). Only this division of the subject, between the material and the formal, the interested and the ethical, or, in the terms of Baudelaire's essay "The Essence of Laughter" ("De l'essence du rire"), on which de Man leans, the inferior and the superior, produces the ethical subject as a formal representative of the human. Accordingly, de Man's assertion that, for Baudelaire, superiority and inferiority "become merely spatial metaphors to indicate a discontinuity and a plurality of levels within a subject that comes to know itself by an increasing differentiation from what is not" (*BI*, 213) is not only erroneous but depends on a significant suppression of the explicitly "universal historical" framework of Baudelaire's essay. Within both the individual man and within humanity in general, Baudelaire contends, the capacity to perceive the comic, and eventually to transcend it in the aesthetic of a "pure poetry [*poésie pure*]," is a product of specifically historical culture. The clarity with which Baudelaire's remark indicates the relation between the double nature of man and the folding over of the history of *l'homme* ("man") with that of *l'humanité* ("humanity")—another mode of "dédoublement"—makes it worth quoting at some length:

The sense of the comic, the ability to laugh, is in him who laughs, and not at all in the object which excites his laughter. It is not the victim of a fall who laughs at his own misfortune, unless, that is, he happens to be a philosopher, in other words, a being who, as the result of long habit, has acquired the power rapidly to become two persons at one and the same time, and can bring to bear on what happens to *himself* the disinterested curiosity of a spectator. . . . If we compare—as we have a perfect right to do—humanity with Man, it becomes clear that the primitive races have, no more than Virginie, any conception of caricature, and know nothing of comedy (the sacred books, no matter to what peoples they may belong, never indulge in laughter). It is, however, as they advance by slow degrees towards the cloudy pinnacles of the intelligence, or bend above the murky flames of metaphysics, that the nations begin to echo the diabolic laughter of Melmoth. If, however, in those same ultra-civilized nations, an intelligence, spurred on by superior ambition, wishes to break through the limits set by worldly pride, and daringly to venture along the road to pure poetry, then it will be found that from such poetry, as limpid and deep as nature itself, laughter will be as completely absent as it is from the spirit of the Sage.[22]

Given its ironic premises, it is all the more striking that this passage should reproduce so accurately the developmental schema of aesthetic history in its movement from the supposed primitive incapacity of self-reflexive disinterest through the division of the subject, and of subject from subject, that this entails, to a possible transcendence of that division in an identity between the purest artifice and nature.

Far from representing a dismantling of the historical form of aesthetics, irony belongs in its very structure within the formal developmental temporality of the aesthetic. It is accordingly interesting to note, insofar as de Man attempts to associate irony with allegory in contradistinction to the symbol, that he evinces a similar blindness with regard to the metaironic structure of symbolist aesthetics itself. For it is an entire misreading of symbolist aesthetics to suggest that in any simple sense, "[i]n the world of the symbol it would be possible for the image to coincide with the substance" or that "the symbol postulates the possibility of an identity or identification" (*BI*, 207). The error is appropriate, since it is precisely the ironic structure of symbolist aesthetics to present every symbol as, in effect, the symbol of an error: that is to say, the reflection upon any sign or object presented as symbolic entails the recognition of its inadequacy to the totality that it is held to represent. Precisely this inadequacy gives way to an ironic *methodology* of symbolism,

which causes the subject to seek to constitute the truth or totality that the object is inadequate to represent. Thus, to cite a
quite representative passage from Coleridge's *The Friend*,
where he is discussing the communication of truth through "a
right though inadequate notion":

Observe, how graciously Nature instructs her human children. She
cannot give us the knowledge derived from sight without occasioning
us at first to mistake images of reflection for substances. But the very
consequences of the delusion lead inevitably to its detection; and out
of the ashes of the error rises a new flower of knowledge. We not only
see, but are enabled to discover by what means we see. So too we are
under the necessity, in given circumstances, of mistaking a square for
a round object; but ere the mistake can have any practical consequences, it is not only removed, but in its removal gives us the symbol
of a new fact, that of distance.[23]

Symbolist pedagogy shares the structure of the exemplary precisely insofar as what is involved in every instance is the production of a disappointment or un-deception. And as becomes
very clear in the above passage, what this involves is always an
ironic relation between the necessarily assumed naive perceiver and the superior consciousness.

It is, of course, the function of a liberal pedagogy to produce
that ironic relation not only *between* subjects, as in the first instance through schooling, but also within each subject as an internalized ethical attitude. We might argue that the condition of
such an ironic disposition is the fundamental prerequisite for
the inculcation of ideology since it assumes, as an internal
mechanism of the most formal and "transferrable" kind, the
subordination of the individual to the universal.[24] It is at this
point that pedagogy necessarily opens onto the political.

Furthermore, though this may seem surprising given the extent to which the ironic mode is habitually associated with a
certain kind of autonomy of judgment, there is an intimate link
between the ironic and the institutional insofar as the ironic is
a *mode* rather than an incidental attitude. Exactly inasmuch as
liberal pedagogy, as a consequence of its exemplary structure, is
drawn toward an ironic disposition (or displacement) of power/
knowledge relations, by the same token irony, as a mode, is in-

separable from a split disposition of superiority/inferiority or of latent and manifest consciousness that must always make an example of someone. The ironic attitude is the internalized modality of the institutional geography of the classroom. The ironic attitude is, accordingly, the subjective counterpart of the idea of the canon, since only in relation to examples subject to a universalizing formalization can an ironic pedagogy take place. As the body of "exemplary products of taste" through which the judgment is cultivated for each subject, a canon is indispensable to that formalization of the judgment whose progressive nature is inspired by its own perpetual inadequacy to that example of examples, the ideal. The subjective relation to the canon implies, therefore, a progressive narrative of aesthetic consciousness whose assimilative force is in no way diminished but rather is augmented by its formal interminability. Paradoxically, however, what the canonical examples exemplify are the "grounds deep-seated and shared alike by all men, underlying their agreement in estimating the forms under which objects are given to them" (*CJ*, 75, sec. 17). There is a tension, if not a contradiction, in other words, between the *function* of the canon as a body of examples subjected to judgment to the end of its development and the *lesson* of the canon, which is the transhistorical identity of equivalence of judgments of taste as of products of genius.[25] This paradox, which perhaps marks the transition from the historical relativism of the Enlightenment to the developmental universal histories of the nineteenth century, is only resolvable by subordinating a spatial distribution of differing cultural products and judgments to a temporal model of aesthetic development that entails an ethical judgment as to the adequacy of any given historical product or judgment to the ideal. The manner in which any judgment takes place always remains identical; the development of judgment takes place through the increasing autonomy of its sphere, in the individual or in the species. Out of this paradox and its resolution will emerge the explicitly developmental aesthetic pedagogies that run through the nineteenth century from Schiller to Arnold, though these will in turn come to be haunted by the fundamental aporia of aesthetics, namely, the difficulty, given their historical claims, of accounting for the continuing appeal of ancient artifacts.[26]

This slippage from the aesthetic to the ethical is, as we have seen, not a misreading of the aesthetic but an elaboration of a productive contradiction that is an inevitable consequence of the universalizing claims of aesthetic philosophy even where it seems most resistant to practical application. There is, accordingly, no clear demarcation between Kant's "philosophical" deduction of the aesthetic and, for example, Schiller's pedagogical *Verwendung* of Kantian ideas: the latter is less a "regression" than, as in Hegel's perception of it, a completion of the logic of the third *Critique*.[27] From its inception, aesthetics gives the example to a pedagogy with which it can scarcely dispense, requiring that pedagogy as the means to constitute the very space that grounds the verisimilitude of its examples. This space being that of "common sense," it provides in turn the fundamental condition both for the formation of political subjects in the specific form of "representative" individuals and for the apparent self-evidence of the canon as a body of representative texts. What this meshing of the aesthetic and the political within the field of pedagogy implies is that any sustained attempt to rethink the nature and function of cultural education from a radical perspective must entail a simultaneous critique of the political culture of representation. In the absence of such a critique, radical pedagogy will continue to reproduce, at the "microscopic" level of its implicit practices, the processes of ideological interpellation that its explicit tendency seeks to disrupt.

The Force of Example

Kant's Symbols

Recent literary theory has raised objections to what appears to be a nearly exclusive concern with "language" in post-structuralist literary criticism. While literary texts are linguistic constructs, so critics have argued, language itself must be seen in a historical and social context. Literary criticism must therefore turn to fields in the social sciences, such as sociology and history, to provide an understanding of the non-linguistic elements that surround and in part determine the language of the texts studied by literary criticism. Otherwise it will be at risk of wrongly imperializing the nonlinguistic world by expounding particular objects of interest, and consequently limiting the understanding of its own object as well.[1]

This objection is important because it raises a question that was at one time not limited to literary criticism but pertained to the nonmathematical sciences in general, that is, whether and in what way they give access to knowledge of the empirical world. The form in which the recent objections concerning literary criticism are raised, however, locates the problem, implicitly, in the *object* of study; the error is seen to be contingent upon the linguistic makeup of the objects with which literary criticism is concerned. If we turn to the philosophical texts in which the question of discursive theoretical knowledge was originally posed, however, we see that the problem does not begin with the nature of the object but with the nature of the theory itself. Indeed, the entire project of Kant's critical philosophy could be considered an attempt to discover whether a philosophy based on principles not simply derived from either mathematics or empirical evidence could provide any systematic knowledge whatsoever. In order to provide any knowledge of objects, philosophy had to be able to systematize itself as rigorously as mathematics does itself. Whether discursive theory could say something about the world depended on what it could say about itself. If we are to remember the questions raised again today in the field of literary theory we must first ask, not "What can a theory of literature know?" but "What can theory know?"

Kant is a good place to examine this question not only because he first asked it in this form but because his critical philosophy has seemed particularly dependent upon nondiscursive science, specifically Newtonian physics.[2] Kant's answer to what philosophy can know, that is, has seemed to be closely linked to what Newtonian physics knows, and it hence appears itself circumscribed by an empirical-historical determinant. But it turns out that in Kant, the particular concept that will eventually allow theory to know is the concept of self-limitation that is best thought in terms of symbolic language. To some extent, then, an examination of the relation between critical philosophy and nondiscursive science will reveal that in order for philosophy to systematize itself, it will first have to symbolize itself in its own self-knowledge.

In the Preface to the second edition of the *The Critique of Pure Reason*, Kant describes the dilemma of a metaphysics fallen into disrepute in the face of the successes of mathematics and natural science. The success of the mathematical sciences, Kant suggests, is that they base their method on an act of rational self-reflection in which the object is recognized as a representation of reason.[3] The structure of scientific method is one of self-recognition; what reason sees in nature is precisely itself. Reason thus makes progress in mathematics and physics because through their objects—number and empirical nature—rational thought learns more and more about itself. In this context, the failure of metaphysics contains a peculiar irony, since it is the science concerned most directly with what would seem purely rational objects, that is, "mere concepts." In the one science in which reason would seem to have the best chance of confronting itself directly, it is the least successful; reason is somehow furthest from itself when it is potentially nearest (*Critique*, 21). It has thus come to recognize itself first of all in the sciences in which it must detour through sensible intuition, through an "application" of concepts to objects, and hence through something exterior to the concept as such.

The successes of the sciences that Kant describes in the second preface are more than a point of comparison for metaphysical failure; in the context in which he is writing, they would seem, indeed, to be the very cause of the metaphysical dilemma. In 1687, Newton had published the laws of motion in his *Principia*, sparking a series of debates that centered around what might be considered the central innovation of the *Principia*: Newton's assertion that the movement of massive bodies separated in space could be explained in terms of an attractive force exerted by these bodies on each other. The concept of attractive force was a breakthrough because it provided a way of explaining and testing Copernican astronomy, which had no way of proving its claims over the Ptolemaic system.[4] But the strength of the concept of gravitation for physics was also its bane for philosophy. The problem that inspired the commentary of Locke, Leibniz, Hume, and others was that while the Newtonian formulas worked effectively in predicting physical phenomena, and seemed to be inductively justified—that is, while the *law* of gravitation seemed perfectly "true"—the *concept* of attractive force as a physical event, an attraction across empty space, made no sense in rational terms. "Action at a distance," or "gravitation," seemed to be a speculative "hypothesis" or, in Leibniz's terms, an "occult quality." Thus the concept of gravitation seemed to achieve scientific (mathematical-empirical) description at the cost of philosophical understanding. The laws of the empirical world were beyond the grasp of a philosophical understanding that was not as rigorous as a mathematically governed system.[5]

It was the innovation of critical philosophy to question the attempt to model philosophical understanding on mathematics or scientific law, by rigorously examining the principle of their difference. Instead of asking "How can philosophy understand the world?" criticism would ask "How is philosophical understanding different from mathematical and scientific understanding?" Thus in the "Doctrine of Method" of the first *Critique*, Kant defines the rigor of philosophical method through its difference from mathematics: "Mathematics and philosophy, although in natural science they do, indeed, go hand in hand, are none the less so completely different, that the procedure of the one can never be imitated by the other. The exactness of mathematics rests upon definitions, axioms and demonstrations. . . . Indeed it is precisely in knowing its limits that philosophy consists" (*Critique*, 585). If the rigor of mathematics consists in the complete and autonomous definition of its objects, the rigor of philosophy consists in the determination, not of an object (including itself), but of its own "limits." What it knows is precisely the ways in which it cannot know objects directly or completely. Such a negative knowledge, therefore, is knowledge not of an object as such but rather of its own *relation* to an object. To know its limits is to know that its knowledge of objects is always relational, a relation between the object and itself. This produces a kind of double limitation. On the one hand, philosophy will know that it can never know objects in themselves, that is, that it "can never transcend the limits of possible experience" (*Critique*, 24); its "transcendental" concepts will always only provide knowledge of the relation between themselves and an empirical "given." On the other hand, the knowledge of this limitation must itself remain limited: it must be understood in terms of a relation to something that is not knowledge. This "something" is precisely the supersensible, which is not grasped by "knowing" (*erkennen*) but only posited by "thinking" (*denken*).[6] What critical philosophy ultimately knows, then, is simply this relation between knowing and thinking: philosophy remains suspended between a direct knowledge of empirical objects and any knowledge of the supersensible, which it can only "think." In this principle of suspension, philosophy's difference from mathematics has been converted from a flaw hindering metaphysical progress into the very ground of its rigor.

Kant thus establishes a link between purely conceptual knowledge and the natural sciences on the basis of the conceptual principle of limitation. That is, the rigorous negativity of conceptual self-reflection is what links it to the rigors of mathematical calculation. Indeed, the relation between natural science and philosophy in Kant's system could be defined in terms of what they *don't* know: while natural science explains the world directly, it gives up the possibility of *understanding* it, and philosophy, while it *understands*, cannot understand *the world*. On this basis Kant develops the elaborate system called the "architectonic," divided between (1) the purely *transcendental* laws, which provide the "conditions of possibility" of experience—for example the law that "every change must have a cause"; (2) the "metaphysical laws," which are based on the transcendental laws as well as on mathematics and empirical "givens" and explain the fundamental features of the material world—for example the law that "every change of matter must have an external cause," that is, Newton's first law of motion;[7] and (3) the physical laws, which concern more specific characteristics of the physical world.[8] Thus, in the case of force, "metaphysics" (which is basically Newtonian physics) need only explain the law mathematically and be able to test and prove its effects experimentally, while philosophy need only explain the transcendental *conditions* for knowing the concept— that is, the law of causality. The centrality of the enigma of force in the most rigorous natural sciences is linked to the centrality of the negative self-reflection of conceptual knowledge in critical philosophy.

Certain problems have arisen, however, concerning this close correspondence of natural science and philosophy, which would seem to be the triumph of critical rigor. Many readers of Kant have suggested that what determines the structure of the system is not, in fact, a conceptual principle but an analogy with the already constituted science of physics, upon which Kant based his conception of philosophy. The most rigorous of defenders of the conceptual independence of the system, Gerd Buchdahl, while insisting on the *general* applicability of the transcendental laws to empirical "givens" (or to "experience"), also notes that in the relation to metaphysics there is "the working of something like analogy," and he concludes that Newtonian physics to some extent "historically conditioned the general construction of the architectonic."[9] Ultimately, then, in spite of its pretensions, the critical philosophy would seem incapable of wresting itself from basically empirical determinants. What philosophical theory knows, in Kant, would still depend on, and to that extent be secondary to, what empirical science knows.

Buchdahl's use of the word "analogy" calls attention to the way in which Newtonian physics, or more specifically, the relation between force and motion, seems to serve as the model for all conceptual relations *within* the transcendental system. The entire concept of relation seems to be modeled, in fact, on the concept of the *event* and its *effects*, or the nonphenomenal occurrence and its representation. Thus, in the first *Critique*, the pure transcendental concepts that Kant defines in his "Table of Categories" are divided into the "mathematical" and the "dynamical," with the three "Analogies of Experience" in the latter corresponding closely to the three laws of motion in the "Metaphysics." The distinction between the mathematical and dynamical categories is itself reiterated in the larger division between the "Analytic" and the "Dialectic" of the first *Critique*, or the analysis of what philosophy can *know* and what it can just *think*. And once again, the division between Analytic and Dialectic in the theoretical realm is repeated in the division between theoretical philosophy and practical philosophy, or the branches of philosophy concerned with the knowledge of nature and with human action. Criticism's own model for its negative self-knowledge would thus appear to be that of a knowledge turned upon itself by the action of a force heterogeneous to, but not separable from, this motion.[10] The entire conceptual structure of critical philosophy, that is, would appear to be *taken over* from Newtonian physics, and thus to look to the empirical world both for the basis of its conceptual structures (modeling its own laws on the laws of physics) and the basis of its own self-representation (representing itself on the model of empirical events). Hence the very knowledge of the *difference* from empirical law that forms the basis of critical thought appears to be, itself, modeled on an empirical event, and the knowledge provided by the discursive theory appears to be traceable, once again, to an *empirical* determinant.

It would be useful, however, before jumping to conclusions, to look somewhat more closely at the actual place in which Kant elaborates, within his critical system, on the principles and foundations of Newtonian physics, the *Metaphysical Foundations of Natural Science*. In the Preface to this work Kant himself comments on the curious dependence of transcendental philosophy on metaphysical law. He sees this dependent relation in the "example":

It is indeed very remarkable (but cannot here be thoroughly entered into) that general metaphysics in all cases where it requires examples [*Beispiele*] (intuitions) in order to provide meaning [*Bedeutung*] for its pure concepts of the understanding must always take them from the general doctrine of body, i.e., from the form and principles of external intuition [*äussere Anschauung*]; and if these instances are not at hand in their entirety, it gropes [*herumtappe*], uncertain and trembling, among mere meaningless concepts. . . . And so a separate metaphysics of corporeal nature does excellent and indispensable service to general metaphysics, inasmuch as the former provides examples [*Beispiele*] (cases in concreto) in which to realize the concepts and propositions of the latter (properly, transcendental philosophy), i.e., to give to a mere form of thought sense and meaning [*Sinn und Bedeutung*].[11]

Kant is concerned here with the fact that transcendental philosophy, as a purely formal structure, "a mere form of thought [*einer blossen Gedankenform*]," depends on something outside of the concept, or "examples," for its "meaning [*Bedeutung*]."[12] What surprises Kant, however, is not the dependence of the "form" on any illustrative "intuition" but rather the dependence of the form specifically on "*external* intuition" or "the general doctrine of body." External intuition, here, is not just a content that gives meaning to the conceptual form, but itself has a "form" and "principles" in the science of dynamics: it is another "form" that is the meaning of the "mere form" of thought. The need for something "external" to thought is thus, here, different from the need for "experience" in general, which Kant emphasizes throughout the first *Critique*: it is another kind of externality represented by the dependence of the form of transcendental philosophy on the form of Newtonian science, a doubling of form and form.

This doubling reappears in the use of the word "external" in the *Foundations* as a whole, in which it comes to stand for two different kinds of relation. In the Preface, Kant first speaks of the doctrine of body as the science concerning objects that "affect" the "external senses" (*Foundations*, 13–14). Here matter, defined as motion, is "external" insofar as it is "given" to the concept; it is that empirical "given" to which the concept must always stand in relation. Yet matter as motion, as Kant writes of it in the main work, is defined by "external relations" in a much more formal sense: the motion of a thing is said to be "the change of its external relations to a given space" (*Foundations*, 21). In this case, "external" refers to relations that can be calculated mathematically. Thus matter, insofar as it affects the "external senses," is what is *given* to them; but insofar as it is determined by "external relations," it is what can be calculated. "External" thus seems to mean both the "philosophical" relation that defines the negativity of conceptual self-reflection and the purely mathematical relation of number. The peculiarity of the metaphysical "example" thus lies in the joining of these two kinds of "external" relations.

The joining of two external relations, it turns out, becomes the very principle of the central law of the *Foundations*. In the "second law of mechanics," Kant reformulates Newton's first law (which, with the other two, gave rise to the theory of gravitation) in terms of the transcendental law of causality. It is thus here that he joins the central principles of transcendental philosophy and metaphysics:

PROPOSITION
Second law of mechanics: Every change of matter has an external cause [*eine äussere Ursache*]. (Every body remains in its state of rest or motion in the same direction and with the same velocity unless it is compelled by an external cause to forsake this state).

PROOF
(In universal metaphysics there is laid down the proposition that every

change has a cause; here there is only to be proved of matter that its change must always have an external cause.) Matter as mere object of the external senses [*aüsserer Sinne*] has no other determination than those of external relations in space [*der äusseren Verhältnisse im Raume*] and hence undergoes no changes except by motion. With regard to such change, insofar as it is an exchange of one motion with another, or of motion with rest, and vice versa, a cause of such change must be found (according to the principle of metaphysics). But this cause cannot be internal [*innerlich*], for matter has no absolutely internal determinations and grounds of determination. Hence all change of matter is based upon an external cause (i.e., a body remains etc.). (*Foundations*, 104–5)

In the "Proposition" Kant reformulates Newton's first law in metaphysical terms in order to show its relation to transcendental principles. In this reformulation, the difference between the "second law of mechanics" and the transcendental law of causality lies primarily in the addition of the word *external*. Its significance is also emphasized by the fact that the reiteration of the law in stricter Newtonian form (in parentheses) replaces Newton's "forces [*viribus*]" with the phrase "external cause."[13] Thus the entire weight of the law, insofar as it articulates metaphysical and transcendental principles, rests on the notion of the "external." In the "Proof," moreover, this term can be seen to involve a double meaning, referring both to the definition of matter and to the explanation of its change. For matter is defined, first of all, in terms of "external relations," in which "external" means purely mathematical calculability. But in the application of the transcendental law to matter, "external" refers to what *affects* "external relations," that is, to what is external to external relations. This latter externality cannot be discovered by empirical means but only by the use of a transcendental concept. Thus at this moment, in the phrase "external cause," "external" is no longer precisely mathematical (or empirical) but conceptual. The example of force as an "external cause" expresses, therefore, the precise point of articulation between metaphysical and transcendental law in terms of a principle of double relation or "externality."

In the "Observation" following the proof, Kant comments on the centrality of this law for natural philosophy. The doubleness of the external as mathematical and as empirical now is given a different name, that of "lifelessness":

> This mechanical law alone must be called the law of inertia (*lex inertiae*); the law that every action has an equal and opposite reaction cannot bear this name. For the latter says what matter does, but the former only what it does not do, and this is better adapted to the expression of inertia. The inertia of matter is and signifies [*bedeutet*] nothing but its lifelessness [*Leblosigkeit*], as matter in itself. Life [*Leben*] means the capacity of a substance to determine itself to act from an internal principle.... Now, we know of no other principle of a substance to change its state but desire and no other internal activity whatever but thought. ... But these determining grounds and actions do not at all belong to the representations of the external senses and hence also not to the determinations of matter as matter. Therefore, all matter as such is lifeless [*leblos*]. The proposition of inertia says so much and no more.... The possibility of a natural science proper rests entirely upon the law of inertia (along with the law of permanence of substance). The opposite of this, and therefore the death of all natural philosophy [*der Tod aller Naturphilosophie*], would be hylozoism. (*Foundations*, 105–6)

The significance of the law of inertia within the critical system is emphasized here in terms of its purely negative character: much like transcendental philosophy itself, it is concerned less with positive assertion than with a kind of limitation. It is this negativity that would essentially bind the metaphysical law to the transcendental one: the expression of what matter does *not* do corresponds to the expression of what transcendental concepts cannot know. This not knowing, moreover, is specifically defined as a suspension of all comparisons between matter, or motion and its causes, to human life: the power of the law to suspend understanding and confine itself to calculation lies in its resistance to any figurations that compare matter with the mind or personify it, as in "hylozoism"; matter "in itself," as the cause of its own movements, remains utterly outside this sort of comprehension. Kant clearly has in mind here the various attempts to explain attractive force in terms of a kind of inner life of matter, but it is significant that he carefully elides the word "force" here and uses instead the word "lifelessness." "Life*less*" (leb*los*) is itself a negative determination that encompasses both the externality of matter as "external relations" in space and the externality of material cause: the *event* of force as a purely calculable and incomprehensible occurrence can only be understood negatively by saying that it is *not* a living action. The word *lifeless* thus represents the full negativity that serves as the hinge for the different parts of the system, the "giving up" of a claim to understanding (in the case of natural science) or of direct knowledge (in the case of transcendental philosophy). "Lifelessness" expresses, that is, the relational quality of all conceptual knowledge that knows in its object only its own *relation* to a "something" that is not fully determined.

The rigor of this use of the word "lifeless" for a purely conceptual negativity gives way further on in the passage, however, to a different kind of language, when Kant informs us that the opposite of *inertia*, or hylozoism, "would be the death of all philosophy." The interest of this phrase is not just that it is meant figuratively but that the figurative meaning turns on the notion of lifelessness, which is now characterized positively, and more humanly, as "death [*Tod*]." If *matter* is characterized as purely inhuman, philosophy dies a very personal death, one that establishes a specific figurative relation between the two: the life of matter is the death of philosophy; the lifelessness of matter is the life of philosophy. The force of the chiasmus compels the reading of a narrative into the relation between matter (or natural law) and philosophy, which gives the "lifelessness" of matter a more personal cast: matter dies, it would appear, *so that* philosophy can have life. The negativity that mediates between metaphysical and transcendental law is no longer purely conceptual but takes the form of a story: what mediates, here, is a death, a sacrifice of one life in the service of another. This story sounds familiar, and can be heard, perhaps, in the original law, when we read that matter only "suffers [*erleidet*]" change by means of external causes: when matter suffers death (*erleidet den Tod*) for philosophy, it mediates between concept and empirical law as Christ's death (*das Leiden Christi*) mediates between fallen man and God. The mediation of limit-thinking has shifted from a purely negative conceptual structure to a story in which negativity is represented in terms of a death.

Our reading of a narrative dimension in the *Foundations*

might seem mere speculation, but Kant's figuration is not confined to the single instance of the "Observation"; it does not seem, that is, to be simply the effect of a moment of imaginative excess. It was already present, in some sense, in the passage on "examples" in the Preface, in which, we recall, it is said that without examples philosophy "gropes, uncertain and trembling, among meaningless concepts." The personification of philosophy here—based on the same word, "gropes [herumtappt]," that is used to characterize it in the Preface to the second edition of the first Critique—suggests that the relation between philosophy and metaphysics is less like a conceptual relation than like a power relation.[14] The dependence of transcendental philosophy on metaphysics, in the "example," is dramatized as the dependence of a master on the "indispensible services [Dienst]" of his servant (in Hegel, notably, Dienst is the word used to describe the function of the slave in the master-slave section of the Phenomenology of Spirit, where death will also be a mediating term). The mediation provided by the example can, therefore, be understood in narrative terms. And this narrative is closely linked to the narrative told in the second law, the story of the death of matter for the life of philosophy, or the "falling" (for the effect of force is the fall of motion) that makes possible negative critical self-consciousness. Force is a kind of death, an occurrence in critical thinking that makes possible the mediation of empirical and conceptual thought and that can no longer be understood in purely empirical terms. Force, or death, would appear to be the narrative figure of the mediation provided by the example, of the relational structure that relates critical knowledge to itself.[15]

The problem that metaphysics presents to transcendental philosophy cannot be understood, therefore, in terms of the dependence of the conceptual model on an empirical law outside of it, or the grounding of the "analogy" in an empirical necessity.[16] Dependence and outsideness or externality are, as we have seen, understandable only within a narrative that robs them of any purely empirical meaning. The extra "externality" of force, or what seems to threaten purely conceptual thought, must also be understood in other terms, as a problem arising from within the very conceptualization of limitation itself. That is, the example, as the structure of relation, first reflects back upon the concept of relation in the notion of the "limitation" of reason as a relation betwen the sensible and supersensible realms. The best place to turn to try to understand this problem better will thus be the part of the system in which the concept of limitation is most carefully discussed, the section called "On the Determination of the Limits of Pure Reason" in Kant's summary of critical philosophy, *Prolegomena to Any Future Metaphysics*. It is also here, in the discussion of the concept of the limit, that we will rediscover the figure, or story, of death. The problems raised by the *Foundations*—the question of the *basis* of transcendental thinking in relation to the empirical world—will thus be best addressed by a look at the determination of the "limit."

The discussion of the limit concept is an attempt to explain, precisely, how self-limitation must be understood in terms of a relation, specifically a relation to the supersensible. In an earlier section, Kant had indicated that the necessity of understanding a relation to the supersensible is implied in all rigorous conceptions of empirical knowledge. He calls this other realm to which knowledge is related, implicit in the relation between concepts and empirical law, the "realm of mere ideas." Not surprisingly, what necessitates the thinking of these ideas is exemplified here by attractive force:

The objects which are given us by experience are in many respects incomprehensible, and many questions to which the law of nature leads us when carried beyond a certain point (though still quite conformably to the laws of nature) admit of no answer. An example is the question: Why do material things attract one another? But if we entirely quit nature or, in pursuing its combinations, exceed all possible experience, and so enter the realm of mere Ideas, we cannot then say that the object is incomprehensible. . . .

Although an absolute whole of experience is impossible, the Idea of a whole of knowledge according to principles must impart to our knowledge a kind of unity, that of a system, without which it is nothing but piecework.[17]

If we think of the "incomprehensibility" of experience as it is described here in terms of the structure of metaphysical example, we can see that Kant is concerned with the grounding of the kind of negative knowledge that transcendental philosophy provides through its rational thinking. As we saw, the power of the system to establish always a knowledge only of a relation, rather than of an object itself, is expressed in the giving up, by transcendental philosophy, of any full knowledge of attractive force, allowing it to represent only the necessity of the relation of the concept of causality to what is "given" to it empirically. Here Kant reminds us that this negative relation is itself only made possible in relation to another relation, the concept of the limitation of the sensible by the supersensible. It is this relation, we recall, that says not only that knowledge is limited *to* the sensible but that the knowledge *of* the limitation is itself limited, is not a full, transparent knowledge of knowledge. Here Kant emphasizes that this final limitation of limitation is precisely what permits the limit concept to provide a principle of epistemological closure, to make critical knowledge into a *system*. The establishment of a relation to supersensible ideas— the kind of thinking Kant calls *denken*—is what permits critical knowledge to *know*, rigorously, that it cannot know itself fully.

The section on the determination of limits is thus concerned with explaining how the concept of the limit establishes a relation to something outside of knowledge. Kant focuses the discussion on the difference between this relational concept and the "mere negations" of Humean skepticism, which is, like all dogmatic (i.e., noncritical) philosophy, still aimed at the direct knowledge of objects, including knowledge itself. Kant thus contrasts the different kinds of negativity in skepticism and criticism in terms of the "boundaries" established by Hume and the "limits" established by criticism:

Our principles, which limit the use of reason to possible experience, might . . . become transcendent and the limits of our reason be set up as limits of the possibility of things in themselves (as Hume's *Dialogues* may illustrate) if a careful critique did not guard the limits of our reason with respect to its empirical use and set a limit to its pretensions. . . .

In all limits [*Grenzen*] there is something positive (for example, a surface is the limit of corporeal space, and is therefore itself a space; a line is a space which is the limit of the surface, a point the limit of the line, but always a place in space), but boundaries contain mere negations. . . . The question now is, What is the attitude of our reason in this connection of what we know with what we do not, and never shall, know? This is an actual connection of a known thing with one quite unknown (and which will always remain so), and though what is unknown should not become in the least more known—which we cannot even hope—yet the concept of this connection must be definite and capable of being rendered distinct.

We must therefore think [*denken*] an immaterial being, a world of understanding, and a Supreme Being. . . .

But as we can never know [*erkennen*] these beings of understanding as they are in themselves, that is, as definite, yet must assume them . . . we are at least able to think [*denken*] this connection by means of such concepts as express their relation to the world of sense.[18]

The "mere negation" of skepticism, Kant implies in these passages, would claim to *know* the world as empty of supersensible beings, because it takes the knowledge of its own limits as absolute, that is, because it believes that the knowledge of limits is not itself limited, that is, is itself supersensible. Kant thus implicitly points to a contradiction in skepticism, that in *negating* all supersensible knowledge, in claiming to *know* that we can only know the empirical world, it relies on the supersensible nature of its *self*-knowledge. The critical insistence on positing a relation to the supersensible thus preserves negative self-knowledge from erroneously attributing a supersensible status to itself. It maintains a completely rigorous negativity by precisely *positing* or "thinking" a *relation* to the supersensible, rather than claiming to know either the presence or absence of this supersensible world. The "thinking" of the relation thus remains, primarily, self-reflexive, because what it says is only that self-knowledge *must* limit itself in a certain way. It says, that is, that criticism can *know* where its knowledge of knowledge stops—it can know the difference between knowing and thinking. It is the rigor of this distinction that permits the negativity of knowledge of limits to produce a closed and systematic philosophy.

The question Kant insists must be answered, however, is that of precisely *how* we can conceive of a relation that is "thought"

rather than known. Kant's discussion of this problem will center, again, on a debate with Hume, concerning one specific
question: whether or not "God," as a supersensible being, can
be thought in a fully critical (i.e., relational) manner. Hume has
insisted, Kant says, that God can only be thought "anthropo-
morphically," that is, by a transfer of qualities from the sensible
world (specifically, understanding), and hence only erroneously,
as a fiction of a supersensible being that is in fact thought entirely in sensible terms. For this reason Hume denies any truth
to this representation. The skeptical "negation," Kant implies,
thus rests on the belief that the representation of God is the attempt to *know* a supersensible object. Kant argues for another
kind of representation:

[W]e stop at this limit [of experience] if we limit [*einschränken*] our
judgment merely to the relation which the world may have to a Being
whose very concept lies beyond all the knowledge which we can attain
within the world. For we then do not attribute to the Supreme Being
any of the properties in themselves by which we represent objects of
experience, and thereby avoid *dogmatic* anthropomorphism; but we
attribute them to the relation of this Being to the world and allow ourselves a *symbolical* anthropomorphism, which in fact concerns language only and not the object itself.

If I say that we are compelled to consider the world *as if* it were the
work of a Supreme Understanding and Will, I really say nothing more
than that a watch, a ship, a regiment, bears the same relation to the
watchmaker, the shipbuilder, the commanding officer as the world of
sense (or whatever constitutes the substratum of this complex of appearances) does to the unknown, which I do not hereby know as it is in
itself but as it is for me, that is, in relation to the world of which I am a
part. (*Prolegomena*, 105–6)

Criticism, Kant suggests, permits a different way of representing God, which is an attempt to know not the supersensible but
only a relation to it. The symbolic anthropomorphism does not
know, but, Kant implies, only thinks God. The difference between skepticism, the most advanced of precritical philoso-
phies, and criticism thus comes down to a difference between
two conceptions of anthropomorphism: dogmatic and symbolic—the representation that claims to know God and the representation that claims only to know the relation to God. With
this distinction, Kant rests the entire weight of the critical sys-

tem—the full rigor of negative thinking—upon the capacity for a certain kind of figuration. Or rather, upon the capacity of criticism to know this figuration, that is, to distinguish between dogmatic and symbolic anthropomorphism, or to define the symbol rigorously and completely. Since the symbol is, ultimately, the form in which thinking as such takes place, the definition of the symbol will amount to the definition of the distinction between knowing and thinking, and will thus constitute the most rigorous form of critical self-knowledge.

What is most significant in the definition of symbolic anthropomorphism is its self-reflexive capacity, made possible by its purely relational character. Where dogmatic anthropomorphism transfers properties from the world of sense to God, Kant says, symbolic anthropomorphism transfers only relations. The symbol claims to know not God but only something about our relation to this being. Since the knowledge of relation is, however, always a knowledge of knowledge, the symbolic representation of the supersensible will also be a reflection on the very establishing of the symbol, a symbol of symbolic thinking. To think a symbolic relation is thus to represent the supersensible in terms of the very act of thinking that makes this representation possible. The symbol, that is, always remembers that it is only a symbol. It knows, one could say, that it posits. The symbol thus mediates between thinking and knowing, or the negativity of knowledge and the knowledge of that negativity. It is this self-mediation that gives rise to the possibility for criticism to distinguish itself over against skepticism, to distinguish between what is and what isn't a symbol. In the symbol, criticism first knows itself as what knows the difference between knowing and thinking. All other points of articulation in the system, such as the structure of exemplification, in which concepts reflect systematically on their own relation to their sensible objects, refer back to and are grounded upon this knowledge of thinking made possible by the symbol.

In defining the rigorous negativity of symbolic representation, however, Kant does not confine himself to a discussion of knowledge, but introduces another term as well, "language [*die Sprache*]": symbolic anthropomorphism, he says, "in fact concerns language only and not the object itself." The symbol, that is, reminds us not only that it is given by thought but that it is given by language. It is not entirely clear what it means, here, to concern "language only," since the relation between the knowing/thinking distinction and language has not been defined. It would appear, however, that the introduction of this term indicates that the knowledge of the symbol cannot be contained completely by the terminology of thought. The thinking of the symbol has put a certain pressure on the critical argument that compels it to change its terms. At this point, the burden of the argument shifts from the attempt of critical thinking to know itself in symbols to the attempt of critical language to represent itself in symbols. The unity of philosophy as a discursive science could be said to depend upon the possibility of this achievement.

This pressure on the argument concerning symbolic anthropomorphism, the sense that it requires a different kind of definition, is also felt in the following paragraph of the section, which provides a reformulation of the definition in terms of analogy: "Such a cognition is one of analogy and does not signify (as is commonly understood) an imperfect similarity of two things, but a perfect similarity between two quite dissimilar things" (*Prolegomena*, 106). The concept of analogy presumably represents the relational character, the self-reflexive capacity, of the symbol, which has just been defined in the previous paragraphs. But the reformulation of the definition in terms of analogy brings with it new examples as well, as if the examples that have just been provided were not fully adequate. These new examples are given in a footnote:

There is, for example, an analogy between the juridical relation of human actions and the mechanical relation of moving forces. . . . Here right and moving force are quite dissimilar things, but in their relation there is complete similarity. By means of such an analogy, I can obtain a notion of things which absolutely are unknown to me. For instance, as the promotion of the welfare of children (= a) is to the love of parents (= b), so the welfare of the human species (= c) is to that unknown character in God (= x), which we call love; not as if it had the least similarity to any human inclination, but because we can suppose its relation to the world to be similar to that which things of the world bear to one another. But the concept of relation in this case is a mere category, namely, the concept of cause, which has nothing to do with sensibility. (*Prolegomena*, 106 n.1)

These examples differ from those in the main text in an interesting way: they are both linked closely to the categories that bind transcendental philosophy to metaphysics, that is, to the "analogies" linked to the three laws of motion. Thus they would appear to have a special status, a privileged place in the linkages that make up the system: they seem to correspond directly to the exemplary structure that Kant finds so "remarkable" and that is also so troubling for the system. This would be the case, in particular, for the symbol representing God's relation to man in terms of "love," since this is based on the concept of causality and is thus the symbolic correlate of the example of inertia. The special status of this particular analogy in representing the symbol links the "remarkable" quality of the metaphysical example with the concept of analogy by which the self-reflexivity of symbolic language is represented. The narrative that emerges in the discussion of the law of inertia—the story of matter dying as a sacrifice to philosophy—would thus seem to point to this extra symbol in the footnote, the symbol of God's love.

The privileged place of this symbol seems to be represented, moreover, by its particular term of comparison, *love*, since love would appear to be the relation par excellence, in particular the love of a parent for a child. Yet the analogy remains somewhat unclear, because it is less the feeling of love that represents God's relation to man than the causality of love, the causal relation of parental love to the child's welfare. Of all symbols to exemplify a causal analogy, love does not seem to be the most obvious. The impact of the figure of love in the symbol does not seem congruent, that is, with its strictly conceptual function as a relation of causality. As was the case in the example of inertia, the symbol of love seems to say more than the causal analogy suggests.

Kant indeed came back to this symbol ten years later in *Religion Within the Limits of Reason Alone* (1793). Here again he discusses the necessity of representing supersensible ideas in sensible form, or "the personified idea of the good principle." In a footnote to this discussion he writes:

It is indeed a limitation of human reason, and one which is ever insep-arable from it, that we can conceive of no considerable moral worth in the actions of a personal being without representing that person, or his manifestation, in human guise. This is not to assert that such worth is in itself (κατ' ἀλήθειαν) so conditioned, but merely that we must al-ways resort to some analogy to natural existences to render supersen-sible qualities intelligible to ourselves. . . . The Scriptures too accom-modate themselves to this mode of representation when, in order to make us comprehend the degree of God's love for the human race, they ascribe to Him the very highest sacrifice which a loving being can make, a sacrifice performed in order that even those who are unworthy may be made happy ("For God so loved the world ..."); though we can-not indeed rationally conceive how an all-sufficient Being could sacri-fice a part of what belongs to His state of bliss or rob Himself of a pos-session. Such is the *schematism of analogy*, with which (as a means of explanation) we cannot dispense. But to transform it into a *schema-tism of objective determination* (for the extension of our knowledge) is *anthropomorphism*, which has, from the moral point of view (in reli-gion), most injurious consequences.[19]

The "schematism of analogy" that Kant attributes to Scripture here is an extension of the analogy discussed in the *Prolego-mena*: there, God is represented symbolically by comparing his relation to man with the loving relation of parent and child; here, God's love for man is further represented in terms of the specific means by which this love is responsible for man's wel-fare (i.e., how God's love makes man "happy"). The analogy here, that is, explains the specific application of the causal cat-egory in the symbolic love-relation. This causal efficacy of pa-rental love is represented in terms of the operation of the sacri-fice. It is God's sacrifice that permits "even those who are un-worthy" to be made happy, that is, to be "saved." It is thus the specific structure of a sacrificial relation that permits the crea-tion of the symbolic analogy between the phenomenal causal relation and the relation to the nonphenomenal being. That is, the structure of the symbol as a symbol of symbol is linked, not to *any* causal relation, but specifically to the sacrificial one. God's "love" has a privileged status as a symbol because it is de-fined by this structure.

The appropriateness of the sacrificial structure as the privileged symbol would seem to lie in its representation of the negative character of symbolic self-knowledge: the sacrifice is a loss suffered in the service of a gain.[20] In its broadest outlines in the footnote, this relation appears to be the loss suffered by God, robbing himself of a possession, or sacrificing part of his state of bliss, in order for man to be made "happy" or to achieve his own state of bliss. The sacrifice thus establishes a relation between God and man that is structured like a chiasmus, or an inverted analogy in which God and man exchange the properties of bliss and unhappiness through the agency of the sacrifice. Put in terms of the parent-child relationship of the earlier analogy, the chiasmus would appear as follows:

Parent's bliss   Parent's unhappiness

Child's unhappiness   Child's bliss

This figure represents the negative relation between man and God (the bliss of one is the unhappiness of the other) as the principle of the unity between them. The symbol thus represents its own negativity in terms of a loss of the knowledge of God regained as the knowledge of the mere thinking of God, that is, the knowledge of the limit.

If we examine the footnote carefully, however, the notion of the sacrifice does not appear to be entirely straightforward. The passage Kant cites from the Gospel of John reminds us that the loving sacrifice for the human child also involves another parent-child relationship:

For God so loved the world, that he gave his only begotten Son, that whosoever believeth in him should not perish, but have everlasting life.
    For God sent not his Son into the world to condemn the world; but that the world through him might be saved.[21]

God's loving relation to man as his child depends on a relation to another child, the only true child. The parental relationship between God and man is mediated through the parental relationship between God and Christ. But in this mediating relation, the "sacrifice" is not the sacrifice *by* the parent but rather *of* the child: in sending his true son into the world so that the world might be saved "through" him, God is sending his first son to his death. The loving relation between parent and child now depends upon a relation in which the parent sends another child to its death: man is only related to God as the beloved child by being the second, foster child, the one that comes after the first child is eliminated. If "parent and child" represent the two-term relationship par excellence, the introduction of the Christ story suggests that there is an extra child somewhere that had to be eliminated in order for parental love to be established. The balance of the four terms of the analogy, or of the two relations, depends on the suppression of another relation that makes the establishment of the analogy possible in the first place.

This other relation creates an imbalance that can be thought of in terms of the chiastic structure of the sacrifice. The extra child, or rather the death of the extra child, creates an asymmetry in this structure, which must be reformulated now not in terms of bliss and unhappiness but in terms of life and death:

Parent's life ⟍   ⟋ Other child's death

Child's death ⟋   ⟍ Child's life

The appearance of the other child's death in the analogy displaces the structure from its position between the terms *God* and *man* to a position "outside" of them, where it cannot be considered an act *of* either of them. Similarly, the agent of this *death,* or the other child, since it appears *only* in function *of* its death, cannot be considered a child in any understandable sense of the word (one could say that Christ, insofar as he appears here only as a child to be sacrificed for the parental love of man, is already dead, and hence not a "beloved" child from the beginning). The other relations within the analogy are thus placed in relation to an "event" that cannot be understood as either sensible or supersensible, an act or property of man or of God. The negativity of this other relation—represented as death—thus remains incomprehensible, since it cannot be properly associated with either term: for man, it is God's death; for God it is Christ's death. This other relation is not, therefore, comprehensible in terms of any kind of thought or knowable difference. If God's relation to the living child becomes comprehensible through the relation to the dead one, the latter cannot be considered a "relation" in any known sense of the term. The other's death, as it were, holds a place for man in the analogy; it opens up the relation in which a place will be reserved for man, even as it closes off the complete understanding of itself as a comprehensible event.[22]

This imbalance within the symbolic analogy, which both permits it to work and makes its complete self-closure impossible, indicates the impossibility for the symbol to represent itself adequately as language. What remains after the symbol has symbolized itself is always another term that is not contained within the symbolic structure. Thus the examples of the symbol given in the main text of the *Prolegomena* produce the examples in the footnote, and these generate other examples in other texts. The movement from symbol to symbol marks the excess of the language of the system in relation to its conceptualization, or the excessiveness of language as occurrence in relation to its self-representation. The division between thinking and knowing in the system, which takes the form of a self-closing structure, might thus be considered a displacement of the difference between event and representation in language, a difference that does not permit systematization as a structure. The attempt to contain this difference, this lag between the event and its representation, would produce, within the structure of the division between knowing and thinking, the narratives that emerge at points of articulation within the system. Thus, while the parent-child analogy in the first symbol of love is understandable in terms of a structure of comparison, the introduction of the Christ child is possible only through a narrative, a relation between a "first" and a "second" child, a life and a death that have already taken place. The temporal ordering of this narrative would attempt to contain the difference that cannot be systematized in conceptual structures. Like the narrative that appears in the metaphysical part of the system, this narrative exceeds the conceptual structure of the critical argument. But its emergence in the symbol indicates that the temporality of the narrative does not derive from an empirical model. The story that emerges at the joints of the system tells of the impossibility for the language of the system to close upon itself in its representation, a nonclosure that appears as the irrevocable "priority" of an event.

We might think of this nonclosure in terms of the difference between the symbol and its concept, or the symbol and its representation as an analogy. If the symbol represents the thinking of the relation of the sensible to the supersensible, the concept of the symbol—the definition of the symbol in critical discourse—enacts a kind of positing that cannot be recuperated symbolically. This nonrecuperation would be marked by the proliferation of examples, not "empirical" examples, but examples in the argument, linguistic examples, which would always eventually take the form of a narrative. The concept of the limit that structures the system would thus be made possible by the symbol and impossible by its concept. The articulation of parts of the system by the symbol would be made possible and impossible by the disarticulation of the symbol with itself. The limit, we might say then, is divided between the structure the symbol symbolizes and the story its example tells.[23]

We recognize this story, moreover, in the metaphysical example. If we reexamine the exemplary relation between transcendental philosophy and metaphysics in terms of the workings of the symbol, the narrative that emerges in the former—the death of matter for philosophy—appears to retell, or repeat, the symbolic sacrifice. Force, or the conceptualization of motion as continually falling, must be read not only in reference to a scientific calculation, but also in reference to the "fall" narrated in the symbol. But this latter reference is not a purely conceptual foundation of the example in the symbol, or the exemplary structure of empirical knowledge in knowledge of limits; for the "death" in this story is not part of a system of conceptualized relations. Rather, the "death" of matter, as the event of "force," re-marks the event in the self-symbolization of the system that founds and yet also exceeds its own knowledge. The enigmatic externality of the event called "force," its exemplary position as an empirical example, marks an event that occurs not in the empirical world but "in" the system itself as language. The threat of the metaphysical example, that the conceptual system might be determined by something outside of it, is not therefore a threat that comes from the empirical world.[24] The externality upon which the system relies is to a certain extent, that is, only *figured* by the empirical world. The narrative that emerges in this figuration says very little indeed about the empirical world as such, and a good deal about the "externality" of the system to itself.[25]

The "remarkable" quality of the metaphysical example, in particular the example of inertia, thus lies in its double relation to physical science on the one hand and to the symbol on the other. While on the one hand the example of inertia exemplifies the articulation between the discursive science of philosophy and the laws of the empirical world, on the other hand it tells of a disarticulation of the discursive system with itself in the symbol. The relation between philosophy and empirical science is thus disrupted by the relation between the symbol and the example, a relation that would be akin to the relation between the *linguistic* examples of the symbol in the text of the *Prolegomena* and the different examples in its footnotes. The empirical example becomes, in this context, yet another linguistic example of a symbol. It tells less about the relation between discursive and nondiscursive knowledge than about the impossible relation of discursive knowledge to itself.

This double aspect of the exemplary-symbolic structure sheds some light on the split between "experience" and "empirical science" in Kant's system. For if "empirical science" refers to observation and mathematics, "experience" refers first of all to a philosophical vocabulary, the vocabulary of empirical philosophy (and in particular that of Hume). "Experience" is not a concept derived from empirical observation but a figure generated by discursive arguments to supplement their own self-representation. "Experience" thus functions as the linguistic example that always accompanies the empirical example. One could thus say that no matter how much it wants to and indeed does refer to empirical law, a discursive text must also say "experience." And in saying that, it has left the empirical realm altogether and is telling the same old story of love and death, a story with neither a purely experiential nor purely spiritual meaning.

The impossibility of fully symbolizing itself thus turns philosophical criticism into something like a literary criticism. This is not a failure, indeed, but a form of rigor, the rigor that exhibits the necessity and impossibility of linking the laws of language to the laws of the empirical world, or of achieving systematic access to a "world" through language. To the extent that all discursive theory is subject to these necessities, the knowledge of theory will always fall into a similar pattern. What discursive theory knows will always be that it cannot know, entirely, what it is: and to this extent its object will always be "linguistic."[26] That is, in Kant's symbolic terms, there can be no *falling*, in theory, that is not also falling *"in love."* And the story of this love is not only a recollection of the world we know but also a repetition of the event that divides us from it.[27]

Of the Eye and the Law

> The way in which the other presents himself, exceeding *the idea of the other in me*, we call the face.
> —Emmanuel Levinas, *Totality and Infinity*

> They take pleasure in keeping under their eyes the living image of this people whom they execrate.
> —Jean-Paul Sartre, *Anti-Semite and Jew*

I begin by recalling a photograph that perhaps everyone has seen at one time or another. Apparently it was taken by National Socialist forces during the destruction of the Warsaw Ghetto. A child, he cannot be much older than eight or nine years of age, is holding up his hands before what must be (they are off camera) weapons directly pointed at him. The child is wearing one of those hats for which we remember Jackie Coogan. There is no star on the child's coat. Unlike the well-fed soldiers in the background—and even one of these is obliquely pointing a rifle at the child—the boy with raised hands is not well nourished. His expression is serious, but not defiant. Certainly his face registers considerable anguish, much more than the faces of the arrested adults and other children in the background, who appear to be somewhat bewildered. Unlike the others with raised arms, this child stands out from the group, alone and vulnerable in the foreground. His expression is so self-possessed that it suggests that only he intuits not only the moral perversity but the extreme danger of this situation. Clearly, in the figure of this terrified child a decidedly moral conscience comes to appearance.

Since the Shoah, this photograph has become exemplary of what must never be repeated. And yet, what does it mean to consider the exemplary in this way? What philosophical assumptions are valorized when one privileges a very specific moment as representative for countless other moments very much like it? And in what sense does a photographic example assume a unification of existential horizons, not to say the presencing of a subject who transcends himself and the temporality of a moment? Indeed, the raising of such a moment to exemplary status may obstruct an approach to the religious understanding of what Emmanuel Levinas has viewed as the relation between the ethical and the infinite, a relation that transcends the presence or simple here and now of any given event and, in so doing, breaks with a unified representation of existential and ethical horizons. That is, our culture's attempt to grasp the ethical import of its immediate past by way of photographic documentation is radically challenged by the kind of phenomenological interrogation undertaken by Levinas. For such a phenomenological interrogation resists the pictorial recoverability of a historical event as a mimetic unification of existential and ethical horizons. In the light of such an alternative understanding of exemplarity, I wish to consider how a photograph can be viewed against the grain of an appearance that presupposes the unified existential horizons of a subject's presence, and to situate this consideration in terms of some Judaic perspectives phenomenologically developed by Levinas.

In 1960, Maurice Merleau-Ponty delivered a paper entitled "The Child's Relations with Others" ("Les Relations avec autrui chez l'enfant"). I am particularly struck by the following passage:

When we considered the child's imagination, it appeared likewise that we could not assimilate what is called the image of the child to a kind of degraded, weakened copy of preceding perceptions. What is called *imagination* is an emotional conduct. Consequently, here again we found ourselves, as it were, beneath the relation of the knowing subject to the known object. We had to do with a primordial operation by which the child organizes the imaginary, just as he organizes the perceived.[1]

One might immediately wonder how we are to detect the way in which the Jewish child in the photograph imaginatively organizes or figures the perceived. Of course, this way of putting matters emphasizes an epistemological if not psychological

"Mit Gewalt aus den Bunkern herausgeholt (Pulled from the bunkers by force)." From *The Stroop Report*; see note 6 to this essay. Photo courtesy YIVO Institute for Jewish Research.

mode of analysis. However, my concern is in breaking with an analysis that would, first of all, depend upon a hermenuetic re-construction of an interiorized consciousness or psychology of the child. That is, we might begin by considering the phenome-nological position of Merleau-Ponty with respect to Emmanuel Levinas's point that in our relation with the Other, our being is not determined or conditioned on the basis of a representational framework through which an individual psychology of the sub-ject or reconstruction of consciousness can be made. Of course, this would bear not only on psychology but on those categories through which we traditionally consider notions like character, plot, or scene, narrative terms that not only give access to cer-tain interpretations of agency and image but, more generally, to history itself as a sequence of moral examples. In short, by way of Levinas and Merleau-Ponty we may begin to rethink many of the concepts which underwrite our usual understanding of history, representation, and psychology insofar as a phenomenological approach may be capable of a dismantling of representational reconstructions that would stand for the historical, a dismantling that extends to the construction of historical examples.

It almost goes without saying that to consider the Shoah in terms of such a dismantling would demand the kind of reflection and development that goes far beyond the scope of an essay. Even Levinas, who himself reflects on this question, has never mounted an extensive or systematic meditation that considers historical particulars or examples. Of course, in an essay one can only work out a very small aspect of this vast field of inquiry, and in doing so I wish to interrogate a peripheral moment that has taken on exemplary moral force in terms of its appearance as a photograph that has, since World War II, become world famous. In part, I wish to find ways in which to describe what a term like Merleau-Ponty's "imaginary" might mean once we agree, however provisionally with Levinas, that in the act of baring one's face before the other, an undetermined concept of being is disclosed, a concept not reducible to an interiorized notion of exemplary consciousness or psychology wherein subjecthood is recovered as a transparent historical and political reality. If we were to speak of a psychology or consciousness, perhaps it would necessarily be one constituted in an exteriority of relationships in whose correspondences a photograph as trace comes to appearance, even as it is left behind.

Let us return to the figure of the child in the photograph. It is striking how the child's raised hands and facial expression are outward signs of what Merleau-Ponty is calling the imagination as emotional conduct. In fact, it is precisely this "emotional conduct" that calls for interpretation. Most curious about the image of this child is that its gesture and expression are peculiarly unchildlike, as if the child were acknowledging that he fits the role of someone who could be a threat to the Third Reich. In part, this is underscored by the photograph's composition, in which the child is seen as isolated from the group, an isolation or unprotectedness which suggests that perhaps he is being singled out for punishment. Indeed, whereas the other persecuted figures are standing near one another for support— some children peer at the camera from behind the adults—the composition of the photograph suggests that the child with raised hands in the foreground is incongruously taking the brunt of something he cannot possibly understand. The incongruity between the person who is the child and the expression which he bears, in addition to his unprotected isolation from the group and the violence he confronts, allows us to perceive a coming to appearance of an emotional comportment whose signs or traces are politically and historically made manifest even as the being of the child *as* child is undetermined with respect to its revealed image. Here, of course, one departs from an understanding of the example which presumes an identification of being and appearance, an identification that presumes not only a psychologization of the figure, but also an existential presencing, the kind presupposed in the Stroop Report in which this photograph was included. Indeed, from the perspective of the report, Sartre's apt pronouncement on the Nazis holds true: "Actually they take pleasure in protecting these few persons through a sort of inversion of their sadism: they take pleasure in keeping under their eyes the living image of this people who they execrate."[2] In other words, this photograph, which was taken in part for Heinrich Himmler's pleasure, sets the child aside as one who is spared under gun point, as one who is protected through an inverse sadism wherein a sentimental notion of childhood plays a very central role.

My argument, however, is that the photograph does not entirely submit to such a gaze, since the figure of the child is so ambiguously situated that its expression or appearance transcends the very notion of childhood, which is necessary for the anti-Semite to take pleasure in keeping a living image under his eyes by means of photography. Indeed, the photograph of the Warsaw child resists the reductive gaze of the Nazi camera eye by refusing to surrender to a commonplace mental construction of childhood, a refusal that accompanies its surrender to the undetermined: the Shoah. This resistance is nothing less than the imaginary resistance to being-in-the-world-as-a-child, a resistance that betokens the existential collapse of appearance and being. In fact, the child's appearance—his position and expression—might be said to overshoot the person that is the child, which is to say, it overshoots exemplarity itself. What Levinas helps us consider is the way in which an auxiliary appearance like a photograph surreptitiously irrupts into the world and in so doing interrupts an event from a transcendental and ethical standpoint. Our consideration of the photograph, then, would mark a position from beyond or outside the event that nevertheless irrupts into the phenomenality of its historical unfolding. Whereas in Husserl one would attempt to reconstruct the intersubjective intentionalities of the represented agencies in the photograph for the sake of establishing how consciousness constitutes or objectifies meanings, in Levinas one would turn to a transcendental phenomenon whose ethical irruption into history disturbs that synchronicity or unity which we ordinarily take as a precondition to interpret consciousness as self-identical with the meanings it constitutes. The photograph, then, in registering the unprotected isolation of the child and his peculiarly mature expression manifests the supplementary trace structure through which the ethical comes into appearance. Consequently the "emotional conduct" revealed in the face of the photographed child comprises an imaginary structure that does not originate in the child himself but in the irruption of the photographed image or trace which has been captured by an other.

By means of such a transcendental irruption of the photograph, the victim is projected beyond the finitude of being, not to say, the ipseity of childhood. Moreover, the victim is projected beyond the familiar historical understanding of the exemplary as that self-identical construction which embodies or objectifies immanent conditions of being, appearance, and, too, action. In contrast to the exemplary considered as a complete but unusual circumstance that solicits direct identification for didactic purposes, the image of the Warsaw child enters history as if it could stand for a self-conscious agency capable of maturely bestowing or comprising those responsibilities that, properly speaking, lie beyond its grasp or its existential horizons. In other words, the image's exemplary appearance is intuited in an imaginative horizon that manifests itself beyond the ipseity of the image per se. To use Merleau-Ponty's words, we find ourselves "beneath the relation of the knowing subject to the known object." The composition of the child's image, then, elicits correspondences that break with those horizons of existential and circumstantial unification which the photograph in its usual mimetic exemplary sense would suggest. It is, then, the correspondences between an imaginary ethical relation and the world which would take the place of a fixed relation between knowing subject and a known object. If Merleau-Ponty remarks that with respect to the child "we [have] to do with a primordial operation by which the child organizes the imaginary, just as he organizes the perceived," I would like to suggest that in the photograph of the Warsaw child such an organization depends on the exemplary irruption of a representation eluding ipseity in which a child's imagination is transcendentally constituted from beyond the being of the child.

In *Totality and Infinity*, Levinas writes: "The relations of transcendence lead to the other, whose mode the idea of Infinity has enabled us to specify."[3] Levinas's work takes into account how it is we can objectify transcendental relationships which are characterized by the ways in which doing, labor, and thinking imply a relation with that other in whose shadow the determinacy of the subject is exceeded and an infinity of possible relations are opened up, an infinity in terms of which the subject disappears as that which is merely self-identical. For Levinas the broaching of the infinite yields a solitude beyond the representable that is the effect of the subject's exceeding itself. Levinas argues that the solitude of the subject's transcendence cannot be thematically recovered within a totality of relationships in which the merely finite is expressed. The subject, therefore, cannot thematically present itself as an example for others in the familiar moral sense. For Levinas there are no saints: "The movement from me to the other could not present itself as a theme to an objective gaze freed from the confrontation of the other, to a reflection."[4] For this reason, the photograph we are considering would not be thematically recoverable, since its ethical relations cannot be localized or exemplified in terms of finite subjects. Indeed, "experience, the idea of infinity, occurs in the relationship with the other. The idea of infinity is the social relationship."[5] Yet, this relationship is not identifiable as the moral sort of exemplary relationships outlined by someone like Polonius in *Hamlet*, or Cephalus in *The Republic*, two figures who presuppose their self-certainty in a determinate totality of social and political relationships.

Levinas's invocation of the infinite has the political aim of resisting the totality of the state and its apparatuses of representation, which, in the photograph we are considering, places emphasis on exemplary ipseity, finitude, or totality. Certainly the photograph, as Nazi document, reflects a hostile perspective maintained by an other which regards the child through a pitiless gaze wherein the impossibility of any relation except that to death or the finitely inert can be established. Clearly, the camera has been used obscenely to document not only the child's destruction, but the gazer's pleasure, which, in part, emanates from the secure sovereignty of the viewer, a sovereignty which we are being tempted to share especially when photographs of the Shoah disclose themselves as voyeuristic glances into the freakish and the grotesque. Such imaginary constructions attempt to suggest otherness through a deprecation that draws on a theatrical or cinematic banality, one that accedes to the hideously supernatural or otherworldly. Without doubt one could say that this is a hollow metaphysical gesture whose effect is to reduce the other to what is ineluctably finite and degradable, that is to say, to *an example* which is comprehensible in terms of total domination and determination.

This is what Levinas would see as the self-certainty of the image that is achieved through the mimetic deprivation of an other's ability to survive. For the Nazis, the promotion of a hollow metaphysics of death is meant to falsify the historical by estranging the image to such a degree that it is no longer capable of being thought as something that could be real, even as the camera validates the exemplary truth that pictures tell. In *Difficult Freedom* (*Difficile liberté*), Levinas calls this pagan: a culture that searches for the closure that makes possible an abandonment of the face of the other. Indeed, the photograph we are considering was taken for the purposes of documenting the liquidation and became part of a well-known report ordered by Heinrich Himmler.[6] Yet, the photograph could also be said to represent an aspect of Nazi photojournalism, which, like all photojournalism, searches for exemplary closure in the irony that from the gazer's remote and safe position the unthinkable is shown to be real. It is only when a filmmaker like Ingmar Bergman uses the photograph of the Warsaw child in *Persona* within a film language that resists such photojournalistic closure, that we begin to glimpse the moral objectionability of representational logocentrism.

Yet, even in a National Socialist image we can perceive a heteronomy of imaginary relays that are nevertheless embedded or entangled in the scene of exemplification. For example, the finitude of the Nazi gaze is ruptured by what Julia Kristeva in *Powers of Horror* calls the psychology of abjection wherein the infinite is linked to a construction of the "abject object" in terms of the death drive and its various political articulations. Here the gaze, so desirous of validating the destruction of the abject object, facilitates the impulse to kill, to destroy the figure it is so anxious to keep before it. As Kristeva summarizes the Nazi position, "The Jew: a conjunction of waste and object of desire, of corpse and life, fecality and pleasure . . . *Abjection itself.*"[7] In terms of the Shoah the construction of the abject relates to the puzzling ways in which the Nazis meticulously documented and, at the same time, expunged traces of the Shoah. That such imaginary relays are chiastically bound, even as they resist the totalization of the glance of consciousness, underscores the heteronomy of the imaginary of the photograph. Certainly we could map other heteronomous aspects of the photographic imaginary: that of our own glance, that of the child's glance, that of the camera's eye, that of the omniscient historical witness, that of the other child figures, and so on. To consider this photograph fully one would have to entertain the imaginary comportments of these gazes and to interrelate them along the lines set forth by not only Levinas but Merleau-Ponty in *The Visible and the Invisible*, wherein the Kantian assumption of a "unity of apperception" is thoroughly undermined by vigorously putting into question a stable distance and self-identity of the gaze, which would validate "that central vision that joins the scattered visions . . . that *I* think that must be able to accompany all our experiences."[8]

In the photograph of the Warsaw child, the figure of the boy, which we can now begin provisionally to understand as opening onto a manifold of imaginary constructions that resist totalization, is exemplary insofar as it stands for a being that "cannot be integrated into the identity of the same," a condition underscored by the boy's standing apart from the other hostages as if he alone were answerable. Levinas writes, "The exteriority of the infinite being is manifested in the absolute resistance which by its apparition, its epiphany, it opposes to all my powers. Its epiphany is not simply the apparition of a form in the light, sensible or intelligible, but already this *no* cast to powers: its logos is: 'You shall not kill.' "[9] This quotation leads me to wonder whether the photograph of the child is not a trace through which we imagine an ethical epiphany or law, a persistent showing that iconoclastically interdicts a unification of gazes. Could the photograph not be understood as an epiphany or baring of the face which prohibits the gaze from becoming a totalizing and unifying agency of apprehension? And as such does the epiphantic not serve as the phenomenological horizon which brings into correspondence the emotional, the imaginary, the perceptible, the ethical, and the exemplary? The photograph of the child, then, would mark the tracing of a structure that facilitates a coming into appearance of such an epiphany. Though not epiphantic, like a work of art, the photograph is the residue of an epiphany that has come to appearance. As such it points to where the epiphantic has come to pass as that which brings correspondences or attunements to consciousness.

That our gaze may not be reducible to a finite apprehension is interdicted not merely by the resistance of epiphantic disclosure to totalization but by the historical given that perception of the child's face cannot ignore its numberless likenesses in the faces of those children who perished. Yet, the paradox from a Levinasian position is that even if exemplary of the liquidation of countless other Jewish children, the image, which cannot be divorced from its being perceived, is too heteronomous to function as a mere example or cultural cliché. In the coming to appearance of this face to consciousness, a power makes itself known which escapes the exercise of brutality: the power not of the individual to survive catastrophe or to meet his or her fate with honor, but the power of the ethical to persist in its exceeding the life of the individual wherein it appears as only a momentary epiphany, as nothing more than the appearance of a face before an other, of what Levinas calls the *me voici*. And this *me voici*, of course, suggests itself through the figure's isolation from the group, its coming to pass as a vulnerable and unprotected appearance that incipiently acknowledges the annihilating capacity of the other. That an ethical principle may live on at the cost of an individual's own sacrifice is commonplace enough. But in the photograph the child's image does not actively sacrifice itself in such an exemplary manner, rather, it passively stands forth in its isolation, perplexity, anguish, and incomprehension. Given the photograph's compositional structure, the figure of the child is so ambiguous that, to some extent, it situates itself outside of an exercise of power and only passively discloses itself in its infinitude to the extent that its nudity and destitution are not strategically placed before an enemy for the sake of engaging him in a struggle in which a principle is put at stake, but that, rather, the disclosure of the figure escapes and exceeds thought even as it manifests itself as the coming to appearance of a meaningful image. This establishes the exemplary in terms of what Merleau-Ponty calls the imaginary. However, unlike a Bachelardian notion of imagination, this transcendent imagination as a showing of the child's face and hands is not thematizable, and what it tells us of an emotional disposition certainly cannot be reducible to a determined notion of subjectivity or childhood. The figure of the child, then, as a transcendentally constituted imagination, is that trace of the infinite wherein ethics is constituted and persists even in the murderous gaze of an Other.

In *L'Au delà du verset* (Beyond the verse) Levinas states: "the revelation of the [holy] name is not solely the corollary of the unity of a being; it carries us much further. Perhaps to the beyond of being."[10] Since there is no word that is proper to God alone, the Talmudic tradition considers names capable of functioning as signs that refer to the holiness of God. These proper names for God are said to be heteronomous because they signify from the beyond of being. They cannot be thought in terms of essence and therefore "trace themselves as a modality of transcendence."[11] Elsewhere, Levinas speaks of the appearance of the face in terms of a visitation of the Other, and one ought to be struck by the parallels this suggests in terms of that name which is not the corollary of the unity of being, but which carries us further—to the beyond of being. For the appearance of the face is similarly not reducible to any one proper name but signifies from beyond the name even as its appearance shines forth as self-identical and capable of disclosing an ethical manifold of relationships in its becoming unconcealed before others. Indeed, the photograph of the Warsaw child meets the condition of a bearing of the face as a trace structure surviving the passing of the face, what is its destitution or death. Yet, the disclosure of the face, a disclosure transpiring in the absence of the name, brings before us questions of responsibility, obligation, and justice. "The presence of a face thus signifies an irrecusable order, a command, which puts a stop to the availability of consciousness."[12] That is, in the bearing of the face a certain "law" is revealed instead of an interiorized psychology of individual will or resistance. This is why Levinas insists, "The 'absolutely other' is not reflected in consciousness."[13]

Similarly, Merleau-Ponty's notion of "emotional conduct" transcends notions of interiorized consciousness and also suggests the possibility of an imaginary disclosure of the absolutely other by means of a residual coming to appearance. Such an appearance occurs not merely in a photograph but through the photograph as trace structure, and it is this coming to appearance of the trace which is indicative of the name signing for that which is beyond being. The "emotional conduct," as we have noticed, transpires in the coming to appearance of the face, though it is an appearance that comes from beyond the bearing of the face itself. Of significance is not merely that a religious-ethical command or law can inhere in a politically suspect representation, but that this command or law has been disclosed by the face of the Warsaw child from a position exterior to itself which consciousness is obliged to imagine. The fact that consciousness is obliged to imagine this is possible only because "the face, still a thing among things, breaks through the form that nevertheless delimits it."[14] Levinas continues:

The nudity of a face is a bareness without any cultural ornament, an absolution, a detachment from its form in the midst of the production of its form. A face *enters* into our world from an absolutely foreign sphere, that is, precisely from an absolute, that which in fact is the very name for ultimate strangeness. The signifyingness of a face in its abstractness is in the literal sense of the term extraordinary, outside of every order, every world. How is such a production possible? How can the coming of the other, the visitation of a face, the absolute not be—in any way—converted into a revelation, not even a symbolism or a suggestion? How is a face not simply a *true representation* in which the other renounces his alterity? The answer, we will have to study the exceptional signifyingness of a trace and the personal "order" in which such a signifyingness is possible.[15]

What establishes an ethical horizon that resists exemplary objectification is not the face itself but its nudity or coming to appearance before consciousness as what is vulnerable. The face as "emotional conduct" is ultimately strange and unassimilable within the context of what Husserl calls the "natural attitude" even as it obliges us to remember what has come to pass concretely in history. Since consciousness for Levinas concerns consciousness of the sacred, a photograph, such as we are considering, can be understood as a coming to perception of a trace that signs for alterity, not unlike a sacred name that is not "proper." Indeed, if such a historical trace of the Shoah signs for the approach of a face, it still has a residual exemplary and representational function: to announce the otherwise than being.

Such an appearance to consciousness of the otherwise than being "is a non-synchronizable diachrony, which representation and thematization dissimulate by transforming the trace into a *sign* of a departure, and then reducing the ambiguity of the face either to a play of physiognomy or to the indicating of a signified. But thus opens the dangerous way in which a pious thought, or one concerned with order, hastily deduces the existence of God."[16] These remarks in *Otherwise Than Being Or Beyond Essence* remind us that one must not assume congruity or identity between the image as trace and the alterity for whose approach it can be said to sign or name. Hence we must not conclude, simply, that God reveals himself in the face of a victim. This, of course, is representative of how profound the differences are between Judaic and Christian traditions, the latter being predicated on precisely the epiphantic disclosure of God in the face of the crucified. Rather, for Levinas the trace merely signs for a being that cannot be said, but in whose very momentary posture an ethical comportment or law asserts itself in the bringing into correspondence of what Husserl called the "intentional correlates" of consciousness, that is, the noema.[17]

What interested Levinas already in his early work on Husserl, *The Theory of Intuition in Husserl's Phenomenology*, is the difference between phenomenological signification, which only points to an object, and intuition, which in fact reaches or possesses an object. Intuition, however, concerns the grasping of objects that are "merely thought," objects that are given to intuition as part of a perceptual experience through which the object is actually constituted by means of being faced. Intuition, then, concerns "an intentionality whose intrinsic meaning consists in reaching its object and facing it as existing."[18] In Levinas's later work the question of facing becomes key to an intuition of the holy that depends upon an understanding of ethics (rather than a privileging of ontology) as a bringing into correspondence of intentional correlates in terms of their intuitive significance. But if such an intuition grasps its object, it does not do so by making thought adequate to things, that is, by establishing identity or resemblances.[19] Rather, the "object" is grasped only insofar as it is phenomenologically experienced or faced by perception as a manifold of correspondences that cannot be homogeneously "resolved into relations." In a very important statement, given the studies that would follow decades later, Levinas writes, "The *existence* of the world cannot be reduced to the categories which form its essence but lies in the fact of being, so to speak, met by consciousness."[20] Levinas hints that given the irreducibility of the existence of the world to categories, its being faced by a consciousness aware of this irreducibility is already an occasion for the transcendence of Western ontology and an intuitive grasping of the otherwise than being.

The intuition of the photograph of the Warsaw child is, of course, subject to a similar stricture: that even as example the child is not reducible to onotological categories of resemblance or exemplarity. A consequence of this would be that the photograph of the child would not be comprehensible in terms of what Aristotle calls "practical wisdom."[21] Christian morality, of course, has always relied on the Ancient Greek assumption of parallel illumination and the revelation of moral universals, and these depend upon ontological categories that allow for substitutability, resemblance, and identification. That is, the question of moral exemplarity is directly tied to notions of imitation and identification which presume the universality of the human subject. Hence in Dante's *Divine Comedy*, we are not surprised to discover that Dante the pilgrim is, as universal moral subject, potentially capable of being in the position of any one of the souls he meets in the afterworld. Similarly, in the medieval play *Everyman*, the protagonist is a moral agency whose exemplary force depends upon philosophical assumptions concerning substitutability, resemblance, and identification. Levinas's intuitive phenomenology, however, undercuts such ontological and moral assumptions. Indeed, already a Renaissance figure like Montaigne criticizes Christian understanding of the moral example when in the "Apology for Raymond Sebond" he writes: "The participation that we have in the knowledge of truth, whatever it may be, has not been acquired by our own powers. God has taught us that clearly enough by the witnesses that he has chosen from the common people, simple and ignorant, to instruct us in his admirable secrets."[22] By wryly recalling the commonly held assumption that we directly learn what God wants us to know through commonplace examples rather than through abstract philosophical or theological reflection, Montaigne points to the strangeness of moral examples and their nonsynchronizable alterity, hinting that they require reflective reconciliation.

Levinas, of course, would not want to suggest that the exemplary bearing of the face is simply perplexing and in need of reflective reconciliation, though he would want to convey the idea that an ethical grasp cannot be embodied in a conceptual system that strongly valorizes the rules of a practical wisdom which derive from mimetic examples. That is, for Levinas the Judaic notion of the law is an antimimetic or iconoclastic imperative. And yet, even in a moment such as the breaking of the tables in *Exodus*, something concrete comes to appearance in history, albeit from the otherwise than being.

The concrete is defined by Levinas as the "il y a," the terrifying coming to pass of an event which is not reducible to ontology but which nevertheless leaves traces of its immanence in the wake of its having happened. The *il y a*, then, is not strictly something that can be interiorized and held fast as personal conscious experience, though it can be phenomenologically intuited. In *Existence and Existents*, which addresses the Shoah, Levinas says that the *il y a* is horror: "The rustling of the *il y a* . . . is horror. We have noted the way it insinuates itself in the night, as an undetermined menace of space itself disengaged from its function as receptacle for objects, as a means of access to beings."[23] Here, as elsewhere, the *il y a* is radically estranged from those conditions out of which a world could be made up. The horror of the *il y a* is the coming to pass of an ethical catastrophe whose moments are countless and whose participants are themselves put in the position of having to make moral decisions in the midst of what appear as anonymous crowds or faces: people without proper names. In short, the *il y a* is the most concrete and agonizing perception of what our moral duty is in conditions that violently and sadistically militate against our human limitations and capacity to obey the laws of God.

"[Such] horror is somehow a movement which will strip consciousness of its very 'subjectivity.' "[24] That is, the *il y a* transpires beyond the realm of subjective experience, beyond the humanly thinkable. The *il y a*, if one had to find a name for it in *Existence and Existents*, could be signed for only by the word "Shoah" in its most concrete senses. At the same time, Levinas is arguing that in the horror of the *il y a* we are not released from our obligation to stand in proximity to the Jewish law, which points to the otherwise than being as divine alterity. If the *il y a* marks the event of a liquidation of existence, it nevertheless marks in the most concrete terms the having come to pass of a law from on high, a law that survives a catastrophe which was intended to liquidate that law itself. Needless to say, there is no cause for rejoicing which might justify the horrors that were endured. Rather, there is only the preception that if we are to talk about representation and exemplification, it has to be in terms of the *il y a* through which mankind comes into a terrifying and murderous correspondence with the law, an *il y a* marked by horrific traces that approach the condition of those names which are not the corollary of the unity of being.

In *Difficult Freedom* Levinas writes, "ethics is an optics."[25] And in *The Book of Questions: Aely*, by Edmond Jabès, we are told: "Within the word *oeil*, eye, there is the word *loi*, law. Every look contains the law."[26] In the photograph of the Warsaw child the law comes to appearance as the face, and yet, as Levinas specifies, the face has already withdrawn to that which is beyond our worldly order of being. It appears before us only as trace, the *il y a* of the coming to pass of a being from the beyond of being. As this *il y a*, the face persists as vestige of an ethical encounter which we are obliged to acknowledge as exemplary insofar as we are obliged to understand and follow divine law. This is not to say that the photograph incarnates a divine manifestation of the law, but that it reveals those conditions under which we can intuit the coming to pass of an ethical order, what Levinas calls the otherwise than being. When we say that the ethical encounter is something we must take as exemplary, we are, however, still breaking radically with the classical and Christian traditions which persist in those sections of Martin Heidegger's *Being and Time* which Levinas rejects.[27]

We recall that in *Being and Time* Heidegger writes: "Dasein can thus gain an experience of death, all the more so because Dasein is essentially Being with Others. In that case, the fact that death has been thus 'Objectively' given must make possible an ontological delimitation of Dasein's totality."[28] Although Heidegger is questioning the notion of Dasein's finitude or totality by suggesting that in Dasein's proximity to the Other's death the categories of being are disrupted and hence refuse Dasein its existential closure, there is still the insistence that "*Here* one Dasein can and must, within certain 'limits' *be* another Dasein."[29] In other words, one Dasein can be substituted by another, and, as Heidegger notes, it is by means of such exemplary substitution that the existential category of concern or care emerges. Levinas's philosophy is aggressively and self-consciously reacting against precisely these passages in *Being and Time*, because Levinas believes Heidegger is subordinating ethics to a mimetic notion of exemplification wherein one's relation to an other is ontologically determined. Instead of privileging what Judaic tradition views as the law, Heidegger privileges ontological difference and derives from it existential and moral notions such as care or being-with-others. In *La Dette impensée* (The debt that is unthought), Marlène Zarader, in comparing Heidegger to Levinas, points out that "insofar as philosophy is defined as ontology . . . it ceaselessly looks for the Other without ever being able to reach it, since it never quits the field of being which is the field of the Same." And ontological difference, of course, would be the law that ensures a return to the same in which the other is not akin to what Levinas calls the "Tout-Autre." For Levinas, then, it is in proximity with the "absolutely other" that Dasein loses its finitude and the mimetic structures of identification through which we come to know ourselves in the examples of others. As Zarader points out, this surpassing of finitude is marked by Levinas in terms of the "pure expression" of the face, which reveals the infinite beyond any system of totalized relationships. Moreover, she rightly argues that this visage or "trace of the infinite" cannot

be introjected within Western thought but concerns the He-
braic law, which is defined in terms of those obligatory conditions laid down to those who fall under the shadow of an other's
coming to appearance from the "otherwise than being."[30]

Near the outset of this essay, I was asking what Merleau-
Ponty's notion of the imaginary might possibly be, given what
he writes about the child and its emotional conduct, and I suggested, at one point, that the imaginary is phenomenologically
posed exterior to the *cogito*, which is to say, from beyond the existential horizons of the subject's exemplary presence. The
imaginary, I contended, is not reducible to an interiorized consciousness but must be considered in terms of ethical relations
which come to pass in the coming to appearance of the trace.
Furthermore, only through such a coming to appearance can we
speak of a phenomenon that brings to consciousness a souvenir
of what once was, for example, the Shoah. Of course, in our attempt to remember or commemorate this past we have been required to reflect on a photograph, and in so doing we have intuited a moral responsiblity towards an other which is given
from outside an ontological network of conceptual relations
which presupposes the ability of one Dasein to " 'be' another
Dasein" within "certain limits." That is, in distancing ourselves from a figure such as Heidegger we have, with the guidance of Levinas, come to understand a law which comes to appearance not because we perceive ourselves to be inherently
identical with others, but because of our hard-won *failure* to
imagine this identification. This leads to the surprising consequence that in not being able to comprehend the identity between an other and myself a certain ethical law comes to the
fore.

This point can be better clarified if we turn to Merleau-
Ponty's *Phenomenology of Perception*, in which the argument
is made that perception is grounded not in identification but the
persistence of what is seen "as an unequal distribution of influences." Merleau-Ponty specifies that one's body experiences
disequilibrium to the extent that it is incapable of projecting its
visual existence into that which is apprehended. In a chapter on
the *cogito*, Merleau-Ponty states that the " 'I' is a field, an expe-

riencing." And he insists that the "I" never occupies a fixed position in terms of which identifications are established but is always subject to being reinscribed within a new "possibility of situations."[31] Samuel B. Mallin summarizes Merleau-Ponty's position as follows:

My body experiences a disequilibrium because it cannot implant its visual existence fully in its [the object's] milieu. It cannot clearly encompass the otherness that faces it by means of one of its structures, and thus it cannot bring it to its maximum visibility. The object side of this situation can be described as the unequal distribution of influences, because otherness is unable to precisely trigger and specify the one structure that would have accommodated it had it been proximal.[32]

Yet, if we experience disequilibrium, this experience is coupled, according to Merleau-Ponty, with the perception that the object persists as something constant. What is constant, however, is neither the identification of subject with object nor the identification of the object with itself as such. What remains constant is the object's persistence as a coming to appearance which resists such identifications. What persists, in other words, is that which "resides in exteriority" and is given to perception by the other as that which can never be encompassed by the me.

If we were to speak of the imaginary conditions of the photograph of the Warsaw child, it would have to be in terms of this nonreciprocity in which, from Levinas's perspective, the law is given in its radical alterity. Indeed, what Merleau-Ponty's phenomenology of perception contributes to is the coming to imaginary appearance of the face as an effect of the ethical constancy or persistence of the law, a Talmudic law which, in fact, speaks to us from the depths of an exemplarity that resists identification and conceptual closure. To put it in this way is to postulate that a photograph such as that of the Warsaw child can be considered to be like a Talmudic redaction—that is to say, the providing of a historical example which serves as the occasion for interpreting the law—in which the emotional comportment of a child is imaginatively given exterior to both our identification with him and his self-identification. His face speaks to us from beyond the finitude of its appearance and from the beyond of its being. And what speaks to us, then, is sacred insofar as what comes to appearance from beyond is the persistence of a law that says "you shall not kill." This persistence requires us to consider the coming to pass of an Other whom we cannot know or represent as such, even as we are obliged to heed him under the dictates of an irrecusable order.

For Levinas the epiphany of the other's approach

reveals as it were *horizontally*, on the basis of the historical world to which it belongs. According to the phenomenological expression, it reveals the horizons of this world. But this mundane signification is found to be disturbed and shaken by another presence, abstract, not integrated into the world. His presence consists in coming unto us, *making an entry*. This can be stated in this way: the phenomenon which is the apparition of the other is also a *face*.[33]

Of this world, the face is nevertheless perceived retroactively in the traces preserved by its annihilators, as if it were destined to survive and signify from beyond the time of its arrest in this world. The face therefore transcends the being of the subject as the coming of presence from somewhere which is not integratable into this world. To perceive the world in a worldly manner and still recognize that perception must consider the "otherwise than being" is, for Levinas, a most basic phenomenological condition, upon which depends our capacity to remember and commemorate the past. Certainly, such perception is entirely congruent with the main outlines of Merleau-Ponty's phenomenological investigations. But in terms of the main occasion for which this essay has been written—the consideration of exemplarity—Levinas's position suggests that only in the transcendence of the moral example can there come to pass an intuition of the law, mediated by a phenomenology of perception, that imaginatively recollects an emotional comportment speaking to us undecidably from within and without the limits of exemplification.

Reference Matter

Notes

Gelley: Introduction

1. *Aristotle on Rhetoric: A Theory of Civic Discourse,* trans. George A. Kennedy (New York: Oxford University Press, 1991), p. 41.

2. See *Historisches Wörterbuch der Philosophie,* ed, J. Ritter et al. (Basel: Schwabe, 1971–92), vol. 7, cols. 74–76.

3. *Aristotle on Rhetoric,* p. 44.

4. *Aristotle on Rhetoric,* p. 44 n. 65. See also Gerald A. Hauser, "Aristotle's Example Revisited," *Philosophy and Rhetoric,* 18 (1985): 171–80; here, p. 179.

5. I am mindful that etymological arguments can never be more than a heuristic, a way to get started. I have already indicated that the Latin *exemplar* took over the Greek *paradeigma,* and clearly this brought into play a very different semantic field. For a discerning survey of the complex semantic context see John D. Lyons, *Exemplum. The Rhetoric of Example in Early Modern France and Italy* (Princeton, N.J.: Princeton University Press, 1989), pp. 9–12. On the connection of mashal to example and *paradeigma* see Daniel Boyarin's essay below.

6. Lyons notes the historical association of *eikon* with *exemplum,* one consequence of which is that "the visual form of example leads to the ontological consequence that examples have the quality of seeming rather than of being, they are associated with *species* and *imago,* and are therefore within the realm of all that is specious and imaginary." *Exemplum,* p. 10.

7. See previous note. See also Roland Barthes, "L'Ancienne rhétorique," in his *L'Aventure sémiologique* (Paris: Seuil, 1985), p. 129.

8. Hugo Friedrich, *Die Rechtsmetaphysik der Göttlichen Komödie* (Frankfurt a.M.: V. Klostermann, 1942), pp. 27–28. (Translations of passages from foreign sources cited here and below are my own unless otherwise indicated.)

9. Hans-Robert Jauss, "Sketch of a Theory and History of Aesthetic Experience," in his *Aesthetic Experience and Literary Hermeneutics* (Minneapolis: University of Minnesota Press, 1982), pp. 107–8.

10. Reinhart Koselleck, "*Historia Magistra Vitae*: The Dissolution of the Topos into the Perspective of a Modernized Historical Process," in his *Futures Past—On the Semantics of Historical Time*, trans. Keith Tribe (Cambridge, Mass.: MIT Press, 1985), pp. 27–28.

11. Cf. the citation from Hugo Friedrich above. More recently Hans Ulrich Gumbrecht, in a detailed investigation of the status of example in medieval conceptions of history, has demonstrated how little modern criteria regarding evidence and facticity were operative in that period: see his "Menschliches Handeln und göttliche Kosmologie: Geschichte als Exempel," in *La Littérature historiographique des origines à 1500*, ed. H. U. Gumbrecht et al., vol. 11 of *GRLMA, Grundriss der Romanischen Literaturen des Mittelalters*, ed. Hans-Robert Jauss et al. (Heidelberg: Carl Winter, 1986), pp. 869–950.

12. See Hans Blumenberg, *The Legitimacy of the Modern World*, trans. Robert M. Wallace (Cambridge, Mass.: MIT Press, 1985), pp. 65–69.

13. Walter Benjamin, "Der Erzähler," originally published in 1936, now in his *Gesammelte Schriften*, vol. 2, ed. Rolf Tiedemann et al. (Frankfurt a.M.: Suhrkamp, 1977), p. 442.

14. Walter Benjamin, "Franz Kafka. Zur zehnten Wiederkehr seines Todestages," originally published in 1934, in *Gesammelte Schriften*, 2: 427. In translating *Dichtung* as *fiction* I am aware that I narrow the meaning of the German word, which also signifies literature and poesy in a wider sense. It is the etymological sense of *fiction*—from Latin *fingere*, to form, invent—that brings it close to *Dichtung*.

15. See *Aristotle on Rhetoric*, pp. 179–80.

16. Karlheinz Stierle, "Story as Exemplum—Exemplum as Story: On the Pragmatics and Poetics of Narrative Texts," in *New Perspectives in German Literary Criticism*, ed. Richard E. Amacher and Victor Lange (Princeton, N.J.: Princeton University Press, 1979), pp. 389–417. This citation, p. 398.

17. The status of example in Kant is treated in Günther Buck, "Kants Lehre vom Exempel," *Archiv für Begriffsgeschichte*, 11, no. 2 (1967): 148–83, and by Ingeborg Heidemann, "Die Funktion des Beispieles in der kritischen Philosophie," in *Kritik und Metaphysik—Studien*, Festschrift Heinz Heimsoeth (Berlin: de Gruyter, 1966), pp. 21–39.

18. Immanuel Kant, *Kritik der reinen Vernunft* (Hamburg: Meiner, 1956), cited below as *CPR*, by section number.

19. Immanuel Kant, *Metaphysik der Sitten*, ed. W. Weischedel (Frankfurt a.M.: Suhrkamp, 1977), cited in Buck, "Kants Lehre vom Exempel," pp. 150–51.

20. See Buck, "Kants Lehre vom Exempel," pp. 174–75; Theodor W. Adorno, *Negative Dialectics* trans. E. B. Ashton (New York: Continuum, 1987), p. 226n; and Claudia J. Brodsky, *The Imposition of Form* (Princeton, N.J.: Princeton University Press, 1987), pp. 68–86, which discusses the striking instance from the *Critique of Practical Reason*, A 54, "Suppose that someone pretended that his lust were irresistible to him ... "

21. Immanuel Kant, *Kritik der Urteilskraft* (Hamburg, Meiner, 1959). In this work (cited below as *CJ*) Kant argues that what is truly exemplary in a genius is what cannot be imitated, the manifestation of artistic freedom, the capacity to fashion "a new rule for art," one that implicitly demolishes the exemplary instance, the prior rule (*CJ*, sec. 49). On this issue see also Jacques Derrida, "Economimesis," in *Mimesis des articulations*, ed. Sylviane Agacinski (Paris: Flammarion, 1975), esp. pp. 70, 79, 87.

22. Jacques Derrida, *The Truth in Painting*, trans. Geoff Bennington and Ian McLeod (Chicago: The University of Chicago Press, 1987), p. 63.

23. Jacques Derrida, "The Law of Genre," *Glyph: Textual Studies*, 7 (1988): 206. The remark on the word *enigma* refers to its Greek root: *ainos*, tale, fable.

24. I have limited myself here to Derrida in relation to Kant on the issue of exemplarity. For more extensive treatments of Derrida in this connection see Gregory Ulmer's review of *La Carte postale*, *Diacritics*, 11 (Fall 1981): 39–56, and the essays by Irene E. Harvey and Michael B. Naas discussed below.

25. Derrida, *The Truth in Painting*, p. 78 (translation modified).

26. Derrida, "The Law of Genre," p. 206.

27. Jean-Luc Nancy, "Lapsus judicii," in his *L'Impératif catégorique* (Paris: Flammarion, 1983), pp. 35–60; here, p. 39, below, p. 40.

28. Irene E. Harvey, "Derrida and the Issues of Exemplarity," in *Derrida—A Critical Reader*, ed. David Wood (Cambridge: Blackwell, 1992), pp. 193–217. This essay will be cited below in text by page number.

29. Michael B. Naas's strongly argued introduction to Derrida's *The Other Heading—Reflections on Today's Europe* (Bloomington: Indiana University Press, 1992) covers some of the same ground as Harvey's essay, though Naas's position is diametrically opposed to hers. He

considers that Derrida's recurrent interrogation and displacement of example, his ability to diagnose the "complicity between the example and the universal" (p. xxx) in the philosophical tradition, enables Derrida to identify "himself, his situation, his time" with an "irreducible singularity, with what can have no example" (p. lv). But this argument, in my view, too facilely disposes of the kind of problematic that Harvey has put forward. See also p. 348, n. 1, below.

30. In Jean-François Lyotard, *The Differend*, trans. Georges Van Den Abbeele (Minneapolis: University of Minnesota Press, 1988), p. 132.

31. Ludwig Wittgenstein, *Philosophical Investigations*, trans. G. E. M. Anscombe (New York: Macmillan, 1958), sec. 210. The German here for "drift" is *Tendenz*. This work will be cited below as *PI*.

32. Plinio Walder Prado, Jr., states the issue in the following terms: "by raising the question 'How does one follow the rule in this case?,' the Wittgensteinian Sceptic not only signals the structural discontinuity which lies between the rule (the general) and the case (the particular), he suggests at the same time that it is a part of the logic of the rule (of what it 'means,' of its *meinen*) to be undetermined, to be unable to assure its determination." In "The Necessity of Contingency. Remarks on Linkage," *L'Esprit créateur*, 31 (1991): 90–106; here, p. 100.

33. See J. L. Austin, *How to Do Things with Words* (Cambridge, Mass.: Harvard University Press, 1975), pp. 116–20.

34. A number of people were kind enough to read and comment on this part of the introduction. The responses of Gregory Lambert, Jean-François Lyotard, Martin Schwab, and Ewa Ziarek have been especially helpful. I have also profited from the remarks of one of the anonymous readers for Stanford University Press.

35. Louis Marin, *Food for Thought*, trans. Mette Hjort (Baltimore: Johns Hopkins University Press, 1989), p. 6.

36. Louis Marin, *Portrait of the King*, trans. Martha Mittonle (Minneapolis: University of Minnesota Press, 1988), p. 13.

Boyarin: Take the Bible for Example

I wish to thank Robert Alter, Ken Frieden, Alexander Gelley, Chana Kronfeld, Mark Steiner, and Meir Sternberg for reading a draft of this essay and commenting on it. I have taken some of their advice—and ignored some, probably at my peril.

1. Robert Alter, *The Art of Biblical Narrative* (New York: Basic Books, 1981), p. 24.

2. Meir Sternberg, *The Poetics of Biblical Narrative: Ideological*

Literature and the Drama of Reading, Indiana Studies in Biblical Literature (Bloomington: Indiana University Press, 1985), p. 34.

3. Daniel Boyarin, "Placing Reading: Ancient Israel and Medieval Europe," in *The Ethnography of Reading,* ed. Jonathan Boyarin (Berkeley: University of California Press, 1993), pp. 10–37.

4. Robert Alter, "Biblical Imperatives and Literary Play," unpublished paper, n.d., pp. 9–10. I thank Prof. Alter for allowing me access to a prepublication copy of this paper.

5. Michael Riffaterre, *Fictional Truth* (Baltimore: Johns Hopkins University Press, 1990), p. xii.

6. This term when capitalized refers to the rabbinical authorities who produced the talmudic literature (which includes midrash). They were active in Palestine and Babylonia in the first four centuries of the Christian era, thus paralleling in time the Church Fathers.

7. For the mashal (parable) as a hermeneutic form see Gerald L. Bruns, *Inventions: Writing, Textuality, and Understanding in Literary History* (New Haven, Conn: Yale University Press, 1982), p. 31. I agree completely and my discussion below will suggest further that for the Rabbis, fiction is par excellence an interpretative practice. If in our culture fiction is that which requires interpretation, for them fiction is that which interprets. On this see also Daniel Boyarin, *Intertextuality and the Reading of Midrash* (Bloomington: Indiana University Press, 1990), especially the chapters entitled "Interpreting in Ordinary Language: The Mashal as Intertext," "The Sea Resists," and "The Song of Songs: Lock or Key?" David Stern, "Rhetoric and Midrash: The Case of the Mashal," *Prooftexts,* 1 (1981): 261–91, offers a very valuable analysis that is quite different from mine and perhaps corrective of it. See further my discussion of the mashal below.

8. The two terms are used interchangably in Hebrew in certain collocations. Thus, one can say either "lᵉmashal" or "lᵉdugma" to mean "for example," but only "dugma" to mean "pattern" or "sample" and (in later Hebrew) only "mashal" to mean "parable."

9. The word for "handles" and the word "proved" come from the same root in Hebrew. "Handles" is being used in a sense very similar to that of the modern English colloquial phrase "I can't get a handle on that idea," i.e., a place of access.

10. *Song of Songs Rabba,* ed. S. Dunsky (Jerusalem, 1980), p. 5. All translations of rabbinic texts in this essay are mine.

11. Babylonian Talmud Sanhedrin 92 b. On this text, see also Raphael Loewe, "The 'Plain' Meaning of Scriptures in Early Jewish Exegesis," *Papers of the Institute of Jewish Studies,* 1 (1964): 172–75.

12. Nelson Goodman, "Routes of Reference," *Critical Inquiry*, 8, no. 1 (Autumn 1981): 121–32.

13. *Tanhuma*, ed. S. Buber, 2 vols. (Jerusalem, 1964–65), 2:96.

14. On this form, see Joseph Heinemann, "The Proem in the Aggadic Midrashim: A Form-Critical Study," *Scripta Hiersolymitana*, 22 (1971): 100–122; and David Stern, "Midrash and the Language of Exegesis," in *Midrash and Literature*, ed. G. Hartman and S. Budick (New Haven, Conn.: Yale University Press, 1986), pp. 105–27, just to give two citations of works in English.

15. *Song of Songs Rabba*, p. 49.

16. This is paralleled in later Hebrew by the same semantic development of the Persian loan word "gaun," "color," which also forms a preposition "kegon," meaning "according to the likeness of" and also "for example." The great eleventh-century French Bible commentator Rashi already anticipated this semantic comparison in his gloss on this verse of Song of Songs. See also Sarah Kamin, "Dugma' in Rashi's Commentary on the Song of Songs" (Hebrew), *Tarbiz*, 52 (1983): 48 n. 27 and p. 47, who cites similar use of Latin "color" as a synonym for "figura, exemplum, similitudo," etc., in medieval Christian hermeneutics.

17. Thus: "This is what the verse says, *God will not diminish the eye of the righteous* (Job 36:7). What does this mean? God does not take away from the righteous their *dugmaterin* [an alternate Greek form equivalent to "dugma"]. Know this, for Abraham begat Isaac in his likeness, for it says, 'These are the generations of Isaac the son of Abraham, Abraham begat Isaac.' And Jacob begat Joseph in his likeness, for it says, 'These are the generations of Jacob, Joseph,' it does not say, Reuben, Simeon, but only Joseph. And furthermore it says 'For he is the son of his old age [*ben zequnim*]'; the very form of his *ikonin* is he to him. And this is *God will not diminish the eye of the righteous.*" (*Tanhuma*, 1:136. For those who may be using other editions, this midrash is found very near the end of the Book of Exodus.) The midrash wonders, why is it that when the generations of these two patriarchs are being recounted only one of their children is mentioned? The tacit answer is that the one who is mentioned is the one who was similar to his father, that is, the one who inherited the father's dugma. We learn that the intention is to refer to the physical form from the following text, which says explicitly (by a typical midrashic pun on "zequnim") that the son had exactly the "ziv ikonin," the son is the *eikōn* of the father, he has the physical *figura* of the father. The dugma of the father thus continues to exist; hence, God does not take away from the righteous their *dugmaterin* when they die. But we find "dugma" also as "figura"

in the spiritual or moral sense in a parallel midrashic text: "*God will not diminish the eye of the righteous. His dugma.* Leah held onto the quality of praising God and confessing to Him (i.e., when she said, 'This time will I praise God'), and therefore she had children who praised [God] . . . David—*Praise God for He is good* [Psalms 107:1]; Daniel—*To You my God I praise and sing* [Daniel 2:23]." The dugma in the first case is the appearance, the physical form, while in the second case it is the behavior, the character, a quality of the human being. The reward for being righteous is that one's descendants are created in one's likeness, pattern, or form.

18. See also Kamin's important discussion in her " 'Dugma' in Rashi's Commentary."

19. Goodman, "Routes of Reference," pp. 124–25.

20. Ibid., p. 127.

21. This dugma also contains perlocutionary force, as in a classic exemplum. It is not so much that Israel belongs to the class of light-bringers exemplified by the dove, but that Israel ought to belong to this class. And therefore, "command the children of Israel that they bring me pure olive oil!" On the perlocutionary force of the exemplum, see Susan Rubin Suleiman, *Authoritarian Fictions: The Ideological Novel as a Literary Genre* (New York: Columbia University Press, 1983), pp. 25–54. In the way that I am analyzing the mashal and related forms here, the perlocutionary force is facultative and not necessary to the form. However, Kamin exaggerates when she says that dugma in the sense of "example to be followed" does not occur in classic rabbinic sources (" 'Dugma' in Rashi's Commentary," p. 49). A dugma as a sample or example can also become naturally an example to follow, someone whose actions or fate serve as an exemplum to others, teaching them some truth or leading them to a certain kind of opinion or behavior. We find this usage in the following midrashic text: "*But God was angry with me for your sakes and did not hear me, and He said to me: It is sufficient for you* [Deuteronomy 3:26]: He said to him, Moses, you serve as a dugma for the judges, that they should say: If indeed Moses (who was the wisest of the wise and the greatest of the great) God did not forgive him for having said, 'Hear now, ye rebels; are we to bring you forth water out of the rock?' [Numbers 20:11], and it was decreed that he would not enter the Land, those who delay and distort judgment, all the more so [*Sifre* Deuteronomy 29]." This text requires some background. At this point in Deuteronomy, Moses is addressing the People of Israel and summarizing the events of the past years. He has told them in the previous verses that he begged of God to be allowed to

enter the Land of Israel, "but God was angry with me for your sakes and did not hear me." The midrash is attempting to explain what it means to say that God did not forgive Moses for the sake of the people. Their explanation is that Moses's punishment is to be exemplary for the people. The word for "sufficient" also means "great," so God is taken to mean in His address to Moses: Since you are great, if I punish you for the sin of bringing water improperly out of the rock, then they will know that your wisdom and greatness did not serve to grant you forgiveness for your sin, and they will say to themselves that they would certainly be punished for theirs.

The structure of this text as representation of a speech act is almost identical to the structure of the exemplum as described by Suleiman, *Authoritarian Fictions.*

22. Goodman, "Routes of Reference," p. 128.

23. *The Midrash on Psalms*, ed. S. Buber (New York, 1947), p. 452.

24. This text may very well be a polemic against those sects of mystical Jews whose religious life centered around attempts to see God, understand His nature, and describe it in terms of measurements. See Moshe Idel, *Kabbalah: New Perspectives* (New Haven, Conn: Yale University Press, 1988), pp. 116–17.

25. "Finding His ḥêqer," the biblical phrase, is resolved in the midrashic gloss into the verb from which ḥêqer is derived and "dugma" as its object. "Dugma," therefore, must be held to have much of the semantic weight of ḥêqer, if not all.

26. *Song of Songs Rabba*, pp. 72–73.

27. For a fuller discussion of this topos, see "The Song of Songs," in my *Intertextuality and the Reading of Midrash.*

28. For this notion and terminology see Meir Sternberg, "Gaps, Ambiguities, and the Reading Process," in his *Poetics of Biblical Narrative*, pp. 186–229.

29. The pearl is yet another image for the hermetic Torah, that which was possessed but is now lost.

30. Hence, the analogy between Solomon and the rabbis. Solomon is a sort of proto-rabbi for the midrash.

31. The order of the books mentioned here deviates from both the chronological and canonical orders because this passage is an introduction to the midrash on *Song of Songs*, and its author wishes therefore to end his discourse by mentioning that book.

32. Goodman, "Routes of Reference," p. 126.

33. Perhaps it would be best to translate "mashal" as "exemplification," that is, as a name for the entire syntagm and not either of its ar-

guments. This may be supported by the fact that the early rabbinic literature that includes the texts being considered here has no separate word for the application of the parable. That word, "nimšal," only developed much later in the history of the language. This ambiguity is often expressed and effaced in the critical literature by referring to the fictional tale as the "mashal proper."

34. For the interpretation of this orthography see below.

35. *Mekilta De-rabbi Ishmael,* ed. J. Z. Lauterbach, 3 vols. (Philadelphia: Jewish Publication Society of America, 1933), 1: 224–25. The text given here has been drawn from my new edition of the *Mekilta.* This text has been completely corrupted in current editions, both vulgate and critical, and may only be restored by recourse to the manuscripts.

36. Whether or not we accept the designation of this narrative as historiography or as fiction, Sternberg certainly is correct that the narrative radically banishes all thought of its not being true.

37. Brevard S. Childs, *The Book of Exodus* (Philadelphia: Westminster Press, 1974), p. 220.

38. Late in the course of revising this paper I came across prototype semantic theory, as developed by Eleanor Rosch and others, which may provide a way of elegantly capturing both of these senses without resorting to polysemy. However, rather than attempt to integrate such analysis at the last moment, I prefer to leave it for a future study. For an excellent summary of work in this field, see George Lakoff, *Women, Fire, and Dangerous Things: What Categories Reveal About the Mind* (Chicago: University of Chicago Press, 1987).

39. Louis Marin, "On the Interpretation of Ordinary Language: A Parable of Pascal," in *Textual Strategies: Perspectives in Post-Structuralist Criticism,* ed. Josue Harari (Ithaca, N.Y.: Cornell University Press, 1979), p. 246.

40. See Stern's response to my paper "Rhetoric and Interpretation: The Case of the Nimshal," *Prooftexts,* 5, no. 3 (Sept. 1985): 270–76. The response appears there on pp. 276–80), and see esp. p. 280, n. 5.

41. Robert Johnston, "Parabolic Interpretations Attributed to Tannaim" (Ph.D. diss., Hartford Seminary Foundation, 1977), p. 299.

42. This description also fits the parable that Marin analyzes (see "On the Interpretation of Ordinary Language"), for there Pascal tells his parable in the context of a real colloquy with a young man, and it is this young man's history (certainly "real") that the parable designates, as Marin says explicitly.

43. I am not claiming that these are notational variants; they in-

volve a controversy about historiography that I simply do not need to get into here.

44. This may give us a different way of looking at another recent theoretical problem of fictional mimesis. Lubomír Doložel has analyzed two extant models for the logical relation of fictional objects and entities in the real world:

1. Fictional particular P/f represents actual particular P/a.
2. Fictional particular P/f/ represents actual universal U/a.

Doložel argues that neither of these models is adequate. The first fails whenever there is a fictional particular that corresponds to no actual particular, while the second (which he attributes to Erich Auerbach) does not account for the particulars of fiction at all. The perhaps unique feature of the rabbinic discourse we are considering is that it found a way, owing precisely to the productive double meaning of dugma, to make sense of narrative without positing a system of abstract universals. Their primary hermeneutic procedure was to gather disparate instances in the text into groups in which the various concrete instances reveal each other's meaning. For the Rabbis discourse is a matter not of propositions and universals in the first place but of particulars and of rules for their comparison. The operation of the intellect is the association of particulars with each other such that they illuminate each other. Mimesis is understood, then, not as representation at all but as a statement that:

> Fictional particular P/f is like or analogous to actual particular P/a/, and thereby interpretive of it.

It is interesting to speculate whether this is reducible to Doložel's own solution that:

> Actual source S/a represents (i.e. provides the representation) of fictional particular P/f/.

45. Hayden White, *Tropics of Discourse: Essays in Cultural Criticism* (Baltimore: Johns Hopkins University Press, 1978), p. 58.

46. Ibid., p. 59.

Nichols: Example Versus *Historia*

I would like to thank Professors Michael Riffaterre of Columbia University and Faith Beasley of Dartmouth College for inviting me to read earlier and very different versions of this paper at confereces they organized in 1985 and 1988. I am grateful to Professor Alexander Gelley of the Program in Comparative Literature at U.C. Irvine for encouraging the present version.

1. Michel de Montaigne, *Essais*, in *Oeuvres complètes*, ed. Albert Thibaudet and Maurice Rat (Paris: Gallimard, Bibliothèque de la Pléiade, 1962), p. 693a. All citations from the *Essais* below will give page numbers from this edition. Translations are my own unless otherwise identified. Other translations will be from *The Complete Essays of Montaigne*, trans. Donald Frame (1958; reprint, Stanford, Calif.: Stanford University Press, 1966), and will be identified by page number given in italics following the page number from the French edition.

2. Eric Havelock, *Preface to Plato* (New York: Grosset and Dunlap, Universal Library, 1967), pp 62–64.

3. Ibid., p. 63.

4. Ibid., p. 63.

5. Hesiod, *Theogony*, ll. 100–101; Havelock, *Preface to Plato*, p. 64.

6. Homer, *The Iliad*, trans. Robert Fitzgerald (New York: Anchor Press/Doubleday, 1975), ll. 1–3. All *Iliad* citations in text below are from this edition.

7. Havelock, *Preface to Plato*, p. 64.

8. "Readers of the *Odyssey* will remember the well-prepared and touching scene in book 19, when Odysseus has at last come home, the scene in which the old housekeeper Euryclea, who had been his nurse, recognizes him by a scar on his thigh. . . . [T]he basic impulse of the Homeric style: to represent phenomena in a fully externalized form, visible and palpable in all their parts, and completely fixed in their spatial and temporal relations." Erich Auerbach, *Mimesis: The Representation of Reality in Western Literature*, trans. from the German by Willard Trask (New York: Anchor/Doubleday, 1957), pp. *1, 4*.

9. Havelock, *Preface to Plato*, p. 109.

10. See Antoine Compagnon's brilliant book on this subject: *La Seconde main ou Le Travail de la citation* (Paris: Seuil, 1979).

11. *Phaedrus*, 275d–e, in *Plato: The Collected Dialogues*, ed. Edith Hamilton and Huntington Cairns, Bollingen Series 71 (Princeton, N.J.: Princeton University Press, 1982), p. 521. All *Phaedrus* citations in text below will be from this edition.

12. "We have defined . . . representation by the two words *mimesis* and *semiosis*. Should representation be conceived as a reproduction, specular in nature, of a formal model, or as a 'mise en sens' of an enigma to be deciphered, a symbolic construct belonging to the world of signs? Between the mode of production of images and the mode of production of meaning there are interferences that are bound to create ambivalence and confusion." Claude-Gilbert Dubois, "Problems of

'Representation' in the Sixteenth Century," in *Medieval and Renaissance Representation: New Reflections*, ed. Stephen G. Nichols and Nancy J. Vickers, special issue of *Poetics Today*, 5 (1984): 471.

13. "Je n'ay dressé commerce avec aucun livre solide, sinon Plutarque et Seneque, où je puyse comme les Danaïdes, remplissant et versant sans cesse. J'en attache quelque chose à ce papier; à moy si peu que rien" ("I have not had regular dealings with any solid book, except Plutarch and Seneca, from whom I draw like the Danaïds, incessantly filling up and pouring out. Some of this sticks to this paper; to myself, little or nothing," 144c; *107*).

14. *Historia* was a medieval form of history writing based on the classical model of the doing-and-saying paradigm but with the added intention of rewriting phenomenal reality—events in the world—according to a pattern of divine intentionality. *Historia* was thus ancillary to the hermeneutics of the Logos, helping people to understand it and how it related to their world. For a fuller discussion see my book, *Romanesque Signs: Early Medieval Narrative and Iconography* (New Haven, Conn.: Yale University Press, 1963 and 1985).

15. Jean Pépin, "*Mysteria* et *Symbola* dans le commentaire de Jean Scot sur l'Évangile de saint Jean," in *The Mind of Eriugena: Papers of a Colloquium*, ed. John J. O'Maera and Ludwig Bieler (Dublin: Irish University Press, 1973), pp. 17–18.

16. On the innovative quality of Eriugena's commentary in respect to Augustine's (whom he explicitly acknowledges), see the notes to Jeauneau's edition, *Jean Scot: Commentaire sur l'Évangile de Jean. Introduction, texte critique, traduction, notes et index*, ed. Édouard Jeauneau, Collection *Sources Chrétiennes*, no. 180 (Paris: Les Éditions du Cerf, 1972), and the indispensable article by Jean Pépin cited above. Jeauneau's edition will be cited below by page number in italics, following page numbers from the *Patrologia Latina* (*PL*) edition: John Scotus Eriugena, *Commentarius in s. evangelium secundum Joannem*, ed. Henricus Floss and J.-P. Migne, in vol. 122 of *Patrologia Latina* (Paris: J.-P. Migne, 1853).

17. This is Gerald Prince's definition of the "disnarrated, a narrative category that constitutes a powerful source of information about a particular narrative's view of narrative and of itself." An early version of the concept may be found in his article "The Dis-narrated," *Style*, 22 (Spring 1988): 1–8. I quote from a subsequent version with the categories more fully elaborated, "L'Alternarré," *Strumenti Critici*, n.s., 4, no. 2 (1989): 223–31. All translations are mine.

18. Prince, "L'Alternarré," pp. 227–28.

19. For further discussions of *historia*, see my book, *Romanesque Signs*, and articles: "Romanesque Imitation or Imitating the Romans?" in *Mimesis: From Mirror to Method, Augustine to Descartes*, ed. John D. Lyons and S. G. Nichols (Hanover, N.H.: University Press of New England, 1982), pp. 36–59; "Remodeling Models: Modernism and the Middle Ages," in *Modernité au moyen âge: Le défi du passé*, published by Brigitte Cazalles and Charles Méla (Geneva: Librairie Droz, 1990), pp. 45–72; "Periodization and the Politics of Perception: A Romanesque Example," *Poetics Today*, 10, no. 1 (1989): 127–54.

20. Virgil, *The Aeneid*, trans. C. Day Lewis (New York: Doubleday Anchor Books, 1953). All *Aeneid* citations in text below will be from this edition.

21. Montaigne's focus on a mode of behavior that does *not* happen here falls within the category of "alethiological expressions of virtuality (unrealized)" in Prince's taxonomy cited above.

22. See also Montaigne's "C'est folie de rapporter le vray et la faux a nostre suffisance," in *Essais*, p. 179a.

23. See also the remarks scattered through the essays deprecating his "scientific" understanding, a modesty topos that has the effect of enhancing the sense of the essay as a causerie, an instructive conversation, spontaneous and seemingly unreflective. For example: "J'ay un esprit primesautier. Ce que je ne voy de la premiere charge, je le voy moins en m'y obstinant. Je ne fay rien sans gayeté; et la continuation (c) et la contention trop ferme (b) esbloüit mon jugement, l'attriste et le lasse. . . . (a) . . . Je dy librement mon advis de toutes choses, voire et de celles qui surpassent à l'adventure ma suffisance, et que je ne tiens aucunement estre de ma jurisdiction. *Ce que j'en opine, c'est aussi pour declarer la mesure de ma veuë, non la mesure des choses*" ("I have an impulsive mind. What I do not see at the first attack, I see less by persisting. I do nothing without gaiety; continuation (c) and too strong contention (b) dazes, depresses, and wearies my judgment. . . . (a) . . . I speak my mind freely on all things, even on those which perhaps exceed my capacity, and which I by no means hold to be within my jurisdiction. And so the opinion I give of them is to declare the measure of my sight, not the measure of things," 389a, b, c; 297–98).

24. "Qu'on voye, en ce que j'emprunte, si j'ay sçeu choisir de quoy rehausser mon propos. Car je fay dire aux autres ce que je ne puis si bien dire, tantost par foiblesse de mon langage, tantost par foiblesse de mon sens. Je ne compte pas mes emprunts, je les poise" ("Let people see in what I borrow whether I have known how to choose what would enhance my theme. For I make others say what I cannot say so well, now

through the weakness of my language, now through the weakness of my understanding. I do not count my borrowings, I weigh them," 387c; *296*).

25. Indeed, in an interesting passage in I:27, *C'est folie de rapporter le vray et le faux a nostre suffisance*, Montaigne even has recourse to Augustine and medieval examples to assert the folly of questioning matters of faith (180a). "C'est une hardiesse dangereuse et de consequence, outre l'absurde temerité qu'elle traisne quant et soy, de mepriser ce que nous ne concevons pas. . . . Or ce qui me semble aporter autant de desordre en nos consciences, en ces troubles où nous sommes de la religion, c'est cette dispensation que les Catholiques font de leur creance. . . . Ou il faut se submettre du tout à l'authorité de notre police ecclesiastique, ou du tout s'en dispenser. C'est n'est pas à nous à establir la part que nous luy devons d'obeïssance" ("It is a dangerous and fateful presumption, besides the absurd temerity that it implies, to disdain what we do not comprehend. . . . Now, what seems to me to bring as much disorder into our consciences as anything, in these religious troubles that we are in, is this partial surrender of their beliefs by Catholics. . . . We must either submit completely to the authority of our ecclesiastical government, or do without it completely. It is not for us to decide what portion of obedience we owe it," 180–81a; *134*).

26. "En cette practique des hommes, j'entends y comprendre, et principalement, ceux qui ne vivent qu'en la memoire des livres. Il practiquera, par le moyen des histoires, ces grandes ames des meilleurs siecles. C'est un vain estude, qui veut; mais qui veut aussi, c'est un estude de fruit inestimable; (c) et le seul estude, comme dit Platon, que les Lacedemoniens eussent reservé à leur part" ("In this association with men I mean to include, and foremost, those who live only in the memory of books. He will associate, by means of histories, with those great souls of the best ages. It is a vain study, if you will; but also, if you will, it is a study of inestimable value, (c) and the only study, as Plato tells us, in which the Lacedaemonians had kept a stake for themselves," 155a, c; *115*).

27. Frederick H. Russell, *The Just War in the Middle Ages* (Cambridge, Eng.: Cambridge University Press, 1977), p. 17.

28. Ibid., pp. 19–20.

29. "Apologie de Raimond Sebond": "Puisque les sens ne peuvent arrester nostre dispute, estans pleins eux-mesmes d'incertitude, il faut que ce soit la raison; aucune raison ne s'establira sans une autre raison: nous voylà à reculons jusques à l'infiny" ("Since the senses cannot decide our dispute, being themselves full of uncertainty, it must be rea-

son that does so. No reason can be established without another reason: there we go retreating back to infinity," 585a; *454*).

30. On Eriugena's concept of theosis, see Nichols, *Romanesque Signs*, chap. 2. One should not ignore the corollaries between Montaigne's description of the human ascent toward the divine and the principles illustrated by Dante in *Paradiso*.

31. Frances A. Yates, *The Art of Memory* (Chicago: University of Chicago Press, 1966), p. 176.

32. See Frances Yates's books *Giordano Bruno and the Hermetic Tradition* (1979) and *Lull and Bruno* (1982).

33. Dante Alighieri, *The Divine Comedy*, trans., with a commentary, Charles S. Singleton, 6 vols., Bollingen Series 80 (Princeton, N.J.: Princeton University Press, 1970–75), XII, ll. 14–15. All Dante citations in text below will be from this edition.

34. Singleton, *Inferno: Commentary*, II, p. 189, note to *Inferno*, XII, l. 42.

35. Thomas Aquinas, *In duodecim libros Metaphysicorum expositio*, III, lect. 11, n. 478. Quoted from Singleton, *Inferno: Commentary*, II, pp. 189–90.

36. Ibid., p. 190.

37. Anika Lemaire, *Jacques Lacan*, edition revised by the author and translated by David Macey (London: Routledge and Kegan Paul, 1977), p. 181.

Lyons: Circe's Drink and Sorbonnic Wine

1. Montaigne here cites Manilius in Latin. Textual references to Montaigne's *Essays* give first the pagination from Pierre Villey's edition as reedited by V.-L. Saulnier, *Les Essais de Michel de Montaigne* (Paris: Presses Universitaires de France, 1965) and then the page number, in italics, from Donald Frame's translation, *The Complete Essays of Montaigne* (1958; reprint, Stanford, Calif.: Stanford University Press, 1966). Quotations are given in Frame's English version, occasionally amended to give a more specific and literal translation of terms referring to example.

2. The consensus is very clearly that examples never fit, never prove anything. Claude Blum's statement of this position is among the clearest and most brutal: "dans les *Essais*, la reprise des 'exemples' apparait comme un cas limite dans l'usage sceptique de l'Histoire qui aboutit à la leçon suivante: on ne peut tirer aucun enseignement des 'exemples.' Là où Montaigne affirme le plus nettement sa position, l'Histoire se trouve à la foix soustraite à son expression paradigmatique et à son

expression syntagmatique." "La Fonction du 'déjà dit' dans les *Essais*: Emprunter, alléguer, citer," *CAIEF*, 33 (May 1981), p. 42. Lino Pertile gives a more positive view of this situation: Montaigne's "use of 'exempla' is based on the idea that nothing can be demonstrated beyond dispute. There is no idea for Montaigne that cannot be turned upside down. Therefore, instead of picking only the examples which would illustrate something (and pretend to prove it), he brings in with complete freedom examples that show the impossibility of saying anything definite about anything. Hence his examples are unpredictable, for he gives up from the very beginning the pretense of tidying up and simplifying reality." "Paper and Ink: The Structure of Unpredictability," in *O un amy! Essays on Montaigne in Honor of Donald M. Frame*, ed. Raymond La Charité (Lexington, Ky.: French Forum, 1977), p. 208.

3. Most recently Michael Wood has discussed "Of experience," using the essay to ask perennially fascinating questions: "How do examples behave? How do they misbehave?" "Montaigne and the Mirror of Example," *Philosophy and Literature*, 13, no. 1 (Apr. 1989): 1–15.

4. Gérard Defaux has described the fixed exemplary status of historical and literary characters in a repertory available to writers of the Renaissance in *Le Curieux, le glorieux, et la sagesse du monde dans la première moitié du XVIe siècle* (Lexington, Ky.: French Forum, 1982).

5. As Steven Rendall notes, "Montaigne's formulation is more radical than it at first appears, for it suggests that in some way everything resembles not merely something else but *everything* else." Rendall, *Distinguo* (Oxford: Clarendon Press, 1992), p. 30.

6. The most complete treatment to date of example in Montaigne is given by Richard Regosin, "Le Miroüer Vague: Reflections of the Example in Montaigne's *Essais*," *Oeuvres & Critiques*, 8, nos. 1–2 (1983): 73–86.

7. Aristotle, *The Art of Rhetoric* (Loeb Classics), II, 20, 1393a–b.

8. Frame translates "exemple" here as "experience."

9. This "uncoupling" belongs to the same family of discursive strategies that Stephen G. Nichols, in his contribution to this volume, calls "disnarration." Disnarration reorients the fragmentary or unjoined narrative element from what I have called horizontal integration toward integration into another realm that can be called symbolical.

10. Montaigne's comments on the learning available from study of others appear in "Of Experience" itself, and the habit of thinking about ancient sages and heroes gave a cast to his thought that permitted him to study himself with something akin to a doubling of himself into viewer and viewed. He claims in this chapter that he learned in child-

hood how to see his own life reflected in another's (1076; *824*). For a fuller consideration of both Machiavelli's and Montaigne's thoughts on example see my *Exemplum: The Rhetoric of Example in Early Modern France and Italy* (Princeton, N.J.: Princeton University Press, 1989).

11. Lawrence Kritzman has written of the creation of the essay as form out of a structure of discursive destruction in his *Destruction/découverte* (Lexington, Ky.: French Forum, 1980).

12. "Whatever is divided into dust is confused." Seneca, *Epistolae morales ad Lucilium*, letter 89.

13. "The experience of human unity . . . triggers off an identity crisis which necessitates the stating of one's difference, for to postulate one's identity is indeed to proclaim one's otherness. . . . Book Three revolves around the problematics of the self/other issue and maintains at all levels the necessity of establishing an *équilibre* in order to remain *libre.*" Patrick Henry, "The Self and the Other," in his *Montaigne in Dialogue* (Saratoga, Calif.: Anma Libri, 1987), pp. 101–21.

14. This passage is an illustration of an internal split in which Montaigne's "mind" dialogues with "himself" by using examples in a classically rhetorical manner, including (in a later part of this mental oration) the traditional appeal to "those men of times past" who put on a *display* of their constancy in the face of suffering. But the thrust of Montaigne's argument undermines appeals to such displays on the grounds that no one knows what suffering is really like merely on the basis of appearance.

Marin: The Discourse of the Example.

1. I have used Thomas Spencer Baynes's translation of Antoine Arnauld and Pierre Nicole, *The Port-Royal Logic* (Edinburgh and London: William Blackwood and Sons, 1851), and I have modified it where I thought necessary.—TRANS.

2. Letter of March 1, 1665, in Nicholas Poussin, *Lettres et propos sur l'art*, ed. Anthony Blunt (Paris: Hermann, 1964), p. 163—ED.

3. As a result of the second criterion of division of signs, the logicians establish four maxims. The third one states, "it is very possible that one thing may hide and reveal another thing at the same time"; and the fourth one states, "since the nature of the sign consists in exciting in the senses, by means of the idea of the thing signifying, that of the thing signified, so long as that effect remains, the sign remains."—TRANS.

Keenan: Fables of Responsibility

An early version of this essay was presented at a panel organized by Alexander Gelley at the meeting of the International Association for Philosophy and Literature, University of Washington, Seattle, in May 1986. I am grateful to him and many others, including especially Elissa Marder and Alexander Garcia-Düttmann, for their comments on this text.

1. Closing moral of *The Gliders*, dir. Paul Terry, in the animated series *Aesop's Film Fables*, produced by Fables Pictures, 1992 (available in the film collection of the Museum of Modern Art, New York).

2. On this remaining of the fable, in the case of Sade, see my "Freedom, the Law of Another Fable," *Literature and the Ethical Question*, issue of *Yale French Studies*, 79 (1991): 231–51.

3. Jacques Derrida, *Limited Inc.* [1977] (Paris: Galilée, 1990), p. 196; translated as *Limited Inc.*, trans. Samuel Weber (Evanston: Northwestern University Press, 1988), p. 106. Further references to these two editions, indicated by the abbreviation *LI*, will be given in text, with the French pages in roman type following by the English pages in italics. Translations will be modified when necessary.

4. Joseph Jacobs, *The Fables of Aesop* [1894] (New York: Shocken Books, 1966), pp. 93–94. Jacobs refers to the source of this version as "Extravagantes v. 15" in Caxton, although the version of that fable in Caxton differs from his in rather extraordinary ways (see my note 17, below). Jacobs also points to Matthew 7:15, which in the King James Version reads: "Beware of false prophets, which come to you in sheep's clothing, but inwardly they are ravening wolves."

5. As this essay is being revised in January 1992, a major new rap music disk is being released by a group called Black Sheep, titled *A Wolf in Sheep's Clothing*. The first single and video is called "The Choice Is Yours," and posits the choice in the refrain as "you can go for *this*, or you can go for *that*." The video track offers two possible images in the case of each choice, and withdraws the incorrect one to make the lesson clear.

6. La Fontaine, *Oeuvres complètes*, vol. 1 (Paris: Gallimard; Bibliothèque de la Pléiade, 1954), pp. 75–76; translated as *The Fables of La Fontaine*, trans. Marianne Moore (New York: Viking Press, 1954), p. 60. The fable is no. 3 in Book III.

7. Jacques Derrida, "Psyché: Invention de l'autre," in his *Psyché* (Paris: Galilée, 1987), pp. 11–61, esp. 17–35; translated as "Psyche: Invention of the Other," trans. Catherine Porter, in *Acts of Literature*, ed. Derek Attridge (New York: Routledge, 1992), pp. 310–43, esp. 318–37.

The quoted passage is on p. 24 of the French edition, pp. 324–25 of the English. Further references to these two sources, indicated by the abbreviation P, will be given in text, with the French pages in roman type followed by the English in italics.

8. G. W. F. Hegel, *Vorlesungen über die Aesthetik*, vol. 1, Theorie Werkausgabe Bd. 13 (Frankfurt a.M.: Suhrkamp Verlag, 1970), pp. 492–501; translated as *Aesthetics: Lectures on Fine Art*, vol. 1, trans. T. M. Knox (Oxford: Clarendon Press, 1975), pp. 383–90. The quotation is on p. 497 of the German, p. 387 of the English. See also Paul de Man, "Hegel on the Sublime," in *Displacement: Derrida and After*, ed. Mark Krupnick (Bloomington: Indiana University Press, 1983), pp. 139–53.

9. Hegel, *Vorlesungen*, p. 497; idem, *Aesthetics*, p. 387.

10. "The Life: The Book of Xanthus the Philosopher and Aesop His Slave, or The Career of Aesop," trans. Lloyd W. Daly, in *Aesop Without Morals*, ed. Lloyd W. Daly (New York: Thomas Yoseloff, 1961), pp. 29–90; Greek manuscript printed as "Vita Aesopi: Vita G," in *Aesopica*, vol. 1, ed. Ben Edwin Perry (Urbana: University of Illinois Press, 1952), pp. 35–77. The English edition will be cited below in text by the abbreviation *A*.

11. Philippe Lacoue-Labarthe, "La Fable," in his *Le Sujet de la philosophie* (Paris: Aubier-Flammarion, 1979), pp. 7–30 (the question is on p. 25). This essay will be cited below in text by the abbreviation F. See also Jean-Luc Nancy "Mundus est fabula," in his *Ego sum* (Paris: Aubier-Flammarion, 1979), pp. 95–127; Paul de Man, "Rhetoric of Tropes," in his *Allegories of Reading* (New Haven, Conn: Yale University Press, 1979), pp. 103–18; Jacques Derrida, "Déclarations d'indépendance," in his *Otobiographies* (Paris: Galilée, 1984), pp. 11–32, esp. 22; Derrida, "Psyché," pp. 17–35; and Andrzej Warminski, "Towards a Fabulous Reading: Nietzsche's 'On Truth and Lie in the Extramoral Sense,'" *Graduate Faculty Philosophy Journal*, 15, no. 2 (1991): 93–120 (which came to my attention only after this essay was written).

12. My translation. Also see Horace, *Satires*, trans. Niall Rudd (Harmondsworth, Eng.: Penguin Books, 1987), p. 41 (Bk. 1, Satire 1): "change the name and you are the subject of the story."

13. Maurice Blanchot, *L'Écriture du désastre* (Paris: Gallimard, 1980), translated as *The Writing of the Disaster*, trans. Ann Smock (Lincoln: University of Nebraska Press, 1986). References to these two editions, indicated by the abbreviation *D*, will be given in text, with the French pages in roman type followed by the English in italics.

14. Jacques Derrida, *L'Autre cap* (Paris: Munuit, 1991), p. 43. My translation.

15. Friedrich Nietzsche, *Zur Genealogie der Moral. Eine Streitschrift* [Liepzig, 1887] (Munich: Wilhelm Goldmann Verlag, n.d.), p. 46; translated as *On the Genealogy of Morals*, trans. Walter Kaufmann (New York: Vintage Books, 1969), p. 58. Further references to these two editions, indicated by the abbreviation *G*, will be given in text, with the German pages in roman type followed by the English in italics.

16. And the rest of Nietzsche's animals—in "On Truth and Lie," "How the True World," *Zarathustra*, and even the birds of prey in the *Dithyrambs of Dionysus*—will have to be left out here as well.

17. *Caxton's Aesop*, ed. R. T. Lenaghan (Cambridge, Mass.: Harvard University Press, 1967), pp. 165–66. The German and Latin sources of Caxton's translation can be found in *Steinhöwels Aesop*, comp. Hermann Oesterly, in *Bibliothek des Literarischen Vereins*, vol. 117 (Tübingen: L. F. Fues, 1873), pp. 243–44. The fable numbered 98 by Steinhöwel ("Fabula prima de aquila et corvo," "Die erste fabel von dem adler, lamp, und rappen") can also be found, in different versions, under the titles "Eagle, Jackdaw, and Shepherd" (Daly, no. 2), "Le Corbeau voulant imiter l'aigle" (La Fontaine, Bk. II, no. 16), and "The Jackdaw Who Would Be an Eagle" (Babrius, no. 137, trans. Ben Edwin Perry, *Babrius and Phaedrus*, Loeb Classical Library [Cambridge, Mass.: Harvard University Press, 1965], pp. 180–81; and Handford, no. 69, in *Fables of Aesop*, trans. S. A. Handford [Harmondsworth, Eng.: Penguin Books, 1964], p. 73). The versions differ significantly.

18. For a striking parallel, see Caxton's version of the "wolf in sheep's clothing," in which a wether (ram) dresses up as a guard dog, only to be forced to chase a marauding wolf and lose its borrowed skin. The wolf "forthwith retorned ageynste him / and damaunded of hym / what beest art thow / And the wether ansuered to hym in this maner / My lord I am a wether whiche playeth with the / And the wulf sayd / . . . I shalle shewe to the / how thou oughtest not to play so with thy lord / And thenne the wulf took and kylled him / and deuoured and ete hym / And therefore he that is wyse must take good hede / how he playeth with him whiche is wyser / more sage / and more stronge / than hym self is" (*Caxton's Aesop*, p. 161).

19. *Caxton's Aesop*, p. 105.

20. *Fables of Aesop*, trans. Handford, p. 38.

Gelley: The Pragmatics of Exemplary Narrative

1. Gérard Genette, "Frontières du récit," in his *Figures II* (Paris: Seuil, 1969), p. 50. Translations of passages from foreign sources cited here and below are my own unless otherwise noted.

2. Thus in regard to "narrative metalepsis," the breach of narrative levels, the intrusion of voice from one level to another, he remarks: "All these tactics demonstrate, by the intensity of their effort, the importance of the boundary which, in the face of all probability, they persistently seek to transgress, *and which is precisely narration (or representation) itself*; mobile but sacred frontiers between two worlds: that in which one recounts, that of which one recounts." Gérard Genette, *Figures III* (Paris: Seuil, 1972), p. 245.

3. Genette, *Figures II*, p. 66.

4. Susan Rubin Suleiman, " 'Exemplary' Narratives," chap. 1 of her *Authoritarian Fictions: The Ideological Novel as a Literary Genre* (New York: Columbia University Press, 1983), pp. 25–61. This source will be cited by page numbers below in text. An earlier version was published as "Le Récit exemplaire—Parabole, fable, roman à thèse," *Poétique*, 32 (1977): 466–89.

5. Aristotle, *On Rhetoric*, 1356b, in *Aristotle on Rhetoric: A Theory of Civic Discourse*, trans. George A. Kennedy (New York: Oxford University Press, 1991), pp. 40–41. See also Roland Barthes, "L'Ancienne rhétorique—Aide-mémoire," in his *L'Aventure sémiologique* (Paris: Seuil, 1985), pp. 125–26.

6. See Karlheinz Stierle, "Story as Exemplum—Exemplum as Story," in *New Perspectives in German Literary Criticism*, ed. Richard E. Amacher and Victor Lange (Princeton, N.J.: Princeton University Press, 1979), p. 406.

7. This "enigmatic" approach is, of course, a venerable one. Suleiman cites a number of recent critics who develop it: Jean Starobinski, Louis Marin, and Frank Kermode.

8. J. L. Austin, we know, explicitly excluded the "poetical use of language" from consideration in his study of illocutionary effects, *How to Do Things with Words* (Cambridge, Mass.: Harvard University Press, 1975). "Go catch a falling star," an example he cites (p. 104), is clearly an imperative in a grammatical sense, but we cannot conceive a situation where it would have an illocutionary effect, though it might well have a perlocutionary effect. But in a sense one could imagine situations where virtually any statement might have some effect that proceeds indirectly from its propositional content. The category of "perlocution" is of little use here.

9. Translation by Ross Chambers, in his *Room for Maneuver: Reading Oppositional Narrative* (Chicago: University of Chicago Press, 1991; © 1991 by The University of Chicago; permission to reprint is gratefully acknowledged.), p. 61. The French text, "Le Pouvoir des fables," is cited from La Fontaine, *Fables*, ed. René Radouant (Paris:

Hachette, 1929), Book VIII, no. 4. In this fable, the year is 1677. The dedicatee, M. de Barillon, is Louis XIV's ambassador to the court of Charles II in England. His task as he sets out for England is to maintain Charles's alliance with France and forestall any agreement by England with members of the European coalition that are a threat to France.

10. Louis Marin, *Le Récit est un piège* (Paris: Minuit, 1978), pp. 31–32.

11. Marin, *Le Récit est un piège*, p. 32. Ross Chambers's reading of "Le Pouvoir des fables" provides an elaboration and refinement of Marin's argument. What Chambers terms oppositional narrative "is an ironic skill and its name is not trap setting but seduction. Its most prominent feature is that it is through the satisfaction of the other's desire that one simultaneously achieves one's own ends." In *Room for Maneuver*, p. 66.

12. Jean-François Lyotard, *Discours, figure* (Paris: Klincksieck, 1971), pp. 110–14.

13. Paul de Man, "Aesthetic Formalization: Kleist's *Über das Marionettentheater*," in de Man's *The Rhetoric of Romanticism* (New York: Columbia University Press, 1984), p. 276.

14. Jean-François Lyotard, *The Differend*, trans. Georges Van Den Abbeele (Minneapolis: University of Minnesota Press, 1988), p. 123. "Abyss" is an allusion to the introduction of Kant's *Critique of Judgment*.

15. J. W. von Goethe, *Die Wahlverwandtschaften*, in *Goethes Werke*, vol. 6 (Hamburg: Christian Wegner Verlag, 1958), p. 368.

16. Cf. "You give him examples—but he has to guess their drift." Ludwig Wittgenstein, *Philosophical Investigations*, trans. G. E. M. Anscombe (New York: Macmillan, 1958), sec. 210. See also Introduction, above, p. 13.

Miller: Parabolic Exemplarity

This essay was originally published in somewhat different form as "Nietzsche in Basel" in J. Hillis Miller, *Topographies* (Stanford, Calif.: Stanford University Press, 1994).

1. For an exemplary discussion of the way an example is just one example among many, perhaps innumerable, possible examples of the same thing, and always at the same time the example of examples, unique and singular, see Michael B. Naas's brilliant essay "Introduction: For Example," in Jacques Derrida, *The Other Heading*, trans. Pascale-Anne Brault and Michael B. Naas (Bloomington and Indianapolis: Indiana University Press, 1992), pp. vii-lix.

2. See Martin Heidegger, "Wer ist Nietzsche's Zarathustra," *Vorträge und Aufsätze* (Pfullingen: Neske, 1967), translated as "Who Is Nietzsche's Zarathustra," trans. Bernd Magnus, in *The New Nietzsche*, ed. David B. Allison (New York: Dell, 1977), pp. 64–79; and Bernard Pautrat, "Retour à l'est," in *Versions du Soleil* (Paris: Seuil, 1971), pp. 329–61.

3. *The Portable Nietzsche*, ed. Walter Kaufmann (New York: Viking, 1959), p. 103. Further references to this edition and to the German edition, Friedrich Nietzsche, *Werke*, ed. Karl Schlecta (Munich: Carl Hanser, 1966), will be given together in the text with the abbreviation *Z*, followed by the German pages in roman type and the English pages in italics.

4. Quintilian, as cited in *Friedrich Nietzsche on Rhetoric and Language*, ed. and trans. Sander L. Gilman, Carole Blaire, and David J. Parent (New York: Oxford University Press, 1989), p. 63. This edition provides a bilingual version of Nietzsche's lectures on ancient rhetoric and an English translation of his "On Truth and Lies in an Extramoral Sense." Readers should be aware that this edition must be used with circumspection. For a challenge to its accuracy and scholarship see Anton Bierl and William M. Calder, III, "Friedrich Nietzsche: 'Abriss der Geschichte der Beredsamkeit': A New Edition," *Nietzsche-Studien*, 21 (1992): 363–89. For an annotated French version of Nietzsche's early writings on rhetoric, see Friedrich Nietzsche, "Rhetoric et langage," ed. and trans. Jean-Luc Nancy and Philippe Lacoue-Labarthe, *Poétique*, 5 (1971): 99–142.

5. *Nietzsche on Rhetoric and Language*, pp. 62, 63.

6. Ibid., p. 246; the German of "Über Wahrheit und Lüge" is from the bilingual German and French edition: Friedrich Nietzsche, *Das Philosophenbuch / Le Livre du philosophe*, trans. Angèle K. Marietti (Paris: Aubier-Flammarion, 1969), p. 170.

7. I have approached this question from a different direction in "Gleichnis in Nietzsche's *Also Sprach Zarathustra*," *International Studies in Philosophy*, 17, no. 2 (1985): 3–15, reprinted in *Theory Now and Then* (London: Harvester Wheatsheaf; Durham: Duke University Press, 1991), pp. 277–91.

8. See Charles Singleton, "In Exitu Israel de Aegypto," *Dante: A Collection of Critical Essays*, ed. John Freccero (Englewood Cliffs, N.J.: Prentice Hall, 1965), pp. 102–21; Paul de Man, *Allegories of Reading*, p. 205: "The paradigm for all texts consists of a figure (or a system of figures) and its deconstruction. But since this model cannot be closed off by final reading, it engenders, in its turn, a supplementary figural superposition which narrates the unreadability of the prior narration.

As distinguished from primary deconstructive narratives centered on figures and ultimately always on metaphor, we can call such narratives to the second (or third) degree *allegories."*

9. Sigmund Freud, *Beyond the Pleasure Principle,* trans. James Strachey (New York: Bantam, 1967), p. 110. "The Book" is presumably the Koran.

10. Friedrich Nietzsche, *Die Geburt der Tragödie,* in *Werke,* ed. Karl Schlechta, 1:12. The translation is by Carol Jacobs, who quotes this passage as one of the epigraphs to her brilliant essay, "Nietzsche: The Stammering Text: The Fragmentary Studies Preliminary to *The Birth of Tragedy,"* in *The Dissimulating Harmony* (Baltimore: Johns Hopkins University Press, 1978), pp. 3–22.

11. *Nietzsche on Rhetoric and Language,* p. 51.

Ziarek: "The Beauty of Failure"

1. See, for example, Walter Benjamin, "Franz Kafka: On the Tenth Anniversary of His Death" and "Some Reflections on Kafka," in his *Illuminations,* trans. Harry Zohn (New York: Schocken, 1969); Frank Kermode, *Genesis of Secrecy: On the Interpretation of Narrative* (Cambridge, Mass.: Harvard University Press, 1979), pp. 26–33; J. Hillis Miller, "Parable and Performative in the Gospels and in Modern Literature," in *Humanizing America's Iconic Book,* ed. Gene M. Tucker and Douglas A. Knight (Chico, Calif.: Scholars Press, 1982), pp. 58–71; and Heinz Politzer, *Franz Kafka: Parable and Paradox* (Ithaca, N.Y.: Cornell University Press, 1966), pp. 1–23. Subsequent references to the Benjamin edition, indicated by the abbreviation *I,* will be given in the text.

2. Kermode, *Genesis of Secrecy,* p. 23.

3. There exists rich literature on the parable in the Judeo-Christian tradition. Only a few sources important for my argument will be mentioned here: C. H. Dodd, *The Parables of the Kingdom* (New York: Scribner, 1961); Robert W. Funk, *Language, Hermeneutic, and the Word of God* (New York: Harper, 1966); J. Jeremias, *The Parables of Jesus* (New York: Scribner, 1972); Jean Starobinski, "The Struggle with Legion: A Literary Analysis of Mark 5:1–20," *NLH,* 4 (1973): 330–56; and David Stern, "Rhetoric and Midrash: The Case of the Mashal," *Prooftexts,* 1 (1981): 262–91.

4. *The Universal Jewish Encyclopedia,* ed. Isaac Landman, vol. 7 (New York: The Universal Jewish Encyclopedia Inc., 1942), p. 395.

5. For a suggestive reading of this parable, especially of the figure of the outsider, see Kermode, *Genesis of Secrecy,* pp. 28–32.

6. Starobinski, "Struggle with Legion," p. 348.

7. On the difference between the interpretation of the secular and sacred parables, see Miller, "Parable and the Performative," p. 59.

8. Theodor W. Adorno, "Notes on Kafka," in his *Prisms*, trans. Samuel and Shierry Weber (Cambridge, Mass.: MIT Press, 1982), pp. 243–72; Wilhelm Emrich, *Franz Kafka: A Critical Study of His Writings*, trans. Sheema Zeben Buehne (New York: Ungar, 1968), pp. 1–74; Politzer, *Parable and Paradox*, pp. 1–23. For discussion of the relevance of the term "parable" in Kafka criticism see Alan Udoff's Introduction to *Kafka and the Contemporary Critical Performance*, ed. Alan Udoff (Bloomington: Indiana University Press, 1987), p. 3.

9. Politzer, *Parable and Paradox*, pp. 21–22.

10. Ibid., p. 16.

11. The thesis of immanence is most convincingly propagated in Kafka criticism by Gilles Deleuze and Félix Guattari, *Kafka: Toward a Minor Literature*, trans. Dana Polan, (Minneapolis: University of Minnesota Press, 1986). According to them, the three misleading themes in Kafka criticism are "the transcendence of the law, the interiority of guilt, the subjectivity of enunciation" (p. 45), which they juxtapose with the immanence of desire. In their analysis of "the writing machine," Deleuze and Guattari see Kafka's prose as "an unlimited field of immanence instead of an infinite transcendence" (p. 51). Unsatisfied and liberated desire is no longer bound toward the inaccessible transcendent law, but always moves forward, displacing the limits and opening new connectors. For the difference between this approach and Benjamin's, see Réda Bensmaïa "Foreword: The Kafka Effect," in Deleuze and Guattari, *Toward a Minor Literature*, pp. ix–xxi.

12. The text of "Some Reflections on Kafka" in *Illuminations* is based upon Benjamin's letter to Gershom Scholem from Paris, June 12, 1938, published also in Walter Benjamin, *Briefe*, ed. Gershom Scholem and Theodor W. Adorno (Frankfurt a.M.: Suhrkamp, 1993), 2: 756–64.

13. Benjamin's interpretations of Kafka are obviously polemical. In addition to rejecting the theological and psychoanalytical interpretations, Benjamin questions Scholem's understanding of Kafka in the context of Jewish mysticism as well as Brecht's vision of Kafka as a prophetic writer. For an excellent account of the way in which Benjamin negotiates his reading of Kafka with Adorno, Brecht, and Scholem, see Hans Mayer, "Walter Benjamin and Franz Kafka: Report on a Constellation," trans. Gary Smith and Thomas S. Hansen, in *On Walter Benjamin: Critical Essays and Recollections*, ed. Gary Smith (Cambridge, Mass.: MIT Press, 1988), pp. 185–209. For an alternative account of the

influence of Scholem—in particular of his idea of "deferral as constitutive for Judaism"—on Benjamin's reading of Kafka, see Susan A. Handelman, *Fragments of Redemption: Jewish Thought and Literary Theory in Benjamin, Scholem, and Levinas* (Bloomington: Indiana University Press, 1991), pp. 44–52. For an excellent account of the way Benjamin's reading of Kafka anticipates contemporary literary theory, see Henry Sussman, *Franz Kafka: Geometrician of Metaphor* (Madison, Wis.: Coda Press, 1979), pp. 1–41.

14. For an illuminating discussion of Benjamin's own relation to modernity, see Rainer Nägele, *Theater, Theory, Speculation: Walter Benjamin and the Scenes of Modernity* (Baltimore: The Johns Hopkins University Press, 1991), pp. 54–77, 135–66.

15. The German passage is from Walter Benjamin, "Franz Kafka: Zur zehnten Wiederkehr seines Todestages," in *Gesammelte Schriften*, ed. Rolf Tiedemann et al. (Frankfurt a.M.: Suhrkamp, 1972–77), 2: 437.

16. Franz Kafka, *Parables and Paradoxes*, in German and English (New York: Schocken, 1975), p. 175. Subsequent references to this edition, indicated by the abbreviation *PP*, will be given in the text.

17. For a less frequently mentioned aspect of transmission in Benjamin's work, see an excellent discussion of rumor or street talk in Avital Ronell, "Street-Talk," in *Benjamin's Ground: New Readings of Walter Benjamin*, ed. Rainer Nägele (Detroit: Wayne State University Press, 1988), pp. 119–45.

18. By reading these texts—one from the earlier and the other from the later phase of Benjamin's career—against each other, one can avoid reductive interpretations that Benjamin accounts for the changes in modern art solely on the basis of the changes in reproduction techniques. For such a reading see, for instance, Peter Bürger, *Theory of the Avant-Garde*, trans. Michael Shaw (Minneapolis: University of Minnesota Press, 1984), pp. 27–34.

19. Paul de Man, "Conclusions: Walter Benjamin's 'The Task of the Translator,'" in his *The Resistance to Theory* (Minneapolis: University of Minnesota Press, 1986), p. 80, emphasis added. In reference to the title of Benjamin's essay, "Die Aufgabe des Übersetzers," de Man reminds us: "*Aufgabe*, task, can also mean the one who has to give up" (p. 80).

20. What de Man's reading of failure contests is a dialectical notion of modernity as "the overcoming of a certain naiveté and a rise of consciousness to another level." De Man argues that this notion of moder-

nity as a critical overcoming of the past still informs Gadamer's "The Philosophical Foundations of the Twentieth Century." De Man, "Conclusion," pp. 74–77.

21. For an excellent account of the overcoming of "this still natural unity rooted in mythical linguistic relations," see Rodolphe Gasché, "Saturnine Vision and the Question of Difference: Reflections on Walter Benjamin's Theory of Language," in Nägele, *Benjamin's Ground*, pp. 86–92.

22. The figure of the broken vessel and its relation to the idea of *Tikkun* of the Lurianic Kabalah is elaborated by Carol Jacobs, "The Monstrosity of Translation," *MLN*, 90 (1975): 762.

23. See Jacobs, "Monstrosity of Translation," pp. 763–64.

24. De Man, "Conclusions," p. 92.

25. In his essay "The Work of Art in the Age of Mechanical Reproduction," Benjamin directly confronts the complicity between aestheticism, community, and fascism.

26. For an illuminating discussion of pure language as an inexpressible latent ground "something like a trembling or vibration . . . or the rush and trance of Dionysian music," see Rainer Nägele, "Benjamin's Ground," in Nägele, *Benjamin's Ground*, pp. 32–36.

27. Walter Benjamin, "Die Aufgabe des Übersetzers," in his *Gesammelte Schriften*, 4: 20.

28. Such an assimilation would erase for Benjamin a distinction between aesthetics and commodity.

29. In structural terms, Benjamin's understanding of transmissibility "bears a kinship" to Derrida's analysis of iterability ("Signature, Event, Context," in Jacques Derrida, *Margins of Philosophy*, trans. Alan Bass [Chicago: University of Chicago Press, 1982], pp. 307–30). Derrida defines iterability as repetition that is linked to alterity as a result of the transposition of contexts. He points out that in the traditional notion of communication the ideal content is not affected by repetition, by the linguistic or semantic transport. Iteration, however, indicates the essential limitation of the "original" context: "a written sign carries with it a force of breaking with its context, that is, the set of presences that organize the moment of its inscription." Because iterability is an inherent quality of the text, it can always be lifted out of its original context and inscribed or "grafted" onto a number of other possible contexts, other "semantic chains" that will affect the consistency of its "original" meaning. Therefore, no single formula, context, law, or idea can contain the movement of iteration or, by extension,

the meaning of the text. Although iterability subverts the stability of exemplification, this "extraction" from the determining context is what constitutes the possibility of citation, and of exemplification.

30. Franz Kafka, *Letters to Friends, Family, and Editors*, trans. Richard and Clara Winston (New York: Schocken, 1978), p. 289. Probably the most extensive analysis of Kafka's writing as situated on the crossroad of languages and the multiple effects of deterritorialization that they perform can be found in Deleuze and Guattari, *Toward a Minor Literature*, pp. 19–27.

31. "On Parables" has inspired many interesting readings. For its interpretation in terms of psychopoetic structures—the erotic sense of the many corresponding to metonymy and the thanatotic sense of the wise corresponding to the metaphor—see Charles Bernheimer, *Flaubert and Kafka: Studies in Psychopoetic Structure* (New Haven, Conn.: Yale University Press, 1982), pp. 45–55. For "On Parables" in the context of the performative function of language, see Miller, "Parable and Performative," pp. 67–71.

32. Franz Kafka, "On the Tram," in *The Complete Stories*, ed. Nahum N. Glatzer (New York: Schocken, 1971), p. 388. Subsequent references to this edition, indicated by the abbreviation *CS*, will be given in the text.

33. See, for example, Bernheimer, *Flaubert and Kafka*, pp. 50–51.

34. The following commentaries on this biblical text are important to my argument and will be cited in the text by the author's name followed by page number: Umberto Cassuto, *A Commentary on the Book of Genesis*, Part 2, trans. Israel Abrahams (Jerusalem: The Magnes Press, 1974), pp. 225–49; Samson Raphael Hirsch, *The Pentateuch*, vol. 1, *Genesis*, trans. Isaac Levy (Judaica Press, 1976), pp. 204–17; Benno Jacob, *The First Book of the Bible: Genesis*, trans. Ernest I. Jacob and Walter Jacob (New York: Ktav, 1974), pp. 77–79; Gerhard von Rad, *Genesis: A Commentary*, trans. H. Marks (Philadelphia: Westminster Press, 1961), pp. 143–51.

35. Jacques Derrida, "Des Tours de Babel," in *Difference in Translation*, ed. Joseph F. Graham (Ithaca, N.Y.: Cornell University Press, 1985), p. 165–66.

36. In his reflection on "The Burrow" in *Geometrician of Metaphor*, Sussman points out that construction functions as "all-embracing metaphor" in Kafka's works: "We are apprised from the outset that the project under construction is a literary as well as architectural object, bespeaking the same duplicity, illusoriness, impenetrability and limits characteristic of the literary text" (p. 150).

37. For a discussion of "lines of escape" in Kafka's text see Deleuze and Guattari, *Toward a Minor Literature*, pp. 34–42.

38. Sussman, *Geometrician of Metaphor*, pp. 149.

39. For a detailed discussion of the ways in which the claim to the community can assure a stability of meaning in the absence of the epistemological foundation, see Stanley Cavell, *The Claim of Reason* (Oxford: Oxford University Press, 1979), pp. 32–78.

40. Cavell claims that there is no further epistemological grounding available for the claim of the linguistic unity of the community. Since the idea of the mutual agreement of speakers is itself groundless, it can be only acknowledged but not proved: it is open "to question whether a philosophical explanation is needed, or wanted, for the fact of agreement in language human beings use together. . . . For nothing is deeper than the fact, or extent, of agreement itself." *Claim of Reason*, pp. 32.

41. For an excellent discussion of modernity's consciousness of time and of Benjamin's critique of the modern notion of time in his concept of history, see Jürgen Habermas, *The Philosophical Discourse of Modernity*, trans. Frederick Lawrence (Cambridge, Mass.: MIT Press, 1987), pp. 1–22.

42. The connection between transmissibility and critical intervention is emphasized by Benjamin as well. Translation is compared directly to critical epistemology and to literary criticism, and the process of mechanical reproduction situates the audience in the position of the critics.

Harvey: Exemplarity and the Origins of Legislation

1. "Ah! Sien grazie ai Numi!" was Radames's response to the gods' having named him the next leader of Egypt's army.

2. See Plato's *Laws*, trans. Trevor J. Saunders (Harmondsworth, Eng.: Penguin Books, 1976), pp. 178–86.

3. See Jean-Jacques Rousseau's *The Social Contract*, trans. Maurice Cranston (Harmondsworth, Eng.: Penguin Books, 1987), p. 49. The context is significant since Rousseau explicitly denied that he is acting as a legislator in writing the law of the law here for us: "I may be asked whether I am a prince or a legislator that I should be writing about politics. I answer no: and indeed that that is my reason for doing so. If I were a prince or a legislator, I should not waste my time saying what ought to be done, I should do it and keep silent." The Cranston translation will be cited below by the abbreviation *SC*.

4. See Jean-Jacques Rousseau, "Lettres écrites de la Montagne," in

Oeuvres complètes III (Paris: Gallimard, Bibliothèque de la Pléiade, 1964), p. 707. This edition of the *Oeuvres* will be cited below by the abbreviation *OC III*. All translations are my own.

5. Jean-Jacques Rousseau, *Emile*, trans. Allan Bloom (New York: Basic Books, 1979), p. 364. This translation will be cited below by the abbreviation *E*.

6. Rousseau, *OC III*, "Sur le Gouvernement de Pologne," pp. 956–59.

7. See the books of Exodus and Deuteronomy, in particular.

8. On Solon, see Plutarch, *The Rise and Fall of Athens: Nine Greek Lives*, trans. Ian Scott Kilvert (Harmondsworth: Penguin Books, 1986), pp. 43–76.

9. Livy, *The Early History of Rome*, trans. Aubrey de Selincourt (Harmondsworth, Eng.: Penguin Books, 1986), p. 51.

10. See the book of Exodus in the Bible.

11. Xenophon and Plutarch, *The Spartan Rhetra*, comp. and trans. J. E. Longhurst (Lawrence, Kans.: Coronado Press, 1970), p. 22.

12. Plutarch, *Rise and Fall of Athens*, p. 53.

13. Livy, *Early History of Rome*, p. 54.

14. Ibid.

15. For more on the idea that the ordering of the list of examples is itself significant, see Derrida's work "Parergon," in his *The Truth in Painting*, trans. Geoff Bennington and Ian McLeod (Chicago: University of Chicago Press, 1987), p. 105.

16. See Plato, *Socrates' Defense (Apology)*, in *Plato: Collected Dialogues*, ed. Edith Hamilton and Huntington Cairns (Princeton, N.J.: Princeton University Press, 1971), pp. 3–27.

17. Saint Augustine, *The Confessions*, trans. R. S. Pine-Coffin (Harmondsworth, Eng.: Penguin Books, 1986).

18. Jacques Derrida, *Of Grammatology*, trans. G. Spivak (Baltimore: Johns Hopkins University Press, 1976), p. 97.

19. Derrida, *Truth in Painting*, p. 105.

20. Despite their apparent and publicly debated differences, these traits form the common ground between the seemingly opposed hermeneutics represented by Hans Georg Gadamer, especially in his *Truth and Method*, ed. Garrett Barder and John Cumming (London: Sheed and Ward, 1975), and Jürgen Habermas, in his *Knowledge and Human Interests*, trans. Jeremy Shapiro (Boston: Beacon Press, 1971).

21. For more on the notion of intentionality, see Edmund Husserl's *Ideas*, trans. F. Kersten (Dordrecht: Kluwer Academic Publishers Group, 1982).

22. See also Derrida's work on Husserl on this topic in *Speech and Phenomenon*, trans. David B. Allison (Evanston: Northwestern University Press, 1973).

23. "Exemplifier" and "exemplified" are two terms I have coined following the example of Saussure's terms "signifier" and "signified" in order to break open the term sign and analyse its aspects of functioning. See also Ferdinand Saussure, *Course in General Linguistics*, trans. Wade Baskin (Glasgow: William Collins, 1974).

24. See Derrida's work on this notion in *Of Grammatology*.

25. For more on the famous notion of Plato's "Noble Lie," see *The Republic*, in *Plato: Collected Works*.

Lloyd: Kant's Examples

This essay was originally published in *Representations*, 28 (Fall 1989): 34–54, a volume of the journal dedicated to the memory of Joel Fineman; © 1989 by the Regents of the University of California. Permission to reprint is gratefully acknowledged.

1. Immanuel Kant, *Critique of Judgment*, trans. with analytical indexes by James Creed Meredith (Oxford: Clarendon, 1982), p. 227. Pages from this edition, referred to hereafter as *CJ*, will be given in text. Page citations in German from the third *Critique* are from *Kritik der Urteilskraft, Werkausgabe*, vol. 10, ed. Wilhelm Weischedel (Frankfurt a.M.: Suhrkamp, 1974), cited throughout in the text as *KU*. The allusion to Georg Lukács is to his *Theory of the Novel*, trans. Anna Bostock (Cambridge, Mass.: MIT Press, 1971), esp. chaps. 1 and 3; the reference to Mikhail Bakhtin is to his *Dialogic Imagination: Four Essays*, ed. Michael Holquist, trans. Caryl Emerson and Michael Holquist (Austin: University of Texas Press, 1981). Bakhtin remarks typically in the essay "Epic and the Novel": "The epic world knows only a single and unified world view, obligatory and indubitably true for heroes as well as for authors and audiences" (p. 35). It should be remarked from the outset that for Kant the organic nature of such a community is always already the product of an *art*, dependent on the form of the "as if" that, as we shall see, governs all aesthetic productions. It is not, therefore, a primal condition of the human disrupted by the advent of modernity as, with varying affect, it appears for Lukács and Bakhtin. This, as I argue at the end of this essay, is closely related to the ironic structure of exemplary pedagogy.

2. I have discussed the specifically *political* function of aesthetic culture in "Arnold, Ferguson, Schiller: Aesthetic Culture and the Politics of Aesthetics," *Cultural Critique*, 2 (Winter 1985–86): 137–69,

and in "Analogies of Aesthetics: The Politics of Culture and the Limits of Materialist Aesthetics," *New Formations*, 10 (Spring 1990): 109–26. In both I delineate some of the crucial historical determinants on the emergence of a doctrine of aesthetic culture in late-eighteenth-century Germany. For an excellent account of the sociohistorical condition of Germany and of its bourgeois intelligentsia at this epoch, see W. H. Bruford, *Germany in the Eighteenth Century: The Social Background of the Literary Revival* (1935; reprint, Cambridge, Eng.: Cambridge University Press, 1959). See also Georg Lukács, "Zur Aesthetik Schillers," in his *Probleme der Ästhetik, Werke*, vol. 10 (Neuweid and Berlin: Luchterhand, 1969), pp. 18–19, 26–27, on the constraint on the German bourgeoisie to conceive of attaining the results of a bourgeois revolution without engaging in an actual revolution. More generally, see Nicolao Merker, *An den Ursprüngen der deutschen Ideologie: Revolution und Utopie im Jakobinismus*, trans. Manfred Buhr (Berlin: Akademie-Verlag, 1984), on the political situation of the German bourgeois intellectuals. In "Kant und die Wende zur Aesthetik," *Zeitschrift für philosophische Forschung*, 16 (1962): 252, Odo Marquard raises the question, in this context, as to whether the aesthetic should be seen as the instrument or the substitute for the political realization of ethical ideals.

3. I have elaborated the political function of the formalism of bourgeois aesthetics more extensively in "Arnold, Ferguson, Schiller," esp. pp. 166–68, and in "Genet's Genealogy: European Minorities and the Ends of the Canon," *Cultural Critique*, 6 (Spring 1987), esp. pp. 171–72.

4. I have been struck by Cathy Caruth's conclusions on the narrative form of examples in the rather different context of the *Critique of Pure Reason*. As she remarks in her brilliant essay, "The Force of Example: Kant's Symbols" (below in this volume), on account of the personification of philosophy itself, "[t]he mediation provided by the example must, therefore, be understood in narrative terms." I seek here only to extend that remark to the structure of the example as such.

5. Marx makes the celebrated comment in *The Eighteenth Brumaire of Louis Bonaparte* (Moscow: Progress Publishers, 1977), p. 11, that the participants in the French Revolution "performed the task of their time in Roman costume and with Roman phrases." The shift from Roman to Greek models as a crucial element in the formation of post-Enlightenment theories of *culture* has been apparent at least since Walter Pater's essay on Winckelmann in *The Renaissance*. But the most important recent study is Marin Bernal's *The Fabrication of Ancient Greece, 1785–1985*, vol. 1 of *Black Athena: The Afro-Asiatic*

Roots of Classical Civilization (New Brunswick, N.J.: Rutgers University Press, 1987).

6. A full demonstration of the antirepresentational form of barricades and guerrilla warfare would require a full-length essay. Crucial to both, however, is the breakdown of the process of temporal deferral constitutive of the political culture of representation and its replacement by the dramatically spatial disposition of social relations as relations of conflicting forces. T. J. Clark's "The Picture of the Barricade," chap. 1 of *The Absolute Bourgeois: Artists and Politics in France, 1848–1851* (Greenwich, Conn.: New York Graphic Society, 1973), is peculiarly suggestive regarding the difficulties of representing artistically the barricades thrown up by the people at the very point at which the possibility of their being represented politically has collapsed. The breakdown of representative politics is what Marx in *The Eighteenth Brumaire* perceives as the critical element of 1848 and the Bonapartist coup. In more general terms, Michel Foucault remarks programmatically on the necessity to spatialize discursive forms in order to analyze the disposition of power relations: "Once knowledge can be analyzed in terms of region, domain, implantation, displacement, transposition, one is able to capture the process by which knowledge functions as a form of power and disseminates the effects of power. . . . Metaphorizing the transformations of discourse in a vocabulary of time necessarily leads to the utilization of the model of individual consciousness with its intrinsic temporality. Endeavouring on the other hand to decipher discourse through the use of spatial, strategic metaphors enables one to grasp precisely the points at which discourses are transformed in, through and on the basis of relations of power." Foucault, "Questions of Geography," in *Power/Knowledge: Selected Interviews and Other Writings, 1972–1977*, ed. Colin Gordon, trans. Colin Gordon, Leo Marshall, John Mepham, and Kate Soper (New York: Pantheon, 1980), pp. 69–70. I would only contend here, as throughout this essay, that at any given moment the apparently "intrinsic" temporality of the individual is produced, in the present instance pedagogically. The geography of classroom relations is a classic instance of the temporalization of arbitrary power relations in which arbitrary dispositions of authority are legitimated by appeal to the transcendental temporality of the exemplary. What gives this locus of authority its verisimilitude is the folding over of this institutional temporality with what appears as the "intrinsic" temporality of the individual subject.

7. The argument concerning the social and developmental character of taste is made at *CJ* 155–56. I have discussed the relation between

social development and the narrative internal to each act of judgment more fully in "Analogies of Aesthetics." In "Parergon," Derrida makes the suggestive but unfortunately "undeveloped" comment: "Si en revanche une anthropologie determinée intervient dans cette critique du jugement esthétique, toute une théorie de l'histoire, de la société et de la culture décide au moment le plus formellement critique. Elle pèse de tout son contenu sur les cadres." Jacques Derrida, "Parergon," in his *La Vérité en peinture* (Paris: Flammarion, 1978), p. 120. See further my "Race Under Representation," *Oxford Literary Review*, 13 (Fall 1991): 62–94.

8. See again Caruth's "Force of Example," where the life of philosophy is seen to depend on the lifelessness of matter, a chiasmatic narrative that she attaches to a Christian narrative of redemption. The ethical narrative of universal history that informs exemplary pedagogy is easily envisaged as a secular transposition of the redemptive narrative of Christianity and clearly retains much of its temporal figurality.

9. I am indebted for this observation to T. W. Adorno's exposition of the "primacy of the object" in the late essay "Subject and Object," in *The Essential Frankfurt School Reader*, ed. Andrew Arato and Eike Gebhardt, intro. Paul Piccone (New York: Urizen Books, 1978), esp. pp. 502–4.

10. See Immanuel Kant, *Critique of Pure Reason*, trans. Norman Kemp Smith (London: Macmillan, 1978), p. 178.

11. Shoshana Felman's very fine essay "Psychoanalysis and Education: Teaching Terminable and Interminable," in *The Pedagogical Imperative: Teaching as a Literary Genre*, Yale French Studies, 63 (1982): 21–44, is instructive, if not exemplary of ironic accounts of pedagogy, especially in its appeal to the potential *interminability* of teaching. This is open to critique not simply for the formalism of its analysis, which entirely ignores the *matter* of teaching, but also insofar as it overlooks the institutional geography of both psychoanalysis and pedagogy which shores up the effect of mastery, esoteric or not, even in the moment of its self-critique. Satya Mohanty's "Radical Teaching, Radical Theory: The Ambiguous Politics of Meaning," in *Theory in the Classroom*, ed. C. Nelson (Urbana: University of Illinois Press, 1986), pp. 149–76, is a forceful critique of this and several other essays in the same volume for their purely "transcendental" radicalism.

12. Kant, *KU*, 299; *CJ*, 226. I cite the German here as well as the English since the translation of *vormachen* (which my German dictionary defines as, amongst other things, *als Beispiel dienen*) as "illustrate" considerably reduces the semantic field of the original term.

13. Jacques Derrida's "Economimesis," trans. R. Klein, *Diacritics*, 11, no. 2 (Summer 1981): 3–25, is an indispensable analysis of the problematic of genius in the *Critique of Judgment* in relation to the differentiation of the aesthetic sphere. Timothy Gould's "The Audience of Originality: Kant and Wordsworth on the Reception of Genius," in *Essays in Kant's Aesthetics*, ed. Ted Cohen and Paul Guyer (Chicago: Chicago University Press, 1982), pp. 179–93, is a useful account of the relation between the definition of genius and the possibility of the communicability of its productions.

14. Derrida comments on this passage and on the punning differentiation between *Nachahmung* and *Nachmachung* in "Economimesis," pp. 10–11.

15. This formal identity of the mode of judgment can also be seen in terms of principles: cf. Immanuel Kant, *On Education* (Ann Arbor: University of Michigan Press, 1960), p. 9: "Uniformity can only result when all men act according to the same principles, which principles would have to become with them a second nature." That the poet now conforms autonomously to others' judgments is an index that principles of judgment have become second nature in him.

16. The other distinction to be made here is the one Kant makes between genius and science: science can be communicated methodically by sheer imitation, and distinctions in achievement are of degree, not kind; genius can never be communicated. By the same token, science is progressive and indefinitely perfectible whereas genius has reached its limit (*CJ*, 169–70). On this distinction, in all probability, Thomas De Quincey based his famous distinction between the literature of knowledge and the literature of power, designating by the former works of practical information, from cookery to geometry, by the latter works of the imagination. It is perhaps an important index of the reception of Kant in England that De Quincey effectively elides the distinction between taste and genius here: the reader repeats the work of the author and is endowed thereby with some of the latter's "power." See Thomas De Quincey, "Alexander Pope," in *Works*, vol. 8 (Edinburgh: Adam and Charles Black, 1863), pp. 5–9.

17. Thomas Huhn has argued to me (personal communication, 1/16/89) that this argument can be given a positive valence, reading "the paradox of the exemplary" as "the revelation and critique of pervasive mis-identity because it alone refuses to forge yet another mis-identity." This is potentially a very forceful critique of my argument and raises the opportunity to remark that it is precisely the burden of this essay to critique from its very grounds the by now habitual transformation

of "the affirmative character of culture" into its negative, critical but still specular image. For this strategy of leftist aesthetics leaves unbroached the necessary task of critiquing the constitutive role of aesthetic culture within the total formation of the political culture of representation, a task that I take to be fundamental to any current rethinking of the politics of cultural education.

18. In "Parergon," p. 123, Derrida remarks of a similar passage of the *Critique of Judgment*: "La troisième *Critique* dépend de manière essentielle . . . d'une anthropologie pragmatique et de ce qui se nommerait, selon plus d'un sens, un humanisme réfléchissant. Ce recours anthropologiste, reconnu en son instance juridique et formelle, pèse en masse, par son contenu, sur cette déduction prétendument pure du jugement ésthétique."

19. The German word that Kant uses throughout the third *Critique* for "represent" is *vorstellen*. Although Odo Marquard writes extensively and suggestively of a "strikt vertretbare Erkenntnissubjekt" ("Kant und die Wende zur Ästhetik," p. 244), the concept of *vertreten*, with its double valence of exchange and representation, is as yet only implicit in the structure of Kant's thought. Only in Schiller's *Letters on the Aesthetic Education of Man* does the usage of *vertreten* begin to be attached to aesthetic works, and this still precedes the modern political usage of the term for parliamentary representation. I have discussed these terms further in "Analogies of Aesthetics," pp. 120–21.

20. Paul de Man, "The Rhetoric of Temporality," in his *Blindness and Insight: Essays in the Rhetoric of Contemporary Criticism*, 2nd ed., revised, intro. Wlad Godzich (London: Methuen, 1983), pp. 187–228. Cited in the text hereafter as *BI*.

21. Cf. de Man, *BI*, 210. Franco Moretti, in *The Way of the World: The Bildungsroman in European Culture* (London: Verso, 1987), p. 98, emphasizes the linkage between irony and the novel made by Bakhtin and Lotman. I should perhaps remark here that Moretti's account of the relation between irony and the impossibility of achieved reconciliation seems to me far more persuasive than de Man's in its account of the contradictions inherent within ironic representation. De Man's circumvention of the relation between irony and the novel even involves him in what is almost an uncharacteristic moment of inverted literary-historical positivism in remarking that "[i]n Germany, for instance, the advent of a fully-fledged ironic consciousness . . . certainly does not coincide with a parallel blossoming of the novel" (*BI*, 210).

22. Charles Baudelaire, "The Essence of Laughter," trans. Gerard Hopkins, in *The Essence of Laughter and Other Essays, Journals and*

Letters, ed. Peter Quennell (New York: Meridian Books, 1956), pp. 117–18. For the original French, see Charles Baudelaire, "De l'essence du rire et généralement du comique dans les arts plastiques," in *Oeuvres complètes,* preface by Claude Roy, notice and notes by Michel Jamet (Paris: Robert Laffont, 1980), pp. 694–95.

23. Samuel Taylor Coleridge, *The Friend: A Series of Essays to Aid in the Formation of Fixed Principles in Politics, Morals, and Religion, with Literary Amusements Interspersed* (London: George Bell, 1899), p. 26. The "Essays on Method," in the same work, are devoted to the exposition of philosophical method in terms of the continual discovery of the inadequacy of any "idols" to represent the truth. In "Force of Examples," Caruth gives a brilliant demonstration of the relational structure of Kant's symbols that is entirely coherent with this analysis of the methodology of symbolism.

24. In a quite literal sense, John Stuart Mill understands this connection between politics and pedagogy as requiring the agency of the state in the establishment of educational institutions whose principal end is the formation of citizens. See his *On Representative Government,* in *Utilitarianism, Liberty and Representative Government* (London: Dent and Sons, 1910), passim, but esp. p. 280: "universal teaching must precede universal enfranchisement." Central to Althusser's analysis of "ideological state apparatuses" are the schools, a fact often overlooked by discussions of his essay that have tended to emphasize its psychoanalytical dimension. What Althusser grasps most clearly in the concept of interpellation, which indeed has close affinities with the moment of self-consciousness in Baudelaire's pratfalls, is that the formation of hailing of the Subject in any given individual is the formal condition for the transformation of that individual into the ideological form of the citizen. See Louis Althusser, "Ideology and Ideological State Apparatuses (Notes Towards an Investigation)," in his *Lenin and Philosophy and Other Essays,* trans. Ben Brewster (New York: Monthly Review Press, 1971), pp. 152–57, 174 and 180–83.

25. One can see the tension in Baudelaire's "De l'essence du rire" between the comic as index of a "dualité permanente" in humanity and the developmental history of the comic as a version of this crux of the aesthetic. T. S. Eliot's assertion, on the other hand, of an "ideal order" amongst artworks is an extreme version of the attempt to escape this crux, but has as its evident consequence the necessity to substitute myth for history. See T. S. Eliot, "Tradition and the Individual Talent," in his *Selected Prose,* ed. John Hayward (Harmondsworth, Eng.: Penguin/Peregrine, 1963), p. 23. The poetic result of the abandonment

of the developmental function of the aesthetic, correlative to Eliot's political royalism and religious anglicanism, is not so much classicism as the deliberate and defensive deployment of cliché such that it becomes impossible for the reader to claim identification with the "experience" of poet, martyr, or saint, an untraversable gap having been constituted between the postulated inimitable experience and the evacuated forms of the language. *Murder in the Cathedral* and *Four Quartets* are exemplary of this mode both thematically and performatively. The deployment of cliché in this fashion is of course no more than an extension of the dialectic of originality and reproducibility designated ironically as a condition of modern art by Baudelaire's comment that the poet's function is to produce new clichés. Cf. Walter Benjamin, "On Some Motifs in Baudelaire," in his *Illuminations*, ed. and intro. Hannah Arendt, trans. Harry Zohn (London: Fontana, 1973), p. 194: Baudelaire "went so far as to proclaim as his goal 'the creation of a cliché.' In this he saw the condition of every future poet; he had a low opinion of those who were not up to it."

26. The clearest statement of the problem is probably Karl Marx's: "The difficulty we are confronted with is not, however, that of understanding how Greek art and epic poetry are associated with certain forms of social development. The difficulty is that they still give us aesthetic pleasure and are in certain respects regarded as a standard and unattainable ideal." Karl Marx, Introduction to his *A Contribution to the Critique of Political Economy* (Moscow: Progress Publishers, 1970), p. 217. The best discussion of this problem, and the most convincing attempt at its resolution for materialist aesthetics, is Michael McKeon's "The Origins of Aesthetic Value," *Telos*, 57 (Fall 1983): 63–82.

27. Paul de Man, in a late lecture entitled "Kant and Schiller," characterizes receptions of Kant of which Schiller is exemplary as "a regression from the incisiveness and from the critical impact of the original." (Typescript, p. 2. I am indebted to Lindsay Waters for transmitting this unpublished transcript to me.) Hegel's remark on Kant's completion by Schiller can be found in the G. W. F. Hegel, *Introduction to the Aesthetics*, trans. T. M. Knox, with an interpretive essay by Charles Karelis (Oxford: Oxford University Press, 1979), p. 61.

Caruth: The Force of Example

This essay first appeared as a chapter in my book *Empirical Truths and Critical Fictions: Locke, Wordsworth, Kant, Freud* (Baltimore: John

Hopkins University Press, 1990), pp. 58–85. Permission to reprint is gratefully acknowledged.

1. Representative of this current trend are, among other critics, Gerald Graff, in *Literature Against Itself: Literary Ideas in Modern Society* (Chicago: The University of Chicago Press, 1979); Frank Lentricchia, in *After the New Criticism* (Chicago: The University of Chicago Press, 1980): and Edward W. Said, in *The World, the Text, and the Critic* (Cambridge, Mass.: Harvard University Press, 1983).

2. Kant would not characterize Newtonian science as entirely non-discursive; what is significant is the relation to a science that is at least in part dependent on what is materially "given" (see the discussion later in this essay of *The Metaphysical Foundation of Natural Science;* also see note 12, below). Readers of Kant have had difficulty with the nature of the relation to Newtonian science; this is briefly discussed below.

3. Immanuel Kant, *Critique of Pure Reason,* trans. Norman Kemp Smith (New York: St. Martin's Press, 1965), pp. 20–21 (B xiii-xiv). Page references to the first *Critique* are to this edition, and will be given in text. The Preface to the second edition of this work will be referred to as the "second Preface." Translations will be modified occasionally for clarity.

4. Although other scientists before Newton did support the Copernican view, it was Newton's inverse square law (the law of gravitation) that reduced the complicated motion of the planets described by Ptolemy and later Copernicus to a single elegant law.

5. For a discussion of this issue see Gerd Buchdahl, "Gravity and Intelligibility: Newton to Kant," in *The Methodological Heritage of Newton,* ed. Robert E. Butts and John W. Davis (Toronto: University of Toronto Press, 1970). It should be noted that such a problem was recognized by Newton himself and that the distinction between "science" and "philosophy" was not firmly established at this time, although it perhaps developed, in part, around this very issue. On Kant's early concern with force and the debates surrounding this topic, see Irving I. Polonoff, *Force, Cosmos, Monads and Other Themes of Kant's Early Thought,* in *Kantstudien,* Ergänzungshefte, 197 (Bonn: Bouvier Verlag Herbert Grundmann, 1973).

6. A general discussion of this distinction can be found in the second Preface, pp. 27–29.

7. This is discussed in detail below.

8. This is the "theoretical" part of the system, concerned with the

realm of "nature"; the place of the other part of the system, concerned with "freedom," is discussed briefly below.

9. Gerd Buchdahl, "The Kantian 'Dynamic of Reason,' with Special Reference to the Place of Causality in Kant's System," in *Kant Studies Today*, ed. Lewis White Beck (La Salle, Ill.: Open Court, 1969), p. 372; and Buchdahl, "Kant: From Metaphysics to Transcendental Logic," in his *Metaphysics and the Philosophy of Science: The Classical Origins Descartes to Kant* (Oxford: Basil Blackwell, 1969). See also Gordon G. Brittan, Jr., *Kant's Theory of Science* (Princeton, N.J.: Princeton University Press, 1978).

10. This would be the case also for the famous "Copernican Analogy" in the second Preface, along with the footnote on Newton that follows it some pages later. Interesting treatments of the analogy can be found in Hans Blumenberg, "Was ist an Kants Wendung das Kopernikanische?" in his *Die Genesis der kopernikanischen Welt* (Frankfurt a.M.: Suhrkamp, 1975), and in the debate between F. L. Paton, 'Kant's So-Called Copernican Revolution," and F. L. Cross, "Professor Paton and 'Kant's So-Called Copernican Revolution,'" both in *Mind*, 46 (1937): 365–71 and 475–77. A more recent discussion can be found in I. Bernard Cohen, "Kant's Alleged Copernican Revolution," in his *Revolution in Science* (Cambridge, Mass.: Harvard University Press, 1985). The power of this model is so strong, indeed, that the *Critique of Judgment*, which is meant to bridge the "gap" between the theoretical and practical realms, is also divided in the same manner: between aesthetic and teleological judgment, in aesthetic judgment between the beautiful and the sublime, and in the sublime between the "mathematical" and the "dynamical" sublime. On the laws of force and motion as more-than-ordinary examples see Paul de Man, "Phenomenality and Materiality in Kant" (forthcoming in *Aesthetic Ideology*, University of Minnesota Press). Helpful discussions of the architectonic that focus on the place of causality within it can be found in Gordon G. Brittan, Jr., "Kant, Closure and Causality," in *Kant on Causality, Freedom, and Objectivity*, ed. William L. Harper and Rolf Meerbote (Minneapolis: University of Minnesota Press, 1984); Gerd Buchdahl, "The Relation Between 'Understanding' and 'Reason' in the Architectonic of Kant's Philosophy," *Proceedings of the Aristotelian Society*, n.s., 67 (1967): 209–26; A. C. Ewing, *Kant's Treatment of Causality* (London: Kegan Paul, 1924); and Sueo Takeda, *Kant und das Problem der Analogie: Eine Forschung nach dem Logos der kantischen Philosophie* (The Hague: Martinus Nijhoff, 1969).

11. Immanuel Kant, *Metaphysical Foundations of Natural Science*,

trans. James W. Ellington, in *Immanuel Kant: Philosophy of Material Nature* (Indianapolis: Hackett Publishing Co., 1985), p. 16; translation modified. Citations of the *Foundations* will be taken from this edition and will be given in the text, with translations occasionally modified.

12. This passage has been a focus of much debate, since Kant is concerned in his critical philosophy with establishing a complex relation between transcendental conditions and metaphysics that would not normally be considered reducible to an opposition between form and content. It is of all the more interest, then, that the passage seems to suggest such an opposition and thus demands a reading that does not simply dismiss or embrace it in the preestablished terms of the system. On the debate concerning this passage see Hansgeorg Hoppe, *Kants Theorie der Physik: Eine Untersuchung über des Opus postumum von Kant* (Frankfurt a.M.: Vittorio Klostermann, 1969).

13. Newton's first law is translated by Motte as follows: "Every body continues in its state of rest, or of uniform motion in a right line, unless it is compelled to change that state by forces impressed upon it." See Sir Isaac Newton, *Principia*, vol. 1, Motte's transl. revised by Florian Cajori (Berkeley: University of California Press, 1934), p. 1. It is important here to note the difference between "external senses" as a physiological concept and the other uses of "external" in Kant's passage.

14. A similar shift can be found in the *Critique of Judgment*, in the movement to the "dynamical sublime," which begins with the word "power" where one might expect "force." On this particular shift see de Man, "Phenomenality and Materiality in Kant."

15. It is thus interesting that "examples" are also called, in the Preface to the *Foundations*, "*Fälle* in concreto."

16. The problem of force in relation to difficulties of closure within the system as a whole is indicated by the last work of Kant, left as a series of fragments at his death, entitled *Transition from the Metaphysical Foundations of Natural Science to Physics*. This work is concerned with the inadequacy of the *Foundations* to provide a full transition between transcendental concepts and empirical law, leaving open the possibility of a "leap" (*Sprung*) within the system. The *Transition* finally hypothesizes an ether to account for force, an odd solution since this is presumably the sort of hypothesis that criticism is meant to avoid. The language of the justification is particularly interesting: "Without such a principle of the continual excitement of the material world there would be a deathly stillness [*die Todesruhe*] of elastic forces . . . and a complete standstill of moving forces." Here, it is

force itself that is threatened by a death. See Immanuel Kant, *Gesammelte Schriften* (Berlin: Georg Reimer, 1904), vols. 21, 22, *Kants handschriftliche Nachlass*, esp. 21: 310, ll. 19–23. Good recent work on the *Transition* can be found in Eckart Förster, ed., *Kant's Transcendental Deductions: The Three "Critiques" and the "Opus postumum"* (Stanford, Calif.: Stanford University Press, 1989).

17. Immanuel Kant, *Prolegomena to Any Future Metaphysics*, trans. Lewis White Beck, Library of Liberal Arts (New York: The Liberal Arts Press, 1950), pp. 96–97. Quotations of the *Prolegomena* are taken from this edition and will be cited in text. German is supplied from the Philosophische Bibliothek edition, *Prolegomena zu einer jeden künftigen Metaphysik*, ed. Karl Vorländer (Hamburg: Felix Meiner, 1976).

18. *Prolegomena*, pp. 99–103, translation modified: *Grenzen* is translated as "limits," *Schranken* as "boundaries." The word "concepts" in the last line refers here strictly speaking to the ideas of *thinking* rather than the concepts of *knowing*.

19. Immanuel Kant, *Religion Within the Limits of Reason Alone*, trans. T. M. Greene and H. H. Hudson (New York: Harper & Row, 1960), p. 58.

20. It would be worth exploring the relation between the sacrificial figure in the discussion of the symbol and the characterization of the sublime in the *Critique of Judgment*.

21. John 3:16–17, King James Version.

22. The place of Christ in these examples has implications for the traditional understanding of the Christ story as a meaningful redemption of Abraham's sacrifice. Kierkegaard's version of the Abraham story in *Fear and Trembling* is relevant in this context. For a reading of Kierkegaard see Kevin Newmark, "Between Hegel and Kierkegaard: The Space of Translation," *Genre*, 16 (Winter 1983): 373–87.

23. One might need also to reread the relation to "Hume" in the argument that defines the symbolic anthropomorphism as "not" a negation. What exactly is the status of this "not"? This would lead as well to a reconsideration of the role of "error" in general in the understanding of the "ideas": unlike empirical concepts, the ideas are first "given" not from something outside of reason (sensible or supersensible) but in error, i.e., the texts of previous metaphysics. The difference between knowing and thinking is thus a difference not just between a relation to the sensible and a relation to the supersensible, but between a relation to the sensible and a relation to texts.

24. A full development of my reinterpretation of the metaphysical

example would entail an examination of Kant's notion of "intuition" (*Anschauung*), which is the form in which the material world is given to thought. In this context, Jaako Hintikka's work on intuition deserves further attention. He suggests that "intuition" in Kant is not, as it is generally interpreted, a kind of raw sensation but is rather to be understood in terms of Kant's notion of the Euclidean proof, in which the "construction of intuitions" is the diagram drawn by the mathematician to represent the geometrical object being studied. This object is also an example (thus "triangle ABC" is said to represent all isosceles triangles, and so on). Intuition would then be a matter of drawn lines and of an exemplary structure established by the claim that a particular drawn figure stands for all such figures. See Jaako Hintikka, "Kantian Intuitions," *Inquiry*, 15 (1972): 341–45.

25. On the traditional difficulties of linking the verbal and nonverbal sciences see Paul de Man, "The Resistance to Theory," in his *The Resistance to Theory* (Minneapolis: University of Minnesota Press, 1986). An indirectly related argument that is useful for a reading of Kant can be found in de Man's essay, "The Epistemology of Metaphor," in *On Metaphor*, ed. Sheldon Sacks (Chicago: University of Chicago Press, 1978). A fine reading of the problematics of example in another part of Kant's system is to be found in J. Hillis Miller, "Reading Telling: Kant," in his *The Ethics of Reading* (New York: Columbia University Press, 1987).

26. I put the word "linguistic" in quotation marks as a reminder that this term is to be used no longer in a mere opposition to the empirical but rather in relation to an event that cannot be thought strictly within such oppositions.

27. Can we not hear, in Kant's claim in the "Doctrine of Method" (quoted above) that philosophy and mathematics "go hand in hand" (also in the German text), this very love story?

Rapaport: Of the Eye and the Law

1. Maurice Merleau-Ponty, "The Child's Relations with Others," in his *The Primacy of Perception and Other Essays* (Evanston, Ill.: Northwestern University Press, 1964), p. 98.

2. Jean-Paul Sartre, *Anti-Semite and Jew*, trans. George J. Becker (New York: Schocken, 1948), p. 48.

3. Emmanuel Levinas, *Totality and Infinity: An Essay on Exteriority*, trans. Alphonso Lingis (Pittsburgh: Duquesne, 1969), p. 109.

4. Ibid., p. 121

5. Emmanuel Levinas, "Philosophy and the Idea of Infinity," in his

Collected Philosophical Papers, trans. Alphonso Lingis (Dordrecht: Martinus Nijhoff, 1987), p. 54.

6. Jürgen Stroop, *The Stroop Report*, trans. Sybil Milton (New York: Pantheon, 1979). This photograph belongs to the "Pictorial Report" of the *Stroop Report*, Exhibit 275 of the International Military Tribunal, held in Nuremberg, 1946. Several photographs from the *Report* were widely publicized by the international media, this photograph being the most well known. There were 54 photographs in all, and 30 were captioned in Gothic Script. Jürgen Stroop directed liquidation of the Warsaw ghetto, and the deluxe leather-bound copy obtained by the U.S. 7th Army was the one Heinrich Himmler had received. In the report, the term "bunker" is a Nazi euphemism for any residence in the Ghetto, the implication being that the liquidation is part of a declared war between Jews and National Socialist forces. The first German edition of the *Stroop Report* (Luchterhand, 1960) was published at the behest of the novelist and political activist Günter Grass.

7. Julia Kristeva, *Powers of Horror: An Essay on Abjection*, trans. Leon S. Roudiez (New York: Columbia University Press, 1968), p. 185.

8. Maurice Merleau-Ponty, *The Visible and the Invisible*, trans. Alphonso Lingis (Evanston, Ill.: Northwestern University Press, 1968), p. 145. The Kantian "unity of apperception" is discussed by Kant in *Critique of Pure Reason* (B 181) with respect to identifying images with a concept by means of a transcendental schema that brings the sensible and the intelligible into correspondence. For Kant, the mental processes of representation depend upon "synthesis" and "unity of apperception."

9. Levinas, "Philosophy and the Idea of Infinity," p. 55.

10. Emmanuel Levinas, *L'Au delà du verset* (Paris: Minuit, 1982), p. 148.

11. Ibid., p. 148.

12. Emmanuel Levinas, "Meaning and Sense," in his *Collected Philosophical Papers*, p. 97.

13. Ibid.

14. Levinas, *Totality and Infinity*, p. 198.

15. Levinas, "Meaning and Sense," p. 96.

16. Emmanuel Levinas, *Otherwise Than Being Or Beyond Essence*, trans. Alphonso Lingis (The Hague: Martinus Nijhoff, 1981), p. 93.

17. On noesis and noema, see Edmund Husserl, *Ideas I*, trans. F. Kersten (The Hague: Martinus Nijhoff, 1983), pp. 210–35.

18. Emmanuel Levinas, *The Theory of Intuition in Husserl's Phe-*

nomenology, trans. André Orianne (Evanston, Ill.: Northwestern University Press, 1973), p. 84.

19. Ibid., p. 85.

20. Ibid., p. 93.

21. See in particular Aristotle's "Magna Moralia."

22. Michel de Montaigne, *The Complete Essays*, trans. Donald M. Frame (Stanford, Calif.: Stanford University Press, 1958), p. 369.

23. Emmanuel Levinas, *Existence and Existents*, trans. Alphonso Lingis (The Hague: Martinus Nijhoff, 1978), p. 60.

24. Ibid.

25. Emmanuel Levinas, *Difficile liberté, essais sur le judaisme* (Paris: Albin Michel, 1976), p. 33.

26. Edmond Jabès, *The Book of Questions: Yaël, Elya, Aely*, trans. Rosmarie Waldrop (Middletown, Conn.: Wesleyan University Press, 1983), p. 215.

27. See, for example, Levinas, *Totality and Infinity*, p. 109: "In contradistinction to the philosophers of existence we will not found the relation with the existent respected in its being, and in this sense absolutely exterior, that is, metaphysical, on being in the world, the *care* and *doing* characteristic of the Heideggerian *Dasein.*"

28. Martin Heidegger, *Being and Time*, trans. John Macquarrie and Edward Robinson (New York: Harper and Row, 1962), p. 281.

29. Ibid., p. 284.

30. Marlène Zarader, *La Dette impensée* (Paris: Seuil, 1990), pp. 153, 154. On the face, see also Susan Handelman, *Fragments of Redemption* (Bloomington: Indiana University Press, 1991), pp. 208–11. Handelman reminds us that the Hebrew word for face is "panim," whose root is "panah," to turn. Extrapolating from Handelman's analysis, which in my view is much too centered on Rosenzweig, the face in Levinas is a revision of the Heideggerian turn from being to Being.

31. Maurice Merleau-Ponty, *Phénoménologie de la perception* (Paris: Gallimard, 1945), pp. 465–66.

32. Samuel B. Mallin, *Merleau-Ponty's Philosophy* (New Haven, Conn.: Yale University Press, 1979), p. 125.

33. Emmanuel Levinas, "The Trace of the Other," trans. Alphonso Lingis, in *Deconstruction in Context: Literature and Philosophy*, ed. Mark C. Taylor (Chicago: University of Chicago Press, 1986), p. 351.

Index

In this index "f" after a number indicates a separate reference on the next page, and "ff" indicates separate references on the next two pages. A continuous discussion over two or more pages is indicated by a span of numbers. *Passim* is used for a cluster of references in close but not consecutive sequence.

Library of Congress Cataloging-in-Publication Data

Unruly examples : on the rhetoric of exemplarity / edited by Alexander
Gelley.

    p.   cm.

Includes index.

ISBN 0-8047-2400-8 (alk. paper) : — ISBN 0-8047-2490-3 (pbk.) :

1. Rhetoric. 2. Example. 3. Literature—Philosophy. I. Gelley,
Alexander.

PN175.U57   1995   94-26822

808—dc20   CIP